SOUTHDOWN in the 1930s

COLIN DRUCE

Capital Transport

Author's Note

This book would not have been possible without the generous assistance of many people to whom I would like to offer my sincere thanks. Firstly, I am especially grateful to renowned Southdown expert Alan Lambert who has most generously assisted me in resolving numerous queries which have arisen during the course of my research. His detailed knowledge and records have proved invaluable. After much searching I believe that, with Alan's help, it has once again proved possible to add significantly to earlier published information on the company. Anyone interested in more detailed vehicle information is recommended to the excellent Fleet History series produced by the Southdown Enthusiasts Club which have once again been essential for compiling fleet information in this book. John Allpress, long time Chairman of SEC, kindly allowed me access to his very comprehensive Route History records. Many hours were again spent in research at the Omnibus Society library in Walsall and I would like to thank Alan Mills for all his help in quickly providing access to all the material I requested. My long term friend John Card has again accompanied me on research missions for which I am very grateful. And, finally my wife, Betty, has cheerfully accepted several more years of our leisure time with me working in my 'office' researching and drafting this latest project.

I have no personal memories of the 1930s, having been born in 1943. I can, however, recall in the austerity years of the late 1940s hearing my parents talking of the 'good old days, before the war'. As I learnt more about 20th century history at school this description seemed rather at odds with the generally held view of the 1930s as a time of hardship, recession, poverty, unemployment, means testing and slum housing! But, my parents were living reasonably comfortably in Croydon, then a County Borough in Surrey, and both enjoyed secure full time employment, could afford holidays in far off Devon and my father even owned an Austin 7 car! Clearly not all parts of Britain suffered in the same way. Actually the car was lost in an air raid and our family used public transport throughout my childhood so I grew up using buses and coaches for almost all my travel needs.

When I began researching for what eventually became my book entitled 'Southdown at War' I had intended that there would be a chapter covering the 1930s as Southdown's experience during that decade appeared to be very different from that suffered by bus companies in the depressed industrial parts of Britain. The strong growth across its operating territory allowed major investment and renewal of its fleet which certainly helped the company to not only survive the difficult days of war on the very frontline but also make a speedy recovery once peace was achieved. The fleet grew from 459 at the start of 1930 to 720 by the end of 1939.

Several factors clearly worked in Southdown's favour. New service based industries tended to locate around London and in the South of England bringing welcome new all year jobs to the south coast towns. The significant growth in ownership of private housing also helped with many new residential developments especially in the coastal areas. Holidays with pay brought thousands of trippers and holidaymakers to the Sussex Coast while the Southern Railway's electrification of its main lines from London also allowed people to live by the sea and commute to work in London.

Due to the large amount of new information uncovered the chapter on the 1930s could not be included in 'Southdown at War' but now forms the basis of this volume on the company during a very exciting decade of development and expansion.

Photographs

I have again been assisted greatly by Alan Lambert who kindly made available his extensive collection for my perusal and answered many requests for help in identifying locations. The photographic archives of the Omnibus Society and Southdown Enthusiasts Club have also provided photographs and I would like to thank Alan Oxley of OS and Michael Cockett of the SEC for their assistance. The archive held by West Sussex County Council at Worthing Library has also proved useful.

Use of Bold Type and 24 hour clock

In the text, route numbers which were new or being revised are shown in bold type as are commencing dates of new timetable publications. Although the 24 hour clock has been used throughout to avoid confusion between a.m. and p.m. times, Southdown used the 12 hour clock in all its publications during the period covered by this book.

Colin Druce

First published 2017

Published by Capital Transport Publishing Ltd www.capitaltransport.com

Printed by Parksons Graphics

Southdown Motor Services Ltd was incorporated on 2 June 1915 as an amalgamation of Worthing Motor Services Ltd, the London & South Coast Haulage Company and the country services of the Brighton Hove & Preston United Omnibus Company Ltd. The latter retained their town services in Brighton and Hove and entered into an agreement with Southdown not to run beyond certain specified limits. They sold out to Thomas Tilling Ltd in November 1916.

In a timetable dated 26 July 1915 regular daily bus services were being operated between:

Brighton – Newhaven – Seaford – Eastbourne
Brighton – Shoreham – Worthing
Brighton – Bramber – Steyning
Brighton – Falmer – Lewes
Brighton – Hurstpierpoint – Bolney – Cuckfield
Worthing – Findon –Storrington
Tarring – Worthing Town Hall – East Worthing (Half Brick Hotel)

In addition a wide range of Char-a-Banc Excursions was being advertised from Brighton, Worthing and Bognor.

With the progress of the Great War going very badly it was not an auspicious time for a new enterprise. Soon after the amalgamation the government commandeered all the company's best vehicles, and the workshops were adapted to the manufacture of ammunition. Many of the vehicles acquired during the war as replacements were based on relatively obscure chassis and few lasted more than around five years with the company. Towards the end of hostilities it proved possible to take delivery of some Tilling-Stevens TS3 petrol electric vehicles, fortunately a type which the Military Authorities considered unsuitable for service in France, and a few lasted into the 1930s – after several body changes! Despite the many setbacks caused by shortages of manpower and vehicles, the business struggled on until the Armistice in November 1918.

From Worthing Motor Services had come two men who were now to shape the future development of the Southdown company. Firstly, Douglas Mackenzie who was Traffic Manager from 1915 until 1938 and responsible for planning and implementing the intensive network of interconnecting bus services that began once hostilities ended. He was also instrumental in later developing the highly successful programme of luxury 'Coach Cruises' for which Southdown became famous. Following Military Service in The Great War he was once more joined by Alfred Cannon who held the post of General Manager between 1919 and 1947. Mackenzie did not like the word 'bus' and called his vehicles 'cars' – a

description which is used throughout this book.

At the end of the Great War, the wartime coalition government, led by Prime Minister David Lloyd George, was returned to power, famously promising to build 'a land fit for heroes to live in'. But, after a brief spell of postwar prosperity, industrial profits and wages began to fall and soldiers returning from the horrors of war soon found it almost impossible to find jobs. By the summer of 1921 there were over two million people unemployed and strikes were on the increase causing widespread suffering and deprivation. The prospects for the Southdown company were not that promising, often requiring a very flexible and innovative approach to business opportunities although fortunately the south of England was not affected as badly as most of the country. In those early days, no reasonable offer was refused. Charabancs might be changed into lorries by removing their seats and buses often carried churns of milk into town from outlying farms, mail for the Post Office, pigs, goats or calves in pig nets and sides of bacon and carcasses of pig or sheep on the roof rack! Drivers and Conductors had to be resourceful and willing to undertake many and varied tasks in those days!

At the start of the 1920s many people outside urban areas lived, worked and socialised in a very limited locality. Walking, or perhaps cycling and horse riding, were often the only means of getting around the country districts. The coming of a local bus service meant increased mobility and opportunities for those beyond the reach of the established tramways and railways. From 1920 Southdown started to develop new bus routes and began to make territorial agreements with neighbouring companies defining the areas to be served. It quickly secured a territory stretching from Hastings to Fareham by concluding territorial agreements with Maidstone & District and Autocar in the east, Aldershot & District and East Surrey Traction Company to the north and Hants & Dorset to the west. Within these areas, but excluding the urban areas of Portsmouth, Brighton and Eastbourne, Southdown regarded itself as the principal operator of all Stage and Express services along with Excursions and Tours. Full details of developments from 1930 onwards are shown in chapters 2 and 3.

The first of many jointly operated services with Maidstone & District began with service 18 (Brighton – Lewes – Heathfield – Hawkhurst) starting in April 1920 to be followed by service 15 (Eastbourne – Hailsham – Herstmonceux – Bexhill – Hastings) by July 1920 and others started in the 1930s.

Southdown mainly purchased vehicles based on Leyland or Tilling-Stevens chassis during the 1920s and many lasted into the early thirties. It was commonplace for the company to swap bodies and during the lifetime of a chassis these might include all or some of charabanc, double or single deck bus or lorry bodies. Whilst there were some welcome improvements in vehicle design and reliability it was not until Leyland Motors Ltd introduced its new Titan TD1 double deck chassis and Tiger TS1 single deck chassis at the 1927 Commercial Motor Show that truly modern style buses started to appear. They heralded a new era in bus and coach travel allowing operators to confidently expand and develop their services and soon became market leaders. Both had low frame chassis allowing easier access for passengers and were fitted with the smooth and quiet running Leyland six cylinder 6.8 litre overhead camshaft petrol engine. Full details of fleet developments are shown in chapter 4.

As the fleet expanded there was an urgent need to improve garaging and maintenance facilities and during the 1920s Southdown built many garages and small but practical 'dormy' sheds. In 1928 maintenance of the fleet was moved from the Freshfield garage in Brighton to an impressive central overhaul works in Victoria Road, Portslade. The company was less keen on providing its own off street bus stations but most towns across the area had conveniently sited enquiry and parcels offices. In Brighton, bus services moved their terminal from the Aquarium to Pool Valley from 1 July 1929 and despite the narrow entrance road and distance from the main shopping area it remained in use until the 1980s. Details of new and improved premises during the 1930s are in chapter 5.

In the late 1920s discussions began across the UK between the four main railway companies and the principal bus companies about possible economies in operation. In the case of Southdown negotiations were completed in 1930 and the Southern Railway acquired about one third of Southdown's ordinary share holding. Following an Agreement between the Southern Railway and Southdown dated 1 January 1930, a Standing Joint Committee was formed to consider proposals for the co-ordination and development of passenger services within the Area served by Southdown. Over the years much was done to coordinate facilities as closely as possible by connections, combined road/rail season tickets, interavailability of ordinary tickets on Stage and Express services and the provision of buses in substitution for rail services when emergencies arose. The influence wielded by the railway companies seems to have varied greatly across the country and inevitably the intention was to protect railway interests rather than develop any form of real competition between modes of travel. Compared to some, Southdown and the Southern Railway seem to have bumped along reasonably well with bus,

coach and rail often competing for business across the bus company's territory. In the early days of the Road Traffic Act both were very often to be found together vigorously opposing the apparently modest licence applications of independent companies.

From the outset the company had been associated with the British Electric Traction group and since February 1917, following its purchase of the town services of the Brighton Hove & Preston United company in November 1916, Thomas Tilling Ltd. was also represented on the Southdown board. In 1922 Thomas Tilling Ltd. had taken a large holding in the BET's subsidiary, the British Automobile Traction Co. Ltd and in 1928 this arrangement was formalised into a merged holding company – Tilling & British Automobile Traction Ltd – of which Southdown became a subsidiary. This arrangement continued until September 1942.

As the 1920s ended the world was plunged into a serious financial crisis which would bring further unemployment and hardship to Britain. Southdown faced an uncertain time!

Seen working locally in Worthing on service 2 between the Town Hall and Broadwater is car 202 (CD 6835), a Tilling-Stevens TS3A with Tilling 51-seat open top double deck body delivered in January 1923. Southdown continued to buy new Tilling-Stevens Petrol-Electric buses until 1926, by which time more efficient conventional transmission systems were available, and many survived into the 1930s although car 202 was scrapped in early 1929. *Pamlin Prints*

Seen near the Aquarium terminus on Madeira Drive in Brighton is car 102 (CD 3532), a Leyland N chassis new in 1919 with a Dodson 31-seat rear entrance bus body which was fitted in July 1922. A new Tilling open top double deck body was fitted in July 1928 and the vehicle was finally sold in October 1935. It is photographed in October 1922 on a short working on service 12 as far as Seaford. *Pamlin Prints*

In many parts of Britain the 1930s were a time of unemployment, declining industries, hunger, depression and slum housing. The North of England, Scotland and South Wales remained among the worst hit areas. Throughout the 1920s, the UK economy had struggled with low growth, high unemployment and deflation. Then, at the end of the decade came the stock market crash of 1929 which precipitated what became known as the Great Depression. The UK economy relied heavily on world trade so the decline in global demand combined with lower exports led to a damaging recession and widespread unemployment especially among the traditional heavy industries. In the 1930s, unemployment benefit was minimal and to be unemployed left workers at the real risk of absolute poverty. Unemployment peaked at just below three million in 1932 and Britain fared better than many European countries as some economic growth occurred from 1934 onwards with a significant fall in the overall unemployment rate from 15% in 1932 to 8% in 1936. The UK also managed to avoid the social and political upheaval often seen in other parts of Europe and which would eventually plunge Britain into another war. After 1935, unemployment began a steady decline, but it was only with rearmament in the period immediately before the outbreak of the Second World War that the worst of the Depression was finally over for many.

In contrast, parts of London and the Home Counties, including most of the Southdown operating territory, witnessed the growth of new light manufacturing and service industries along with attractive residential developments. The housing boom of the mid-1930s along with the construction of factories, shops, cinemas, schools and other public buildings meant that there were almost one million jobs in the construction and related industries by the late 1930s. New factories sprung up to supply the new home owners with domestic appliances such as cookers, vacuum cleaners, heaters, radios, irons and, still in relatively small numbers, refrigerators and even televisions – all then made in Britain. Despite the gloom in many parts of the country, most people with a secure job actually saw their living standards rise significantly during the 1930s.

By 1939 about 27% of the population of Britain owned their own house whereas in 1900 about 90% of the population rented their home. Of almost four million houses built in England between 1919 and 1939, nearly three million were built by private builders, and just over one million by local authorities despite the early post war intention of building homes fit for working-class 'heroes' as a priority. The first council houses had been built before the Great War – as The First World War was known in the 1930s – with many more following in the 1920s and 1930s allowing much needed slum clearance to take place. Private developers in the area usually added 'on Southdown bus route' to their advertising!

The spread of paid holidays at the end of the decade meant that many more families could now afford to spend a week by the sea and with millions living within easy reach of the Sussex Coast it was not surprising that hotels, guest houses and holiday camps boomed. By April 1937 only around four million manual workers earning £250 a year or less, out of a total workforce of 18.5 million, were entitled to paid holiday with perhaps another million who had also gained the right. In November 1936 the government had set up a committee to examine the whole question of holidays with pay, taking evidence from employers and the trade unions along with representatives from holiday resorts, the transport industry and other interested parties. All sides agreed that workers needed holidays but many doubted whether industry could afford to pay for them. The 1938 Holidays with Pay Act set up a special 'Holiday' branch in the Ministry of Labour to oversee voluntary schemes before legislation which was planned to be introduced in 1940-1. By June 1939 over eleven million white and blue collar workers were entitled to holidays with pay usually amounting to one working week plus bank holidays.

The unprecedented increase in the numbers of holiday makers had far reaching consequences for the appearance of the English coastal towns as they were adapted and improved to cope with increased tourism – although not all residents welcomed the changes. An added bonus for the

New residential developments in the coastal area to the west of Worthing during the interwar years soon effectively joined Goring to Worthing. Here a Short Bros bodied Leyland Titan is heading west along Goring Road past shops and houses that are still recognisable to this day although the area is now fully built up and there is, inevitably, a lot more road traffic!
West Sussex County Council

Southdown area was the Southern Railway electrification of its main lines from London to the Sussex Coast and Portsmouth during the 1930s. Trains ran to frequent regular headway timetables throughout the week with reduced journey times making commuting from the South Coast to London a realistic option for those wanting to live by the sea. Better transport links and increasing social mobility also began to create a demand for holiday homes on the south coast and many smart residential areas were developed in the 1930s.

Portsmouth, however, did not escape the interwar depression as well as other parts of the Southdown area due to the importance of the Naval Dockyard to the local economy. After The Great War Britain signed the Washington Treaty of 1921 to prevent a further arms race and so limit the size and number of ships for each nation. This had a devastating effect on the shipbuilding industries and Royal Dockyards, with few new ships ordered and Portsmouth Royal Dockyard restricted to rebuilding and refitting war damaged battleships. Men returning home from the services and discharges from the Dockyard led to unemployment in the city and brought much suffering to the townspeople of Portsmouth. From 1936 to the outbreak of war the British Government quietly followed a policy of mass rearmament because of the growing threat from Nazi Germany which boosted

demand and economic growth in places such as Portsmouth. But, it was only with the onset of full scale war in 1939 that the city started to see a return to full employment.

In 1920 the boundaries of Portsmouth had been extended to include the village of Cosham just north of Portsea Island and in 1932 further extended to include Drayton and Farlington to the north east. The area was growing rapidly and soon all of these villages became suburbs of the city. In 1934 work began on the Highbury estate south of Cosham and throughout the 1930s many more council houses were built as the slums were cleared from parts of Portsea. By 1939 the population of Portsmouth had reached 260,000.

In the 1930s nearby Southsea promoted itself as the resort for those 'who prefer their seaside stay to be spent among surroundings that are peaceful and refined without being dull'. It could also boast two Victorian piers – South Parade and Clarence – both at times used for the popular steamers to the Isle of Wight. Southsea Common was originally owned by the military until it was bought by Portsmouth Corporation in 1922 and gardens, bowling greens and tennis courts added for the enjoyment of residents and visitors.

On Hayling Island holiday camps proved very popular and Southdown began a new direct coach service to London in 1934. The Civil Service Camp was founded in 1924 and Harry

A busy 1920s scene on the Eastern Esplanade at Bognor. On the left is a Southdown bus on service 31 heading east towards Brighton. It is one of a batch of three shortened Tilling-Stevens TS3 petrol electrics with Brush 29-seat front entrance bus bodies delivered in 1920. It appears that the bus is loading with the entrance facing on to the roadway perhaps indicating the lack of road traffic at this time! *West Sussex County Council*

A typical 1930s scene at Worthing sea front with a Southdown Tilling-Stevens Express B9B coach advertising forthcoming excursions. The folding roof has been opened ready for an exhilarating country drive although many of the strollers look somewhat overdressed by today's standards. All of the company's remaining fleet of Tilling-Stevens single deck buses and coaches were commandeered by the Military authorities in 1940 following the loss of transport and equipment during the evacuation from Dunkirk. *West Sussex County Council*

Warner opened his first holiday camp on Hayling Island at Northney in 1932. Most offered entertainment, sports and leisure facilities as part of an inclusive package unlike hotels and boarding houses. Despite the restrictions imposed by the only road bridge to the mainland being weight restricted, many dwellings appeared at Eastoke, almost entirely old railway carriages, buses and even London trams!

To the east of Chichester Harbour there were new holiday developments at East and West Wittering, Bracklesham Bay and Selsey even requiring Southdown to provide a special direct coach service from London by the end of the 1930s. At nearby Pagham, the Beach Estate, which dated from before the Great War, originally consisted of holiday homes mostly created from redundant railway carriages but gradually these became permanent as new homes were built.

In the Bognor Regis area new housing estates were developed in Aldwick, Middleton-on-Sea and North Bersted with prices for a new house at the latter ranging from £540 to £675. The cost of new houses was actually falling in the 1930s due to lower construction costs and new labour practices which led to fierce competition between building firms. The willingness of building

societies to lend meant that lower middle class people such as elementary schoolteachers and better paid shop assistants were now able to buy their own homes. The combination of an increasing number of people having paid holidays, falling prices and rising standards of living in some regions meant that many seaside resorts were now booming. An estimated £3 to £4 million was spent on improvements to Britain's seafronts every year of the decade, with promenades being extended and entertainment facilities built. In 1936 the Bognor Regis Town Council put forward a proposal for a Winter Garden to replace the modest wooden bandstand and attractive gardens were developed to attract visitors and residents alike. Butlin's had opened an amusement park and zoo in the early 1930s and a holiday camp followed in 1960. Following an operation in 1928 King George V spent some time recuperating in Bognor and when leaving the town he was petitioned to rename it Bognor Regis as a mark of his visit. The famous reply *'Bugger Bognor'* may have been his response although it may also have occurred towards the end of his life when told that he would soon be well enough to revisit the town! Southdown tended to limit the use of the full name to coaching activities such as the covers of London

Express service leaflets. Presumably it also looked more inviting on a chalk board for an afternoon excursion than plain Bognor!

New developments in Littlehampton included the amusement park built by Butlin's and opened in 1933 and by the mid 1930s over 250,000 holidaymakers and day trippers were visiting the resort each year. Nearby Rustington Lido, was built in 1936 as a luxurious holiday camp and gained a direct Southdown coach service to London from 1937. To the east of Littlehampton new homes were built in Angmering, East Preston and Rustington as well as Ferring and Goring prompting a significant increase in Southdown bus services from early in 1939. Across the country 287,500 new private houses were built in 1935 and 275,200 in 1937, the peak years of the 1930s housing boom and the vast majority of these were for sale rather than rent. The number of owner occupied houses in Britain had been around three quarters of a million in the early 1920s but by 1938 it had risen to more than three and a quarter million.

Worthing expanded rapidly in the 1930s as a dormitory town for commuters to Brighton and London and by 1938 some 493 people had season tickets to London and 415 to Brighton from stations within the borough. With many new housing developments to the north of the town centre the resident population grew rapidly reaching 62,000 by the late 1930s. The town also continued to attract elderly and retired people in increasing numbers with many being elderly ladies moving from London. In 1931 41% of its population aged over 14 were either retired or unoccupied, while between 1931 and 1951 the proportion of the population aged 65 or over increased from 14.2% to 24.6 %. Worthing also flourished as a seaside resort in the 1930s and more than 53,000 day trippers visited the town on August Bank Holiday in 1935.

Brighton was already one of Britain's top seaside resorts and especially popular with Londoners. During the 1920s the practice of deliberately exposing the body to the sun for the purpose of acquiring a tan became fashionable. Many local authorities were slow to catch on to the idea of providing facilities for sunbathing and at the start of the 1930s it was only at Brighton beach that men were not required to cover their upper body!

But, even after paid holidays were introduced, a holiday away from home was beyond the reach of many. Full board accommodation in Brighton could cost £1.15s (£1.75) a week, rising to £2.2s (£2.10) at the height of the tourist season. This meant that a family with two children would have to spend at least £6.6s (£6.30) in July or August. With the added cost of travel and spending money the total could come to over £10 which was equal to more than three weeks' wages for most working men. Some might have afforded a hotel but most holidaymakers relied on the traditional seaside boarding houses for their accommodation. Full board was the norm with three meals a day consisting of plain home cooking – and no choice – as most people expected in those days. Taking a bath would often be charged extra – if available at all – and hot running water in bedrooms considered a real luxury in only the very best of establishments! Staying in the bedroom on wet days was not generally permitted!

Between 1920 and 1931 some of the worst slums of Brighton were demolished and new housing estates were built to house the displaced residents. The large council estate at Whitehawk was developed between 1933 and 1937 with some 1200 houses and private developers also started to build new houses on the edge of the town such as at Hangleton and Woodingdean, areas later to be served by Southdown buses. The area of Patcham known as Ladies Mile was another 1930s development and in 1934 a four bedroom house with a garage would have cost £795 cash or £75 deposit with the remaining £720 to be paid over 25 years.

Between 1929 and 1932 the Corporation tried to create jobs during the depression with the building of a new coastal road to Rottingdean, the Marine Drive, and a sea wall with under cliff promenade stretching more than three miles from Black Rock to Rottingdean and Saltdean. In nearby Saltdean the new Mount Estate was a major development of the 1930s and covered a substantial area of downland on the east side of Saltdean Vale. The famous Lido opened adjacent to the main coast road with the imposing 426 bedroom Ocean Hotel providing the backdrop.

Peacehaven stands on the white cliffs at precisely the point where the Greenwich Meridian leaves these shores. In 1915 entrepreneur Charles Neville saw an expanse of derelict land that was ripe for development and bought a number of acres of land and established a company to develop a 'garden city by the sea'. He ran a competition in the national newspapers to give away a plot worth £100 to the person who came up with the best name for his development. It proved exceptionally popular with some 80,000 entries but the winning name was New Anzac-on-Sea in honour of the Australian and New

A busy scene looking east along Madeira Drive in Brighton during the 1930s. Southdown vehicles in view include on the far right a Short Bros bodied Tilling-Stevens B10B2 coach new in 1930 followed by a Harrington bodied Leyland Tiger. Also just visible to the left on Marine Parade is a Tilling-Stevens Express B10A2 bus on service 12. Until July 1929 Southdown had used the section of Madeira Drive adjacent to the Aquarium as its Brighton bus terminus. Although it appears to be a bright day those enjoying a stroll on the prom are very soberly dressed for occasion! *Author's collection*

Zealand Army Corps which had recently joined battle in The Great War. After the tragedy at Gallipoli, the name was quietly changed to Peacehaven around 1917. Building started in the 1920s and Peacehaven would eventually grow into a town larger than the County town of Lewes!

Further along the coast Eastbourne continued to develop as a holiday resort during the 20 years between the wars although remaining a quiet, sedate place with an air of grandeur and, perhaps, a touch of snobbery. Parks and gardens were laid out, the central bandstand was built and 4,000 acres of the Downs purchased by the Council to prevent development. Both private and Council housing estates were built in Old Town, Seaside and Hampden Park.

At nearby Pevensey Bay a fine development of seaside bungalows was built in the later 1930s based on Swedish designs. The original development was to have had shops and a cinema, although sadly, the war intervened and the cinema was never built. The opening of a new direct road across the Pevensey Marshes towards Bexhill in 1934 allowed Southdown to improve bus services in the area and provide a new faster link to Bexhill and Hastings.

One of the finest examples of modern seaside building is the De La Warr Pavilion at Bexhill-on-Sea. In 1933 a competition was announced to design a new pavilion in a simple and modern style. The winning entry was chosen and the Pavilion, which opened in December 1935, fully utilised all the latest building techniques and

Across the Southdown area the Tilling-Stevens Express B10A2 single deck buses were a common sight by the start of the 1930s. Car 607 (UF 3067) was one of 38 delivered during 1928. This example has a Short Bros 32-seat body but others had bodies built by Thomas Tilling and Harrington. When delivered the Short Bros bodied vehicles did not have roof mounted destination screens nor luggage racks as fitted to the later deliveries. Car 607 is seen operating into Brighton on service 12 which was limited to single deck buses until summer 1939. *Alan Lambert Collection*

The so called Carpet Gardens have long been a feature of the Eastbourne promenade and almost all the buildings in view are still recognisable to the present day despite the severe damage inflicted on the town during World War 2. The prominent building in the background is the Queens Hotel while the buildings at the Pier entrance have been extended since this time. Photographs of Southdown's service 97 to Beachy Head were often taken in the wide section of road by the Pier. *Author's Collection*

materials and was one of the first in the UK which employed a welded steel framed structure and supporting plate glass walls.

In the 1930s Hastings and St Leonards were transformed from two rather run down Victorian towns into modern resorts with £100,000 spent on the White Rock Pavilion, £180,000 on a new promenade and underground car park and well over £150,000 on new swimming facilities. Given that in those days you could buy a brand new semi-detached house in the town for as little as £500 these were huge amounts for the local councils to be spending on attracting visitors. As the traditional fishing industry declined the number of boarding houses doubled and beaches were cleared of nets and mooring for fishing boats to be replaced by car and coach parks and a boating lake.

Inland the pace of change was generally slower although towns such as Haywards Heath and Horsham benefited greatly during the 1930s from the new electric train services to London and attracted many new commuters to live in the countryside around. Both county towns – Lewes and Chichester – also benefited from the railway electrification schemes but did not see much

development during the 1930s although the latter's city centre no doubt gained from the opening of the new by-pass road in 1937. Uckfield and East Grinstead missed out and still had steam hauled trains to London at the start of the 1960s! Southdown bus services only reached as far north as Crawley from July 1933 by which time it was already a small but prosperous town, serving a wide rural area and those passing through on the main London to Brighton road. The town centre level crossing caused severe congestion at summer weekends even in the 1930s and a new by-pass road was built in 1937. Many smaller towns and villages across the Southdown area were hardly changed during the period and still retained their charming rural character. Much of Sussex remained thinly populated open countryside and with the decline in agriculture during the interwar years the number of farm workers fell by around 10 per cent between 1921 and 1931. The South Downs stretched from Southdown's western border right across to the sea near Eastbourne and large areas of woodland covered the northern areas offering plenty of fine weather tourist potential but little all your round bus traffic.

For many years Horsham Carfax was the traditional terminus for all buses serving the town. These included Southdown, East Surrey – later London Passenger Transport Board from Dorking and Crawley, Aldershot & District from Guildford along with several local independent operators. In this 1930s scene Southdown Leyland lowbridge bodied Titan TDI car 853 (UF 5653) can be seen awaiting departure for Brighton via Henfield on service 17 while a Southdown Leyland Tiger coach is picking up on the left hand side of the picture. The independent operators running south into Southdown territory were all acquired before the outbreak of war.
West Sussex County Council

In the final years of the 1920s Southdown acquired twelve more small businesses but the purchase of an existing company did not always stop further competition in that area as it remained relatively easy for a new operator to start up soon afterwards. The Road Traffic Act of 1930 brought an end to the opening of such competing services and introduced licensing reforms that many considered to be long overdue. For the bus and coach industry the passing of the Act was arguably the most important event during the 1930s.

Most of the regulations in force at the start of 1930 dated back to the earliest days of motorised transport in the 19th century and were totally unsuited to the new motor age of the late 1920s. Prior to the new Act each separate local authority was a licensing authority under the Town Police Clauses Acts and could impose sometimes arbitrary conditions controlling not only the speed limits to be observed in its area, but also vehicle details such as the number and position of its doors, and also vehicle weight. Often various petty restrictions and modifications were demanded and those responsible for the licensing of vehicles in one area might have completely different ideas to the authorities in another

adjoining district. An unfortunate operator might, therefore, be forced to run their vehicles between two nearby places covered by two distinctly differing sets of regulations. It proved particularly difficult with the development of longer distance services through many separate authorities' areas with opposing views on what was necessary for the safe conveyance of passengers through their district. A plate was affixed to the back of the bus and a vehicle used on a long distance route might display a wide variety of such plates. Drivers also had to be approved and licensed to work in a specific area and had to display a badge when working. Licences for vehicles were renewed every year with a police inspector visiting garages to inspect the cars. There was certainly need for change but what followed in the 1930 Road Traffic Act would now be considered by many to be the start of a bureaucratic nightmare.

The new Act swept away the existing outdated licensing arrangements and divided the country into traffic areas, each having three Commissioners of which the chairman was required to devote the whole of his time to the duties of his office. The Commissioners, who were responsible to the Minister of Transport,

In future Excursions and Tours would be subject to strict licensing and would come under the category of Express Carriages. Detailed routes would need to be specified and backing licences obtained for those Tours which passed through adjoining Traffic Areas. New in June 1936 car 1146 (CCD 746), a Leyland Tiger TS7 with Harrington bodywork, waits for custom on the sea front at Worthing, possibly in the summer of 1939 after its half-length folding roof had been replaced by a folding sunroof and glass cove windows earlier in the year. *Southdown Enthusiasts Club – Clark/Surfleet Collection*

had the power to grant or refuse any licences. In reaching a decision on any application they must have regard to the traffic needs of the whole area and the provision of adequate and efficient services. They should consider the elimination of unnecessary services and the provision, where possible, of services on routes which were not remunerative. Finally, they must consider the co-ordination of all forms of passenger transport including between road and rail services. As the railway companies could, and did, oppose many applications, especially from companies in which they did not have a financial interest, even where an established service could be proven, the so called co-ordination was entirely in favour of rail!

Generally, the Commissioners were to aim at establishing an adequate transport service in their Areas by creating what was described by some at the time as 'a controlled monopoly'. A refusal could easily mean the end of a well managed established business and many small operators soon gave up or sold out to the larger companies who benefited most from the new regime.

In future Road Service Licences, lasting for one year, would be required to authorise the operation of bus and coach services and were divided into three categories.

A Stage Carriage Licence was required for a motor vehicle carrying passengers for hire or reward at separate fares – of which one must be less than 1/- (5p) – and stopping to pick up or set down along its line of route as most bus services operated.

An Express Carriage Licence was required for a motor vehicle carrying passengers for hire or reward at separate fares where no fare was less than 1/- (5p) which covered most long distance coach services, excursions and tours.

A Contract Carriage Licence covered motor vehicles carrying passengers for hire or reward under a contract for the use of the vehicle as a whole at a fixed or agreed rate. This roughly defined a typical private hire operation.

Operators wishing to apply for a Road Service Licence were required to submit timetables and fare tables along with the proposed route and stopping places to the appropriate area Traffic Commissioner in which the service would run. Where a route ran through more than one area, operators were required to apply to the commissioners of each area through which the proposed route was to run. In this case the local area would be issued with a Primary licence and the others as backing licences.

Traffic Courts were to be established where all applications could be considered and objectors had the right to be heard. The Commissioners were required to hear representations from persons other than applicants, any local authority, passenger transport undertakings including the railway companies or other body or person directly interested or affected by the proposed service. They could then approve or reject the application and in the latter case the operator could appeal to the Minister of Transport whose decision would be final. Clearly the intention was to restrict competition and thus reduce the number of vehicles on the road. As the workings of the new Act unfolded it became clear that the interests of the travelling public were rarely considered as uppermost!

Vehicles were subject to inspection and approval and, subject to gaining a Certificate of Fitness (COF) showing that the vehicle complied with the constructional requirements prescribed by the Ministry of Transport, it would then be licensed to ply for hire as a Public Service Vehicle. The COF, unless revoked or cancelled, continued in force for five years, unless the certifying officer considered a shorter period to be appropriate. A vehicle that was licensed as a Stage Carriage could be used as a Contract Carriage and also, subject to any condition attached to the road service licence, as an Express Carriage. A vehicle licensed as an Express Carriage could be used as a Contract Carriage or, subject to the approval of the commissioners of each traffic area in which the vehicle was to run, a Stage Carriage. For instance, Southdown had some difficulty in getting the early Tilling-Stevens Express vehicles licensed for Express work because they did not have a separate emergency exit.

Drivers and Conductors would also have to be licensed by the commissioners but licence badges issued in any one traffic area would be valid throughout the country so removing the previous need for a selection of badges to be worn. Any driver or conductor who did not already hold a licence was required to apply for a licence to become effective on 1 April 1931. New rules governed the conduct of drivers and conductors along with passengers travelling on public service vehicles and usually formed the basis for revised Conditions of Carriage as included by the bus companies in their timetable publications. Drivers and conductors were not allowed to smoke in a vehicle, during the journey or when carrying passengers, and must take all reasonable precautions to ensure the safety of their passengers. Unless essential the conductor must not speak to the driver when the vehicle is in motion and all reasonable precautions must be taken to ensure that routes, fares and destinations are clearly and correctly displayed. Passengers must not use offensive language or conduct themselves in a disorderly manner, and must not make excessive noise, or throw from the vehicle any article likely to cause injury or annoyance.

A maximum speed limit of 30 miles per hour for Public Service Vehicles was introduced under the Road Traffic Act and from 1 January 1933 all vehicles operating as Express Carriages were required to be equipped with efficient speedometers. The matter was extremely controversial at the time especially as a blanket 20mph speed limit, set in the 1903 Motor Car Act, had been repealed for light vehicles in 1930! Modern buses and coaches were becoming safer and easily capable of travelling at higher speeds without endangering the travelling public. By 1934 the mounting death toll on the roads caused a change of heart in government and from 18 March 1935 a 30 mph limit was imposed for all vehicles in built up areas. The limit for Public Service Vehicles remained unchanged until the 1960s!

Although the legislation received royal assent on 1 August 1930 the wide reaching proposals could not be implemented until 1931 and the requirements of the Act were phased in as directed by the Minister. But the Minister did announce that Road Service Licences would be required after 1 April 1931 and that any service started after 9 February 1931 could not continue beyond 31 March 1931. Application for the grant or backing of licences to continue an existing service, with or without modifications, had to be made to the Commissioners before 15 March 1931. An operator was allowed to continue a service – with seasonal variations according to those in 1930 – until applications had been dealt with. If a route was in operation on or before 9 February 1931 the operator could use its existence as an established facility when arguing their case although this did not in itself guarantee that a licence would eventually be issued. Not surprisingly a race began to establish new, or expand existing, services before this date, sometimes in direct competition with established operators. Some companies tried to obtain vehicles as fast as possible and some even started new services after the deadline but many either failed or were eventually forced to withdraw by the Minister of Transport. After 1 April 1931 operators could not vary their services without the approval of the Traffic Commissioners although it took a very long time to process all the applications through the new licensing system.

So far as Southdown was concerned they would principally be dealing with three Traffic Areas which included:

South Eastern Area covering the counties of East Sussex and West Sussex along with those parts of Surrey and Kent outside the Metropolitan Police District. Also the county boroughs of Brighton, Eastbourne and Hastings. All Southdown's bus and coach services other than those operating mainly in Hampshire were licensed in the South Eastern area.

Southern Traffic Area covering the county of Hampshire along with the county borough of Portsmouth. All Southdown's Hampshire operations were licensed in this area. In 1933 The Minister of Transport announced plans to merge the Southern Traffic Area with other areas by making alterations to the South Eastern, Western and East Midland areas. In September 1939 at the outbreak of war the Southern area was resurrected as the newly created Regional Transport Commissioners gained many extra powers and duties.

Metropolitan Traffic Area covering the Metropolitan Police District and City of London. For Southdown this mainly affected backing licences but also some Tour operations starting from London.

Details of applications made to the Commissioners appeared in a new fortnightly publication with the less than snappy title of 'Notices & Proceedings' which apart from a break in wartime is still around today. At first the publication appeared weekly in order to process the many thousands of applications as quickly as possible, issue No 1 appearing in the South Eastern area on 13 March 1931.

During March 1931 the Traffic Commissioners for the South Eastern area issued some guidance to operators stating that applications for road service licences and backings would not be granted as a matter of course, even for existing services. For both unopposed and opposed applications, applicants were advised to attend the public sittings at which their applications were being heard. Where they were unopposed, applicants must still provide evidence to justify their applications, and where they were opposed, applicants and opponents must submit appropriate evidence to the Commissioners. The large companies already had suitably qualified employees while others engaged appropriate persons from the legal profession who were enjoying great demand for their services but the small operator used to the old days could rarely put up much of a fight. Those companies with territorial agreements did not generally oppose each other and the companies in which the Southern Railway had acquired a financial interest were, almost always, spared any railway opposition. Otherwise, looking through early issues of Notices & Proceedings it appears that almost

Vehicles such as car 401 (UF 1001) delivered in July 1926 were built to designs that predated the regulations imposed by the new Road Traffic Act. It was a normal control Tilling-Stevens Express B9B chassis fitted with 29-seat rear entrance Harrington bodywork which had been rebuilt in late 1930 with fixed back and folding sunroof and seen here on a wet day just leaving the Crawley Station bound for London. In 1935 some of the early B9B chassis received new Harrington bodies to a much more modern outline and survived with Southdown until the start of the war. Car 401 passed to West Sussex County Council in April 1940 and later saw service with a Showman. *Stilltime Images*

everyone objected to everyone else! Southdown and the Southern Railway objected to virtually every application by the independent coach operators – and there were literally hundreds in the London area – intent on running services or excursions to the South Coast!

The first Southdown applications appeared in issue No 2 and the first public inquiry in the South Eastern area took place at County Hall, Lewes on 15 April 1931 although only involving Southdown in the role of objector on this occasion. Whatever the original intentions, the Act effectively killed off competition and stifled innovation for decades to come. Worse, it allowed the powerful Railway interests to interfere in the development of the bus and coach industry by allowing them to object to any new services which they considered to be in competition with the railways. Most of the Act's provisions remained in force until at least 1980.

By the standards of the time, car 129 (CD 5129) enjoyed a very long life with Southdown and was finally sold in October 1934 although it must have looked very out of date alongside the latest covered top double deckers. It started life as a Leyland N chassis new in 1920 with single deck body by Goodman but in June 1928 a Short Bros 51 seat body was fitted.
Alan Lambert Collection

An elevated view looking north taken in the 1930s from the Pier Pavilion at Worthing with a 1935 Southdown Short Bros highbridge bodied Leyland Titan TD4c on service 7 proceeding along South Street towards the Pier. In the foreground is a small traffic roundabout with a 'Keep Left' sign. On the left The Arcade, opened in 1925, remains much the same today but the Marine (later Pier) Hotel and Walter Bros. Bazaar are long since demolished.
West Sussex County Council

By the start of the thirties Southdown Motor Services Ltd had been in existence for less than 15 years and yet it had already secured a bus operating territory stretching along the coast from Hastings to Fareham and inland to Petersfield, Horsham, Handcross, Uckfield and Heathfield. Southdown's bus route network was already well established with main trunk routes linking most of the major towns and villages throughout their territory and by summer 1930 many of the services that would survive in familiar form into the 1960s were already in place. A full list of services as at 1 January 1930 appears in Appendix 1.

The Road Traffic Act of 1930 brought many changes to the bus and coach industry but many of the pioneer operators were unprepared for such a strict regime and willingly sold out to larger concerns. Southdown was happy to acquire operators in order to remove competition and consolidate its strong position and even by the start of the 1930s there were very few bus operators remaining totally within the Southdown area. By the start of World War Two a further 44 rival operators had been acquired. In many other large bus company areas there remained a significant number of small operators providing market day services into the main towns but, apart from border towns such as Horsham and East Grinstead, very few survived within the Southdown area by 1939.

Before examining the service developments in detail it is worth looking at some features of bus services at the time. Firstly, almost all services operated on 7 days a week, starting a little later on Sundays, but then generally running to the same timetable as on Weekdays – Mondays to Saturdays in today's jargon – until the last bus. Evening services were provided on almost all routes and as new cinemas appeared even in the smaller towns during the 1930s the demand for evening buses increased. In some cases special late buses were provided which waited for the end of the last performance. BUT, apart from in the larger towns and cities such as Brighton and Portsmouth, first buses often did not arrive until after 0900 and sometimes much later. In Worthing, where the company operated a very comprehensive network of local services, first buses arrived in the town centre from about 0745. Some other examples include the first 12 into Eastbourne arriving at 0900 or the first 91 from Heathfield reaching Eastbourne at 1025 – there were earlier buses from Hailsham! This was because long distance commuting by bus did not really exist in these times and school children were mostly educated in local schools to which they could walk. Although car ownership grew steadily in the 1930s most people still relied on buses for their local travel needs even by the end of the decade.

Many of Southdown's bus services were transporting people between towns and villages so that the average distance travelled was relatively

Car 600 (UF 4300) was a Tilling-Stevens Express B10A2 single deck chassis fitted with Short Bros 48-seat all metal bodywork delivered new in March 1929. It is seen operating on service 11 which ran frequently between Brighton and Goring. Note that 'Bungalow Town' is mentioned on the front destination screen and on two slip boards although in fact buses on this service followed the main coast from Shoreham to Lancing and did not divert to the area later covered by service 21. Although it remained unique in the fleet car 600 enjoyed a very long life with Southdown and was not sold until February 1950.
Alan Lambert Collection

great. By 1939 the average fare paid on Southdown buses was 4d compared to an average of 2½d for the whole bus industry. The longer distance passenger was obviously more likely to be influenced by the weather and seasonality with many services suffering a steep fall in revenue in periods of bad weather and during the winter months. This inevitably resulted in less intensive use of vehicles as compared to those operators running in industrial areas where passenger demand was spread more evenly throughout the year. A large proportion of the Southdown fleet was laid up during the winter months and even in summer the daily mileages on seasonal work were relatively low resulting in fare scales which were higher than those found in more industrial districts.

Southdown did not run 'market day' services on one or two days per week as often found in other counties despite much of the operating area being very rural in the 1930s! Even most country routes ran to a regular headway throughout the day. Connections were provided where possible to increase journey opportunities but in the timetables of the early 1930s the difference between a through bus and a connection was not always very clear – even to your author who quite enjoys reading bus timetables! In a few instances it has proved almost impossible to determine exactly which journeys were in fact provided as a through bus!

Despite some welcome improvements to road surfaces and significant improvement in the performance of buses during the 1930s many services continued with virtually the same running times throughout the decade. On some of the longer trunk routes there were changes. For instance, the 12 between Pool Valley and Eastbourne reduced end to end journey time from 1 hour 40 minutes in 1930 to 1 hour 26 minutes in 1939 thanks mostly to the better hill climbing abilities of the Leyland 8.6 litre powered buses on the route. Over the same period the 31 reduced from 4 hours 30 minutes to 3 hours 58 minutes. Of course, schedules were governed by the 30 miles per hour speed limit imposed under the Road Traffic Act although by the end of the 1930s this speed could easily be exceeded by almost every bus and coach then running!

Some major road projects were started during the 1930s but new construction in Britain failed miserably to keep pace with the rapid growth in the volume of road traffic. In spite of this, most bus services of this era could generally be relied upon to run on time and urban congestion was relatively unknown outside large cities such as London. For Southdown fine days at summer weekends proved a headache as a big increase in motor traffic could often lead to delays on the main roads heading away from the coast in the evenings. Otherwise the frequent delays and congestion that have dogged service reliability, especially in more recent times, were almost unknown during the 1930s.

OFFICIAL TIME TABLE
1st MAY, 1930
PRICE TWOPENCE

Starting on 1 May 1930 a new full colour cover design appeared for the bus timetables which at this time appeared almost every month. Background colours were green and cream/yellow and the four illustrations included an offside view of a Tilling-Stevens Express, Arundel river bridge with the Castle standing prominently above the town Beachy Head and a nearside view of a Leyland bodied Titan TD1. A folded route system map was included and this design continued at frequent intervals until December 1937.

Up until the issue dated 14 April 1930 the front cover of Southdown's bus timetables was dominated by an advert for Sussex Daily News but a new style attractive full colour front cover adorned the issue dated 1 May 1930. It included an offside illustration of a Tilling-Stevens Express single deck bus and a nearside view of a Leyland bodied Leyland Titan TD1 along with two local views. Although updated from 4 April 1938 to include more modern vehicles – a 1400 class Tiger and a lowbridge Titan – this remained the standard up to the issue dated 16 July 1939, the last before the outbreak of war. In addition to the individual route timetables a number of summary timetables were included such as Brighton to Worthing, Southsea to Westbourne, Haywards Heath to Lindfield and Cuckfield and Eastbourne to Hailsham, Some services were only mentioned in these summaries which did not in the early years actually denote which journeys belonged to which service. A list of Company offices and agents along with Passenger Regulations and very detailed fare tables, featuring many by connection, were also included. The cost remained at 2d (less than 1p) throughout the 1930s although the number of pages increased rapidly from around 144 in June 1930 to 368 in July 1939! Throughout the 1930s bus services were grouped in areas typically as follows, but increased as the network grew:

Worthing area 1 to 11
Brighton area 11 to 31
Portsmouth area 31 to 49
Bognor Regis and Chichester area 50 to 66

Littlehampton area 64 to 69
Horsham area 70 to 83
Haywards Heath area 81 to 89
Eastbourne area 90 to 99

Until the issue dated 8 June 1935 the London Express Services were only included in a very brief format with departure times from terminals although the Coastal Express, later South Coast Express, timetables were included, sometimes as a coloured insert. Details of the Southdown Coach Cruises programme were also featured, again usually as a coloured insert.

1930

Significant revisions to the town services in Worthing occurred from **Saturday 1 March**. This was the largest urban area that Southdown did not have to share with a Municipal operator and a very comprehensive network was offered which grew with the residential developments of the 1930s. On service **3** between EAST WORTHING (Ham Hotel) and ELM GROVE all journeys were altered to operate around the East Worthing loop anti-clockwise (Ham Road, Lyndhurst Road, Selden Road) and also all journeys to Elm Grove were diverted between Brighton Road and Chapel Road to operate via Steyne Gardens, Marine Parade, South Street and Chapel Road to serve part of the sea front. The frequency became 15 minutes every day

although no Sunday service ran between 1300 and 1400, a feature of Worthing operations at the time.

Service **4** was extended to operate between EAST WORTHING (HAM HOTEL) and HIGH SALVINGTON via Ham Road, Brighton Road, Steyne Gardens, Marine Parade, South Street, Chapel Road, Railway Approach, Teville Road, Tarring Road, South Street (Tarring), High Street, Rectory Road, Offington Lane, Ashacre Lane, Salvington Road, Durrington Hill and Salvington Hill. Return as outward route reversed to Chapel Road and then via Warwick Street – missing the stop at the Dome – Brighton Road, Selden Road, Lyndhurst Road to Ham Road running clockwise around the East Worthing loop. The frequency became a 15 minute service daily as far as Durrington with alternate journeys extended to and from High Salvington.

The existing service 5 was renumbered **7** (see below) and a completely revised service **5** introduced between WORTHING PIER and EAST WORTHING (THACKERAY ROAD) via South Street, Chapel Road, Broadwater Road, Broadwater Street East and Dominion Road. With a journey time of just 13 minutes the new housing developments to the east of the Broadwater Road gained a 15 minute service daily. As with most other local Worthing services

A view of Worthing's Marine Parade looking towards the Pier Pavilion on the left and the Dome cinema to the right. Several Southdown open top buses are can be seen awaiting departure. For some unknown reason, buses on local services towards East Worthing did not serve the stop outside the Dome but instead proceeded direct from the old Town Hall to Brighton Road through the now pedestrianised Warwick Street. *West Sussex County Council*

at this time it was suspended on Sundays between 1300 and 1400.

Service **6** was diverted between Broadwater Road and Poulters Lane to operate via Northcourt Road, South Farm Road and Poulters Lane. The Sunday service was withdrawn between 1300 and 1400.

New service **7** replaced the former service 5 and ran between WORTHING PIER and SOMPTING (MARQUIS OF GRANBY) via South Street, Chapel Road, Broadwater Road, Broadwater Street East, Forest Road, Southfield Road, Wigmore Road, Kingsland Road, Sompting Road and West Street. With a journey time of 18 minutes a 15 minute service ran as far as Wigmore Road with alternate journeys extended to and from Sompting daily. No Sunday service was provided between 1300 and 1400.

From **Monday 14 April** the through Brighton to Southsea frequency on service **31** was revised to provide a 30 minute service daily. This remained the pattern until 1939 but there were many other supporting routes. The 31A provided an additional 30 minute service from Southsea to Emsworth via Fratton and was from this date extended daily to Westbourne. The 31B provided two extra buses per hour from Southsea South Parade to Havant via Theatre Royal. At the eastern end of the route service 11 provided additional buses every 30 minutes from Brighton as far as Goring Church plus an extra hourly service to Worthing via Sussex Pad and Lancing Station, sometimes referred to as service 11A, perhaps to avoid confusion, but not shown as such in timetables. It was, however, shown as 11A on the route map! As part of these changes service **47** was withdrawn between Portsmouth and Havant and curtailed to operate an hourly service daily HAVANT CHURCH – HAYLING – HAVANT CHURCH with most journeys operating anti-clockwise around the Hayling loop. Services **48** from Waterlooville and **49** from Horndean provided a combined hourly service in the clockwise direction. Among other revisions from this date service **56** was withdrawn between Halnaker, Boxgrove, Tangmere and Chichester being curtailed to operate between CHICHESTER (WEST STREET) and OLD BOSHAM and the frequency improved from every 90 minutes to an hourly service daily. To replace the withdrawn section service **66** was increased to run hourly daily. New service **94** was introduced linking Polegate Station with Wannock where the Tea Gardens were a popular attraction. With a journey time of just 6 minutes the frequency varied but ran at 15 minute intervals during busy times.

Starting from **Sunday 11 May** service **40** was diverted between Purbrook Church and Waterlooville to operate direct via London Road while, as replacement, one journey per hour on service 41 was diverted via Stakes Road and Stakes Hill Road. All journeys on service 41 ran to Southsea via Fratton.

From **Sunday 1 June** service **7** was extended from Sompting to COKEHAM (BALL TREE HOTEL) via Sompting Road and West Street. The frequency became every 15 minutes to Wigmore Road with alternate journeys extended to and from Sompting and with alternate journeys further extended to and from Cokeham daily. No Sunday service ran between 1300 and 1400.

Service **54** was revised to provide a roughly 2 to 3 hourly service daily between Chichester and Compton with six journeys on Monday to Friday, seven on Saturdays and five on Sundays. Three additional journeys each way on Saturdays ran between Chichester and Emsworth Square via Churchers Corner and Westbourne. One Sunday morning journey in each direction operated through from Southsea to Compton via services 46 and 54, otherwise passengers could change at Churchers Corners where connections were made throughout the day. The name of this connecting point appears to have been invented by Southdown as the description does not appear on any maps and is situated north of Westbourne where the B2147 road crosses Common Road at a staggered junction. In a 1926 timetable it was described as Little Hambrook Farm which was run by the Churcher family and subsequently appears to have been named after them by Southdown. Alan Lambert has a vision of Traffic Manager Douglas Mackenzie knocking on the farmhouse door to ask what the corner was called and on being told it didn't have a name decided to call it Churchers Corner! It was not displayed on destination blinds and buses terminating here showed 'Westbourne for Compton' or 'Westbourne for Funtington' depending on the direction of the connecting service.

Full summer services commenced on **Sunday 6 July** with further revisions to Worthing area services. An additional 30 minute frequency was introduced on service **1** between Worthing and Findon during afternoon and evening periods daily. In conjunction with service 2 this provided four buses an hour between Worthing and Findon for the high summer period. Sunday

Car 927 (UF 7427) was a Leyland Titan TD1 with Short Bros 50-seat highbridge bodywork and seen on the steeply cambered road near Petersfield Station. This was the northern terminus of service 40 after August 1933 when it was switched from East Meon. The Walman sliding roof is clearly in the fully open position on what looks like a sunny day. Car 927 passed to Wilts & Dorset in June 1939 and enjoyed a very long life after receiving a new utility body in 1944.
Alan Lambert Collection

Car 71 (CD 4871) is a Petrol Electric Tilling-Stevens TS3 new in October 1919 and seen here opposite The Dome at Worthing in 1927 after fitment of its third body which this time was a 51-seat Tilling double decker. In this scene it is waiting to depart on service 4 to High Salvington and was later fitted with pneumatic tyres surviving in the fleet until September 1931, a very satisfactory performance for a vehicle at this time. *Author's Collection*

services were now provided throughout the day without any lunchtime break on services **3, 5, 6** and **7**. New Service **4A** was introduced between Worthing (Dome) and High Salvington following the same route as the 4 and providing a combined 7/8 minute frequency between these two points from around 1400 until 2100 daily. The Tea Gardens at High Salvington on the edge of the South Downs proved a popular attraction for Worthing residents throughout the 1930s.

Seasonal service **10B** was reintroduced between ARUNDEL SQUARE and BOGNOR PIER via Walberton, Yapton, Bilsham and Middleton-on-Sea. Eight journeys ran each way at irregular intervals daily with four extended between Arundel and Worthing as Service **10A**. Service **11** was extended via Goring Way, Goring Street, Goring Station, Littlehampton Road, Ferring Lane and Ferring Street to operate between BRIGHTON (POOL VALLEY) and FERRING with a 30 minute service throughout daily plus an hourly service between Brighton and Worthing via Sussex Pad. The frequency of service **27** as far as Devil's Dyke increased to 22 journeys each way daily. The all year service to Henfield via the downland villages of Poynings, Fulking and Edburton continued every 3 hours and together this remained the high summer frequency through the 1930s.

Further west the frequency of Hayling Island service **47** was increased for the summer to hourly clockwise and a 30 minute service anti-clockwise daily but no journeys ran through to Portsmouth. Additional clockwise journeys around the Hayling loop were provided by services 48 and 49.

From the same date Southdown introduced new service **95** between EASTBOURNE (PEVENSEY ROAD) and HEATHFIELD (STATION ROAD) via Polegate, Hailsham, Harebeating, Carter's Corner, Cowbeech, Beech Hill, Rushlake Green, Three Cups Corner, Punnett's Town and Cade Street. Three journeys ran each way on Sundays to Fridays with an additional late evening journey each way on Saturdays. Buses served new roads for Southdown in an area once important for chicken farming but the service was withdrawn from 31 December 1931 after the application for a Road Service Licence was refused by the South Eastern Traffic Commissioners. The area was already well served by a daily bus service operated by J Haffenden of Vines Cross.

After 21 September 1930 the extra service **1** journeys between Worthing and Findon were withdrawn along with service **4A** and other seasonal services such as **10B** and **94**. Winter timetables were introduced from **Monday 22 September** with service **14** curtailed to operate between BRIGHTON (POOL VALLEY) and HAYWARDS HEATH STATION, being withdrawn between Haywards Heath and Lindfield. Service **24** was revised to operate as a circular from BRIGHTON (POOL VALLEY) via Patcham, Pyecombe, Muddleswood, Hurstpierpoint, Stone Pound, Hassocks, Keymer, Ditchling, Westmeston, Plumpton, Offham, Lewes, Falmer and Moulscombe. Buses ran 2 hourly each way daily plus one journey each way daily between Henfield, Lewes and Brighton and one journey each way weekdays between Brighton, Lewes and Offham. Apart from garage positioning journeys the main service was withdrawn between Henfield and Hurstpierpoint and rerouted to form a circular service. Presumably the company faced some criticism over this loss of service and a new service 28 was introduced in January 1931 as shown below. Finally, the odd Sunday morning journey in each direction between Southsea and Compton on service 54 was withdrawn at this time.

The company had also hoped to extend service 12 from Pool Valley to Brighton Station from 22 September 1930 but arrangements could not be completed in time. Only the 0620, 0650, 0710, 0730 and 0810 journeys from Seaford on Monday to Saturday were extended to Brighton Station and all buses towards Seaford and Eastbourne started from Pool Valley. A full service to and from Brighton Station commenced from **Saturday 1 November 1930**. The service beyond Seaford to Eastbourne was basically only hourly with a few extra timings added. Between Brighton and Seaford buses ran about every 10 to 15 mins with some Seaford evening journeys continuing to Chyngton Gardens as the last bus to Eastbourne left Brighton Pool Valley at 1920. Eight journeys daily each way ran between Brighton Station and Peacehaven Annexe, the last evening one being provided by diverting a Seaford bus.

Also commencing from this date service 4 was reduced to provide a 15 minute service daily as far as Durrington with only alternate journeys extended to and from High Salvington. On service 11 only one journey per hour ran beyond Goring Church to Ferring. Service 16 was curtailed to operate between BRIGHTON (POOL VALLEY) and GOLDEN CROSS with only garage journeys extended to and from East Hoathly. Connections were made with service 92 at Golden Cross for Uckfield and Eastbourne.

1931

Starting on **Thursday 1 January** a new local service was introduced in Newhaven. Numbered 13C, it ran between NEWHAVEN Bridge Street and DENTON via Bridge Street, Drove Road, Avis Road and Denton Road with three journeys daily at 1035, 1435 and 2035 from Bridge Street returning from Denton 20 minutes later. These journeys were worked in the layover time of the service 13 buses from Brighton via Lewes. On Friday, Saturday and Sunday evenings seven journeys were provided between Bridge Street and Denton between 1730 and 2205. In addition five journeys ran between Bridge Street and the Recreation Ground via High Street, Meeching Road, Dacre Road, South Road and Fort Road.

Further changes to services occurred in this area from **Thursday 29 January** when service 13 was curtailed to operate only between BRIGHTON (POOL VALLEY) and LEWES (COUNTY HALL) and the frequency reduced to just a few early morning and late evening journeys when the country services did not maintain a 12 minute headway between Brighton and Lewes. New service 13A was introduced between LEWES (COUNTY HALL) and NEWHAVEN via Iford, Rodmell, Southease and Piddinghoe with a roughly 2 hourly service daily. Newhaven local service 13C had obviously proved popular and was increased to seven journeys each way weekdays (six on Sundays) between Bridge Street and Denton. Additionally seven journeys each way on weekdays (six on Sundays) ran between Bridge Street and EAST SIDE via Bridge Street, Railway Road, Clifton Road, Norton Road with a journey time of just 4 minutes each way. All of the Denton and East Side journeys could be provided during the layover time of the service 13A bus in Newhaven.

In 1930 the Southern Railway had announced plans to electrify the lines from Purley to Brighton and Worthing using the third rail system already in use on nearly 800 miles of line. The train mileage would be increased by about 150% and Southdown was no doubt mindful of the potential to provide a network of feeder bus routes to and from the principal stations. Haywards Heath gained three new bus services from **29 January 1931** of which two provided purely local facilities. A further link between HAYWARDS HEATH STATION and HORSHAM (CARFAX) was by service 83 running via Cuckfield, Whiteman's Green, Slough Green, Bolney Five Cross Roads, Warninglid, Lower Beeding, Monk's Gate and Mannings Heath with a two hourly frequency. Another service that remained basically unchanged for many years was the 84, a new HAYWARDS HEATH TOWN CIRCULAR operating via Sydney Road, Oathall Road, New England Road, Western Road, Franklyn Road, South Road, Broadway, Muster Green, Boltro Road and Market Place with a journey time of 18 minutes. An hourly service ran each way daily and the first clockwise

This undated leaflet probably covers the period in early 1931 when Southdown were registering new services to beat the forthcoming deadline imposed under the Road Traffic Act. It is believed that Millards Coaches of Fareham ran a limited service to Portchester Castle at this time and no doubt Southdown's comprehensive service was an attempt to force them off the road. Millards did not apply for a licence under the 1930 Act and service 45C was included in the main timetable book from 20 July 1931.

Southdown Motor Services, Ltd.

Bus Service 45c.

FAREHAM and PORTCHESTER CASTLE

This Service connects at Portchester Railway Hotel with buses to and from Southsea and Fareham, and also at Cornaway Lane with buses to Southsea.

NS—NOT SUNDAYS.	WEEKDAYS AND SUNDAYS.												SO—SUNDAYS ONLY.				
	NS	NS	NS	NS	NS	NS											
Fareham			8 58	9 35	10 35	11 35	12 35	1 35	and then at the following minutes past each hour.	35	until	1035	...	...	...	...
Cornaway Lane			9 2	9 39	10 39	11 39	12 39	1 39		39		1039	...	...	...	...
White Hart Inn			9 6	9 43	10 43	11 43	12 43	1 43		43		1043	...	...	...	...
Portchester Castle ...	8 40	9 10	9 46	10 46	11 46	12 46	1 46		46		1046	...	...	...	...
Portchester (Railway Hotel)	8 44	9 12	9 48	10 48	11 48	12 48	1 48		48		1048	...	...	...	...
	NS	NS	NS	NS	NS	NS	NS	SO								
Portchester (Railway Hotel)	8 36	8 44	9 13	9 54	10 54	11 54	1254	1 20	1 54	and then at the following minutes past each hour.	54	until	9 54	...	...	
Portchester Castle arr.	8 38	...	9 17	9 56	10 56	11 56	1256	...	1 56		56		9 56	...	...	
Portchester Castle dep.		8 18	10 7	11 7	12 7	1 7	...	2 7		7		10 7	...	...	
White Hart Inn			9 20	10 9	11 9	12 9	1 9	...	2 9		9		10 9	...	...	
Cornaway Lane			9 24	10 13	11 13	12 13	1 13	...	2 13		13		1013	...	...	
Fareham		8 57	9 31	10 20	11 20	12 20	1 20	1 30	2 20		20		1020	...	...	

FARE TABLE

Fareham (Office). 21.

1	Delme Arms. 20					
1½	1	Down End Road. 19				
2	1½	1	Cornaway Lane. 18			
3	2	2	1	**Council Houses. 17**		
3	2	2	1	1	Office, Bates Brickyard. 16	
4	3	3	2	1	1	Portchester Castle. 15
5	4	4	3	2	2	1	Portchester Railway Hotel. 14

Return Fare : Fareham and Portchester Castle, 7d.

departure arrived at Haywards Heath Station at 0750 in time for a fast train to the City. New roads to the north east of Haywards Heath were served by service **85** which ran between HAYWARDS HEATH STATION and LINDFIELD POST OFFICE via Mill Green Road, College Road, Gander Hill, Sunte Avenue, Hickmans Lane and High Street with a journey time of just 8 minutes. An hourly service was provided daily although this was not the first Southdown bus in the area as service 30 had linked Haywards Heath and Lindfield via Sydney Road, West Common and Black Hill since July 1926. For many years the 85 was only included in the Bus Timetable publications as part of the Haywards Heath to Lindfield summary and described as '85 via The Witch'. The 84 and 85 were timed so they could be provided by one bus.

A number of other new links were introduced from the same date and new service **28** restored the lost section of route between Hurstpierpoint and Henfield referred to earlier. It ran between BRIGHTON (POOL VALLEY) and HENFIELD via Patcham, Pyecombe, Clayton, Hassocks (Stone Pound) Hurst Road, Wickham Hill, College Lane, St. John's College, Chalkers Lane, Danworth Lane, Cuckfield Road, Hurstpierpoint High Street, Albourne, High Cross, Chestham Corner with a two hourly service daily. Following disappointing results the **28** was withdrawn after operation on 31 December 1931 and the link between Hurstpierpoint, Albourne and Henfield lost until much more recent times. Additionally, new service **29** commenced operation between BRIGHTON (POOL VALLEY) and HAYWARDS HEATH STATION via Falmer, Lewes, Offham, Plumpton, Plumpton Station, Plumpton Green, Wivelsfield Green and Wivelsfield. With a journey time of 1 hour 25 minutes buses ran daily every 2 hours and served new roads in Offham, Plumpton and Wivelsfield. The first journey towards Brighton started at Wivelsfield Green at 0805 and reached Brighton at 0918 before returning to Haywards Heath to arrive at 1049!

This large number of alterations and new services all starting on 29 January 1931 may have been influenced by the Minister of Transport's announcement that, under the terms of the new Road Traffic Act 1930, operators would need to have a Road Service Licence after 1 April 1931 and that any service started after 9 February 1931 could not continue beyond 31 March 1931. Where a route was in operation on or before 9 February 1931 the operator could use its existence as an established facility although it did not guarantee that a licence would eventually be issued. In fact Southdown's Traffic Manager had been specifically instructed by the Board to open at once any new routes which in his opinion were advisable to adequately cover roads in the company's operating area.

As part of the agreement with Maidstone & District over the operation of the Coastal Express Service within their territory the two companies agreed in principle to allocate additional workings on jointly operated service 15 between Hastings and Eastbourne. As each company's workings were not specified in the published timetable it is not clear as to how this affected the operation which required two buses from each company. Further details of the Coastal Express Service can be found in chapter 3.

Summer timetables were introduced on **Monday 1 June** with the usual increase in services aimed at the tourist markets such as the **27** to Devils Dyke. In Worthing service **4** was increased to run every 15 minute throughout to High Salvington daily and service **94** reintroduced again between Polegate Station and Wannock. This time no service ran in the morning with buses starting from Polegate Station at 1340 and then running at frequent intervals until early evening.

High summer timetables began on **Monday 20 July** with the frequency of service **12** increased to every 30 minutes throughout between Brighton and Eastbourne and a 10 minute service between Brighton and Seaford daily. Nine journeys ran to and from Peacehaven Annexe. This service was restricted to single deck buses throughout the 1930s as remedial work on Newhaven Bridge was only completed soon after the outbreak of war. For the winter timetable commencing on **Monday 21 September** the frequency was reduced to an hourly service throughout to Eastbourne with a 15 minute service between Brighton and Seaford daily plus eight journeys to Peacehaven Annexe.

THE BATTLE FOR BEACHY HEAD

In Eastbourne, the municipality had tried unsuccessfully to influence the departure times of Southdown buses running in the borough, although the company was eventually to establish an extremely successful base in the town. Whilst the longer country routes were of no interest to Eastbourne Corporation's Motor Omnibus Department there were some, such as those to Wannock, Jevington and Pevensey Bay, which had their termini just beyond the municipal boundary. By far the most contentious route proved to be that to the top of Beachy Head and on 6 August 1931 the Traffic Commissioners for the South Eastern area held a Public Sitting at Eastbourne Town Hall to hear applications for stage carriage licences for this route from six operators including Chapman & Sons, Southdown, Eastbourne Motor Coach Association, Eastbourne Corporation, Southern Glideway Coaches and Keith & Boyle of London SE11. The hearing had been adjourned from an earlier Public Sitting held in Brighton on 20 July 1931 at which all of the applicants were granted short term licences to commence from 22 July and end on 10 August 1931 subject to various conditions including that they used only single deck vehicles and did not pick up and set down the same passengers along the sea front between the Redoubt and foot of Beachy Head. The maximum number of vehicles allowed to be used varied between one and eleven (Chapman) probably in accordance with the operator's previous journeys to Beachy Head

Following the later hearing it was confirmed that a Road Service Licence would be granted to Southdown and commencing **Tuesday 11 August** the famous service **97** began operating between EASTBOURNE (ROYAL PARADE) and BEACHY HEAD HOTEL via Royal Parade, Marine Parade, Grand Parade, King Edward's Parade, Duke's Drive, Upper Dukes Drive and Beachy Head Road. To avoid buses passing in narrow roads in the Meads area they returned from Beachy Head Road via Meads Road, Meads Street, Darley Road and Chesterfield Road to King Edward's Parade. The journey time was 18 minutes and an hourly basic service was operated daily but increased to 20 minutes in fine weather. The maximum number of vehicles to be run on any departure was limited to one. For some unknown reason the service continued to run on short term licences until 30 November 1931 after which the, then, customary one year licence was issued.

Not surprisingly Eastbourne Corporation was very unhappy with the decision and considered an appeal. Instead they decided to oppose the Southdown renewal application in November 1932 and to apply for a licence to operate the service. Despite claiming that the new Southdown service had adversely affected their own service to the foot of Beachy Head the new application was refused and the Southdown licence renewed. The corporation maintained that it had prior rights of operation within its boundaries, but the Commissioners disagreed with the argument and said that it had missed its opportunity in the past and must not complain at other people showing more initiative. Ironically, some years earlier the transport committee of Eastbourne had been requested to run such a service to the top of Beachy Head but refrained from competing with the coach operators based in the town who provided what they considered to be an adequate number of vehicles.

In 1934 Southdown decided that the single deck restriction could be partly overcome by purchasing vehicles of higher seating capacity for this service and introduced the first of four petrol engined three axle Leyland Tigers with Short Bros 40-seat bodywork built to an attractive coach like specification. The service prospered during the 1930s until wartime conditions forced its complete suspension in summer 1940.

1932

Staring on **Friday 1 January** service **31A** was curtailed to operate between SOUTHSEA (SOUTH PARADE PIER) and EMSWORTH SQUARE being withdrawn from Westbourne. In its place Southdown introduced a new local service between EMSWORTH SQUARE and WESTBOURNE (POST OFFICE) via High Street, North Street, New Brighton Road and Westbourne Road. Numbered **44** it had a journey time of just 7 minutes and ran every 30 minutes daily. Apart from one early journey from Emsworth at 0750 on Weekdays the service did not commence until 1227 continuing half hourly until 2227. Westbourne already enjoyed an hourly bus service **46** to Havant and Portsmouth which from this date was increased to an approximately hourly service throughout from Portsmouth to Churchers Corner – just north of Westbourne – plus an hourly service between Portsmouth and Westbourne Cricketers daily. The service was curtailed for the winter at Portsmouth Victoria Hall but subsequently extended to Southsea in summer. Service 54 still provided three journeys on Saturdays which ran from Chichester via Churchers Corner and Westbourne to Emsworth.

In the Eastbourne area the timetable for the Eastbourne to Beachy Head service **97** became a basic two hourly frequency increased to 30 minutes in very fine weather although no service was offered in very bad weather! The advertised timetable varied according to Dull days, Fine Days and Very Fine Exceptional Days!!

From **Thursday 10 March** new service **90** began running between EASTBOURNE (PEVENSEY ROAD) and HEATHFIELD (PRINCE OF WALES HOTEL). It followed existing route 91 to Hailsham and then served Hellingly Mental Hospital, Grove Bridge, Horam, Little London and Heathfield. Three journeys were provided each way daily plus one journey each way between Eastbourne and Little London. From 18 June 1932 the frequency was increased to an hourly service daily for the summer period but from 1 January 1933 it was diverted between Hailsham and Horam to operate via Leap Cross, Upper Horsebridge, Hellingly Hospital, Grove Hill, Marie Green, Horam etc. and the frequency revised to 4 journeys each way daily which became the standard for many years.

Starting on Easter **Saturday 26 March** service **7** was extended from COKEHAM (BALL TREE HOTEL) via West Street, Cokeham Road, Boundstone Lane, Sompting Road, Lancing Station and South Street to LANCING (THREE HORSE SHOES HOTEL). A 15 minute service ran as far as Downland Corner with alternate journeys extended to and from Lancing daily. From the Three Horse Shoes buses followed a turning loop via Brighton Road and Penhill Road back to South Street.

Starting from **Saturday 18 June** Chichester area service **53** was increased to provide a two hourly service each way around the Witterings and Bracklesham Bay loop daily plus two journeys direct to Itchenor daily.

High Summer Timetables commenced on **Monday 18 July** with a number of new features. Instead of just adding to the frequency of service 4 to High Salvington Southdown introduced a

The revised timetable for the Heathfield to Eastbourne services shows the very late arrival of the first bus into Eastbourne each day! Although a very comprehensive daytime frequency was provided it is strange that there was considered to be no demand for earlier travel into Eastbourne. Note that in the pre-LPTB days there were connections at Heathfield for Tonbridge.

In the Eastbourne area the timetable for the Eastbourne to Beachy Head service 97 became a basic two hourly frequency increased to 30 minutes in very fine weather although no service was offered in very bad weather! At a time when, presumably, the Traffic Commissioners accepted such variations the advertised timetable varied according to Dull days, Fine Days and Very Fine Exceptional Days!

Bus Services 90 & 91 EASTBOURNE, HEATHFIELD, UCKFIELD.

With connections at Heathfield to and from Tunbridge Wells and Tonbridge.

SSO—Saturdays and Sundays only.   NS—Not Sundays.   SO—Sundays only.
★ Goes to Cross-in-Hand if required.

	NS																	SSO					SSO	SSO
Eastbourne ...	9 35	1035	1135	12 5	1235	135	235	335	4 5	435	535	6 5	635	735	735	8 35	9 5	9 35	...	11 0
Up. Will'gdn ...	9 45	1045	1145	1215	1245	145	245	345	415	445	545	615	645	745	745	8 45	915	9 45	...	1110
Polegate ...	9 52	1052	1152	1222	1252	152	252	352	422	452	552	622	652	752	752	8 52	922	9 52	...	1117
Hailsham ...	10 5	11 5	12 5	1235	1 5	2 5	3 5	4 5	435	5 5	6 5	635	7 5	8 5	8 5	9 5	935	10 5	...	1130
Horsebridge ...	1010	1110	1210	1240	1 10	210	310	410	440	510	610	640	710	810	810	9 10	940	1010	...	1136
Horeham R. ...	1023	1123	1223	1253	1 23	223	323	423	453	523	623	653	723	823	823	9 23	953	1023	...	1149
Maynards G. ...	1026	1126	1226	...	1 26	226	326	426	...	526	626	...	726	826	826	9 26	...	1026	...	1152
Little L'nd'n ...				1258				458			658				958					
Heathfield ...	810	1037	1137	1237	1 7	1 37	237	337	437	537	637	7 7	737	837	837	9 37	107	1037	1052	12 5
Cross-in-Hd. ...	816	1046	1146	1246	1 46	246	346	446	...	546	646	...	746	846	846	9 46	★	1058	
Blackboys ...	823	1053	1153	1253	1 53	253	353	453	...	553	653	...	753	853	9 53	...	11 5	...
Framfield ...	831	11 1	12 1	1 1	2 1	3 1	4 1	5 1	...	6 1	7 1	...	8 1	9 1	10 1	...	1113	...
Uckfield ...	840	1110	1210	1 10	2 10	310	410	510	...	610	710	...	810	910	1010	...	1123

	NS	SO																	SSO	SSO
Uckfield ...	8 45	...	...	9 45	...	1145	1245	...	1 45	245	345	...	445	545	645	...	7 45	8 45	9 15	1020
Framfield ...	8 53	...	...	9 53	...	1153	1253	...	1 53	253	353	...	453	553	653	...	7 53	8 53	9 23	1027
Blackboys ...	9 1	...	...	10 1	...	12 1	1 1	...	2 1	3 1	4 1	...	5 1	6 1	7 1	...	8 1	9 1	9 31	1035
Cross-in-Hd. ...	9 10	9 10	...	1010	...	1210	1 10	...	2 10	310	410	...	510	610	710	...	8 10	9 10	9 40	1046
Heathfield ...	9 18	9 18	9 48	1018	1118	1218	1 18	1 48	2 18	318	418	...	518	618	718	748	8 18	9 18	9 48	1052
Little L'nd'n ...	...	...	10 1	...	...	...	...	2 1	...			5 1			8 1					
Maynards G. ...	9 31	9 31	...	1031	1131	1231	1 31	...	2 31	331	431	...	531	631	731	...	8 31	9 31	10 1	...
Horeham R. ...	9 36	9 36	10 6	1036	1136	1236	1 36	2 6	2 36	336	436	5 6	536	636	736	8 6	8 36	9 36	10 6	...
Horsebridge ...	9 47	9 47	1017	1047	1147	1247	1 47	2 17	2 47	347	447	517	547	647	747	817	8 47	9 47	10 17	...
Hailsham ...	9 55	9 55	1025	1055	1155	1255	1 55	2 25	2 55	355	455	525	555	655	755	825	8 55	9 55	1025	...
Polegate ...	10 8	10 8	1038	11 8	12 8	1 8	2 8	2 38	3 8	4 8	5 8	538	6 8	7 8	8 8	838	9 8	10 8	1038	...
Up. Will'gdn ...	1015	1015	1045	1115	1215	1 15	2 15	2 45	3 15	415	515	545	615	715	815	845	9 15	1015	1045	...
Eastbourne ...	1025	1025	1055	1125	1225	1 25	2 25	2 55	3 25	425	525	555	625	725	825	855	9 25	1025	1055	...

new summer only service **8** between WORTHING (DOME) and HIGH SALVINGTON which followed the main road north via Broadwater, Offington Corner and Swandean. The frequency of service **11** was further enhanced to provide a 30 minute service throughout between Brighton and Ferring daily plus a 30 minute service between Brighton and Worthing via Sussex Pad. Additionally, an extra 30 minute service between Brighton and Worthing via the Coast Road was introduced but did not run in inclement weather. The half hourly service **31** journeys continued between Brighton and Southsea.

The first development of the Lower Bevendean estate came in the early 1930s when Brighton Corporation extended its housing from South Moulscombe up the valley on Bevendean land. To cater for the new residents Southdown introduced new route **13E** running between BRIGHTON (POOL VALLEY) and BEVENDEAN via Grand Junction Road, Old Steine, Pavilion Parade, Marlborough Place, Gloucester Place, Richmond Place, Richmond Terrace, Lewes Road, The Avenue, Hillside and Widdicombe Way. A 20 minute frequency was provided daily.

From the same date a new summer only service **26A** commenced between SEAFORD (CLINTON PLACE) and ALFRISTON (CROSS) running direct via Alfriston Road and High-and-Over. This was a very challenging route for buses of the time and ran every 40 minutes with departures from Seaford at 1425 until 1945 daily until 18 September. Service 26 already provided an all year round hourly service between Seaford and Alfriston but using the rather less demanding route via Litlington.

In the Portsmouth area service **45** was revised to provide a 10 minute service daily to Fareham with one journey per hour numbered **45C** and diverted in Portchester to operate via East Street, Castle Street, White Hart Lane and Cornaway Lane. One journey per hour continued to run beyond Fareham to and from Warsash. At this time no service was routed via Fratton and journeys beyond Theatre Royal did not start until the 1013 departure from South Parade Pier.

INCREASED SERVICE

Commencing Saturday, 26th March, 1932

Service 97 EASTBOURNE AND BEACHY HEAD.

WEEKDAYS AND SUNDAYS.

	C	ABC	C	BC	C	A C	C	ABC	C	BC	C	ABC	C	BC	BC	C	
Eastb'e (Ryl Pde.)	10 0	1030	11 0	1130	12 0	1230	2 0	230	3 0	330	4 0	430	5 0	530	6 30	7 0	...
Pier ...	10 3	1033	11 3	1133	12 3	1233	2 3	233	3 3	333	4 3	433	5 3	533	6 33	7 3	...
Foot of Beachy Hd	1010	1040	1110	1140	1210	1240	2 10	240	3 10	340	4 10	440	5 10	540	6 40	7 10	...
Beachy Head Htl.	1018	1048	1118	1148	1218	1248	2 18	248	3 18	348	4 18	448	5 18	548	6 48	7 18	...

	C	ABC	C	BC	C	ABC	C	ABC	C	BC	C	ABC	C	BC	BC	C	
Beachy Head Htl.	1020	1050	1120	1150	1220	1250	2 20	250	3 20	350	4 20	450	5 20	550	6 50	7 20	...
Mead Street ...	1028	1058	1128	1158	1228	1258	2 28	258	3 28	358	4 28	458	5 28	558	6 58	7 28	...
Pier ...	1035	11 5	1135	12 5	1235	1 5	2 35	3 5	3 35	4 5	4 35	5 5	5 35	6 5	7 5	7 35	...
Eastb'e (Ryl Pde.)	1038	11 8	1138	12 8	1238	1 8	2 38	3 8	3 38	4 8	4 38	5 8	5 38	6 8	7 8	7 38	...

A. To be run on DULL DAYS.
B. „ „ „ „ FINE DAYS
C. „ „ „ „ VERY FINE EXCEPTIONAL DAYS
IN VERY BAD WEATHER - NO SERVICE

FARE TABLE.

			Adults	Children
Company's Garage (Royal Parade) to Beachy Head Hotel			9d.	6d.
Pier	„	„ „ „ „	8d.	6d.
Grand Hotel (Cab Shelter)	„	„ „ „ „	7d.	5d.
Foot of Beachy Head or Mead St.	„	„ „ „ „	6d.	4d.

YOUR FRIENDS ABROAD will appreciate News and Pictures from the Home County. Send a copy of the "*Southern Weekly News*" every Saturday.

Service **94** was again reintroduced between Polegate Station and Wannock as in summer 1931 and ran until 18 September but did not appear in 1933. This was the first full summer for the Beachy Head service **97** and a much enhanced timetable was offered for the high summer period. Buses ran from Royal Parade at 0950 and every 20 minutes until 2030 returning from Beachy Head 20 minutes later although in inclement weather only an hourly service was provided between 1030 and 1930. What happened on changeable days can only be imagined!

Winter timetables began on **Monday 19 September** and service **11** lost some of its summer enhancement but the journeys via the Old Shoreham Toll Bridge and Sussex Pad Hotel – sometimes referred to on maps as 11A – continued with a 30 minute service, previously hourly in winter. The frequency of service **12** was reduced as in the previous winter. Service **97** reverted to the same timetable as the previous winter along with its variable operating days according to weather conditions.

When Road Service Licences were granted in 1931 several were restricted to the use of single deck vehicles only and where appropriate Southdown started to apply to modify the conditions attached to the licences on renewal to allow the use of double deckers. One that was opposed by Bexhill Corporation was the **15** between Hastings and Eastbourne.

Some further alterations were introduced as from **Monday 17 October** with service **4** reduced for the winter to a 15 minute service daily with just alternate journeys extended to and from High Salvington. Service **45** was curtailed for the winter at PORTSMOUTH (VICTORIA HALL) no longer continuing to South Parade Pier. The frequency between Portsmouth and Fareham was reduced to every 15 minutes daily with one journey per hour – sometimes referred to as 45C – operating via Castle Street.

Also from this date, Southdown acquired the goodwill of G. Tate of Felpham who traded as Red Rover Motor Services running a Stage Carriage service between Bognor and Pagham. Service **50** was now extended to operate from ELMER (NEW CITY) to PAGHAM BEACH replacing service 61 between Bognor and Pagham Beach but with an increased 30 minute frequency. Certain journeys diverted at Gossamer Lane to operate via Nyetimber Lane, Pagham Road and Sea Lane.

Finally, Southdown acquired from J. Haffenden of Vines Cross, Horeham Road their Stage Carriage service between Heathfield and Eastbourne via Rushlake Green allowing them to recommence an enhanced service **95**. Buses ran every three hours but were now diverted between Hailsham and Eastbourne to operate via Stone Cross and Friday Street. The original application by Southdown for this service was refused by the Traffic Commissioners as Haffenden had been the established operator on the route.

On 14 December 1932 Southdown acquired the Stage Carriage services and goodwill of S. S. T. Overington trading as Blue Bus Company, Horsham for the sum of £500. The services between Horsham-Handcross-Balcombe and Horsham-Maplehurst were absorbed into the Southdown network with changes which were introduced on 1 January 1933.

1933

Work commenced on the Southern Railway electrification to Brighton and Worthing in 1931 and services were formally inaugurated on 30 December 1932 with full services starting on Sunday 1 January 1933. The new services were very generous compared to the steam services they replaced and would clearly present formidable competition for Southdown's bus and coach services but might also encourage many more passengers on to buses connecting into the principal railway stations.

Service **21** had featured in the timetable index by 1930 running between SOUTHWICK (TOWN HALL) and SHOREHAM BRIDGE but without any details of its timing! By 1 June 1930 it was shown as running three journeys each way on Wednesday and Sunday afternoons presumably for hospital visitors with timing points at Southwick Town Hall, Kingston Lane, Union Entrance, Shoreham Station and Shoreham Office. The 'Union Entrance' was the former Steyning Union Workhouse built in 1835 and now the site of Southlands Hospital. These

journeys became known as service **21B** and from **Saturday 1 January** Southdown introduced a revised service **21** running between SOUTHWICK (TOWN HALL) and BUNGALOW TOWN (Kingston Ferry Road) via Albion Street, Kingston Lane, Upper Shoreham Road, Buckingham Road, Brunswick Road, East Street, High Street, Norfolk Bridge, Brighton Road and King's Drive with an hourly service daily. Shoreham's 'Bungalow Town' was built on a shingle spit of beach extending westwards from the mouth of the Adur. Most of the development took place between the wars when it became a weekend retreat for the comfortably off. The dwellings were often makeshift and haphazard, with many still constructed around redundant railway carriages and at first there was no electricity, gas, or main drainage and water brought from the 'mainland'. Bus number **21** was to be associated with Bungalow Town, later known as Shoreham Beach, for many years.

Service **27** gained one additional 'local' journey each way daily between Brighton Pool Valley and Mill Lane. New housing was extending along Dyke Road Avenue which would provide additional all year traffic for this very seasonal route. At this time the winter service consisted of a three hourly service daily to Henfield and five journeys each way daily as far as Devil's Dyke.

A small package of revisions and new routes started in the Storrington area at this time. Service **65** from Littlehampton via Amberley was curtailed at Storrington with the section onwards to West Chiltington becoming part of new route **60** running between STORRINGTON and PULBOROUGH STATION via Fryern Lodge, Roundabout Cottages, West Chiltington Common Post Office, West Chiltington village, West Chiltington Common Post Office, Heath Mill and Mare Hill. Eight journeys were provided each way daily some of which did not serve West Chiltington village. In addition new service **61** commenced between STORRINGTON and THAKEHAM CROSS ROADS via B2139 covering

Bus Service 21 SOUTHWICK, STEYNING UNION and SHOREHAM.		WEDS.			SUNS.		
Southwick (**Town Hall**) ...	155	...	...	220	...	...
Southwick Green (South side)	157	...	...	222	...	...
Kingston Lane (North End)	2 0	225	...	225	245	...
Union Entrance ...	2 3	228	350	228	248	410
Shoreham Station ...	2 7	232	354	232	252	414
Shoreham (Norfolk Bridge) ...	210	...	357	235	255	417
		WEDS.			SUNS.		
Shoreham (Norfolk Bridge) ...	215	...	4 0	235	255	420
Shoreham Station ...	218	242	4 3	238	258	423
Union Entrance ...	222	246	4 7	242	3 2	427
Kingston Lane (North End)	225	...	410	245	...	430
Southwick Green (South side)	...	...	413	...	...	433
Southwick (Town Hall) ...	...	...	415	...	...	435

more new roads for Southdown. With a journey time of 13 minutes there were seven journeys each way on weekdays and six journeys each way on Sundays.

As already stated Southdown had acquired the goodwill of S. S. T. Overington t/a Blue Bus Company, Horsham on 14 December 1932 including the Stage Carriage services between Horsham–Handcross–Balcombe and Horsham–Maplehurst although Overington continued to run coaches until 1935. In replacement Southdown introduced new service **80** running between HORSHAM CARFAX and MAPLEHURST (WHITE HORSE) via Mannings Heath, Monks Gate and Nuthurst with a 2/4 hourly frequency. Service **81** which provided a long cross country link from Haywards Heath to Wisborough Green was curtailed at BILLINGSHURST and revised to provide a three hourly frequency daily.

Southdown already operated service **82** between Haywards Heath and Horsham via Cuckfield and Handcross and this was now curtailed to operate between BALCOMBE (HALF MOON) and HORSHAM (CARFAX) via Handcross, Ashfold Crossways Plummer's Plain, Lower Beeding, Monk's Gate and Mannings Heath. An hourly service ran daily between Handcross and Horsham with three journeys operating to and from Balcombe. The first and last journeys continued to operate as garage workings to and from Haywards Heath. Service **83** still maintained a link between Haywards Heath and Horsham via Bolney.

Finally, among the January changes service **96** was curtailed to run between EASTBOURNE (PEVENSEY ROAD) and PEVENSEY BAY (BAY HOTEL) via Stone Cross, no longer returning via Pevensey Bay Road and Seaside to form a circular service. But, the frequency was significantly increased from seven journeys daily to hourly.

Starting on Easter **Saturday 15 April** service **11** was revised with a 30 minute service throughout between Brighton and Ferring via the Coast Road. The service between Brighton and Worthing via Sussex Pad was reduced to hourly and formally renumbered **11A** although in compensation a new hourly service was introduced between Lancing Manor (Old Shoreham Road/Grinstead Lane) and Worthing numbered **11B**. Also from this date a new service **98** commenced running between EASTBOURNE (PEVENSEY ROAD) and PEVENSEY (OLD MINT HOUSE) via Seaside and Pevensey Bay Road in replacement for the withdrawn coastal section of service 96 lost in January. At first just three journeys were provided each way daily but from 3 June 1933 an hourly summer service ran daily reverting to three journeys in winter.

Summer services were introduced from Whit **Saturday 3 June** and brought some enhancements to services. The changes to the **11** group in April were short lived and a 30 minute service was again provided between Brighton and

Worthing via Sussex Pad numbered **11A** while service **11B** was withdrawn. On service **27** the short journeys between Brighton and Devils Dyke increased to 12 journeys each way daily and in Portsmouth services **45** and **46** were once again extended through to SOUTHSEA (SOUTH PARADE PIER).

The London Passenger Transport Bill received royal assent on 13 April 1933 with the new London Passenger Transport Board (LPTB), assuming control from midnight on 1 July 1933. The new Board's defined London Passenger Transport Area (LPTA) extended approximately 25 to 30 miles from Charing Cross including an area of almost 2,000 square miles reaching Baldock in the north, Gravesend and Brentwood in the east, Horsham, Crawley and East Grinstead in the south and Guildford and Slough to the west. In some parts the boundary line caused some illogical splitting of routes which took many years to satisfactorily resolve. As far as Southdown was concerned much of the southern boundary was based on the former East Surrey operating boundary, a company with which it already had a territorial agreement. Within the LPTB 'Special Area', which in the territory adjoining Southdown passed about five to ten miles north of the LPTA boundary, the board enjoyed unrestricted monopoly rights and no operator was permitted to run a local bus service without its permission. Fortunately this did not affect any existing Southdown operations. In addition the Board was granted certain running rights to cross the LPTA boundary such as its service 409 between East Grinstead and Forest Row although Southdown was allowed to extend its services north to East Grinstead. The Board was not permitted to operate outside the LPTA area and any existing express services or excursions and tours crossing the border were

Car 693 (UF 6593), a Tilling-Stevens Express B10A2 with Short Bros bodywork dating from 1930, is seen laying over at Horsham Carfax before departure on service 80 to Steyning via Partridge Green to which it was extended in January 1935 after Southdown acquired the business of Carter Bros of Monks Gate. Despite the delivery of the 1400 class Leyland Tigers from 1935 onwards many of the large fleet of Tilling-Stevens buses survived until the outbreak of the war with car 693 being requisitioned by the Military Authorities in July 1940. *A.Duke, Omnibus Society*

Until July 1933 Southdown only served the town of East Grinstead on its London to Eastbourne express services. In this tranquil early 1930s scene showing the High Street looking south towards Eastbourne there appears to be an alarming number of parked cars and no provision for buses to stop! From 1 July 1933 services 28, 30 and 92 loaded on the left near the white shop awnings and the company soon established a booking office in the town. In later years bus stops for services 36 and 87 were also established on the right near the Memorial. *West Sussex County Council*

usually handed over to the nearest relevant companies with which it had area agreements – including Southdown. The fleet name London Transport was adopted in 1934 but throughout the 1930s operations were controlled by the LPTB and this was the legal owner shown on its vehicles.

Commencing on **Saturday 1 July** Southdown gained significant new territory as services south of Crawley and East Grinstead previously provided by London General Country Services which were outside the defined LPTA were transferred to Southdown. These included the sections between Crawley and Handcross and also East Grinstead and Uckfield resulting in several existing services being extended and many new links introduced that were to prosper for many years. East Surrey had first reached Handcross as long ago as 21 February 1916 following an agreement with Southdown. This defined the boundary between the two companies as a line from Haslemere in the west to Crowborough in the east, through Horsham and Handcross with the East Grinstead to Uckfield road being neutral territory and open for use by either operator. East Surrey had to fight for the Handcross and Crowborough concessions and never reached the latter throughout its history. Southdown was

fortunate in that unlike its neighbours Maidstone & District and Aldershot & District it did not have to compulsorily pass any services or garages over to LPTB. Service **23** was extended northwards from HANDCROSS via Pease Pottage to CRAWLEY (GEORGE HOTEL) with a two hourly service daily replacing London General Country Services route 426 over this section.

East Surrey service S9 from West Croydon was extended to Uckfield from 19 October 1922 and renumbered 409 from 1 December 1924. The LPTA boundary passed just to the south of East Grinstead which now became the border town although LPTB were allowed to operate their 409 as far as Forest Row. Southdown's replacement of the Uckfield to East Grinstead section was initially rather more complex. Firstly, service **30** from Brighton was extended northwards every two hours from Chelwood Gate via Wych Cross, Forest Row and Ashurst Wood to EAST GRINSTEAD (CROWN HOTEL). The Eastbourne to Chailey service **92** was withdrawn between Uckfield and Chailey and diverted via Ringles Cross, Maresfield, Nutley, Chelwood Gate, Wych Cross, Forest Row and Ashurst Wood to EAST GRINSTEAD (CROWN HOTEL). A two hourly service was provided throughout between Eastbourne and East Grinstead plus a two hourly service between Eastbourne and Chelwood Gate daily which connected with service 30.

Finally, new service **89** between UCKFIELD and CHAILEY (KING'S HEAD HOTEL) via Ringles Cross, Maresfield, Piltdown and Newick replaced this section of service 92 and provided an hourly service daily. There were no changes at the border town of Horsham as a result of the formation of LPTB and several small independent companies continued to serve the town for many years to come.

The high summer timetable commenced on **Saturday 15 July** and service **8** was once again reintroduced between Worthing and High

Sometime after service 92 was diverted northwards, East Grinstead High Street is the setting for car 658 (UF 4658), a Tilling-Stevens Express B10A2 with Short Bros bodywork dating from 1929 which is about to set off on the long run to Eastbourne. This was Southdown's standard single decker bus for the first half of the 1930s and many survived until the outbreak of the war. *C.F.Klapper, Omnibus Society*

Salvington as in 1932. A 30 minute service throughout between Brighton and Eastbourne was restored daily on service **12**. Summer only service **26A** was reinstated and extended from Alfriston via Berwick and Polegate to EASTBOURNE (PEVENSEY ROAD). Buses ran hourly with departures from each end between 1420 and 2020 daily. The frequency of service **45** between Southsea and Fareham was again increased to a 10 minute service daily with one journey per hour diverting via Castle Street in Portchester as in summer 1932.

In 1932 the highways committee of Littlehampton Urban District Council had asked Southdown to discuss the provision of additional bus services in the town and, presumably in response, a new summer only LITTLEHAMPTON TOWN SERVICE numbered **63** commenced from this date starting from the Nelson Hotel and running via Pier Road, Surrey Street, Arundel Road, Wick Street, Worthing Road, Horsham Road, St Flora's Road, Norfolk Road and South Terrace every 40 minutes in each direction daily. Also new was service **66A** which ran between LITTLEHAMPTON (EAST STREET) and WICK (GLOBE INN) via East Street, Horsham Road and Worthing Road with a journey time of seven minutes. A 30 minute frequency was provided daily. Beachy Head service **97** was increased in line with the 1932 summer timetable to provide an hourly basic service daily increased to 20 minutes in fine weather.

Among revisions in the Portsmouth area from **Thursday 3 August** service **40** was withdrawn without replacement between Clanfield and East Meon and diverted to Petersfield Station via Hog's Lodge Inn and Buriton Cross Roads. This replaced one journey an hour on service **42** which became hourly throughout between Southsea and South Harting daily plus additional journeys on summer Saturdays and Sundays between Southsea and Snells Corner. Further to the recent enhancement of service **45** the Saturday morning frequency was reduced from 10 to 15 minutes.

In addition Hayling Island service **47** was once again extended from Havant to SOUTHSEA (SOUTH PARADE) via Fratton restoring the direct link lost in April 1930. A 30 minute service daily was provided with all journeys operating anti-clockwise around the Hayling loop plus a 30 minute service daily between Havant Station and Hayling operating clockwise around the loop and with alternate journeys diverted between Langstone Road and Stoke via Northney. The extension was probably made possible by the delivery in July of a further six lightweight TSM Express buses which were able to cross the restricted Langstone Bridge between Hayling Island and Havant. After many years services **48** from Waterlooville and **49** from Horndean no longer served Hayling and both were curtailed at Havant where connections could be made with the 47 and through fares remained available.

Car 523 (UF 3023) is one of a batch of five Dennis 30cwt chassis with all metal Short Bros 18-seat bodywork new in March 1928. Although suitable for one man (there were no female drivers with Southdown at this time) operation there is clearly a two person crew in evidence in this scene at Littlehampton on the local circular service 63. This vehicle passed to Brighton, Hove & District for further service in March 1936. *Alan Lambert Collection*

In the 1930s Hayling Island was becoming a popular destination for families who wanted to stay in the new 'holiday camps'. In August 1933 Southdown acquired two operators who were both running summer stage carriage services between Eastoke Post Office and Hayling Ferry connecting with the ferry to and from Southsea. These were G.W. Meekings of Bentley, Hampshire and P.C. Bellier of Portsmouth and to meet the growing demand from holidaymakers Southdown introduced new summer only service **46**. Although there is a reference to this service in the bus timetable no details were included but for the 1934 season it ran between HAYLING FERRY and EASTOKE HOUSE via Ferry Road, St Catherine's Road, Station Road, Beach Road, Sea Front and Southwood Road. An hourly basic service was increased to half hourly on fine days. On 'very fine days' when many Portsmouth residents wished to travel across to Hayling Island an increased service was provided between the Ferry and South Hayling Beach. As a result the Westbourne to Southsea service 46 was renumbered to **43** while the existing 43 between SOUTHSEA (SOUTH PARADE PIER) and FARLINGTON CHURCH was renumbered **31C**.

In this early 1930s scene car 935 (UF 8375) is seen waiting at South Harting which was the northern terminus of service 42 from Southsea until January 1935 when it was cut back to Petersfield Station and replaced by a new localised service 61. The vehicle is a Leyland Titan TD1 with Short Bros highbridge body dating from 1932 which remained in service with Southdown until September 1940 before passing for further service to Cumberland Motor Services. The distinctive building behind the bus is still in place. *C.F.Klapper, Omnibus Society*

PETERSFIELD, CLANFIELD, WATERLOOVILLE, HAVANT AND HAYLING ISLAND

WEEKDAYS AND SUNDAYS.

		NS																		
Petersfield (Station)	...	...	1013	...	1213	...	2 13	...	4 13	...	6 13	...	8 13	...	...	...	...			
Clanfield		...	1032	...	1232	...	2 32	...	4 32	...	6 32	...	8 32	...	...	...	...			
Waterlooville ... arr.		...	1052	...	1252	...	2 52	...	4 52	...	6 52	...	8 52	...	...	...	...			
Waterlooville ... dep.	9 19	1053	1119	1253	1 19	2 53	3 19	4 53	5 19	6 53	7 19	8 53	9 19							
Havant (Church) ... arr.	9 29	11 3	1129	1 3	1 29	3 3	3 29	5 3	5 29	7 3	7 29	9 3	9 29							
Havant (Church) ... dep.	9 34	11 4	1134	1 4	1 34	3 4	3 34	5 4	5 34	7 4	7 34	9 4	9 34							
Hayling Beach ... arr.	9 55	1125	1155	1 25	1 55	3 25	3 55	5 25	5 55	7 25	7 55	9 25	9 55							

	NS																			
Hayling Beach ... dep.	8 1	9 55	1025	1155	1225	1 55	2 25	3 55	4 25	5 55	6 25	7 55	8 25							
Havant (Church) ... arr.	8 22	1022	1052	1222	1252	2 22	2 52	4 22	4 52	6 22	6 52	8 22	8 52							
Havant (Church) ... dep.	8 52	1029	11 5	1229	1 5	2 29	3 5	4 29	5 5	6 29	7 5	8 29	9 5							
Waterlooville ... arr.	9 2	1039	1115	1239	1 15	2 39	3 15	4 39	5 15	6 39	7 15	8 39	9 15							
Waterlooville ... dep.	...	1116	...	1 16	...	3 16	...	5 16	...	7 16	...	9 16								
Clanfield ... ,,	...	1136	...	1 36	...	3 36	...	5 36	...	7 36	...	9 36								
Petersfield (Station) ,,	...	1155	...	1 55	...	3 55	...	5 55	...	7 55	...									

FARE TABLE.

THROUGH RETURN FARES.

Waterlooville. 30.
3 | Loxter. 26.
4 | 1 | Bedhampton Halt. 15.
5 | 2 | 1 | Havant. 14.

Petersfield and Hayling	... ...	3/6
Clanfield and Hayling	... ...	2/9
Waterlooville and Hayling	... ...	2/-

For Fares between Waterlooville and Petersfield see page 128
" " " Havant and Hayling see page 143

After the changes of 3 August 1933 the new timetable for service 48 makes no clear distinction between the main service between Havant and Waterlooville or connections to Petersfield and Hayling. It replaced an equally confusing version which combined the 47, 48 and 49 but was in practice a simplification of services in the Havant area following the resumption of through journeys between Southsea and Hayling Island.

Winter timetables began on **Monday 18 September** and in Worthing service 8 to High Salvington via Offington Corner was withdrawn and would not reappear in this form again. Service **12** was reduced in line with the previous winter's timetable becoming hourly beyond Seaford to Eastbourne. Devils Dyke journeys on service **27** were once again reduced to six journeys each way daily plus the one journey each way daily from Brighton to Mill Lane. In Littlehampton the recently introduced local service **63** was seasonally withdrawn but reintroduced in a revised form in 1934. Summer only

services **10B**, **26A** and **46** ceased for winter but at Eastbourne service **97** retained its summer timetable for another month. Its operation varied according to the state of the weather!

Further changes occurred from **Monday 16 October** and services **11** and **11A** reverted to the timetable introduced on 15 April 1933 which meant the daily reintroduction of the **11B** between Worthing and Lancing Manor. In Portsmouth service **45** was reduced to a 15 minute service on Sundays to Fridays and Saturday mornings but kept a 10 minute service from noon on Saturdays as far as Fareham. Along with the 43 it was not cut back from Southsea for this winter as in the past. Hayling service **47** was curtailed to operate just HAVANT STATION – HAYLING – HAVANT STATION running both ways around the Hayling loop. There was an hourly service each way including a two hourly service via Northney. Service **48** was extended from HAVANT to HORNDEAN via Rowlands Castle, Woodhouse Ashes and Woodhouse replacing service **49** over this section. Two journeys per hour were provided between Havant and Waterlooville and one journey between Havant and Horndean.

In Eastbourne service **97** reverted to its winter timetable of an hourly basic service daily but increased to 30 minutes in exceptionally fine weather and this remained the standard until the war. Service **98** between Eastbourne and Pevensey via the Coast Road and Pevensey Bay was reduced from hourly to just three journeys each way daily.

Seen here on bus service 97 at Eastbourne Pier car 1083 (UF 9783) is a Leyland Tiger TS4 with Harrington coach body dating from 1933. Judging by the lack of passengers and traffic it is a quiet winter day and demand for Beachy Head is limited! The coach was requisitioned for Military service in June 1940 but reacquired by Southdown in February 1946 and was later modernised with a longer Covrad radiator.
C.F.Klapper, Omnibus Society

1934

Some further revisions to the services in Worthing commenced as from **Thursday 29 March** with the existing service **5** between Goring Church and Broadwater being renumbered 8 and revised to run between WORTHING PIER and BROADWATER (THACKERAY ROAD) via South Street, Chapel Road, Broadwater Road, Broadwater Street East and Dominion Road. A new circular service **5** ran THOMAS A'BECKET HOTEL – PIER – A' BECKET AVENUE via Poulters Lane, South Farm Road, Northcourt Road, Broadwater Road, Chapel Road, South Street, Marine Parade, West Buildings, Crescent Road, Clifton Road, South Farm Road, Pavilion Road, Becket Road, South Street, Rectory Road and Littlehampton Road. A 15 minute service was provided daily with buses operating only in this direction as service **6** was revised to run the opposite way around the loop at the same frequency. At the same time the through service between Brighton and Ferring on the **11** was increased to run every 30 minutes.

From the early 1900s Pevensey Bay started to emerge as a holiday resort although much of the coastline development came in the 1930s. But, the old marsh road, which snaked its way from Eastbourne to Hastings was only a narrow cart road with bends and sharp corners totally unsuited to the traffic needs of even the 1920s. As a result the only bus link between the towns ran via Hailsham and Ninfield. It took over a decade before any action was taken but in the summer of 1933 a new direct road was finally opened across Pevensey Marsh. In October 1933 Southdown, along with Maidstone & District, made an application to run a new Stage Carriage service between Eastbourne and Hastings via the new road which would allow a shorter journey and, as a result cheaper fares, which they claimed would encourage more passengers to travel. The companies proposed to run six journeys in each direction daily but did not intend to introduce the new service until the Thursday before Easter 1934 – 'so that the surface of the new road should be properly set'. Despite some objections the Traffic Commissioners granted a daily service all the year round as applied for.

Starting on **Thursday 29 March** it was finally possible to introduce a direct service **99** between EASTBOURNE (PEVENSEY ROAD) and HASTINGS (WELLINGTON SQUARE) via Pevensey Bay, Little Common and Bexhill. The service obviously prospered and at the end of the year an application was made for an increased service between Eastbourne and Bexhill. At the hearing before the Traffic Commissioners the Southern Railway stated that the electrification of the Eastbourne to Hastings line had reached an advanced stage and full services would be run from July 1935 with the existing number of trains increased from 18 to 51 on weekdays and 8 to 36 on Sundays. The Commissioners decided that the evidence given by Southdown appeared

to justify an increase in the bus service, but they felt bound to take account of the greatly improved facilities to be offered by the railway company so only a slight increase was granted. This was a fairly rare case of the Southern Railway opposing Southdown expansion in the Traffic Courts.

Southdown had acquired an Express Carriage service from H J Sargent of East Grinstead on 30 June 1933 and from Whit **Saturday 19 May** it was licensed as a Stage Carriage service and gained the number **28** with northbound journeys from Brighton which started at Steine Street diverted via Pool Valley. Three journeys per day were provided with departures from East Grinstead at 0845, 1345 and 1745 and from Brighton at 1200, 1600 and 2045 daily normally worked with coaches. Local fares were introduced between East Grinstead and Lewes and it was advertised as running Limited Stop between Chailey and Brighton where alternative Southdown services were available.

The start of summer timetables from **Saturday 16 June** saw the return of service **46** between HAYLING FERRY and EASTOKE HOUSE which had first appeared in August 1933. An hourly basic service was increased to 30 minutes on fine days while on very fine days an increased service was run between Hayling Ferry and South Hayling Beach. Service **47** was extended from Havant Station to SOUTHSEA (SOUTH PARADE) via Fratton as in summer 1933. Service **93B** between Eastbourne and Polegate Station was renumbered **94** from the same date.

A very large programme of revisions and improvements began with the high summer timetable on **Saturday 14 July**. Recently revised Worthing services **5** and **6** both had their frequencies increased from a 15 minute to 10 minute service daily. In addition a number of complicated changes were introduced on services between Brighton and Worthing although they helped to simplify the confusion over service 11 routeings. Service **10** between Worthing and

Bus Services 98 & 99 EASTBOURNE, PEVENSEY, BEXHILL, HASTINGS

Worked jointly by buses of Southdown and Maidstone Companies.
For additional buses between Eastbourne, Bexhill and Hastings, see page 65.

WEEKDAYS AND SUNDAYS.

	NS									
Eastbourne (Pevensey Road) ...	8 10	9 30	1130	1230	1 30	2 30	3 30	5 30	6 30	8 30	...
Eastbourne (Archery) ...	8 15	9 36	1136	1236	1 36	2 36	3 36	5 36	6 36	8 36	...
Coastguards Cottages ...	8 22	9 44	1144	1244	1 44	2 44	3 44	5 44	6 44	8 44	...
Pevensey Bay (Bay Hotel) ...	8 26	9 48	1148	1248	1 48	2 48	3 48	5 48	6 48	8 48	...
Pevensey (Old Mint House) ...	8 31	9 53	1153	1253	1 53	2 53	3 53	5 53	6 53	8 53	...
Barnhorn Lane (Constable's Farm) ...		10 2	12 2	1 2	...	3 2	4 2	6 2	7 2	9 2	...
Little Common (Wheatsheaf) ...		10 9	12 9	1 9	...	3 9	4 9	6 9	7 9	9 9	...
Sutherland Avenue (Bottom) ...		1014	1214	1 14	...	3 14	4 14	6 14	7 14	9 14	...
Bexhill (Marina) ...		1019	1219	1 19	...	3 19	4 19	6 19	7 19	9 19	...
Hastings (Wellington Square) ...		1044	1244	1 44	...	3 44	4 44	6 44	7 44	9 44	...

Hastings (Wellington Square) ...		10 9	11 9	1 9	...		2 9	4 9	5 9	7 9	8 9
Bexhill (Marina) ...		1034	1134	1 34	...		2 34	4 34	5 34	7 34	8 34
Sutherland Avenue (Bottom) ...		1039	1139	1 39	...		2 39	4 39	5 39	7 39	8 39
Little Common (Wheatsheaf) ...		1044	1144	1 44	...		2 44	4 44	5 44	7 44	8 44
Barnhorn Lane (Constable's Farm) ...		1051	1151	1 51	...		2 51	4 51	5 51	7 51	8 51
Pevensey (Old Mint House) ...	10 0	11 0	12 0	2 0	2 25	3 0	5 0	6 0	8 0	9 0
Pevensey Bay (Bay Hotel) ...	10 5	11 5	12 5	2 5	2 30	3 5	5 5	6 5	8 5	9 5
Coastguards Cottages ...	10 9	11 9	12 9	2 9	2 34	3 9	5 9	6 9	8 9	9 9
Eastbourne (Archery) ...	1017	1117	1217	2 17	2 42	3 17	5 17	6 17	8 17	9 17
Eastbourne (Pevensey Road) ...	1023	1123	1223	2 23	2 48	3 23	5 23	6 23	8 23	9 23

This timetable shows the enhanced services between Eastbourne and Hastings for the 1935 summer season although once again it is notable that no early morning services are included. Until services ceased in July 1940 buses on service 99 operated a double run to the Old Mint House at Pevensey. At this time Southdown and Maidstone & District were each providing one bus for the jointly run service.

Car 1067 (UF 8837) is a Leyland Tiger TS4 with Harrington coachwork dating from 1932 and seen here at the terminus in East Grinstead High Street of Limited Stop service 28 to Brighton. Coaches were normally used and advance bookings were available. The service ended abruptly soon after the start of war and car 1067 was requisitioned by the Military in June 1940. It was reacquired by Southdown in September 1946 but fitted with a lorry body in 1947 and survives in preservation. *J.F.Parke, Omnibus Society*

Angmering Green was renumbered **9** and extended eastwards from WORTHING (DOME) to SHOREHAM (BRIDGE HOTEL) via Brighton Road, South Lancing, Lancing Station, North Lancing, Sussex Pad Hotel, A27 and Old Shoreham Toll Bridge. It was also increased in frequency from two hourly to hourly and, along with the revised service 10, replaced the service **11A** journeys that ran via Sussex Pad Hotel. Service **10A** between Worthing and Arundel was renumbered **10** and extended from WORTHING (DOME) to BRIGHTON (POOL VALLEY) via the same route as the 9 to Shoreham and then A259 to Brighton. The frequency was increased from two hourly to hourly and when combined with service 9 increased the daily frequency via Sussex Pad Hotel to half hourly. Summer only service **10B** between Bognor and Arundel was reintroduced with a two hourly service daily but no journeys ran through to Worthing. Service **11** was extended from FERRING to ANGMERING-ON-SEA via Langbury Lane, Littlehampton Road, Worthing Road, North Lane and Sea Road to its junction with Sea View Road. The section

of route via Sussex Pad Hotel (**11A**) was replaced by the extensions of services 9 and 10 and all journeys now ran via the coast road. A 30 minute service was provided daily which combined with service 31 to offer a 15 minute frequency between Brighton and Worthing.

The frequency of service **12** increased to every 30 minutes throughout between Brighton and Eastbourne with a 10 minute service between Brighton and Seaford plus nine journeys between Brighton and Peacehaven Annexe. Service **21** was extended from Southwick Town Hall to Brighton Pool Valley via the A259 and ran every 30 minutes daily. Service **28** was increased to run every two hourly daily for the summer but in winter was reduced to three journeys each way daily and this became the pattern of operation until total suspension soon after the outbreak of war. The replacement services introduced in July 1933 on the formation of LPTB were simplified with the **30** being curtailed daily at CHELWOOD COMMON (PILLAR BOX) where connections were made with an hourly **92** which was now extended through to East Grinstead. Additional journeys were run in summer on Saturday and Sunday afternoons between Uckfield and East Grinstead.

To serve new housing developments to the west of the town and adjoining the Esplanade a new Bognor Regis local service was introduced. Service **55** ran between BARRACK LANE (SOUTH END) and NORTH BERSTED CHURCH via Barrack Lane, Aldwick Road, Esplanade, York Road, High Street, London Road, Station Road, Linden Road, Collyer Avenue, Hampshire Avenue and Chichester Road with a 30 minute service daily.

Littlehampton local service **63** was reintroduced but revised to start from WICK (GLOBE INN) although following the same circular route around the town in both directions but now

Southdown took into stock its last batch of Leyland Titans TD1 models in 1932. All had Short Bros highbridge bodies and car 940 (UF 8380) is seen about to cross the Norfolk Bridge at Shoreham heading west on service 11 to Angmering-on-Sea, which variation applied between July 1934 and January 1939. In November 1943 the original body was removed at Portslade Works and car 940 was then sent to East Lancs for a new body to be fitted in January 1944. *A.Duke, Omnibus Society*

Bus Service 6 A BECKET AVENUE (Littlehampton Road), THOMAS-A-BECKET, BECKET ROAD, PIER, SOUTH FARM ROAD, THOMAS-A-BECKET									
WEEKDAYS AND SUNDAYS.									
A Becket Avenue ...	...	...	**8 19**	**8 34**	**8 49**	**9 4**	**9 19**	**9 34**	**9 49**
Thomas-a-Becket ...	...	...	**8 21**	**8 36**	**8 51**	**9 6**	**9 21**	**9 36**	**9 51**
Glebe Road	...	...	8 24	8 39	8 54	9 9	9 24	9 39	9 54
Becket Road	...	...	8 26	8 41	8 56	9 11	9 26	9 41	9 56
Clifton Arms	...	...	8 29	8 44	8 59	9 14	9 29	9 44	9 59
West Buildings ...	...	...	8 32	8 47	9 2	9 17	9 32	9 47	10 2
Pier	**8 5**	**8 20**	**8 35**	**8 50**	**9 5**	**9 20**	**9 35**	**9 50**	**10 5**
Norfolk Hotel ...	8 8	8 23	8 38	8 53	9 8	9 23	9 38	9 53	10 8
Cecilian Avenue ...	8 10	8 25	8 40	8 55	9 10	9 25	9 40	9 55	1010
St. Lawrence Avenue...	8 13	8 28	8 43	8 58	9 13	9 28	9 43	9 58	1013
Thomas-a-Becket ...	**8 19**	**8 34**	**8 49**	**9 4**	**9 19**	**9 34**	**9 49**	**10 4**	**1019**

A Becket Avenue ...	and then at the following minutes past each hour	**4**	**19**	**34**	**49**	until	**11 4**	**1119**	**1134**
Thomas-a-Becket ...		**6**	**21**	**36**	**51**		**11 6**	**1121**	**1136**
Glebe Road		9	24	39	54		11 9	1124	1139
Becket Road		11	26	41	56		1111	1126	1141
Clifton Arms		14	29	44	59		1114	1129	1144
West Buildings ...		17	32	47	2		1117	1132	1147
Pier		**20**	**35**	**50**	**5**		**1120**	**1135**	**1150**
Norfolk Hotel ...		23	38	53	8		1123	—	—
Cecilian Avenue ...		25	40	55	10		1125	...	...
St. Lawrence Avenue...		28	43	58	13		1128	...	...
Thomas-a-Becket ...		**34**	**49**	**4**	**19**		**1134**	...	...

Sundays.—This Service starts from the Pier at 9.50 a.m. and from A Becket Avenue at 10.19 a.m.

FARE TABLE.

A Becket Avenue (Littlehampton Road). 5.															
1	**Thomas-a-Becket. 6.**														
1	1	Glebe Road. **7.**													
1½	1	1	Athelstan Road. **9.**												
1½	1	1	1	Becket Road. **11.**											
1½	1	1	1	1	Lanfranc Road. **12.**										
2	1½	1	1	1	1	Woodside Road. **14.**									
2	1½	1½	1	1	1	1	Pavilion Road Corner or Clifton Arms. **19.**								
2	1½	1½	1½	1	1	1	1	Cobden Arms. **20.**							
2½	2	2	2	1½	1½	1½	1	1	Bandstand. **27.**						
2½	**2**	**2**	**2**	**1½**	**1½**	**1½**	**1**	**1**	**1**	**Pier (30) or Old Town Hall. 23**					
3½	3	3	3	2½	2½	2½	1½	1½	1	1	Norfolk Hotel. **21.**				
3½	3	3	3	2½	2½	2½	2	2	1½	1	1	Cecilian Avenue. **18.**			
4	3½	3½	3½	3	3	3	2½	2½	2	1½	1	1	S. Lawrence. Av. **17**		
4½	4	4	4	3½	3½	3½	3	2½	2	2	1½	1	1	East Corner of Poulters Ln. **16.**	
4½	**4**	**4**	**4**	**3½**	**3½**	**3½**	**3**	**3**	**2½**	**2**	**1½**	**1½**	**1**	**1**	**Thomas-a-Becket. 6**

Bus Service 5 THOMAS-A-BECKET, SOUTH FARM ROAD, PIER, BECKET RD., THOMAS-A-BECKET, A BECKET AVENUE (Littlehampton Road)										
WEEKDAYS AND SUNDAYS.										
Thomas-a-Becket	...	...	...	**8 26**	**8 41**	**8 56**	**9 11**	**9 26**	**9 41**	**9 56**
St. Lawrence Ave.	...	...	...	8 32	8 47	9 2	9 17	9 32	9 47	10 2
Cecilian Avenue ...	...	...	...	8 34	8 49	9 4	9 19	9 34	9 49	10 4
Norfolk Hotel ...	...	...	...	8 36	8 51	9 6	9 21	9 36	9 51	10 6
Pier	**7 55**	**8 10**	**8 25**	**8 40**	**8 55**	**9 10**	**9 25**	**9 40**	**9 55**	**1010**
West Buildings ...	7 58	8 13	8 28	8 43	8 58	9 13	9 28	9 43	9 58	1013
Clifton Arms ...	8 1	8 16	8 31	8 46	9 1	9 16	9 31	9 46	10 1	1016
Becket Road ...	8 4	8 19	8 34	8 49	9 4	9 19	9 34	9 49	10 4	1019
Glebe Road ...	8 6	8 21	8 36	8 51	9 6	9 21	9 36	9 51	10 6	1021
Thomas-a-Becket	**8 9**	**8 24**	**8 39**	**8 54**	**9 9**	**9 24**	**9 39**	**9 54**	**10 9**	**1024**
A Becket Avenue...	**8 11**	**8 26**	**8 41**	**8 56**	**9 11**	**9 26**	**9 41**	**9 56**	**1011**	**1026**

Thomas-a-Becket	and then at the following minutes past each hour	**11**	**26**	**41**	**56**	until	**1056**	**1111**	**1126**	**1141**
St. Lawrence Ave.		17	32	47	2		11 2	1117	1132	1147
Cecilian Avenue ...		19	34	49	4		11 4	1119	1134	1149
Norfolk Hotel ...		21	36	51	6		11 6	1121	1136	1151
Pier		**25**	**40**	**55**	**10**		**1110**	**1125**	**1140**	**1155**
West Buildings ...		28	43	58	13		1113	—	—	—
Clifton Arms ...		31	46	1	16		1116	...	...	...
Becket Road ...		34	49	4	19		1119	...	...	...
Glebe Road ...		36	51	6	21		1121	...	...	...
Thomas-a-Becket		**39**	**54**	**9**	**24**		**1124**	...	...	...
A Becket Avenue...		**41**	**56**	**11**	**26**		**1126**	...	...	...

Sundays.—This Service starts from the Pier at 9.55 a.m. and from Thomas-a-Becket at 10.11 a.m.

FARE TABLE.

Thomas-a-Becket. 6.															
1	East Corner of Poulters Lane. **16.**														
1	1	St. Lawrence Avenue. **17.**													
1½	1	1	Cecilian Avenue. **18.**												
1½	1½	1	1	Norfolk Hotel. **21.**											
2	**2**	**1½**	**1**	**1**	**Old Town Hall (23) or Pier. 30.**										
2½	2	2	1½	1	1	Bandstand. **27.**									
3	2½	2½	2	1½	1	1	Cobden Arms. **20.**								
3	3	2½	2	1½	1	1	1	Clifton Arms or Pav. Road Corner. **19.**							
3½	3½	3	2½	2½	1½	1½	1	1	Woodside Road. **14.**						
3½	3½	3	2½	2½	1½	1½	1	1	1	Lanfranc Road. **12.**					
3½	3½	3	2½	2½	1½	1½	1	1	1	1	Becket Road. **11.**				
4	4	3½	3	3	2	2	1½	1	1	1	1	Athelstan Road. **9.**			
4	4	3½	3	3	2	2	1½	1½	1	1	1	1	Glebe Road. **7.**		
4	**4**	**3½**	**3**	**3**	**2**	**2**	**1½**	**1½**	**1½**	**1**	**1**	**1**	**1**	**Thomas-a-Becket. 6.**	
4½	**4½**	**4**	**3½**	**3½**	**2½**	**2½**	**2**	**2**	**2**	**1½**	**1½**	**1½**	**1**	**1**	**A Becket Ave. 5.**

Hopefully the timetables and faretables for services 5 and 6 will help explain the complex nature of these operations! Note that first buses on Weekdays arrived at Worthing Pier soon after 0830 although a comprehensive 15 minute frequency then applied until after 2300 each day.

every 45 minutes each way. Service **66** was extended at its eastern end from LITTLEHAMPTON to RUSTINGTON CHURCH via Sea Road and at its western end from CHICHESTER to SUMMERSDALE. Here it ran in a loop from Broyle Road via Wellington Road, Summersdale Road, The Drive, The Avenue, Lavant Road, The Broadway, Summersdale Road and Wellington Road. An hourly service ran daily with alternate journeys operating via Boxgrove and Halnaker or direct via A27. Service **66A** between Littlehampton and Wick was withdrawn as part of these changes. Service **67** which had formerly only been included in the summary of journeys between Littlehampton and Arundel was extended from LITTLEHAMPTON to RUSTINGTON CHURCH via Sea Road and now included in full, running hourly between Rustington, Littlehampton and Arundel. There was no early morning service with first buses departing Rustington Church at 0935 and Arundel Square at 0906 daily. Previously it had largely existed to maintain the 15 minute frequency between Arundel and Littlehampton. Services **68** and **68A** were extended in Arundel to terminate at ARUNDEL (FORD ROAD) and provided a combined 30 minute service daily.

Winter timetables were introduced from **Monday 17 September** with the by now usual seasonal reductions on several services in the coastal towns. The newly revised Worthing services **5** and **6** had their frequencies reduced to a 15 minute service daily. In addition summer only routes such as **10B**, **26A**, **46** and **63** were withdrawn.

Following the successful introduction of service 13E in July 1932 Southdown now consolidated their position in the housing estates which were springing up bordering the Lewes Road with a new service **13F** running between BRIGHTON (POOL VALLEY) and LOWER BEVENDEAN (HAPPY VALLEY) via Grand Junction Road, Old Steine, Pavilion Parade, Marlborough Place, Gloucester Place, Richmond Place, Richmond Terrace, Lewes Road and The Avenue. From **Monday 15 October** there were two journeys per hour daily – although not half hourly – but from 24 July 1935 the frequency increased to three journeys per hour daily and a regular 20 minute daily service was provided from 4 June 1938.

An interesting development came in November 1934 when Basil Williams, later to form the Hants & Sussex company but then only 20 years of age, applied to the South Eastern Area Traffic Commissioners to run a daily bus service between Emsworth and Thorney Island. Not surprisingly the application was opposed by Southdown, who were keen to stop any new competition in their established territory, but also West Sussex County Council mainly due to the poor state of the roads, and the application was refused. This was not to be the last time that Southdown would be opposing the expansion plans of Basil Williams and his Hants & Sussex company.

1935

Early in the New Year several major revisions to services took place right across the Southdown area from Portsmouth to Horsham and Haywards Heath. In the west of the area the Portsdown and Horndean Light Railway finally gave up the unequal struggle with Southdown's Leyland Titans and closed after operation on 9 January 1935. The line had opened on 2 March 1903 running from Cosham, just south of the railway station following the line of the present day Northern Road passing Queen Alexandra Hospital and then climbing the side of Portsdown hill until it joined the road at 'The George'. The track passed through Purbrook, Waterlooville and Cowplain, where the tram depot stood, and then continued on the old main A3 road until its terminus in Horndean. It ran on reserved track to the east of the A3 between Waterlooville and Horndean and traces of the route can still be seen as extra wide verges in several locations. From 1923 the Light Railway extended into Portsmouth and by 1927 it ran to both the Clarence and South Parade Piers. Although the system had quite an influence on the growth of the Waterlooville, Cowplain and Horndean areas, the introduction of trolleybuses in Portsmouth in the 1930s reduced the available routes for trams.

It was therefore decided to abandon tramways in the area, and the Light Railway Company was sold to Southdown with the last tram running on 9 January 1935. From **Thursday 10 January** the frequencies of several services along the A3 corridor were improved as a result with the **40** becoming hourly throughout plus an hourly service between Southsea and Clanfield, Drift Lane daily. Service **41** was increased from 2 to 3 buses per hour with a new service from Theatre Royal and an extra bus per hour via Stakes becoming an hourly service via Theatre Royal and then direct along the A3 plus a 30 minute service via Fratton and Stakes. Finally, the **42** was curtailed at PETERSFIELD STATION being replaced between Petersfield and South Harting by new service 61. The frequency was increased

to hourly throughout daily plus two journeys per hour daily between Southsea and Snell's Corner. New service **61** was introduced between PETERSFIELD STATION and ELSTED CHURCH replacing the 42 as far as South Harting and then continuing via Turkey Island to Elstead with an hourly service daily.

Following the opening of the impressive new bus and coach station in High Street, Bognor Regis services were revised and rerouted to serve the new terminal. Service **59** was curtailed to operate between BOGNOR RAILWAY STATION and PETWORTH and the service between BOGNOR and PETERSFIELD renumbered from 59 to **60**. Both services ran two hourly providing a combined hourly service between Bognor and Midhurst. Additional journeys ran on Saturdays between Midhurst and Petersfield. The section of route between Midhurst and Horsham was covered by new service 77 – see below. The two local routes in the Storrington area were renumbered with service 60 to PULBOROUGH STATION becoming **70** and service 61 to THAKEHAM CROSS ROADS altered to **71**.

By the mid-1930s the market town of Horsham was still served by a variety of small independent bus operators in addition to the main interurban services provided by Southdown, Aldershot & District and LPTB. Southdown had already acquired the services of Blue Bus Company in December 1932 and now took the opportunity to remove competition on the routes running south from Horsham. One of the most important operators in and around Horsham was W.H. Rayner & Son who traded as Horsham Bus Service providing both local town services in Horsham and rural routes from their base at Barns Green. But, a disastrous fire on the night of Sunday 31 July 1934 destroyed their garage along with four coaches, two buses and Mr Rayner's car. Next day the only Rayner vehicle fit for use was the Harrington bodied Dennis 30cwt PX5776 which had been outside the garage and this ran the service to Horsham via Christ's Hospital. The following day the Coneyhurst and Barns Green routes were operated by Southdown vehicles loaned as an emergency measure. They were garaged initially in Parkers Yard, Barns Green, although later a small 'Dormy Shed' was constructed. The business was formally acquired completely by Southdown on 2 January 1935 with the revised services starting on 10 January.

The three Horsham Town Services became **72** between THE COMMON, Carfax and HIGHLANDS ESTATE, **72B** between HORSHAM CARFAX and THE COMMON and **73** between THE COMMON, Carfax and ST LEONARD'S HOTEL. On the 72 a 20 minute service ran daily with an additional 20 minute service on Saturdays from 1600 to 2100 between The Common and Carfax. From 12 October 1936 the frequency was reduced on Thursday (early closing day) and Sunday afternoons when a 40 minute service operated. The 72B was irregular workings only but a regular

In a specially posed scene two of Southdown's Leyland Titan TD2's with Short Bros bodywork are seen apparently passing a tramcar on the Horndean Light Railway. It nicely illustrates the difference in passenger amenities provided by the competing forms of transport! Cars 930 on the left and 927 on the right were both new in June 1931 and sold to Wilts & Dorset in June 1939. They were also both rebodied during the war and went on to lead very long lives. *Portsmouth Evening News*

20 minute service operated on Saturday afternoons and evenings while the 73 had a 2 hourly frequency daily. For many years one man operated Leyland Cubs were used on the local Horsham town routes.

The former Rayner country services were numbered **74** between HORSHAM CARFAX and COOLHAM via London Road, Worthing Road, Southwater, Buckbarn Cross Roads, Lodge Farm, Green Street and Scolliers Corner with a three hourly service daily. From 18 April 1935 the service was extended to CONEYHURST and the frequency reduced to two journeys each way daily plus one journey each way daily between Horsham and Coolham and one additional journey each way throughout on Saturdays and Sundays. After leaving the main A24 it served some sparsely populated roads and was withdrawn completely on 31 December 1938. In addition the **75** ran between HORSHAM (CARFAX) and BILLINGSHURST following a more promising route via Christ's Hospital, Itchingfield, Barns Green, Brooks Green, Coolham and Coneyhurst with two journeys each way daily plus irregular journeys to and from Barns Green or Brooks Green. To compensate for the reductions to the 74 from 18 April 1935 service **75** was increased to provide five journeys each way plus irregular journeys to and from Barns Green or Brooks Green.

Replacing the northern part of service 59 was a new service **77** between HORSHAM STATION and MIDHURST via Broadbridge Heath, Slinfold, Five Oaks, Billingshurst, Wisborough Green, Petworth, Tillington, Cowdray Park and Easebourne. A two hourly service ran daily but the 77 was short lived and from 1 January 1937 it was replaced, in a succession of route number changes, by extending service 63 northwards from Petworth to Horsham. Other changes in the area on the same day included new service **78** between SLINFOLD and HANDCROSS (RED LION) via Broadbridge Heath, Horsham Carfax, Mannings Heath village, Monks Gate, Lower Beeding and Ashfold Crossways. This partly replaced service 82 but was extended across Horsham to Slinfold. Service **82** was renumbered **79** and extended from Horsham to Slinfold via Broadbridge Heath to operate from BALCOMBE (HALF MOON) to SLINFOLD with three journeys each way daily. A generous hourly service was operated daily between Handcross and Slinfold in conjunction with service 78.

Another Horsham area independent to be acquired at this time was T. W. Carter of Monks Gate trading as Carter Bros Southdown took over the Stage Carriage service between Horsham and Steyning by extending existing service **80** southwards from Maplehurst to STEYNING (WHITE HORSE) via West Grinstead Station, Littleworth, Partridge Green and Ashurst. Five through journeys ran each way Monday to Friday and six journeys each way on Saturdays and Sundays. Operating out of

Horsham along East Street and Queen Street under the low railway bridge meant that the 80 was always associated with single deck buses notably the 1400 class Tigers which gave way to ECW bodied PS1s and later Royal Tigers.

The Haywards Heath area also witnessed some changes to its route network. Service **20** was curtailed to operate between BRIGHTON (POOL VALLEY) and HAYWARDS HEATH (RAILWAY STATION) being withdrawn between Haywards Heath and Balcombe. Service **81** which provided a rural cross country link between HAYWARDS HEATH STATION – BOLNEY – COWFOLD – BILLINGSHURST had its frequency increased to an hourly service daily between Haywards Heath and Cowfold and three hourly to and from Billingshurst. Two new services commenced running between HAYWARDS HEATH STATION and BALCOMBE (HALF MOON HOTEL). The **86** ran via Borde Hill whilst the **87** served Cuckfield, Whiteman's Green and Brook Street. Both services ran two hourly and replaced service 20 which had run alternately via Brook Street or Borde Hill. And, finally, Eastbourne service **94** was extended hourly from POLEGATE STATION via Pevensey Road, Polegate to DITTONS WOOD CORNER.

The quaintly named Hundred of Manhood and Selsey Tramway which opened in 1897, running between Chichester and Selsey, finally closed on 19 January 1935. The name had been changed to West Sussex Railway in 1924. There were

The one man operated Leyland Cubs were a familiar sight on the local town services at Horsham Carfax for many years until replaced by larger buses after the war. Cars 19 to 26 (ECD 519-526) were all Leyland Cub KPZ2 models with Park Royal 20-seat bodywork which was the maximum capacity then permitted for operation without a conductor. Most survived with Southdown until late 1956 and one (car 24) has been fully restored at Amberley Museum. *J.F.Parke, Omnibus Society*

No complaints about 'invading anyone's privacy' as the crew of car 830 (UF 5530) happily pose for the camera! It was a Leyland Titan TD1 with Leyland lowbridge 48-seat bodywork new in December 1929 and seen at Storrington when operating on the hourly service 1 to Worthing. Like many others of this batch it was sold in June 1938 and saw further service in Scotland. *Alan Lambert Collection*

This level of service applied on the 39 from the time of takeover until shortly after the outbreak of war although from October 1935 it was extended daily to Southsea (South Parade Pier). Note the much earlier arrival time of first journeys in Portsmouth where employment and business provided plenty of demand for such facilities.

Bus Service 39 — HAMBLEDON, DENMEAD, WATERLOOVILLE, PORTSMOUTH.

WEEKDAYS AND SUNDAYS. NS.—Not Sundays.

	NS	NS	NS	NS							NS						
World's End	§	§	...	...	...	8 35	...	...	...	...	...	...	...	...	...	1 35	...
Hambledon Village	5 40	6 25	7 15	7 45	8 15	8 45	9 15	9 45	1015	1045	1115	1145	1215	1245	1 15	1 45	215
Denmead	5 50	6 35	7 25	7 55	8 25	8 55	9 25	9 55	1025	1055	1125	1155	1225	1255	1 25	1 55	225
Waterlooville	6 4	6 49	7 35	8 5	8 35	9 5	9 35	10 5	1035	11 5	1135	12 5	1235	1 5	1 35	2 5	235
Purbrook Church	6 8	6 53	7 39	8 9	8 39	9 9	9 39	10 9	1039	11 9	1139	12 9	1239	1 9	1 39	2 9	239
Portsdown (George)	6 13	6 58	7 44	8 14	8 44	9 14	9 44	1014	1044	1114	1144	1214	1244	1 14	1 44	2 14	244
Cosham Gates	6 17	7 2	7 48	8 18	8 48	9 18	9 48	1018	1048	1118	1148	1218	1248	1 18	1 48	2 18	248
North End	6 24	7 9	7 55	8 25	8 55	9 25	9 55	1025	1055	1125	1155	1225	1255	1 25	1 55	2 25	255
Portsmouth (Th. Roy)	6 33	7 18	8 4	8 34	9 4	9 34	10 4	1034	11 4	1134	12 4	1234	1 4	1 34	2 4	2 34	3 4

World's End	...	...	...	...	...	...	5 35	...	...	...	8 0	...	...	...	...
Hambledon Village	2 45	3 15	3 45	4 15	4 45	5 15	5 45	6 15	6 45	7 15	7 45	8 15	8 45	9 15	9 45
Denmead	2 55	3 25	3 55	4 25	4 55	5 25	5 55	6 25	6 55	7 25	7 55	8 25	8 55	9 25	9 55
Waterlooville	3 5	3 35	4 5	4 35	5 5	5 35	6 5	6 35	7 5	7 35	8 5	8 35	9 5	9 35	10 5
Purbrook Church	3 9	3 39	4 9	4 39	5 9	5 39	6 9	6 39	7 9	7 39	8 9	8 39	9 9	9 39	10 9
Portsdown (George)	3 14	3 44	4 14	4 44	5 14	5 44	6 14	6 44	7 14	7 44	8 14	8 44	9 14	9 44	1014
Cosham Gates	3 18	3 48	4 18	4 48	5 18	5 48	6 18	6 48	7 18	7 48	8 18	8 48	9 18	9 48	1018
North End	3 25	3 55	4 25	4 55	5 25	5 55	6 25	6 55	7 25	7 55	8 25	8 55	9 25	9 55	1025
Portsmouth (Th. Roy)	3 34	4 4	4 34	5 4	5 34	6 4	6 34	7 4	7 34	8 4	8 34	9 4	9 34	10 4	1034

§On journeys marked § passengers change buses at Waterlooville.

Seen outside the fine new Bognor Bus Station opened in January 1935 is car 133 (BUF 233) a Leyland Titan TD4 with Short Bros highbridge 50-seat body operating an eastbound service 31 journey. The bus has been specially decorated for celebrations marking the Silver Jubilee of King George V during 1935. In the postwar rebodying programme a new East Lancs body was fitted in May 1946 and car 133 then remained in service until sale in February 1961.
Alan Lambert Collection

intermediate halts at Hunston, Chalder, Sidlesham and Ferry and in later years the service had been operated by petrol engined rail-cars. Given the irregular and slow nature of the service it was, presumably, not felt necessary to augment the bus service in replacement.

Not deterred by the unsuccessful bid to run a service to Thorney Island, Basil Williams considered other unserved areas and this time chose Woodmancote to the east of Westbourne. Together with H.W. Eades, the local coal merchant, he applied to the Traffic Commissioners in March 1935, for a licence to operate a daily service from Emsworth Station via Southbourne using a 14-seat bus. The application was in the name of Hants & Sussex Motors, a grand sounding title for a new bus operator, but obviously one with expansion in mind. The proposed route was along roads already covered by Southdown's service 31 and once more there was an objection from the company which resulted in the application being withdrawn.

Southdown further strengthened their dominance along the A3 corridor from **Thursday 21 March** when they acquired the Stage Carriage service between Portsmouth and Hambledon – plus some vehicles – from F. G. Tanner trading as Denmead Queen Motor Services, Denmead. New service **39** ran between PORTSMOUTH (THEATRE ROYAL), HAMBLEDON and WORLD'S END via Portsdown, Purbrook Church, Waterlooville and Denmead. A 30 minute service ran daily to Hambledon with a few journeys operating to and from World's End.

Summer timetables were introduced from **Saturday 8 June** and service **1** once more gained an additional 30 minute frequency daily between Worthing and Findon providing four buses per hour over this section in conjunction with service 2. Although not shown as such in public timetables these journeys were referred to as service 1B. Worthing cross town service **3** was extended westwards from ELM GROVE along Goring Road to terminate at GORING CHURCH with a 10 minute frequency daily. Service **7** was extended to operate as a circular WORTHING PIER – LANCING – WORTHING (DOME) via the previous route to Lancing, South Street and then along the Coast Road via Brighton Road, Steyne Gardens and Marine Parade. A 10 minute frequency was provided as far as Sompting via Broadwater with alternate journeys extended to and from Worthing Dome daily. There were the usual additions to popular services in the coastal towns and service **26A** between Seaford, Alfriston and Eastbourne reappeared as in 1934. Hayling service **46** was reintroduced and, although there was no change to the basic service, the additional fine weather journeys were operated throughout to provide a 30 minute frequency. The frequency of service **47** was enhanced as in summer 1934.

The Southern Railway now turned its electrification plans to the lines to Seaford, Eastbourne, Hastings and Ore and also decided to electrify the short section from Haywards Heath to Horsted Keynes via Ardingly. Full public services started on 7 July 1935 but further west the Midhurst to Chichester branch line closed to passengers although it remained open for freight as far as Lavant.

The high summer timetables started from **Saturday 13 July** and service **9** was extended beyond Angmering Green to ANGMERING (CRUNDENS CORNER) via The Square, Station Road and Angmering Station. On Bank Holidays this service was unusual in that it was extended to start from BRIGHTON (POOL VALLEY). Service **12** was increased in line with summer 1934 but the Peacehaven Annexe journeys were transferred to service **21** which was extended eastwards from Brighton Pool Valley to PEACEHAVEN ANNEXE via the A259 and Roderick Avenue. An hourly service ran throughout plus an hourly service between Bungalow Town and Peacehaven (Rosemary) daily. Service **12** had previously included up to nine journeys a day that served Peacehaven Annexe.

The summer only service between ARUNDEL SQUARE and BOGNOR PIER via Walberton, Yapton and Middleton was reintroduced and renumbered **62** continuing to run every year until withdrawal at the start of the war. A two hourly frequency operated daily. Littlehampton town service **63** appeared again running as in 1934 but this was its last year of operation.

To reduce traffic congestion in Cosham High Street a new one way system for buses was introduced with all Portsmouth and Southsea bound journeys on services **31, 31A, 31B, 31C, 39, 40, 41, 42, 43, 45** and **47** diverted via Northern Road. This also avoided the level crossing which could cause delays to buses.

With the newly delivered three axle Leyland Tigers offering greater capacity on the

Seen outside Royal Parade garage is car 51 (AUF 851) a Leyland Tiger TS6T with Short Bros B40C 'coach style' bodywork delivered new in August 1934 especially for the service to Beachy Head. Apart from during the wartime suspension of the 97 they were a familiar sight on this route until withdrawal in 1952 although after the war they were more profitably employed in Portsmouth during the winter months.
Alan Lambert Collection

The acquisition of Blue Motor Services (Southwick) Ltd of Boarhunt brought regular operation of Southdown buses to Clarence Pier at Southsea until it was cut back soon after the outbreak of war in September 1939.

Bus Service 38 SOUTHSEA, SOUTHWICK, BOARHUNT, WICKHAM, DROXFORD, MEONSTOKE, HAMBLEDON															

WEEKDAYS AND SUNDAYS.

						Sats.					Sats.			★
Southsea (Clarence Pier)...	...	...	9 0	1030	*12 0*	1 30	2 30	4 30	5 30	*6 30*	7 30	9 30	11 5
Theatre Royal ...	...	...	9 5	1035	*12 5*	1 35	2 35	4 35	5 35	*6 35*	7 35	9 35	1110
North End Office ...	...	...	9 14	1044	*1214*	1 44	2 44	4 44	5 44	*6 44*	7 44	9 44	1119
Cosham Gates ...	...	...	9 21	1051	*1221*	1 51	2 51	4 51	5 51	*6 51*	7 51	9 51	1126
Portsdown (The George)...	...	...	9 25	1055	*1225*	1 55	2 55	4 55	5 55	*6 55*	7 55	9 55	1130
Southwick (Church)...	...	...	9 37	11 7	*1237*	2 7	3 7	5 7	6 7	7 7	8 7	10 7	1142
Boarhunt (Garage) ...	7 55	8 0	9 46	1116	*1245*	2 16	3 16	5 16	6 16	*7 16*	8 16	1016	1151
Wickham (The Square) ...	8 5	8 10	9 55	1125	*1255*	2 25	3 25	5 25	6 25	*7 25*	8 25	1025	12 0
Roebuck Inn ...		8 15	10 0	1130		2 30			6 30		8 30		
The Bold Forester ...		8 20	10 5	1135	...	2 35	...	...	6 35		8 35	...	...
The Plough Inn ...		8 21	10 6	1136	...	2 36	...	...	6 36		8 36	...	...
Chapel Road ...		8 23	10 8	1138	...	2 38	...	...	6 38		8 38	...	...
Soberton (The Falcon) ...		8 25	1010	1140	...	2 40	...	...	6 40		8 40	...	...
Soberton (White Lion) ...		8 31	1016	1146	...	2 46	...	...	6 46		8 46	...	...
Droxford (Railway Stn.)...		8 36	1021	1151	...	2 51	...	...	6 51		8 51	...	...
Droxford (The Square) ...		8 40	1025	1155	...	2 55	...	...	6 55		8 55	...	...
Meonstoke (Buck's Head) ...		8 50	1035	12 5	...	3 5	...	...	7 5		9 5	...	...
Droxford (Railway Stn.)...		...	...	1210	...	...	...	...	7 10		...	...	...
Bushy Down Farm ...		...	...	1213	...	...	...	...	7 13		...	...	...
Race Course Corner ...		...	...	1215	...	...	...	...	7 15		...	...	...
Hambledon (The Square) ...		...	...	1223	...	...	...	...	7 23		...	...	...

Sats.—Saturdays only.   ★Waits until after second performance at Hippodrome.

Eastbourne to Beachy Head service **97** the peak summer frequency was increased still further to an hourly basic service daily but increased to 15 minutes in fine weather.

On 1 August 1935 Southdown finally gained complete control of the country routes into Portsmouth from the north when they acquired the Stage Carriage service between Hambledon and Portsmouth of Blue Motor Services (Southwick) Ltd of Boarhunt. Starting with the winter timetable on **Monday 16 September** new service **38** ran between SOUTHSEA (CLARENCE PIER) and HAMBLEDON SQUARE via Cosham, Portsdown Hill Road, Southwick Hill Cross Roads, Southwick Road, Southwick, Wickham Square, Soberton, Droxford Station, Droxford Square, Meonstoke (Bucks Head), Droxford Station, Bushy Down Farm and Race Course Corner. Two through journeys were provided each way daily plus five journeys each way daily between Southsea and Meonstoke and four journeys each way Sunday to Friday (six on Saturdays) between Southsea and Wickham. Summer only services were withdrawn from this date and the winter operation on Beachy Head service **97** was reduced to a two hourly basic service increased to 30 minutes in fine weather. This remained the level of operation each winter until the outbreak of war in 1939.

Starting on **Monday 14 October** service **7** was curtailed at LANCING (THREE HORSE SHOES) and the terminal loop working in Lancing reintroduced. The frequency was revised to a 10 minute service as far as Downland Corner with a 30 minute service to and from Lancing.

Since 1928 Southdown had been providing a daily service **27** along Dyke Road and Dyke Road Avenue in Brighton and from 1 January 1933 had introduced one additional journey each way daily as far as Mill Lane in addition to the three hourly service to Henfield plus numerous short journeys to Devils Dyke according to season. Between 1932 and 1934 the developers, Braybons, started building the Valley Drive estate with smart modern semi-detached houses costing £895 freehold. As a sign of things to come the houses were among the first to be provided with a matching garage to house the Austin 7 which it was presumably assumed the man of the house would drive to work from his home on the outer edge of Brighton. Undeterred by such a threat, Southdown clearly saw potential to expand their operations in this area and extended service **12** from Brighton Station to terminate at TONGDEAN LANE (WOODLAND DRIVE) running via Junction Road, Terminus Road, Buckingham Place, Seven Dials, Dyke Road and Dyke Road Avenue. Initially the frequency comprised a 30 minute through service to Eastbourne plus a 30 minute service to Seaford daily.

Some revisions to services in the Portsmouth area included service **39** which was extended from Portsmouth (Theatre Royal) to SOUTHSEA (SOUTH PARADE) and diverted between

Purbrook and Waterlooville via Stakes. All journeys on service **41** reverted to operate via Fratton Road and then direct along the A3 no longer serving Theatre Royal or Stakes. The frequency was reduced to a 30 minute service daily which became the standard for many years to come.

1936

Some minor alterations to services in Lewes and Newhaven began on **Wednesday 1 January** with certain journeys on service **13A** being extended in Lewes to LEWES (NEVILL CRESCENT). An approximately two hourly service was provided daily with additional journeys on Saturday evenings between County Hall and Rodmell. Service **13C** was extended at the Denton end of route to run from Bridge Street via New Road, Avis Road, Denton Road, Heighton Road, Heighton, South Heighton and New Road to Bridge Street. In addition the journeys between NEWHAVEN (BRIDGE STREET) and EAST SIDE via Bridge Street, Railway Road, Clifton Road, Norton Road became part of new service **13D**. Buses returned via Norton Terrace, Baker Street, Railway Road and Bridge Street with a journey time of four minutes. There were seven journeys each way on Weekdays and six on Sundays. On Friday, Saturday and Sunday evenings five journeys also operated between Bridge Street and Gibbon Road. Apart from the latter all journeys on services 13C and 13D were provided as part of the layover time at Newhaven on service 13A.

In addition to the regular network Southdown were also licensed to provide on demand late evening services within a specified radius in most of the towns it served. These were to cater for those attending social events, dances and concerts, etc that finished after the last buses and normally double fares were charged on such operations. Separate licences were held for each of the towns covered.

On 27 March 1936 Southdown paid to Maidstone & District M S Ltd the sum of £6,000 in respect of a Stage Carriage service between

Uckfield Bus Station is the setting for car 860 (UF 5660) a Leyland Titan TD1 with Leyland lowbridge body new in 1930 heading south on service 92 to Eastbourne. Alongside is car 105 (BUF 205) a Leyland Titan TD4 with Short Bros lowbridge body dating from 1935 on the joint service 119 between Brighton and Tunbridge Wells which was shared with Maidstone & District. Both services required the use of low height buses due to low bridges at Stone Cross on route 92 and Lewes on route 119.
J.F.Parke, Omnibus Society

Tunbridge Wells and Uckfield acquired from Autocar Services Ltd, Tunbridge Wells and from **Thursday 9 April** extended service **19** from UCKFIELD to TUNBRIDGE WELLS via Ringles Cross then either Five Ash Down or Maresfield and Duddleswell, then Crowborough Broadway, Eridge and Eridge Green to terminate at Monson Road. On journeys towards Brighton buses started from the War Memorial. This replaced part of the Maidstone & District service which had once run from Uckfield via Tunbridge Wells and Tonbridge to Sevenoaks and been operated by Autocar and Redcar until these companies were fully absorbed by M&D during 1935. An hourly joint service with Maidstone & District numbered **119** now ran daily with alternate journeys via Maresfield and certain journeys via South View Road in Crowborough. The first bus from Uckfield to reach Brighton arrived at 0935 whilst the first bus into Tunbridge Wells arrived at 0928, rather later than would be expected today, although the Southern Railway ran an irregular train service over the route.

Saturday 30 May marked the start of the summer timetable and service **12** was increased to provide:

 2 buses per hour between Tongdean and Eastbourne
 2 buses per hour between Tongdean and Seaford
 2 buses per hour between Brighton Station and Seaford
 Journeys to Peacehaven Annexe were now part of service 21

The Hayling Island sea front service **46** was reintroduced and the increased frequency on service **47** also commenced from this date

The high summer timetable commenced on **Sunday 5 July** with the reintroduction of summer only services **26A** and **62** and improvements to services in coastal towns. Certain journeys on service **45** were diverted between South Parade Pier and London Road to operate via South Parade, Clarence Parade, Palmerston Road, Grove Road South, Elm Grove, Victoria Road North, Fratton Road, Kingston Road to London Road. The frequency was increased to provide:

 3 buses per hour between Southsea and Fareham via Theatre Royal
 2 buses per hour between Southsea and Fareham via Fratton
 2 buses per hour between Southsea and Fareham via Theatre Royal and Castle Street
 1 bus per hour between Southsea and Warsash via Theatre Royal

On Saturday and Sunday afternoons one of the Fratton journeys was extended to and from Warsash.

New service **63** was introduced between PETWORTH SQUARE and CHICHESTER STATION via Petworth Station, Duncton, Upwaltham, Halnaker, Maudlin and Westhampnett. This provided a new direct link and covered new roads

for Southdown between Duncton and Halnaker. Four journeys each way were provided daily with a later journey on Saturdays. Buses departed Petworth Square at 1013, 1313, 1513, 1713 plus 1913 on Saturdays and from Chichester Station at 1218, 1418, 1618, 1818 plus 2018 on Saturdays.

Commencing with the winter timetable on **Monday 14 September** service **23** was curtailed to operate between BRIGHTON (POOL VALLEY) and HAYWARDS HEATH RAILWAY STATION being replaced between Haywards Heath and Crawley via Handcross by a new service **82**. A two hourly service daily continued as on the 23. First bus from Handcross into Crawley arrived at 0838, quite early for this period, so Crawley clearly had some commercial importance before expanding as a New Town after the war. Last bus from Crawley as far as Handcross was at 2045 except on Wednesdays, Saturdays and Sundays when it was 2245 presumably to cater for the patrons of the Imperial Cinema.

The usual seasonal services and enhancements ended at this time and no further changes of any significance occurred during 1936 making this a relatively quiet year.

1937

Starting on **Friday 1 January** service **59** was revised to provide a two hourly service throughout between Bognor and Petworth plus a two hourly service from Midhurst to Petworth. Together with service 60 and Aldershot & District buses on service 19 there was an hourly frequency between Bognor and Midhurst. But, as service 19 replaced the 59 or 60 every three hours and ran direct between Chichester and Bognor via Bersted rather than Rose Green it meant some two hour gaps in the service via the latter. Service **63** was now extended northwards from Petworth to Horsham in place of service 77 to operate between HORSHAM STATION and CHICHESTER STATION. A two hourly service ran between Horsham and Petworth with four journeys (five on Saturdays) operating through to

Car 821 (UF 4821) Leyland Titan TD1 with Brush 51-seat open top body delivered new in June 1929 is seen here on summer only service 62 heading from Arundel towards Bognor probably in summer 1936 whilst still in original livery. During 1937 the open top fleet was repainted with cream upper decks and used mainly on seasonal services where passengers might still appreciate the open air ride! After being fitted with a temporary top cover for wartime use it returned to summer open top form after the war and was finally sold in February 1951!
D.W.K. Jones

In this service 97 timetable which was introduced from 25 March 1937 journeys are still run according to weather conditions although at least a basic two hourly service is provided on wet days. The last round trip is shown as running only on 'Exceptional fine days' and would require considerable confidence in one's weather forecasting skills if planning a walk along the South Downs in time for this final departure of the day!

Service 97 — EASTBOURNE AND BEACHY HEAD.

WEEKDAYS AND SUNDAYS.

	BC	ABC	C	BC	C	ABC	C	ABC
Eastbourne (Royal Parade)	9 45	10 30	11 0	11 30	12 0	12 30	2 0	2 30
Pier	9 48	10 33	11 3	11 33	12 3	12 33	2 3	2 33
Foot of Beachy Head	9 55	10 40	11 10	11 40	12 10	12 40	2 10	2 40
Beachy Head Hotel	10 3	10 48	11 18	11 48	12 18	12 48	2 18	2 48

	C	BC	C	ABC	C	BC	BC	C
Eastbourne (Royal Parade)	3 0	3 30	4 0	4 30	5 0	5 30	6 30	7 0
Pier	3 3	3 33	4 3	4 33	5 3	5 33	6 33	7 3
Foot of Beachy Head	3 10	3 40	4 10	4 40	5 10	5 40	6 40	7 10
Beachy Head Hotel	3 18	3 48	4 18	4 48	5 18	5 48	6 48	7 18

	BC	ABC	C	BC	C	ABC	C	ABC
Beachy Head Hotel	10 5	10 50	11 20	11 50	12 20	12 50	2 20	2 50
Mead Street	10 13	10 58	11 28	11 58	12 28	12 58	2 28	2 58
Pier	10 20	11 5	11 35	12 5	12 35	1 5	2 35	3 5
Eastbourne (Royal Parade)	10 23	11 8	11 38	12 8	12 38	1 8	2 38	3 8

	C	BC	C	ABC	C	BC	BC	C
Beachy Head Hotel	3 20	3 50	4 20	4 50	5 20	5 50	6 50	7 20
Mead Street	3 28	3 58	4 28	4 58	5 28	5 58	6 58	7 28
Pier	3 35	4 5	4 35	5 5	5 35	6 5	7 5	7 35
Eastbourne (Royal Parade)	3 38	4 8	4 38	5 8	5 38	6 8	7 8	7 38

A. To be run on WET DAYS. B. To be run on NORMAL DAYS.
C. To be run on EXCEPTIONAL FINE DAYS.

FARE TABLE.

				Adults	Children
Company's Garage (Royal Parade) to Beachy Head Hotel				9d.	6d.
Pier	,,	,,	,,	8d.	6d.
Grand Hotel	,,	,,	,,	7d.	5d.
Foot of Beachy Head or Mead St.	,,	,,	,,	6d.	4d.

and from Chichester. There was still no bus northwards from Chichester until 1205. From the same date Haywards Heath local service **84** was rerouted away from Sydney Road and Outhall Road and diverted via Muster Green in both directions.

Service **21B** was revised to run between BRIGHTON (POOL VALLEY) and SHOREHAM BRIDGE as from **Thursday 25 March.** It ran only irregularly on Wednesdays and Sundays to serve Southlands Hospital and also as a connecting service at both Kingston Lane (north end) and Shoreham Bridge.

Since the original application by Basil Williams for a bus service to Thorney Island, work had started in 1937 on the construction of an airfield and so in May 1937 the new Hants & Sussex company applied for a Stage Carriage licence to operate three return journeys a day, with an additional late journey on Saturdays and Sundays. Once again objections were lodged by Southdown and by West Sussex County Council who did so because of the unsuitability of the road. A public enquiry was held in July 1937 but the hearing was adjourned and nothing further occurred until November 1938 when Southdown submitted an application to extend their Westbourne to Emsworth service **44** to Thorney Island. West Sussex County Council maintained their objection because of the unsuitability of the road but they had already granted Hants & Sussex a contract in April to convey schoolchildren from Thorney Island to Emsworth! Hants & Sussex was also providing a contract service for the RAF Institute as there was no other means of transport for RAF personnel to reach

the mainland. Southdown claimed that their Emsworth local service 44 was running at a loss and needed the Thorney extension to increase revenue, but both the Commanding Officer of RAF Thorney Island and the Havant & Waterloo

Service 7 had been developed during the 1930s to serve the expanding new residential districts of Sompting and Lancing and now provided a 10 minute frequency via Broadwater and a 20 minute frequency via the Coast Road to Lancing. Once again the full service ran until last buses with no reductions during the evening or on Sundays as would be expected nowadays.

SOUTHDOWN MOTOR SERVICES, Ltd.

INCREASED SERVICE

Commencing SATURDAY, 17th JULY, 1937

Bus Service 7 — WORTHING PIER, BROADWATER, SOMPTING, LANCING, WORTHING DOME

CIRCULAR SERVICE. CLOCKWISE. WEEKDAYS AND SUNDAYS.

Stops: Pier, Norfolk Hotel, Broadwater Church, Wigmore Road, Downland Corner, Sompting, Cokeham, Lancing Manor, Lancing Station, Lancing (3 Horse Shoes), Worthing (Dome).

This Service connects at Lancing Manor with Services 9 & 10 to and from Shoreham and Brighton.

Bus Service 7 — WORTHING DOME, LANCING, SOMPTING, BROADWATER, WORTHING PIER

CIRCULAR SERVICE. WEEKDAYS AND SUNDAYS. ANTI-CLOCK.

Stops: Worthing (Dome), Lancing (3 Horse Shoes), Lancing Station, Lancing Manor, Cokeham, Sompting, Downland Corner, Wigmore Road, Broadwater Church, Norfolk Hotel, Pier.

This Service connects at Lancing Manor with Services 9 & 10 to and from Shoreham and Brighton.

Urban District Council supported the Hants & Sussex application in preference to the one from Southdown. Finally, the Traffic Commissioner granted a licence to Hants & Sussex for six return journeys a day. Southdown appealed unsuccessfully against this decision although they could not have imagined the battles that lay ahead in the Traffic Courts, even in wartime when such niceties were officially suspended for the duration.

Summer timetables commenced on **Saturday 12 June** and saw the reintroduction of seasonal services **26A** and **46** along with enhanced frequencies on some routes such as the **4** running every 10 minute throughout to High Salvington daily.

At the company's 23rd ordinary general meeting held on Monday 14 June 1937 the Chairman announced that 63 out of the 94 services operated were unremunerative. Presumably the rest were very successful as the company was returning a satisfactory profit each year.

Work on electrification of the Southern Railway lines from Hampton Court Junction to Guildford and Portsmouth had commenced in October 1935 with full public services from Waterloo to Alton and Portsmouth commencing on 4 July 1937.

Southdown acquired from H. J. Sargent of East Grinstead their Stage Carriage service running between East Grinstead and Ashdown Forest and on **Saturday 17 July** commenced operation of new service **87** between EAST GRINSTEAD (CROWN) and ASHDOWN FOREST (GOAT INN) via Dunnings, Sainthill Green, Kingscote Station, Selsfield, West Hoathly, Sharpthorne and Tyes Cross. Six journeys were

provided each way on Monday to Friday with seven on Saturdays and four on Sundays. In consequence the existing service 87 between Haywards Heath and Balcombe via Cuckfield was renumbered to **86A**. Seasonal service **62** was also reintroduced between Bognor and Arundel and on service **27** from Brighton to Devil's Dyke no less than 23 journeys ran each way daily. The Brighton to Mill Lane journeys were withdrawn as service 12 was now serving this area four times an hour daily.

Winter timetables commenced from **Monday 27 September** with the usual seasonal reductions but more interesting changes were to follow in December. On 10 November 1937 Southdown acquired from R. J. Smart (trading as Ferring Omnibus Services) the Stage Carriage service between Ferring-on-Sea (South Drive) and Ferring Crossing (Henty Arms) with limited journeys on to Goring-by-Sea Railway Station. In replacement from **Thursday 2 December** service **11** was withdrawn between Brighton and Worthing and a new section added in Ferring to FERRING-ON-SEA (SOUTH DRIVE) via Ferring Street, Ferringham Lane and Ocean Drive returning via South Drive, West Drive and Ferringham Lane. There was some opposition from the parish council as Mr Smart had been running his bus service over private roads by permission of the owners who questioned whether he had the right to sell. While a more frequent service as proposed by Southdown was desirable, there were fears that the larger Tilling-Stevens Express buses on the proposed through route from Worthing would be too heavy for the estate roads. Rather confusingly hourly services on the 11 were now provided daily from Worthing both to Ferring-on-Sea and

In summer 1938 car 691 (UF 6591), a Tilling-Stevens B10A2 with Short Bros body new in 1930, is seen operating on the new section of service 11 which was extended to Ferring-on-Sea following the takeover of R J Smart's stage carriage service in November 1937. The much improved service was not welcomed by all the local residents, fearing damage to the estate roads, and in 1940 invasion scares led to the curtailment of service 11 some way from the sensitive sea front areas.
Alan Lambert Collection

The Titans fitted with Torque Convertors were usually to be found on the busy local services in and around Worthing. Car 120 (BUF 220) was a Leyland Titan TD4c with Short Bros highbridge body delivered in May 1935. During this period service 3 was a busy cross town link between East Worthing and Goring with a daily frequency of every 10 minutes. Car 120 was rebodied by Beadle in August 1947 and finally withdrawn in February 1959. *S.L. Poole*

After almost eight years a new and improved full colour cover design for bus timetables first appeared with the issue dated 2 December 1937. In fact editions were printed for this date with BOTH the old and new cover designs! Buses were now a 1400 class Leyland Tiger and Beadle bodied lowbridge Leyland Titan with scenes depicting Beachy Head and Arundel river bridge also included. The last prewar timetable with this cover design appeared for services commencing 13 July 1939.

Angmering-on-Sea with an additional hourly local service daily between Ferring (Ferring Lane/Langbury Lane) and Ferring (South Drive). To replace service 11 east of Worthing a new service **31F** was introduced running from BRIGHTON (POOL VALLEY) to WORTHING (DOME) every 30 minutes daily. Could the choice of service number 31F indicate an intention to run a Brighton to Ferring-on-Sea service once the protests had subsided? This somewhat complex arrangement lasted until 1 January 1939 when the Angmering section of service 11 was sensibly renumbered **31G**.

Further improvements were also made to most of the Worthing local services with service **3** extended at its eastern end to EAST WORTHING (HAM HOTEL) and revised to operate via Ham Road direct to Brighton Road and then as existing route to Goring Church. A 10 minute frequency operated daily and following the reconstruction of Ham Bridge buses were able to continue northwards from Ham Hotel as service 8 via Broadwater to Worthing Pier. Service 4 was revised and extended to operate between EAST WORTHING (BROOKDEAN ROAD) and HIGH SALVINGTON via Brougham Road, Lyndhurst Road, Selden Road, Brighton Road, Steyne Gardens, Marine Parade, South Street, Chapel Road and then as previously. The return route from Chapel Road was via Warwick Street, Brighton Road, Selden Road, Lyndhurst Road and Brougham Road not serving the sea front stop by The Dome. This replaced service 3 via Lyndhurst Road and Selden Road. A 10 minute service was provided daily to Durrington with alternate journeys extended to and from High Salvington.

The rather complex overlapping circular services **5** and **6** were simplified with service **5** revised to commence at WORTHING PIER and follow the western side of the loop to Thomas A'Becket Hotel and then continue northwards from Rectory Road via Offington Lane to OFFINGTON CORNER. Service **6** was revised to commence at WORTHING PIER and follow the eastern side of the loop to Thomas A'Becket Hotel and then continue a short distance along Littlehampton Road to terminate at RINGMER ROAD. The frequency of each route was every 10 minutes daily and with the circular services withdrawn buses now operated in both directions.

Service **8** was extended from Dominion Road via Ham Road to EAST WORTHING (HAM HOTEL) with buses then continuing from Ham Hotel as service 3 to Goring Church. A 10 minute frequency was provided daily. Following road widening services **9** and **10** were diverted between Chapel Road, Worthing and Offington Corner to operate via Teville Road, South Farm Road and Warren Road instead of direct via Broadwater.

Service **21** was withdrawn between BRIGHTON (POOL VALLEY) and PEACEHAVEN ANNEXE, this section being once more covered by service 12. On the same day a new local service **21A** began operation between SOUTHWICK (TOWN HALL) and SHOREHAM STATION via Albion Street, Kingston Lane, Upper Shoreham Road, Mill Lane, Victoria Road, High Street, East Street and Brunswick Road. With a journey time of 18 minutes it ran every 30 minutes daily and covered some previously unserved roads north of Shoreham such as Mill Lane and Victoria Road. Very low railway bridges on the main line between Brighton and Worthing meant that these routes were always restricted to single deck buses.

1938

On 4 March 1938 the company paid the sum of £150 to M.H.W. Garlick of East Hoathly in respect of their Stage Carriage service between East Hoathly and Uckfield. Only minor adjustments were made to Southdown's existing service 92 between these points.

From the start of the summer timetables on **Saturday 4 June** service **13E** was extended to run from HIGHER BEVENDEAN to EAST MOULSCOMBE via Hodshrove Road, Moulscombe Way and Shortgate Road returning via Appledore Road and Moulscombe Way. The frequency was also increased from four journeys per hour to every 12 minutes daily. The land was acquired by the borough in 1922 and the estate of Moulscombe was gradually developed from 1924 onwards in the form of a garden city with winding roads, large grass verges and big gardens. In South Moulscombe the earliest buildings were effectively an adjunct to the existing housing opposite Preston barracks but the later extensions in North and then East Moulscombe took the estate out into relatively remote countryside. The development was an attempt by the borough to rehouse families from some of the slums that existed in inner Brighton. Service **13F** between Brighton and Lower Bevendean had its frequency revised to a regular 20 minute service daily.

Also in the Brighton area, additional journeys on service **12** were introduced between BRIGHTON STATION and SALTDEAN MOUNT via the main service 12 route to Saltdean (Marine Drive) then along Longridge Avenue, Wicklands Avenue, Chichester Drive and Saltdean Vale to its junction with Tumulus Road. The new Mount Estate covered a substantial area of downland on the east side of Saltdean Vale. Initially buses could only reach the imposing Ocean Hotel as the roads were not yet suitable but from 16 July 1938 the service was able to reach the terminus at Saltdean Mount with a 30 minute service daily.

Finally, service **20** was withdrawn between Haywards Heath and Chailey and the **89** extended to HAYWARDS HEATH STATION via Scaynes Hill in replacement. Summer only services **26A** and **46** also reappeared from this date.

Following the success of earlier schemes the Southern Railway announced the electrification of the Mid Sussex Line south of Horsham as well as the coast line westwards from West Worthing to link with the newly electrified Portsmouth line near Havant. Trial trains commenced operation in May 1938 with full public services starting on 3 July 1938. This was to be the last such electrification affecting the Southdown area and post war railway developments mainly involved the abandonment of the remaining non-electrified lines especially after the Beeching Report.

High summer timetables commenced as from

Bus Service 62	BOGNOR, YAPTON, WALBERTON & ARUNDEL

Connecting at Arundel with buses to and from Worthing and Brighton.

WEEKDAYS AND SUNDAYS.

		1	2	3	4	5	6	7	8	9
Bognor (Pier)	dep	1013	1213	2 13	4 13	6 13	8 13	...	...	...
Felpham (Post Office)	,,	1021	1221	2 21	4 21	6 21	8 21	...	...	...
Middleton	,,	1026	1226	2 26	4 26	6 26	8 26	...	...	...
Yapton (Black Dog)	,,	1035	1235	2 35	4 35	6 35	8 35	...	...	...
Walberton (Blacksmith's Shop)	,,	1041	1241	2 41	4 41	6 41	8 41	...	...	...
Arundel (Square)	arr	1056	1256	2 56	4 56	6 56	8 56	...	...	...
Arundel (Square) ...	dep	11 3	1 3	3 3	5 3	7 3	9 3			
Worthing (Dome) ...	arr	1145	1 45	3 45	5 45	7 45	9 45			
Brighton (Pool Valley) ...	,,	1238	2 38	4 38	6 38	8 38	1038			
Brighton (Pool Valley) ...	dep	9 45	1145	1 45	3 45	5 45	7 45			
Worthing (Dome) ...	,,	1040	1240	2 40	4 40	6 40	8 40			
Arundel (Square) ...	arr	1121	1 21	3 21	5 21	7 21	9 21			
Arundel (Square) ...	dep	1127	1 27	3 27	5 27	7 27	9 27	...	...	...
Walberton (Blacksmith's Shop)	,,	1142	1 42	3 42	5 42	7 42	9 42	...	...	...
Yapton (Black Dog)	,,	1148	1 48	3 48	5 48	7 48	9 48	...	...	...
Middleton	,,	1157	1 57	3 57	5 57	7 57	9 57	...	...	...
Felpham (Post Office)	,,	12 3	2 3	4 3	6 3	8 3	10 3	...	...	...
Bognor (Pier)	arr	1211	2 11	4 11	6 11	8 11	1011	...	...	...

TRAVEL BY BUS

Saturday 16 July and on service **47** four additional journeys were introduced each way on weekdays only between SOUTHSEA (SOUTH PARADE) and EASTOKE HOUSE via Theatre Royal, Havant Church (not Havant Station), Manor Road, Bus Station, Sea Front, Rails Lane, Southwood Road. This supplemented the usual summer frequency for Hayling Island which included a 30 minute frequency from Southsea via Fratton.

And, from the same date a new and rather strange little service **49** appeared in Bognor. Described as the BOGNOR WATERFRONT SERVICE it ran from the East Car Park via the Pier and Aldwick Road Post Office to the West Car Park with a journey time of 10 minutes and a 30 minute frequency. Services started at 0941 from the Pier and continued until mid-evening. Withdrawn on 18 September 1938 it did not re-appear for the 1939 season.

The Saturday only Chichester to Emsworth Square journeys on service **54** were finally withdrawn but four additional journeys on Saturdays only were introduced between Chichester and Hambrook Lane (South End) via the existing route to East Ashling then via Chapel Corner, West Ashling, B2146, Mount Noddy, Scant Road, Hambrook Post Office, Hambrook House and West Ashling.

Seasonal service **62** between Bognor and Arundel was reintroduced and to the east of the area service **95** was extended over previously unserved roads from HEATHFIELD to WALDRON (STAR INN) via Cross-in-Hand, Roser's Cross and Waldron Cross Ways. A three hourly service ran daily plus one journey each way on Wednesdays only between Heathfield and Hailsham.

A Mr L. Cherriman operated a long established Stage Carriage service between Hassocks Station and Hurstpierpoint (Western Road) and after the electrification of the railway in 1933 introduced an hourly service with six journeys operating to and from the Chinese Gardens

Summer only service 62 was usually operated by an open top Leyland TDI and continued to terminate at Bognor Pier after most other Southdown services had moved to the Bus Station. It became an early casualty of the war and in postwar days was absorbed into an all year service 69 extended to run between Bognor and Horsham.

Considering the rural nature of much of Southdown's operating territory it is surprising that so few routes were considered suitable for one man operated buses. Car 22 (ECD 522) was one of eight Leyland Cub KPZ2 models with Park Royal 20-seat body delivered new in late 1937 although the final three were not actually registered for service until much later with the last – car 26 (ECD 526) – appearing in January 1939! All were petrol engined although car 22 was fitted with a Leyland 4.7 litre diesel engine in December 1950. All were withdrawn from service by the end of 1956 and car 24 survives in preservation with the Southdown Omnibus Trust at Amberley. *Park Royal Vehicles*

Hotel. Southdown acquired the goodwill and introduced new service **34** on **Thursday 15 September** running between HASSOCKS STATION and HURSTPIERPOINT (WESTERN ROAD) via Stone Pound, Cuckfield Road and Western Road using a one man operated Leyland Cub. Some late evening journeys were operated between Hassocks Cinema and Hurstpierpoint. But, with a first bus from Hurstpierpoint at 0815 (0755 on Mondays) it was obviously not intended for any rail commuters to London who needed to start work at 09.00! Connections with Southdown buses on services 23 and 30 were advertised at Hassocks, Stone Pound.

In the midst of the grave Munich crisis as trench shelters were being dug in local parks the winter timetables were introduced on **Monday 26 September**. The winter frequency for service **12** now became:

2 buses per hour between Tongdean and Eastbourne
2 buses per hour between Tongdean and Seaford
2 buses per hour between Brighton Station and Saltdean Mount
1 bus per hour between Brighton Pool Valley and Peacehaven Annexe

To serve new housing developments west of Bognor service **50** had certain journeys diverted at Gossamer Lane to operate via Nyetimber Lane and Pagham Road to Sea Lane. The frequency was reduced to run every hour daily. But from the same date new service **50A** began operating between ELMER (NEW CITY) and NYETIMBER (LAMB INN) via the same route as service 50 to Gossamer Lane and then via Rose Green Road and Pagham Road. An hourly service was provided daily.

The story of Worthing's Tramocars has been told in detail in the publication 'An Anthology of the Worthing Tramocars' published by the Southdown Enthusiasts Club in 2002. Services began in 1924 using small low loading Shelvoke & Drewry buses and by February 1935 there were two services running along the sea front. Route 1 ran between SPLASH POINT (MARINE PARADE) and LIBRARY via Marine Parade, West Parade, Wallace Avenue, Elm Grove, Ripley Road, Tarring Road, Heene Road, Cowper Road, Wykeham Road and Richmond Road returning via Chapel Road, Stoke Abbott Road, Christchurch Road, Richmond Road and then as outward route reversed. A frequent 10 minute service was provided. Route 2 operated from SPLASH POINT to WEST WORTHING STATION via Marine Parade, Western Place, Rowlands Road, Grand Avenue and Tarring Road every 10 minutes on Weekdays and every 15 minutes on Sundays. The terminus at Splash Point was on the sea front at the junction of Marine Parade and Warwick Road.

In February 1938 Mr Gates offered the business to Southdown and agreement was reached with the company to purchase Tramocars Ltd on 1 April 1938 for £15,750. At first Southdown retained the Tramocars timetable except that

the vehicles started and finished their day at the Pier instead of Heene Road, now being garaged at the Worthing depot in Library Place. In the Southdown timetable dated 26 September 1938 they were shown as being allocated numbers **T1** between SPLASH POINT (MARINE PARADE) and LIBRARY as the former Tramocars 1 and **T2** from SPLASH POINT to WEST WORTHING STATION as the former Tramocars 2 although this numbering had actually taken place on 1 August 1938.

With increasing competition from buses on Southdown service **27** which went right to the summit, the Devils Dyke railway line closed on 31 December 1938. In the winter 1938 timetable there were eight trains each day to and from The Dyke taking 20 minutes for the journey with some additional services as far as Rowan Halt. The branch was opened on 30 September 1887 and the branch line climbed on an almost continuous gradient of 1 in 40 to a point 200ft below the summit leaving visitors with a stiff half mile climb to the hotel. After the introduction of bus services traffic on the line fell steadily with very few travellers using the trains in winter. At first service 27 continued unchanged but, at the request of the Southern Railway, Southdown introduced a replacement service **32** from 7 April 1939 although the outbreak of war ensured its early demise.

January to August 1939 – Prelude to War

The start of 1939 brought a tidying up of several services in the Brighton, Worthing, Littlehampton and Arundel areas. The company's Traffic Notices which advised operating staff of any changes to routes, times, allocations, fares or connections have survived for the period from January to August 1939 and it has been possible to add some extra detail to this section. From **Sunday 1 January** service **9** between SHOREHAM (BRIDGE HOTEL) and ANGMERING was extended to ARUNDEL SQUARE. An hourly service was provided daily and the extension replaced service 66 over this section. At the same time the unusual extension on Bank Holidays only to Brighton (Pool Valley) was withdrawn. In addition new Service **9A** was introduced between ANGMERING-ON-SEA and ARUNDEL SQUARE via Sea Road, Preston Street, Worthing Road, Station Road, Ash Lane and then as service 9. This service ran hourly daily and combined with service 9 to provide a half hourly service between Angmering and Arundel. One journey operated to Angmering Village and was numbered **9B**. The 9 and 9A were interworked at Arundel and required five lowbridge double deckers with three allocated to Littlehampton and two at Worthing.

As a result of these changes services **68** and **68A** were curtailed to operate as circulars running ARUNDEL SQUARE – RUSTINGTON – ARUNDEL SQUARE via Crossbush, Lyminster, Littlehampton and the inland route to Rustington. Service **68** operated around the Rustington loop via Horsham Road, Worthing Road, North Lane, Rustington Street, The Street, Ash Lane, Mill Lane and Worthing Road to Horsham Road in this direction only with journeys in the reverse direction numbered **68A**. The Angmering Green section of route was now covered by services 9/9A while Ford Road journeys in Arundel were mostly replaced by an extension of service 10 although one journey continued to serve Ford Road. Two highbridge double deckers were required for the revised 68/68A both allocated to Littlehampton.

Also in connection with the above changes,

Opposite Tramocars no 4 halts for the camera at Worthing Pier probably in the mid-1920s and was clearly carrying registration PX 1592 but was altered to PX 1593 by the time it was taken over by Southdown in April 1938. It was a Shelvoke & Drewry Freighter with Hickman 20-seat rear entrance body new in March 1925. It only lasted in service until sale in September 1938. *West Sussex County Council*

Right A rear view of car 854 (UF 5654), one of a large batch of Leyland Titan TD1s with Leyland 48-seat lowbridge body new in January 1930. It is seen in the High Street in Arundel opposite the Norfolk Arms Hotel when traffic levels allowed buses to terminate in the middle of the wide street. Service 10 actually needed lowbridge buses due to a restricted railway bridge in Shoreham and ran hourly to Brighton mostly using the direct route along the A27 to the outskirts of Worthing continuing in this form for many years until the 1971 cutbacks. *Frank Wilson*

Car 1206 (UF 6806) was another of Southdown's large fleet of Tilling-Stevens Express B10A2 models with Short Bros 31-seat bodywork. Delivered new in October 1930 it is seen in Chichester operating on five times daily service 58 which during the 1930s ran northwards to the village East Dean on the edge of the South Downs. This vehicle survived in the fleet until July 1940 when it was requisitioned by the Military Authorities.
Alan Lambert Collection

service **66** was curtailed to operate between ARUNDEL SQUARE, CHICHESTER and SUMMERSDALE being replaced between Rustington and Arundel by services 9 and 9A although the first and last journeys daily still operated to and from Rustington Church. An hourly service was provided daily with alternate journeys operating via Halnaker. The service was now operated by two single deckers, one based at Chichester and one at Littlehampton. Service **67** between Rustington and Arundel was withdrawn as a result of the changes. The regular 15 minute headway between Angmering, Crundens's Corner and Littlehampton via the Coast Road was now provided by services 9, 9A and 31 while the regular 15 minute headway between Littlehampton and Arundel was now provided by 9, 9A, 68 and 68A.

Service **10** was extended in Arundel to FORD ROAD via High Street, Tarrant Street, Chichester Road and Ford Road to its junction with Priory Road. The **10** interworked at Brighton with service 22 and required nine lowbridge double deckers of which one each was allocated to Brighton, Littlehampton, and Steyning and two each to Worthing, Pulborough and Petworth.

The Angmering section of service **11** was renumbered 31G leaving this once important trunk route to run just hourly between WORTHING (PIER) and FERRING-ON-SEA (SOUTH DRIVE) only. Just one single decker was now required and based at Worthing. The regular 15 minute headway between Brighton and Worthing via the Coast Road was now provided by services 31, 31F and 31G. A 30 minute headway via Sussex Pad was maintained by service 10 and a connection between 9 and 22 at Shoreham.

The timetable for service **21** was revised although retaining the basic half hourly frequency. Four single deck buses were required for this operation with three based at Brighton but one now allocated to Worthing. The timings between Brighton Pool Valley and Shoreham were included in the Brighton to Worthing time-table summary for the first time.

In the first of several route variations in this area, service **31** was diverted between Goring Station and Roundstone Gates to operate via Goring Street, Littlehampton Road, Ferring Lane, Langbury Lane, Littlehampton Road and Worthing Road, replacing service 11 journeys via Langbury Lane. The duty schedules provided for all journeys between Southsea and Bognor Pier to be worked by Portsmouth, Emsworth or Chichester crews while journeys between Bognor Pier and Brighton were worked by Brighton, Worthing, Littlehampton or Bognor crews. Meal reliefs were normally only taken at Theatre Royal, Portsmouth – situated close to Hyde Park Road garage – or Pool Valley, Brighton. Crews arriving at Bognor Pier at 17 and 47 minutes past the hour would normally turn round and work straight back at 20 and 50 minutes past each hour!!

New service **31G** was introduced hourly between BRIGHTON (POOL VALLEY) and ANGMERING-ON-SEA running as service 31 to Worthing then via Marine Parade, Heene Road, Mill Road, Goring Road, Mulberry Lane, Goring Way, Goring Street, Littlehampton Road, Worthing Road, North Lane and Sea Road to its junction with Sea View Road. This replaced one journey per hour on the **31F** between Brighton and Worthing – which became hourly – and service 11 journeys to Angmering-on-Sea. The regular 15 minute headway between Worthing and North Ferring Corner was now provided by 11, 31 and 31G. Services 31, 31F and 31G were jointly allocated and required a total of 21 double deck buses based at Brighton 3, Worthing 5, Littlehampton 3, Bognor 2, Chichester 4, Emsworth 1 and Portsmouth 3.

Emsworth local service **44** was now run by a one man operated Leyland Cub in place of a crew operated single decker. The Traffic Notice suggests that Southdown were still hoping to extend this service to Thorney Island despite the imminent start of operation by Hants & Sussex. Some journeys on service **48** between Havant and Rowlands Castle were withdrawn while others were reduced to run at weekends only and the whole service in the hands of a one man operated Leyland Cub.

Service **53** journeys between Chichester and Itchenor were apparently renumbered **53A** although the Traffic Notice did not differentiate. Two journeys were provided each way on Weekdays departing Chichester at 1140 and 1410 with an extra journey each way on Sundays departing Chichester at 1735. On Saturdays the Hambrook journeys on service **54** were diverted via Scant Lane to Hambrook Post Office. Although not shown as such in the public timeta-bles these are referred to as service **54A** in the Traffic Notice. In Bognor the local service **55** was slightly altered at the North Bersted end of route by its diversion along the newly extended Collyer Avenue to South Way and then via the south end of Central Avenue to Chichester Road instead of running direct via Hampshire Avenue. Service **64** was extended every 2 or 3 hours daily from Yapton (Sparks Corner) via unclassified roads to terminate at FORD AERODROME GATES where it connected with service 31 to and from Littlehampton.

Service **70** was a minor route between PULBOROUGH and STORRINGTON – later to be absorbed into service 1 – and from this date the frequency was revised to eight journeys each way daily with all but one journey serving West Chiltington village. Timings were revised to make better connections at Pulborough with the fast trains to London now operating on the newly electrified Mid Sussex line. Traffic Notice No 6 states that from Tuesday 17 January the 1640 journey from Storrington will be retarded to 1705 in order to make a connection with the 1616 service 1 from Worthing – for the benefit of children attending Worthing High School! It is reassuring to know that such glitches could happen even in a very 'connection conscious' company like Southdown!

Service **71** between STORRINGTON and THAKEHAM CROSS ROADS gained one additional journey each day making eight on Weekdays and seven on Sunday. The bus that worked services 70 and 71 was changed each day with the service 65 vehicle from Littlehampton arriving in Storrington at 1044 as there were no fuelling facilities at Storrington garage.

Further north the former Rayner service **75** between BILLINGSHURST and HORSHAM via Barns Green gained an increased frequency with five journeys each way daily to Billingshurst plus one journey each way daily to Coneyhurst and various additional short journeys running between Horsham and Barns Green or Brooks Green. A new link was provided by two journeys each way daily diverting at Coolham to and from Scolliers Corner, Shipley partly replacing service **74** which was withdrawn.

Starting on **Thursday 19 January** services **78** and **79** were completely revised. Most journeys on service **78** were diverted in Horsham to pass under the low railway bridge in East Street to operate via Carfax, North Street, Park Street, East Street, Queen Street and Brighton Road. One journey each way continued via Station Road. At the same time the frequency was reduced on Monday-Friday to seven journeys each way, on Saturdays to eight journeys each way and on Sundays to six journeys each way while not all journeys operated to and from Slinfold. Certain journeys on Wednesdays, Saturdays and Sundays ran as Service **79** and continued beyond Handcross to Balcombe but ran direct between the Water Tower and Balcombe rather than via Cowdray Corner. The combined frequency had previously been hourly from Handcross to Horsham and Slinfold. A single one man operated Leyland Cub based at Handcross could now cover the whole service on both routes. Previously one bus had been based

at Haywards Heath and ran in service as additional journeys on service **82** between Handcross and Haywards Heath. The latter service was now revised to start and finish at Haywards Heath and the one lowbridge double decker allocated to Haywards Heath instead of Handcross. Finally, service **86** was extended from Balcombe via St. Mary's Church and Balcombe Lane to operate between HAYWARDS HEATH STATION and STONEY LANE covering roads no longer served by service 79. A two hourly service was provided daily. These changes were covered by the issue of a further timetable marked **Sunday 1 January 2ⁿᵈ Edition** although it is not clear why these were added as an apparent after thought given the complexity of changes in other parts of the area.

Owing to the reconstruction of the bridge over the River Cuckmere near Alfriston service **26** was unable to serve Litlington from Monday 30 January and was instead diverted via the route of summer only service 26A via High and Over. From 17 February Southdown provided a special shuttle service on Fridays and Saturdays only between Seaford and Litlington departing Seaford at 1418, 1718 and 2118 and returning from Litlington 18 minutes later. The works obviously took longer than expected and continued until 11 May 1939.

Commencing on **Thursday 2 February** service **31** was rerouted in Bognor and no longer ran via The Pier. After the opening of the Bus Station it had continued to run in a loop via York Road, Esplanade and Waterloo Square but was now diverted via the High Street to load and unload in the Bus Station. Storrington area services **70** and **71** also had revised timetables again, having been previously amended from 1 January 1939.

The Hants & Sussex service to Thorney Island referred to earlier finally commenced on 27 February 1939. In a further touch of irony Hants & Sussex purchased two former Southdown Tilling-Stevens Express buses in the spring of 1939, and, after repainting in their cream and

Seen at Storrington Square on service 70 to Pulborough via West Chiltington is car 683 (UF 5683) a Tilling-Stevens Express B10A2 with Short Bros B31R bodywork new in December 1931. Just arriving is a Leyland Titan on service 22 heading towards Brighton which is not due to connect with the 70 although connections are scheduled here with service 1 to and from Worthing. The tall buildings in the background are still recognisable today.
Frank Wilson

black livery put them to work on the Thorney Island service!

A few minor timing changes were introduced starting **Thursday 6 April** and from this date the summary timetables, Brighton to Lewes, Southsea to Horndean and Southsea to Havant and Westbourne helpfully included the route number above each column except for inbound Portsmouth journeys where no number was carried on destination displays. This was later extended to all summary timetables. Devil's Dyke short journeys on service **27** were increased to seven each way daily as in spring 1938. On service **45** journey times and frequencies were revised as follows:

1 journey per hour Theatre Royal – direct – Fareham – Warsash

2 journeys per hour Bradford Junction – Fratton – Castle Street – Fareham

2 journeys per hour Theatre Royal – Castle Street – Cornaway Lane, Portchester

2 journeys per hour Theatre Royal – direct – Cornaway Lane, Portchester

3 journeys per hour Theatre Royal – direct – Fareham

As compared to Winter 1938/9 the service via Fratton was reduced from three buses per hour to two while Fareham was reduced from eight buses per hour to six. The full service now required an allocation of 18 double deckers of which two were outstationed at Warsash. Of the remainder 11 were garaged at Hyde Park Road and five at Hilsea.

A NEW SERVICE, starting on April 7, 1939

will run between

BRIGHTON STATION AND THE DEVIL'S DYKE HOTEL

in place of the former train service, as shown below :—

32	BRIGHTON STATION	Hove Station	DEVIL'S DYKE	32
	(For other daily buses to the Devil's Dyke see Route 27)			

GOOD FRIDAY, April 7th, to EASTER MONDAY, April 10th (incl.)
and then EVERY SAT. AND SUN. until Whitsuntide.

					†				†	
Brighton Station S.R. ...	1010	1110	1210	2 10	3 10	4 10	5 10	6 10		
Seven Dials ...	1013	1113	1213	2 13	3 13	4 13	5 13	6 13		
Hove Station S.R. ...	1019	1119	1219	2 19	3 19	4 19	5 19	6 19		
Portland Road ...	1022	1122	1222	2 22	3 22	4 22	5 22	6 22		
Old Shoreham Rd Nevill Rd	1024	1124	1224	2 24	3 24	4 24	5 24	6 24		
West Blatchington ...	1026	1126	1226	2 26	3 26	4 26	5 26	6 26		
Mill Road ...	1029	1129	1229	2 29	3 29	4 29	5 29	6 29		
Brighton & Hove Golf Club	1033	1133	1233	2 33	3 33	4 33	5 33	6 33		
Devil's Dyke Hotel ...	1038	1138	1238	2 38	3 38	4 38	5 38	6 38		
				†				†		
Devil's Dyke Hotel ...	1040	1140	1240	2 40	3 40	4 40	5 40	6 40		
Brighton & Hove Golf Club	1045	1145	1245	2 45	3 45	4 45	5 45	6 45		
Mill Road ...	1049	1149	1249	2 49	3 49	4 49	5 49	6 49		
West Blatchington ...	1052	1152	1252	2 52	3 52	4 52	5 52	6 52		
Old Shoreham Rd Nevill Rd	1054	1154	1254	2 54	3 54	4 54	5 54	6 54		
Portland Road ...	1056	1156	1256	2 56	3 56	4 56	5 56	6 56		
Hove Station S.R. ...	1059	1159	1259	2 59	3 59	4 59	5 59	6 59		
Seven Dials ...	11 5	12 5	1 5	3 5	4 5	5 5	6 5	7 5		
Brighton Station S.R. ...	11 8	12 8	1 8	3 8	4 8	5 8	6 8	7 8		

†Will not run on wet days.

						Brighton Station.						
5						Seven Dials. 2						
5	5					Holland Road. 3			SINGLE FARES			
5	5	4				Hove Station. 4						
5	5	4	4			Coleridge Street. 5						
5	5	4	4	4		Old Shoreham Road or Droveway. 6						
5	5	4	4	4	3	West Blatchington. 7						
5	5	4	4	4	3	1	Mill Road. 8					
5	5	4	4	4	3	2	1	Saddlescombe Road. 9				
5	5	5	4	4	3	2	2	Brighton and Hove Golf Club. 10			
6	5	5	5	5	4	3	2	2	Poynings Road Corner. 11		
7	6	6	6	6	5	4	3	2	1	Devil's Dyke Hotel. 12	

Brighton Railway Station.	RETURN FARES
—	Hove Station.
—	Old Shoreham Road.
—	Saddlescombe Road.
10	8	6	Brighton & Hove Golf Club.
1/-	10	8	Poynings Road Corner.
1/2	1/-	10	Dyke Hotel.

(left margin caption)

Service 32 was a somewhat half-hearted response by Southdown to replace the Dyke branch line which had been finally withdrawn at the end of 1938. Contemporary accounts suggest that in effect Southdown had already replaced the trains by running a frequent bus service 27 right to the summit which proved far more attractive than the infrequent trains to a terminus that left visitors with a stiff half mile climb to the hotel! It was an obvious early casualty of the war and quietly dropped from any postwar plans.

To replace the Dyke branch line which had been withdrawn on 31 December 1938 the Southern Railway requested Southdown to provide a new bus service. Starting on **Good Friday 7 April** service **32** ran from BRIGHTON STATION to DEVIL'S DYKE HOTEL via Terminus Road, Buckingham Place, Seven Dials, Goldsmid Road, Davigdor Road, Cromwell Road, Denmark Villas, Station Approach, Hove Station, Goldstone Villas, Clarendon Villas, Sackville Road, Nevill Road, King George VI Avenue and Dyke Road. An hourly service was provided daily although during wet weather the frequency was reduced to two hourly. Traffic Notice No 10 makes clear that it is the responsibility of the Inspector or Regulator on duty at Brighton Station to decide what constitutes a wet day. If the weather was just showery or changeable the full service would run. One double decker was required to run an hourly service and the open top Leyland TD1s dating from 1929 were often allocated to the service which ran on short term licences throughout its brief existence operating over the Easter holiday, then Saturdays and Sundays until Whitsun and daily from 25 May until it was suspended on 14 September due to wartime conditions.

Starting on **Thursday 27 April** service **12** timings between Old Steine and Dyke Road, Tivoli Crescent were co-ordinated with the new Brighton Corporation services 51 and 52 and a composite timetable issued showing all journeys. Southdown continued to provide four journeys each hour over this section as part of the through service to Seaford and Eastbourne. Some Southdown fares between Tongdean and Brighton Station were reduced as a result of the new arrangement but there were no return fares or interavailability of tickets between the operators at this time. From late July a 7d return fare was introduced between Tongdean and Pool Valley and also available for use on service 27. The Traffic Notice stressed the need for punctuality in view of the new co-ordination. On 1 May 1939 trolleybuses of Brighton Corporation started to replace more tram routes until the final abandonment came on 31 August 1939 just days before war was declared.

With war now almost inevitable the last full summer timetable to be introduced for seven long years commenced on **Thursday 25 May**. Some further high season enhancements to frequencies were introduced as usual in July by which time the prospects of peace seemed even less promising. Several services would be appearing for the last time in their present form and some would be lost forever. On Worthing local service **4** between East Worthing and High Salvington the full 10 minute frequency was extended to High Salvington daily as in summer 1938.

A new service **11A** provided by a one man operated Leyland Cub was introduced between NORTH FERRING CORNER and FERRING

An unusually quiet Pool Valley in Brighton is the setting for car 1401 (BUF 981) a Leyland Tiger TS7 with attractive Harrington 'dual purpose' bodywork as delivered in 1935. A number of modifications were made to these buses at the start of the war and the cream roofs were painted dark green to make them less visible to enemy aircraft. The 1400 class Tigers formed the mainstay of the important Brighton to Haywards Heath routes – which were restricted to single deck operation – until the arrival of Royal Tiger buses in 1952/3. Unlike many in its class this vehicle was not converted to perimeter seating during the war and was withdrawn in 1955. A.Duke, Omnibus Society

(SOUTH DRIVE) via the same route as service 11 but following the Ferring loop in the opposite – clockwise – direction. The journey time was a mere 8 minutes and an hourly frequency provided daily between 0952 and 1852 with no evening service. This supplemented service 11 within Ferring and also covered for the withdrawal of service 31 via Ferring Lane – see below. Buses connected at North Ferring Corner with services 31 or 31G to or from Worthing and in the event of a missed connection one morning journey could extend to Goring Station if there were any passengers for the 0924 train to London! The 11A was due to run for the summer period until 24 September but may have been affected by the outbreak of war. On service 12 there was no general change to frequency at this date although the Peacehaven Annexe journeys were renumbered 12A and Saltdean Mount journeys renumbered 12B.

Summer only service 26A was reintroduced between Seaford and Eastbourne via High & Over and Alfriston. Two single deckers were required to provide the service, one based at Eastbourne and one at Seaford. It was withdrawn in September 1939 'for the duration' but soon became the main all year round service between Seaford and Alfriston after the war while the service 26 via Litlington was reduced to run three hourly. The busy service 27 as far as Devils Dyke had a frequency increase with 12 journeys each way daily similar to summer 1938. Two double deckers were allocated to the Devil's Dyke short journeys and the open top TD1s could usually be found on these.

Service 31 was diverted between Goring Station and Roundstone Gates to operate direct via Goring Street, Littlehampton Road and Worthing Road omitting the route via Ferring Lane and Langbury Lane introduced on 1 January 1939. New service 11A shown above provided some replacement but not for Langbury

Lane. The duty schedules were amended so that all journeys between Southsea and Littlehampton were worked by Portsmouth, Emsworth, Chichester or Bognor crews while journeys between Littlehampton and Brighton were worked by Brighton, Worthing or Littlehampton crews.

To serve the popular holiday camps on Hayling Island the frequency of service 47 was again improved. Seven lightweight 26-seat single deckers were required to operate the service of which five were based at Emsworth. Sadly within a few weeks the visitors would be gone and the camps closed for the duration. In the Bognor area service 50A gained an extension from Nyetimber via Pagham Road to Pagham Beach providing four buses per hour daily between Elmer, Bognor and Pagham in conjunction with service 50. Six double deckers were allocated to Bognor for these services.

Commencing on **Saturday 10 June** summer only service 46 was reintroduced every 30 minutes. The 2230 departure from Hayling Bus Station awaited the end of the performance at

Service 26A had been a popular summer route with tourists during the 1930s but made its last appearance in the July 1939 timetable becoming an early casualty of war. The ability of modern buses to cope with the steep hills between Alfriston and Seaford led to Southdown changing its route pattern after the war when the 26A became the 126 and ran daily throughout the year. It wasn't such good news for the residents on the parallel route through Litlington who saw their service reduce from hourly to three hourly!

26a	Seaford, High-and-Over, Alfriston, Eastbourne										26a	
Seaford Clinton Place ...	...	...	11 20	12 20	2 20	3 20	4 20	5 20	6 20	7 20	8 20	
Cemetery ...	...	...	11 25	12 25	2 25	3 25	4 25	5 25	6 25	7 25	8 25	
High and Over ...	...	...	11 31	12 31	2 31	3 31	4 31	5 31	6 31	7 31	8 31	
Frog Firle	...	...	11 34	12 34	2 34	3 34	4 34	5 34	6 34	7 34	8 34	
Alfriston Cross ...			11 38	12 38	2 38	3 38	4 38	5 38	6 38	7 38	8 38	
Berwick *R.A.C. Box*	...		11 46	12 46	2 46	3 46	4 46	5 46	6 46	7 46	8 46	
Wilmington	...		11 52	12 52	2 52	3 52	4 52	5 52	6 52	7 52	8 52	
Polegate *Horse & Groom*			11 58	12 58	2 58	3 58	4 58	5 58	6 58	7 58	8 58	
Lower Willingdon	...		12 0	1 0	3 0	4 0	5 0	6 0	7 0	8 0	9 0	
Upper Willingdon *School*	...		12 2	1 2	3 2	4 2	5 2	6 2	7 2	8 2	9 2	
Eastbourne Pevensey Road			12 14	1 14	3 14	4 14	5 14	6 14	7 14	8 14	9 14	
Eastbourne Pevensey Road	...		11 20	12 20	2 20	3 20	4 20	5 20	6 20	7 20	8 20	
Upper Willingdon *School*	...		11 32	12 32	2 32	3 32	4 32	5 32	6 32	7 32	8 32	
Lower Willingdon	...		11 34	12 34	2 34	3 34	4 34	5 34	6 34	7 34	8 34	
Polegate *Horse & Groom*	...		11 36	12 36	2 36	3 36	4 36	5 36	6 36	7 36	8 36	
Wilmington	...		11 42	12 42	2 42	3 42	4 42	5 42	6 42	7 42	8 42	
Berwick *R.A.C. Box*	...		11 48	12 48	2 48	3 48	4 48	5 48	6 48	7 48	8 48	
Alfriston Cross ...			11 56	12 56	2 56	3 56	4 56	5 56	6 56	7 56	8 56	
Frog Firle	...		12 0	1 0	3 0	4 0	5 0	6 0	7 0	8 0	9 0	
High and Over ...	...		12 3	1 3	3 3	4 3	5 3	6 3	7 3	8 3	9 3	
Cemetery ...	...		12 8	1 8	3 8	4 8	5 8	6 8	7 8	8 8	9 8	
Seaford Clinton Place ...			12 14	1 14	3 14	4 14	5 14	6 14	7 14	8 14	9 14	

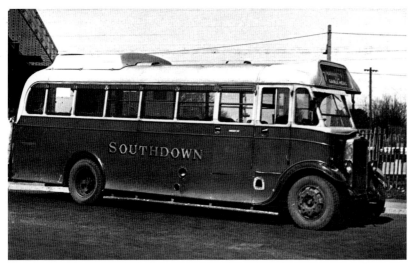

During 1936/7 Southdown took delivery of six 'forward control' Leyland Cub SKPZ2 models with lightweight Park Royal 26-seat rear entrance bodies for use on the Hayling Island services which crossed a weight restricted bridge on the only road to Havant. Car 8 (DUF 8), delivered in March 1937, is seen on service 47 at Havant Station in original livery with cream roof and survived with the company until 1956 and the opening of the new bridge to the mainland. *Southdown Enthusiasts Club – Clark/ Surfleet Collection*

the Regal Cinema while the final service 47 from Portsmouth continued to Eastoke House arriving at the, in those far off days, very late hour of 12 minutes past midnight! A unique feature of service **47** was the Special Church journeys on Sundays from 11 June 1939. The first departed Eastoke House at 0740, Eastoke Post Office at 0745 and Hayling Bus Station at 0749 and ran via Sea Front and Manor Road to St Marys Church returning at 0845. The second departed Eastoke House at 0805, Eastoke Post Office at 0810 and Hayling Bus Station at 0814 and ran via Sea Front and Manor Road to St Patrick's R.C. Church returning at 0915. These journeys were withdrawn soon after the outbreak of war and not reintroduced.

With little chance of further local expansion Hants & Sussex chose to acquire the businesses of existing independent operators. The first such purchase came on 1 July 1939 with the business of Gavin of Midhurst which operated services from Midhurst to Graffham on Mondays, Wednesdays, Thursdays and Saturdays and from Graffham to Chichester on Wednesdays and the first Saturday of the month. Gavin also held a licence to operate between Midhurst and Lurgashall but this was not operating at the time. The application to acquire the Road Service licences, in the name of B.S. Williams, was opposed by Southdown, Aldershot & District and the Southern Railway. The Commissioner issued two short period licences to enable the services to be maintained pending a public hearing but, before this could be arranged, war had been declared. Under the Emergency Regulations public inquiries were no longer allowed and Road Service licences were replaced by Defence Permits resulting in these services operating on Permits throughout the war.

Some further enhancement of Southdown services commenced on **Thursday 13 July** with most broadly in line with those operated in summer 1938. This was to be the last full peace-time timetable for seven years and the last in the format which had appeared throughout the

1930s. In Worthing the Lancing Manor journeys on service **7** were transferred to a new service **7A** which ran every 20 minutes daily between WORTHING PIER and LANCING MANOR as service 7 to Sompting, West Street then via Busticle Lane, Upper Brighton Road and Manor Road.

An additional composite timetable – as referred to earlier – was added for service **12** showing Brighton Corporation services 51 and 52 between Dyke Road and Old Steine along with the Southdown journeys between Tongdean and Old Steine. There were already timetables for the complete service between Seaford and Tongdean including 12A and 12B plus a separate timetable for through journeys to Eastbourne! The frequency of service **12** was increased to provide:

2 journeys per hour between Tongdean and Eastbourne
1 journey per hour between Tongdean and Peacehaven (Rosemary)
4 journeys per hour between Brighton Station and Seaford.

As a result the frequency to Tongdean was reduced from four to three buses per hour compared to summer 1938 but in replacement service **12A** was extended from Brighton Station to Tongdean. Four highbridge double deck buses had commenced operation on journeys running as far east as Peacehaven Annexe or Peacehaven Rosemary from 10 June 1939. But, further work was required at the Southern Railway's bridge at Newhaven – which they considered unable to cope with the weight of double deck buses – before the through service to Seaford and Eastbourne could be converted. In the meantime it meant that on some journeys it was necessary for passengers to change from single to double deckers or vice-versa at Brighton Station, Old Steine or Pool Valley. Some 22 buses were required to provide the summer service as follows – Eastbourne 2 single deckers, Seaford 5 single deckers, Brighton 4 double deckers and 10 single deckers plus an additional bus not required on service 12 after 0754.

On service **27** the short journeys to Devil's Dyke were increased to 23 each way daily similar to summer 1938 although on fine days when traffic required the service could be increased to run every 15 minutes. Buses departed Pool Valley between 0900 and 2130 returning from Devils Dyke 30 minutes later. Two double deckers based at Brighton were allocated to the Devil's Dyke short journeys and one single decker each to Brighton and Henfield for the through service. The former Sargent's service between Brighton and East Grinstead, numbered **28**, was again increased for the summer to provide six journeys each way daily on a roughly two hourly frequency similar to 1938. Two vehicles were allocated to the service, one from East Grinstead and one from Brighton. It was to be an early casualty of the wartime cuts being suspended from 14 September and one of the few that failed to reappear in post war years. Leyland Cub operated service **34** was rerouted in Hurstpierpoint via Cuckfield Road due to an obstruction with the terminal point becoming HURSTPIERPOINT (CHINESE GARDENS HOTEL).

Four additional journeys each way between Southsea (South Parade Pier) and Eastoke House were added to service **47** on weekdays only, similar to summer 1938. The normal all day service ran from South Parade Pier via Fratton but these additional journeys operated via Theatre Royal. Although referred to in the public timetables as part of service 47 they are referred to as 47A in Traffic Notice No 17. One additional 26 seater rear entrance Leyland Cub or lightweight Tilling-Stevens Express was required for this operation. An interesting feature of the timetable book was the inclusion in the Portsmouth section of timetables for Portsmouth to Winchester connecting services changing to Hants & Dorset at Fareham and Southsea to

Aldershot and Guildford changing to Aldershot & District at Petersfield along with through fares.

On service **53** the full summer timetable was introduced including an extra hourly journey each way between Chichester and East Wittering via Earnley. This route interworked with service 57 at Chichester and required a total of four double deckers of which one was based at Wittering, two at Chichester and one at Bognor.

Service **60** was curtailed to operate hourly between MIDHURST (GRAMMAR SCHOOL) and PETERSFIELD STATION being withdrawn between Bognor and Midhurst. The latter section of route was covered by service 59 which ran every one or two hours sharing the route with Aldershot & District's service 19 running between Aldershot and Bognor. The 19 operated every 90 minutes and so filled the two hour gaps in the 59 timetable but also added some 30 minute frequencies during the day.

For the 1937 season the open top Leyland TDIs dating from 1929 had been repainted with cream upper deck panels and allocated for seasonal work. This ensured that the complete batch survived until after the war even though later covered top Titans were mostly sold in 1938/9. Car 801 (UF 4801) with Brush 51-seat body and open staircase is seen awaiting departure from Pool Valley at Brighton on a short working on the popular service 27 to Devils Dyke. Alongside is a 1400 class Leyland Tiger on frequent local service 13E to Higher Bevendean. *A.Duke, Omnibus Society*

After the opening of the new Bus Station in Bognor High Street at the beginning of 1935 most services were altered to terminate at the conveniently sited facility but hourly service 57 from Chichester via Tangmere and Westergate continued to run to Bognor Pier until the war made such extensions superfluous. Car 843 (UF 5643), a Leyland Titan TDI with Leyland lowbridge bodywork is seen on The Esplanade in Bognor. *Alan Lambert Collection*

Car 1414 (BUF 994) was a Leyland Tiger TS7 with attractive Harrington 'dual purpose' bodywork delivered in 1935. It is seen on service 99 in original condition with roof mounted luggage rack and rear corner side glasses. Along with many others of this class it was converted to perimeter seating during the war to permit up to 30 standees although service 99 was suspended 'for the duration' from late July 1940. S.L.Poole

Summer only service **62** was reintroduced – for what was to be its last ever season – between Bognor Pier and Arundel via Middleton, Yapton and Walberton running every 2 hours daily. Buses departed Bognor between 1004 and 2004 and returned from Arundel between 1122 and 2122. The timetable allowed some 37 minutes stand time at Arundel and the Traffic Notice suggested that this might be used to provide a relief working to Littlehampton if needed. Connections were made at Arundel with service 10 to Worthing and Brighton. This service had premium fares and those wishing to use their service 31 returns to travel back on service 62 were obliged to pay a supplement of 6d. One double decker was allocated to Bognor for this operation and there is photographic evidence of open top TD1s being used on occasions.

To the east of the Southdown area there were the usual summer frequency increases broadly in line with those of summer 1938 although the extra Uckfield to East Grinstead Saturday and Sunday afternoon short journeys on service **92** were not reintroduced as in past years. These had been a feature of this service since its extension northwards in July 1933 at the formation of LPTB. Passengers holding return tickets on the coach service between Eastbourne and East Grinstead or intermediately were allowed to return by bus without further payment. The frequency of the popular Beachy Head service **97** was increased to an hourly basic service daily and further enhanced to every 15 minutes in fine weather similar to summer 1938. Departures from Royal Parade were between 0945 and 2045

The last prewar timetable for services 98 and 99 provided enhanced services between Pevensey and Eastbourne via the Coast Road including a journey into Eastbourne before 0900. These services were reduced after the outbreak of war and both routes suspended at the end of July 1940 when a German invasion along this part of the coast seemed a distinct possibility. A limited inland service between Eastbourne and Pevensey Bay was provided by the 96 running via Stone Cross.

– except no journeys ran at 1300 and 1315 – returning from Beachy Head 20 minutes later. Three of the four Leyland Tigers specially purchased for this service were required to provide the summer service. Service **98** from Eastbourne to Pevensey via Pevensey Bay was increased to provide an approximately hourly service daily in conjunction with the 99 as far as Pevensey, Old Mint House while service **99** from Eastbourne to Hastings via Bexhill was increased to run every 1 to 2 hours with a total of eight through journeys daily. Departures from Eastbourne were between 0935 and 2035 and from Hastings between 1012 and 2012. Passengers holding return tickets between Eastbourne and Bexhill or Hastings were allowed to return by service 15 via Hailsham on payment of a 1/- supplement. Southdown provided two single deckers for the interworked services 98 and 99, both based at Eastbourne.

Given the growing international tension, summer was celebrated as best possible but few could have doubted that, despite the hopes following the Munich Agreement in September 1938, another European war was looming. Most people probably wanted to just enjoy a last holiday before war was declared. There was little doubt that any new war would involve bombing of civilians and various contingency plans for public shelters became apparent to even the most optimistic among the population as August progressed. Southdown were inevitably involved in planning for the coming conflict as the continuation of essential transport services would be a priority. If war had not been declared on Sunday 3 September the summer timetables would have continued in force until **Sunday 24 September.**

Bus Services **98 & 99** EASTBOURNE, PEVENSEY, BEXHILL, HASTINGS

Worked jointly by buses of Southdown and Maidstone Companies.
For additional buses between Eastbourne, Bexhill and Hastings, see Service 15.

WEEKDAYS AND SUNDAYS.

		NS									
Eastbourne (Pevensey Road)	...	8 10	9 35	1135	1235	1 30	2 35	2 50	3 35	3 50
Eastbourne (Archery)	...	8 15	9 41	1141	1241	1 36	2 41	2 56	3 41	3 56
Coastguards Cottages	...	8 22	9 49	1149	1249	1 44	2 49	3 4	3 49	4 4
Pevensey Bay (Bay Hotel)	...	8 26	9 53	1153	1253	1 48	2 53	3 8	3 53	4 8
Pevensey (Old Mint House)	...	8 31	9 58	1158	1258	1 53	2 58	3 13	3 58	4 13
Barnhorn Lane (Constable's Farm)	...		10 7	12 7	1 7		3 7		4 7	
Little Common (Wheatsheaf)	...		1014	1214	1 14		3 14		4 14	
Sutherland Avenue (Bottom)	...		1019	1219	1 19		3 19		4 19	
Bexhill (Marina)	...		1024	1224	1 24		3 24		4 24	
Hastings (Wellington Square)	...		1049	1249	1 49		3 49		4 49	
Eastbourne (Pevensey Road)	...	4 50	5 35	5 50	6 35	6 50	7 50	8 35	8 50	9 50
Eastbourne (Archery)	...	4 56	5 41	5 56	6 41	6 56	7 56	8 41	8 56	9 56
Coastguards Cottages	...	5 4	5 49	6 4	6 49	7 4	8 4	8 49	9 4	10 4
Pevensey Bay (Bay Hotel)	...	5 8	5 53	6 8	6 53	7 8	8 8	8 53	9 8	10 8
Pevensey (Old Mint House)	...	5 13	5 58	6 13	6 58	7 13	8 13	8 58	9 13	1013
Barnhorn Lane (Constable's Farm)	...		6 7		7 7			9 7		
Little Common (Wheatsheaf)	...		6 14		7 14			9 14		
Sutherland Avenue (Bottom)	...		6 19		7 19			9 19		
Bexhill (Marina)	...		6 24		7 24			9 24		
Hastings (Wellington Square)	...		6 49		7 49			9 49		

Bus Services **98 & 99** HASTINGS, BEXHILL, PEVENSEY, EASTBOURNE

Worked jointly by buses of Southdown and Maidstone Companies.
For additional buses between Hastings, Bexhill and Eastbourne, see Service 15.

WEEKDAYS AND SUNDAYS.

		NS									
Hastings (Wellington Square)	...		1012	1112	1 12		2 12			4 12
Bexhill (Marina)	...		1037	1137	1 37		2 37			4 37
Sutherland Avenue (Bottom)	...		1042	1142	1 42		2 42			4 42
Little Common (Wheatsheaf)	...		1047	1147	1 47		2 47			4 47
Barnhorn Lane (Constable's Farm)	...		1054	1154	1 54		2 54			4 54
Pevensey (Old Mint House)	...	8 33	10 0	11 3	12 3	2 3	2 25	3 3	3 25	4 25	5 3
Pevensey Bay (Bay Hotel)	...	8 38	10 5	11 8	12 8	2 8	2 30	3 8	3 30	4 30	5 8
Coastguards Cottages	...	8 42	10 9	1112	1212	2 12	2 34	3 12	3 34	4 34	5 12
Eastbourne (Archery)	...	8 50	1017	1120	1220	2 20	2 42	3 20	3 42	4 42	5 20
Eastbourne (Pevensey Road)	...	8 56	1023	1126	1226	2 26	2 48	3 26	3 48	4 48	5 26
Hastings (Wellington Square)	...		5 12		7 12		8 12			
Bexhill (Marina)	...		5 37		7 37		8 37			
Sutherland Avenue (Bottom)	...		5 42		7 42		8 42			
Little Common (Wheatsheaf)	...		5 47		7 47		8 47			
Barnhorn Lane (Constable's Farm)	...		5 54		7 54		8 54			
Pevensey (Old Mint House)	...	5 25	6 3	6 25	7 25	8 25	9 3	9 25	1025
Pevensey Bay (Bay Hotel)	...	5 30	6 8	6 30	7 30	8 30	9 8	9 30	1030
Coastguards Cottages	...	5 34	6 12	6 34	7 34	8 34	9 12	9 34	1034
Eastbourne (Archery)	...	5 42	6 20	6 42	7 42	8 42	9 20	9 42	1042
Eastbourne (Pevensey Road)	...	5 48	6 26	6 48	7 48	8 48	9 26	9 48	1048

During the 1930s virtually every town, suburb and major new housing development enjoyed at least one smart new cinema while many older cinemas were modernised to compete with the newcomers. In the era before television, the cinema was one of the main forms of entertainment in the UK, a chance to escape from economic depression and escalating political tensions across Europe.

A survey in 1938 showed that 31% of the population went to the cinema once a week with 13% attending twice, 3% three times, and 2% four or more times providing an important source of passengers for evening bus services. In addition some traditional theatres still offered variety shows throughout the year. It is not surprising, therefore, that the time of the last bus was often determined by the finishing time of local cinema performances.

An interesting event occurred in February 1939 when the last service 24 bus from Brighton to Henfield via Hurstpierpoint had to be altered so that it could operate an additional journey from Hassocks Cinema at 2205 or the close of the last performance in order to help relieve pressure on the last service 34 bus! Such was the demand in those days!

All places of entertainment were closed at the outbreak of war due to fears of serious loss of life if a cinema or theatre received a direct hit. By the middle of September 1939 most had been allowed to reopen once the expected bombing did not materialise but the effect of the blackout reduced evening travel except where absolutely necessary. Below are examples of buses serving cinemas and theatres from the Southdown timetable dated 13 July 1939.

Service   Depart   (as described in timetable)

Service	Depart (as described in timetable)
T1	Special late cars leave the Connaught Theatre after the last performance
T2	Special late cars leave the Plaza Cinema at the conclusion of the last performance
9A	2212 from Angmering-on-Sea diverts via Littlehampton Pavilion at 2235
12A	2159 from Brighton Station waits at Peacehaven for end of performance at Peacehaven Cinema
31	2305 from Theatre Royal waits until after second performance at Hippodrome
31A	2257 from South Parade Pier waits at junction of Elm Grove and Victoria Road for conclusion of performance at the Kings Theatre
34	2243 from Hassocks Stone Pound operates from Hassocks Cinema
38	2305 from Clarence Pier waits at Theatre Royal until after second performance at Hippodrome
39	2255 from South Parade Pier waits at Theatre Royal until after second performance at Hippodrome
42	2305 from Theatre Royal waits until after second performance at Hippodrome
44	2227 from Emsworth awaits conclusion of performance at Emsworth Cinema
45	2305 from Theatre Royal waits until after second performance at Hippodrome
46	2230 from Hayling Bus Station waits end of performance at Regal Cinema
47	2305 from Theatre Royal waits until after second performance at Hippodrome
	2149 from South Parade Pier waits end of performance at Havant Cinema
57	2245 from Bognor Pier awaits conclusion of the last performance at the Theatre and Pictures
61	2215 from Petersfield Station waits at Petersfield Square until conclusion of Cinema
92	2300 from Eastbourne leaves Devonshire Park Theatre after the performance (not later than 2300)
96	2300 from Eastbourne leaves Devonshire Park Theatre after the performance (not later than 2300)

Bus Service 96   EASTBOURNE AND PEVENSEY BAY.

★Leaves Devonshire Park Theatre after the performance (not later than 11.0 p.m.).
For additional buses between Eastbourne and Pevensey see page 314.

WEEK DAYS & SUNDAYS.

	NS	NS														★
Eastbourne (Pevensey Road)	8 10	9 13	9 40	1013	1113	1213	1 13	2 13	3 13	4 13	513	613	713	813	913	11 0
Eastbourne (Archery)	8 16	9 19	9 46	1019	1119	1219	1 19	2 19	3 19	4 19	519	619	719	819	919	11 6
Hide Corner	8 22	9 25	9 52	1025	1125	1225	1 25	2 25	3 25	4 25	525	625	725	825	925	11 12
Stone Cross	8 25	9 28	9 55	1028	1128	1228	1 28	2 28	3 28	4 28	528	628	728	828	928	11 15
Westham (Railway Hotel)	8 30	9 33	10 0	1033	1133	1233	1 33	2 33	3 33	433	533	633	733	833	933	11 20
Pevensey (Old Mint House)	8 33	9 36	10 3	1036	1136	1236	1 36	2 36	3 36	4 36	536	636	736	836	936	11 23
Pevensey Bay (Bay Hotel)	8 38	9 41	10 8	1041	1141	1241	1 41	2 41	3 41	4 41	541	641	741	841	941	11 28

	NS	NS													
Pevensey Bay (Bay Hotel)	8 26	9 43	1043	1143	1243	1 43	2 43	3 43	4 43	5 43	6 43	7 43	8 43	9 43	11 30
Pevensey (Old Mint House)	8 31	9 48	1048	1148	1248	1 48	2 48	3 48	4 48	5 48	6 48	7 48	8 48	9 48	11 35
Westham (Railway Hotel)	8 34	9 51	1051	1151	1251	1 51	2 51	3 51	4 51	5 51	6 51	7 51	8 51	9 51	11 38
Stone Cross	8 39	9 56	1056	1156	1256	1 56	2 56	3 56	4 56	5 56	6 56	7 56	8 56	9 56	11 43
Hide Corner	8 42	9 59	1059	1159	1259	1 59	2 59	3 59	4 59	5 59	6 59	7 59	8 59	9 59	11 46
Eastbourne (Archery)	8 48	10 5	11 5	12 5	1 5	2 5	3 5	4 5	5 5	6 5	7 5	8 5	9 5	10 5	11 52
Eastbourne (Pevensey Road)	8 55	1011	1111	1211	1 11	2 11	3 11	4 11	5 11	6 11	7 11	8 11	9 11	1011	11 58

In August 1938 Adolf Hitler threatened to invade Czechoslovakia. The British government was ill prepared for a war with Nazi Germany and Prime Minister Neville Chamberlain ordered that Air Raid Precautions (ARP) volunteers be mobilised. During September 1938 cellars and basements were requisitioned for air raid shelters and late season holidaymakers watched as trenches were dug in the parks of towns along the south coast. Gas masks were issued to the civilian population for fear of sudden gas attacks in the event of war and the government prepared detailed plans for the evacuation of children from Britain's large cities – including Portsmouth. Here the plans involved road, rail and sea with Southdown being required to provide 134 buses to evacuate just over 7,000 children from twelve schools on the western side of Portsea Island while the Corporation would operate 130 buses for schools on the eastern side. Others would go by rail but the plan was later amended as more children were sent by steamer to the Isle of Wight and Southdown did not participate in the main scheme. Although the immediate danger of war was averted by the agreement reached in Munich between Chamberlain and Hitler at the end of September 1938 another European war now seemed inevitable.

On 15 March 1939 German troops occupied the remainder of Czechoslovakia in violation of the Munich Agreement of the previous September. Initially, the British and French governments made only weak protests in response. On 31 March France and Britain declared that they would stand by Poland following further threats from Hitler. Not everyone, though, appeared concerned by developments in Europe. The MP for Eastbourne, Charles Taylor, speaking at a meeting in the spring of 1939 said 'I do not think Eastbourne need worry about being bombed in time of war – the attackers, whoever they might be, would not go to the trouble of carrying high explosive bombs for the purpose of bombing Eastbourne.' Sadly for the residents of the town his optimistic view of the looming conflict proved hopelessly wrong. In fact the drift towards war started to accelerate on 3 April as Hitler issued a directive to the Army High Command to prepare for an attack on Poland by 1 September. Britain and Poland signed a mutual assistance pact on 6 April with Britain pledging support should she be threatened by another country.

As a further sign of the deteriorating international scene a trial blackout was ordered as a preparation for war and took place across a large area of Eastern England including the whole of the Southdown area between midnight and 0400 on Friday 11 August after having been rather confusingly cancelled at short notice on the previous night due to adverse weather conditions. Overall the results were pronounced a

Posed for the camera in the village of South Harting are a group on evacuees – probably from London – who will have travelled by train and then special Southdown buses from Petersfield Station which acted as a main distribution point for the local area. The impact of so many new arrivals on village schools and local bus services led to many improvised changes in the first few weeks of war although by the end of September Southdown had halved the frequency of service 61 which linked the village with Petersfield! *Portsmouth Evening News*

success but, despite warnings to the public to keep off the darkened streets, it also attracted thousands of sightseers in London, who treated the event as if it was an entertainment rather than a preparation for war!

On Wednesday 23 August Nazi Germany and Soviet Russia signed a non-aggression pact thus ending any remaining hopes of Britain and France reaching some agreement with Russia. In Germany, Hitler gave orders for the invasion of Poland to begin on the 26 August 1939. The Emergency Powers (Defence) Bill was passed in one day on Thursday 24 August giving full authority of law to 'defence regulations' issued by the British government. ARP workers were put on alert as Britain started to call up military reservists. Hitler set a new date for the invasion of Poland of Friday 1 September. The public had been urged to carry on as normal during the past weeks but the international crisis now began to affect everyday life as Britain started to mobilise its Armed Forces which, for Southdown, included the sudden loss of experienced members of the staff.

With war now inevitable, the Government issued the order to 'Evacuate forthwith' at 1107 on Thursday 31 August. Prepared plans for evacuation from the towns and cities at risk of bombing would commence at dawn on 1 September 1939 with the Government estimating that 3,500,000 people would be evacuated in a four day period. In fact only 1,500,000 people took up the offer to move to safer areas away from the major towns and cities. For example, in Chichester some 9000 mothers and children were expected but under 5000 actually arrived.

The first major impact on Southdown was the arrival in Sussex of thousands of evacuees starting on Friday 1 September as parties of school children, mainly from the London area, were taken by train to all the main towns along the coast from Hastings to Bognor Regis and inland from Crowborough and East Grinstead in the east to Horsham, Petersfield and Chichester in the west. Many were moved by Southdown buses and coaches from the railway stations to their billets, often in outlying villages.

Not all evacuees were heading *into* Southdown territory though. In Portsmouth, which had been declared an evacuation area, the first of some 12,000 children along with their teachers were taken by special trains to reception centres in places such as Winchester, Salisbury and the New Forest or on boats to the Isle of Wight. The Southern Railway provided 16 special services from Clarence Pier and a total of 5,281 adults and children were carried to the Isle of Wight. The 1938 plans were changed and in the event Southdown was only involved in some smaller evacuation movements in Portsmouth and able to run normal services. In contrast the Corporation had to reduce services and run feeder buses to the main trolleybus routes in order to release sufficient buses for the evacuation exercise.

Southdown were, however, required to provide buses at Petersfield to help transport evacuees from the railway station to the reception areas situated between the Meon Valley and Rowlands Castle.

Later, as dusk fell on Friday 1 September 1939 Britain was officially plunged into complete darkness as all street lighting was turned off although for the first few days the results were far from satisfactory in some places. The total darkness meant that trying to get around after dark was confusing, frightening and often dangerous. Going out in the blackout was very soon restricted to journeys of necessity and, inevitably, bus patronage in the evenings reduced dramatically especially as places of entertainment were all temporarily closed down at the outbreak of war. Road accidents were quickly on the increase and in September 1939, despite much reduced traffic on the roads, the total number of people killed increased by nearly one hundred per cent. Southdown was soon affected. On Sunday 10 September a man was killed by a bus whilst walking along Commercial Road in Portsmouth near the junction of Hyde Park Road. It was dark with heavy rain and the man, who was deaf, did not hear the approaching bus. The Coroner returned a verdict of Accidental Death and exonerated the bus driver.

In a BBC radio broadcast at 1115 on Sunday 3 September Prime Minister Neville Chamberlain announced that the country was again at war with Germany. Following Chamberlain's broadcast, there were a series of short official announcements including an unexpected one instructing listeners that all theatres, cinemas, music halls and other places of entertainment were to be closed forthwith, and football matches and other events that attracted large crowds were forbidden – measures intended to minimise the chances of a large number of people being killed by a single bomb. This concern was later proved by subsequent events in Brighton, Portsmouth and East Grinstead when cinemas received direct hits resulting in many casualties. For the second time in its history Southdown now faced all the uncertainties of a war with Germany and this time it was clear that civilians would be in the frontline.

Despite the war at sea taking a toll on shipping, the expected air attacks on Britain's cities did not materialise during 1939 allowing some degree of normality with the reopening of many cinemas and theatres by mid-September. Children who had been evacuated earlier in the month from Portsmouth soon began to drift back to their homes in ever increasing numbers even though most schools in the city remained closed. At the same time many of the evacuees from London to Sussex returned home despite official advice to the contrary. *Further information about the period from 1940 to 1947 can be found in 'Southdown at War' also published by Capital Transport*

At the outbreak of war Southdown's full summer timetable had just three weeks operation remaining. The inevitable drift towards war over several months had given the company some time to prepare its plans for bus services in the hostile conditions that were expected. Among the immediate changes the Traffic Commissioners became Regional Transport Commissioners (RTCs) with the South Eastern Area based at Tunbridge Wells. The Southern Area – including Portsmouth and Fareham – which had earlier been abolished was resurrected under wartime regulations at Reading and continued in existence until the end of the hostilities. Their duties were vastly expanded and included supervision of the evacuation of children and others if and when necessary. The RTCs had the power to curtail bus and coach services that were mostly intended for pleasure and to allow new services to be started under a wartime Defence Permit without reference to a traffic court as the normal licensing regulations were suspended. They also allocated the much sought after petrol and diesel fuel coupons initially using a basic allowance linked to the route miles that each operator covered in 1938 plus a discretionary amount for new essential routes to strategic locations. They could issue a permit to any person to act as a driver or conductor of a public service vehicle for a period of one year from the date of the permit. Defence Permits costing £2 per vehicle and £1 per service per annum replaced the PSV licensing system but modifications to existing road service licences were free.

Most Southdown Stage Carriage licences expired on 28 February 1940 and those that remained in operation were replaced by Defence Permits starting next day (29 February 1940) in the South Eastern area and from 1 March 1940 in the Southern area which gained reference numbers prefixed by the letter 'J'. The Permit for service 31 was issued only in the South Eastern area but Permits for all other services in Portsmouth, Havant, Emsworth and Hayling Island were issued in the Southern area. The fortnightly publication of 'Notices and Proceedings' ceased at the outbreak of war and the Traffic Courts procedure established since 1931 was suspended for the duration leading to some dissatisfaction on the part of smaller operators such as Hants & Sussex who felt they had been cheated under the new system.

During the wartime period many amendments to services were introduced at short notice to meet the changing travel needs. Given the loss of traffic as holiday visitors returned home and with normal places of entertainment closed it appears that reductions to Southdown bus services began in early September particularly affecting evening frequencies and times of last buses which were generally brought forward by around an hour.

The evacuation from the cities which began on Friday 1 September was completed on the first working day of war, Monday 4 September, and hailed a great success although the numbers of school age children choosing to remain in the danger areas such as Portsmouth was soon to cause problems for the authorities. Starting on **Tuesday 5 September** winter timetables were introduced on some services including (at least) **11, 12, 27, 31G, 38, 47, 50, 50A, 52, 53, 55, 98** and **99** while services **62** between Bognor Regis and Arundel and **65** between Littlehampton and Storrington were temporarily suspended. The withdrawal of service **65** left the village of Amberley dependent on the Southern Railway and made travel from Storrington to Arundel a lengthy affair.

In addition, all Southdown and Portsmouth Corporation services departing from Southsea after 2030, were withdrawn due, according to the local press, to Police complaints about interior lights. This, despite the fact that Portsmouth's official response to the blackout was regarded by the authorities as 'wholly unsatisfactory' with motorists still openly driving around using dipped headlights without covers. The following day all Corporation and Southdown buses running within Portsmouth were withdrawn after 2030, although passenger demand had in any case virtually collapsed due to the closure of all entertainment in the city. Meanwhile the Police and Air Raid wardens were patrolling the

BLACK-OUT

★

YOU can help the Bus-Driver— by hailing the bus boldly, preferably with something white (or light-coloured) in your hand.

YOU can help the Conductor, too—by stating your destination clearly, and by tendering him the exact amount of your fare.

YOU may be sure that both will do their best to help you.

31	PORTSMOUTH, CHICHESTER, BOGNOR, LITTLEHAMPTON, WORTHING AND BRIGHTON												
Southsea *South Parade Pier*	...	...		3 52	4 22	4 52	5 22	5 52	6 22	6 52	7 22	7 52	8 22
Portsmouth *Theatre Royal*	...	...		4 2	4 32	5 2	5 32	6 2	6 32	7 2	7 32	8 2	8 32
Cosham *Station*	...	...		4 18	4 48	5 18	5 48	6 18	6 48	7 18	7 48	8 18	8 48
Havant *Church*	...	...		4 37	5 7	5 37	6 7	6 37	7 7	7 37	8 7	8 37	9 7
Emsworth *Square*	...	...		4 45	5 15	5 45	6 15	6 45	7 15	7 45	8 15	8 45	9 15
Thorney Corner	...	...		4 47	5 17	5 47	6 17	6 47	7 17	7 47	8 17	8 47	9 17
Nutbourne *Bell*	...	...		4 53	5 23	5 53	6 23	6 53	7 23	7 53	8 23	8 53	9 23
Bosham *Swan*	...	...		5 0	5 30	6 0	6 30	7 0	7 30	8 0	8 30	9 0	9 30
Fishbourne *Post Office*	...			5 7	5 37	6 7	6 37	7 7	7 37	8 7	8 37	9 7	9 37
Chichester *West Street*	...	arr.		5 12	5 42	6 12	6 42	7 12	7 42	8 12	8 42	9 12	9 42
Chichester *West Street*	...	dep.		5 13	5 43	6 13	6 43	7 13	7 43	8 13	8 43	9 13	9 43
Merston Corner	...	...		5 23	5 53	6 23	6 53	7 23	7 53	8 23	8 53	9 23	9 53
North Bersted *Post Office*	...			5 32	6 2	6 32	7 2	7 32	8 2	8 32	9 2	9 32	10 2
Bognor *Station S.R.*	...			5 39	6 9	6 39	7 9	7 39	8 9	8 39	9 9	9 39	10 9
Bognor *Bus Station*	...	arr.		5 42	6 12	6 42	7 12	7 42	8 12	8 42	9 12	9 42	1012
Bognor *Bus Station*	...	dep.		5 44	6 14	6 44	7 14	7 44	8 14	8 44	9 14	9 44	...
Felpham *South Downs Hotel*	...			5 54	6 24	6 54	7 24	7 54	8 24	8 54	9 24	9 54	...
Yapton *Sparks Corner*	...			6 3	6 33	7 3	7 33	8 3	8 33	9 3	9 33	10 3	...
Littlehampton *East Street*	...	arr.		6 17	6 47	7 17	7 47	8 17	8 47	9 17	9 47	1017	...
Littlehampton *East Street*	...	dep.		6 20	6 50	7 20	7 50	8 20	8 50	9 20	9 50	...	...
Rustington *Church*	...			6 31	7 1	7 31	8 1	8 31	9 1	9 31	10 1	...	...
Angmering *Crunden's Corner*	...			6 36	7 6	7 36	8 6	8 36	9 6	9 36	10 6	...	...
Ferring *Henty Arms*	...			6 44	7 14	7 44	8 14	8 44	9 14	9 44	1014	...	...
Goring *Church*	...	arr.		6 51	7 21	7 51	8 21	8 51	9 21	9 51	1021	...	...
Worthing *Dome*	...	arr.		7 3	7 33	8 3	8 33	9 3	9 33	10 3	1033	...	...
Worthing *Dome*	...	dep.		7 5	7 35	8 5	8 35	9 5	9 35	10 5	1035	...	...
Shoreham *Bridge Hotel*	...			7 24	7 54	8 24	8 54	9 24	9 54	1024	1054	...	...
Brighton *Pool Valley*	...	...		7 51	8 21	8 51	9 21	9 51	1021	1051	1121	...	...

This extract from the afternoon and evening service 31 timetable illustrates the drastic reductions imposed soon after the outbreak of war in the Southsea area after 2030. Eventually some common sense prevailed and later services were resumed but not to prewar levels and from early 1943 a ban on all journeys departing from towns and cities after 2100 was introduced across the country outside the Metropolitan Regional Transport area.

city trying to enforce the blackout regulations! On Friday 8 September it was reported that Southdown were attempting to solve the interior lights problem by painting over the windows. If approved they hoped to be able to resume some evening services soon. Some cinemas in 'safe' areas were permitted to reopen from Saturday 9 September but this did not include Portsmouth although those in nearby Havant and Fareham were allowed. Finally, after much pressure, cinemas in Portsmouth and Southsea were allowed to open again from Friday 15 September subject to closing no later than 2200. The Hippodrome Theatre reopened the following day and other theatres announced they would offering new variety shows soon. It would appear that the interior lighting problems of buses were eventually resolved and some evening bus services restored in time for the reopening of cinemas and theatres.

Evening journeys on service **31** were formally altered from **Saturday 9 September** with the last through bus from Brighton to Portsmouth departing at 1745 instead of 1915. The last bus from Brighton to Bognor became 2045 instead of 2145 and the final bus as far as Littlehampton was half hour earlier at 2145. From Southsea the last bus to Brighton ran 30 minutes earlier at 1922 while the final service as far as Littlehampton was advanced by an hour to 1952. Running times were unchanged at this time. Despite the cutbacks Southdown's evening services still fared better than some with all Maidstone & District services in Hastings terminating by 2100 although East Kent's last bus to Rye left at 2200.

The extra seasonal journeys on the Eastbourne to Beachy Head service **97** were withdrawn from **Tuesday 12 September** and services **28** (Brighton to East Grinstead) and **32** (Brighton Station to Devils Dyke) temporarily suspended from **Thursday 14 September**. Neither of these were reinstated and the service numbers quickly re-used at the end of the war.

Starting on **Saturday 16 September** Hayling Island service **47** was curtailed to operate a circular route between HAVANT STATION and HAYLING no longer running through to Southsea. An hourly frequency ran each way around the loop including a two-hourly service via Northney. The timetable for service **12** was altered from **Sunday 17 September** with the through frequency between Brighton and Eastbourne reduced to hourly. Last buses were brought forward with the final departure from Brighton Station to Seaford advanced from 0004 to 2249 and the last **12B** to Saltdean Mount leaving Brighton Station at 2141 instead of 2309. The last through bus from Eastbourne was advanced from 2200 to 2045. Running times were unchanged at this time. Commencing **Thursday 21 September** service **38** was withdrawn between Droxford, Meonstoke and Hambledon and also between Southsea Clarence Pier and Theatre Royal – Southdown's only link with Clarence Pier at the time. Four through journeys ran daily plus two journeys as far as Wickham.

Whilst food rationing would not commence until January 1940, the rationing of petrol and diesel fuel began on Saturday 23 September 1939 (after being delayed from 17 September) and

Revisions to services in the Midhurst area from 28 September 1939 included the extension of service 59 from Petworth northwards to Horsham to form one of Southdown's longest bus routes. Seen after the war in North Street, Midhurst on a southbound journey to Chichester and Bognor is car 177 (EUF 177), a Leyland TitanTD5 with Park Royal lowbridge body new May 1938. It was rebodied by East Lancs in February 1950 and finally sold to dealer Frank Cowley of Salford in February 1961. *Southdown Enthusiasts Club – Clark/ Surfleet Collection*

large bus companies were obliged to reduce consumption by at least 25% with immediate effect. In the normal course of events some bus services would have been withdrawn or reduced in frequency from **Monday 25 September** when the winter timetable was due to commence. Although, as noted above, many changes had occurred before this date, summer only services **26A** and **46** along with any remaining seasonal journeys were withdrawn no later than Sunday 24 September 1939.

Starting on **Thursday 28 September** evening journeys were reduced on service **22** with the last bus from Brighton advanced from 2220 (2300 on Saturdays) to 2120. Although a

basic hourly daytime service continued to run between Brighton and Petworth the number of buses to Duncton was cut to four. Service **59** gained a lengthy extension over former service 63 from PETWORTH to HORSHAM STATION via Wisborough Green, Billingshurst, Slinfold and Broadbridge Heath. With a journey time of 2 hours 53 minutes it became one of the longest Southdown routes. An hourly service ran between Bognor and Midhurst – partly replacing Aldershot & District's 19 which was curtailed from the north at Midhurst – with alternate journeys continuing to and from Horsham. On the alternate hour buses changed to service 60 at Midhurst and ran to Petersfield. As a consequence service **63** was reduced to run only between PETWORTH and CHICHESTER. The frequency of service **60** running between Midhurst (Grammar School) and Petersfield Station was halved from hourly to two hourly daily. In addition service **61** was curtailed to operate only between PETERSFIELD STATION and EAST HARTING (TURKEY ISLAND) being withdrawn from Elsted Church. The company stated that the service between East Harting and Elsted was for the present entirely suspended.

Although service **81** between Haywards Heath and Billingshurst might have appeared as a strategic cross county link on the route map, the western section traversed some very unpromising bus territory which struggled to support a regular daily service even in the post war boom years. Accordingly, from Thursday 28 September the Cowfold to Billingshurst section was suspended without replacement and the

In the early days of the war changes to services were advertised locally by leaflets and inevitably many have not survived. These two leaflets cover reductions in the Petersfield area to which many young evacuees from London had just been directed. Fuel rationing had started and most people had significantly reduced their travel habits due to the blackout and fear of being caught out in air raids. Soon demand for bus services in the country districts would start to soar as fuel rationing forced more people to give up their car.

SOUTHDOWN MOTOR SERVICES, LTD.

SERVICE 60 : PETERSFIELD—MIDHURST ; REDUCTION OF SERVICE

STARTING ON THURSDAY, SEPTEMBER 28th, 1939

It is regretted that circumstances make it necessary to operate a reduced Service between Petersfield and Midhurst, as shown below. Service 60 buses to and from Petersfield will, with few exceptions, run from and to Chichester and Bognor, *via* Service 59 route.

If traffic requires and circumstances permit, supplementary journeys (not shown on this leaflet) will be run between Rogate and Petersfield on Saturday afternoons.

SOUTHDOWN MOTOR SERVICES, LTD.

SERVICE 61 : REVISION OF TIMES & CURTAILMENT OF ROUTE.

STARTING ON THURSDAY, SEPTEMBER 28th, 1939.

It is regretted that circumstances make it necessary for this Service to be considerably curtailed. A reduced Time Table, as shown below, will be operated between Petersfield and East Harting only. Between East Harting (Turkey Island) and Elsted, the Service will, for the present, be entirely suspended.

frequency of the Haywards Heath to Cowfold section halved to two hourly. Again, the company apologised for the 'considerable curtailment' of the service.

The term 'Phoney War' is usually applied to the period from late September 1939 to April 1940 when, after the successful German attack on Poland at the start of September, little seemed to happen. Many experts in the UK had predicted major German air attacks on towns and cities leading to massive casualties and destruction from the outset of war. The sirens had sounded on a few occasions but the feared bombing did not occur and by October many of the London evacuees who had come to Sussex at the start of hostilities had already returned home to their families.

The next known revision to services occurred on **Thursday 19 October** affecting service **45** which was withdrawn between Southsea South Parade Pier and Theatre Royal or Bradford Junction on Fratton journeys. Journey times were revised and blackout journey times introduced after 1800. The main daytime westbound service consisted of:

1 journey per hour Theatre Royal – direct – Fareham – Warsash
2 journeys per hour Bradford Junction – Fratton – direct – Cornaway Lane, Portchester
2 journeys per hour Theatre Royal – Castle Street – Fareham
2 journeys per hour Theatre Royal – Castle Street – Cornaway Lane, Portchester
3 journeys per hour Theatre Royal – direct – Fareham

There were still ten journeys per hour overall but two extra journeys were extended beyond Cornaway Lane to Fareham while the westbound Fratton journeys no longer served Castle Street. A slightly different pattern of service applied for eastbound journeys.

In January 1939 Southdown had informed the Lewes Chamber of Commerce that a circular service from the Downs Estate to Winterbourne Estate, Southover and Landport Estate could not be introduced as requested at the present time. The reason given was that buses could not travel from the Downs Estate to Landport Estate although they felt it might be possible to strengthen the existing service from Downs Estate to the centre of Lewes and later extend it to Landport once the road surfaces had been improved. The Chamber of Commerce suggested that a smaller operator might be able to provide the service but were informed that Southdown would feel obliged to oppose any such application. Subsequently, by October, a Mr Rugg (a member of the Chamber) applied to the Regional Transport Commissioner for a Permit to operate new services between the Railway Station and the Downs and Nevill Estates with four journeys including one in the morning peak. This extended further into the estates than the existing

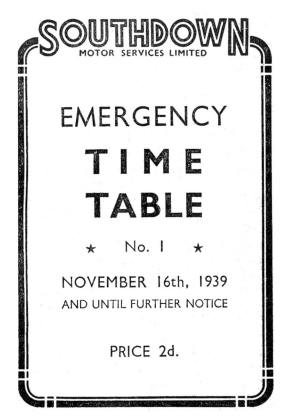

SOUTHDOWN
MOTOR SERVICES LIMITED

EMERGENCY
TIME
TABLE
★ No. 1 ★

NOVEMBER 16th, 1939
AND UNTIL FURTHER NOTICE

PRICE 2d.

Southdown service **13A** journeys. Another was proposed between the Railway Station and Winterbourne with three journeys in the middle of the day covering some roads not served by Southdown. He proposed to use a 20 seater bus for both services. Given the suspension of the normal Road Service Licensing system by this time the Commissioner felt obliged to refer the matter to Southdown who responded that they had already been forced to reduce services due to Fuel Rationing and therefore considered it was unreasonable for a competitor to be allowed to start a new service. The application was refused but the Chamber of Commerce was very concerned at the apparent monopoly situation that Southdown appeared to enjoy in Lewes. A further application was made by Mr Rugg and this was refused in December on the grounds of need to conserve fuel supplies so bringing the matter to an end for the present.

Blackout regulations were making all travel after dark difficult and often hazardous. Southdown had long been renowned for its system of connecting services and in an effort to maintain this facility and cope with the blackout conditions, the company introduced new schedules from 16 November 1939. From this date all timings after 1800 were extended by 10%. Thus a journey of 1 hour would be given 1 hour 6 minutes and one of 90 minutes was rescheduled to take 1 hour 39 minutes. Services departing every 30 minutes would change to every 33 minutes after 1800 and hourly departures would, for example, become 1700, 1806, 1912, 2018, 2124

Car 1478 (GCD 378) was a Leyland Tiger TS8 with Harrington 32-seat rear entrance body new in November 1939. No photographs have been found depicting these buses in the early months of their lives and it is doubtful if they ever carried a cream painted roof as the earlier members of the class. It is seen after the war on service 12B heading for Saltdean Mount – a route that was soon significantly reduced after the outbreak of war. *Author's Collection*

etc. The timetable for Service 31 was complicated as late afternoon journeys would start with a normal running schedule but from 1800 the time was gradually extended.

A complete system timetable book was issued dated **Thursday 16 November** incorporating the new blackout timetables. It was described as *Emergency Timetable No 1* and was the first of the wartime series which were smaller than prewar, measuring 127mm by 87mm but still cost 2d – and no longer included a map, faretables or express coach timetables. The cover was a thin cream card with green print and the first edition ran to 196 pages as compared to 368 pages for the July 1939 publication. In addition to the blackout amendments a number of other changes were introduced throughout the Southdown area although it must be stressed that most probably started earlier.

In Worthing the short journeys on service **1** between Worthing and Findon were reduced to operate during weekday peak periods only and cross town service **3** curtailed to terminate at GEORGE V AVENUE (GORING ROAD) although certain early morning weekday journeys continued to and from Goring Church and the frequency remained at 10 minutes daily. The frequency of service **4** was reduced to 20 minutes throughout daily – the winter service was normally every 10 minutes as far as Durrington. Not surprisingly the former Tramocars routes were also both reduced in frequency with both **T1** and **T2** dropping from a 10 minute service in winter 1938 to a 15 minute service. The short service **11A** between NORTH FERRING CORNER and FERRING (SOUTH DRIVE) was withdrawn – although probably at an earlier date – and service **31** was once more diverted between Goring Station and Roundstone Gates to operate via Goring Street, Littlehampton Road, Ferring Lane, Langbury Lane, Littlehampton Road and Worthing Road thus reversing the change introduced on 25 May 1939.

The daytime frequency of service **12** was revised to provide:

1 journey per hour Tongdean to Eastbourne
3 journeys per hour Tongdean to Seaford
1 journey per hour Tongdean to Peacehaven, Rosemary
1 journey per hour Brighton Station to Peacehaven Annexe (12A)
1 journey per hour Brighton Station to Saltdean Mount (12B)

This represented a reduction of one Eastbourne to Seaford journey per hour compared to winter 1938 whilst the frequency of **12B** was reduced from two buses per hour in the previous winter to an hourly service daily. Service **12A** was again curtailed to operate only between BRIGHTON STATION and PEACEHAVEN ANNEXE. As work on Newhaven Bridge was completed, double deckers began to appear on other journeys and by 1 December 1939 the entire 12 group had been converted except service 12B which retained its 1400 class Tiger saloons. Among many frequency reductions service **13F** between BRIGHTON (POOL VALLEY) and LOWER BEVENDEAN (HAPPY VALLEY) had its frequency reduced from 20 minutes daily to 30 minutes on Weekdays and hourly on Sundays although at this stage other buses along the Lewes Road remained virtually unchanged.

As part of a reduction in frequency to Southsea, services **31B**, **31C** and **43** were withdrawn between South Parade Pier and Theatre Royal. Also in the Portsmouth area service **39** was withdrawn between HAMBLEDON and WORLD'S END. New service **42A** was introduced between PORTSMOUTH (THEATRE ROYAL) and HORNDEAN (SHIP & BELL) operating only late evenings as a renumbering of short journeys on service 42 as far as Horndean. With the cinemas and theatres all fully reopened last buses from Portsmouth were generally at least 30 minutes earlier than prewar departing Theatre Royal at around 2230. In the Chichester area the frequency of service **52** was slightly reduced as compared to winter 1938 with an hourly service via Hunston but only four Selsey bound and five Chichester bound journeys operating via Donnington. The Witterings loop service **53** was reduced to a two hourly service each way daily similar to winter 1938. Service **69** was suspended between Littlehampton and Arundel but the frequency was increased from two hourly to 90 minutes.

In the north of the area service **86A** was curtailed to operate between HAYWARDS HEATH STATION and BROOK STREET being suspended between Brook Street and Balcombe although other services in the Haywards Heath area remained unscathed at this time. At East Grinstead, service **87** was curtailed at TYES CROSS being suspended from its usual terminus in the midst of Ashdown Forest, an area which the Military were soon to use extensively for training purposes.

Further east, the timetable page for the Beachy Head service **97** stated "This service will

During the war both Hastings and Eastbourne would soon be in the front line and suffer significant bomb damage and the voluntary evacuation of many residents including school children. Car 139 (CCD 939) was a petrol engined Leyland Titan TD4 with Beadle 52-seat lowbridge bodywork delivered in May 1936 and is seen here at the Wellington Square terminus of service 15 in Hastings. Buses were required to layover on a steep hill often necessitating chocks to be placed against the front wheels if left unattended. Throughout the 1930s an hourly service was provided jointly with Maidstone & District. J.T.Wilson

be continued as long as circumstances permit, at times announced locally in Eastbourne. It is hoped in any event to maintain a service at fine weekends". The frequency of service **99** was reduced from two hourly daily in winter 1938 to 4 journeys daily with buses departing Eastbourne at 1030, 1230, 1430 and 1830 and Hastings at 1006, 1206, 1406 and 1806. A second edition of *Emergency Timetable No.1* was issued with some minor alterations from **Saturday 25 November**.

At the company Board Meeting on Thursday 30 November 1939 approval was given to purchase the Goodwill of the businesses of H G Bannister (t/a The Blue Bus) of Burgess Hill and Mrs L A Evans (t/a The Red Bus) of Ditchling together with two vehicles for the sum of £300. The vehicles were not used by Southdown and

the Chairman & Managing Director was authorised to order additional Rolling Stock if they considered it necessary. Southdown took over the service from Thursday 1 February 1940.

Fortunately the feared bombing raids on London and other cities did not come during the remainder of 1939 and most places of entertainment were allowed to fully reopen by 17 December in time for Christmas although this in turn often caused problems for bus operators as most evening services had already been much reduced in line with lower demand caused by the blackout. But, anyone hoping to travel over the festive season would have found their journeys difficult, as fuel rationing and restrictions began to affect road and rail services across the country.

To avoid sensitive areas earmarked for Military training service 87 was cut back from it is normal tranquil terminus at a cross roads in the midst of Ashdown Forest about one mile to Tyes Cross 'for the duration'.

87	EAST GRINSTEAD—TYES CROSS										87
	via KINGSCOTE and WEST HOATHLY										
		NS	NS	NS	SO	Sats					
East Grinstead *Crown*	...	8 0	10 5	1 5	2 5	2 35	4 35	6	6	9	5
Sainthill Green ...	...	8 7	1012	1 12	2 12	2 42	4 42	6	14	9	13
Hazeldene *Cross Roads*	...	8 11	1016	1 16	2 16	2 46	4 46	6	18	9	17
Kingscote *Station S.R.*	...	8 16	1021	1 21	2 21	2 51	4 51	6	24	9	23
Selsfield	...	8 22	1027	1 27	2 27	2 57	4 57	6	30	9	29
West Hoathly *The Cat*	...	8 27	1032	1 32	2 32	3 2	5 2	6	36	9	35
Sharpthorne *Post Office*	...	8 30	1035	1 35	2 35	3 5	5 5	6	39	9	38
Tyes Cross	...	8 33	1038	1 38	2 38	3 8	5 8	6	42	...	
		NS	NS	NS	SO	Sats					
Tyes Cross	...	8 35	1050	1 50	2 50	3 20	5 20	6	55	...	
Sharpthorne *Post Office*	...	8 38	1053	1 53	2 53	3 23	5 23	6	59	9	40
West Hoathly *The Cat*	...	8 41	1056	1 56	2 56	3 26	5 26	7	2	9	43
Selsfield	...	8 46	11 1	2 1	3 1	3 31	5 31	7	8	9	49
Kingscote *Station S.R.*	...	8 52	11 7	2 7	3 7	3 37	5 37	7	14	9	55
Hazeldene *Cross Roads*	...	8 57	1112	2 12	3 12	3 42	5 42	7	20	10	1
Sainthill Green ...	...	9 1	1116	2 16	3 16	3 46	5 46	7	24	10	5
East Grinstead *Crown*	...	9 8	1123	2 23	3 23	3 53	5 53	7	32	1013	

NS—Not Sundays.   SO—Sundays only.   Sats.—Saturdays only.

Southdown appeared to get along pretty well with the neighbouring companies which had territorial agreements in place, both before and after the passing of the 1930 Act. These included Hants & Dorset, Aldershot & District, East Surrey – later LPTB – and Maidstone & District. Of course the new Road Traffic Act effectively confirmed the territorial boundaries by the grant of Road Service Licences and prevented any new competition from upsetting the current situation. The same cannot, however, be said of the three municipal operators within the Southdown area, namely Eastbourne, Brighton and Portsmouth.

Eastbourne

The grant of a Road Service Licence to Southdown for the Beachy Head service in 1931 effectively soured relations with Eastbourne Corporation for the remainder of the 1930s and beyond. Southdown was still able to develop its long and medium distance country services including those passing just outside the Eastbourne boundary to places such as Wannock, Hailsham and Pevensey, but it was limited to serving the main roads in and out of the town. The Beachy Head service was not allowed to compete with the Corporation's frequent service along the sea front from Princes Park to the Foot of Beachy Head as the carriage of local passengers over this section was expressly forbidden under the conditions applied to the Beachy Head Licence.

Brighton

The problems encountered with Brighton Corporation and its varied and ambitious plans to control tram, trolleybus and bus services within its boundaries continued throughout the 1930s and only reached a partial conclusion at the end of August 1939. From an early date Southdown had acquired the country routes from Brighton Hove & Preston United Omnibus Company Ltd. An agreement gave Southdown certain specified rights to run bus routes in the area outside the existing Brighton and Hove boundaries which were then mostly rural in nature. Problems arose following the boundary changes from 1 April 1928 which brought a number of outlying areas under Brighton Corporation control. In some cases subsequent housing developments meant that these were, under the original agreement, still part of Southdown's operating area.

In 1930 Brighton Corporation proposed the establishment of a Transport Board to co-ordinate surface road transport within the boroughs of Brighton and Hove and adjoining districts.

The board's area would extend into the Urban District of Shoreham-by-Sea to include the section of Upper Shoreham Road between the western boundary of Southwick and the Red Lion at Old Shoreham. Southdown would be required to surrender to the board all local services presently run within this area although the board would not, without the consent of the company, operate on that part of the Brighton to London main road north of Waterhall Road (just north of Patcham), or on the 'lower road' (presumably A259) between Portslade and Southwick. The board would not object to the company running services into the Brighton and Hove area from points outside along any road on which the company was now running although Southdown would be required to charge higher fares over common sections of route.

Fortunately the passing of the Road Traffic Act 1930 and the new role of the Traffic Commissioners in determining who shall be licensed to operate where brought this proposed scheme to an end. Southdown's growing presence in the town, especially where these appeared to be providing for mainly local journeys would be a source of irritation throughout the 1930s. As the applications for Road Service Licences were heard in 1931 Brighton Corporation lodged 340 objections including 25 for Stage Carriage services, mostly by Southdown, in respect of services operating along roads served by the trams. Protective fares to safeguard the tramway undertaking were also requested.

At the end of 1931 the Corporation proposed another scheme to develop its own network of bus services. With the expansion of the borough boundaries in 1928, the council believed it should be in a position to provide transport for the new housing areas. The first three included one to Moulscombe – already operated by Southdown, a new route along Hollingbury Road which was not then served and the Coombe Road route, operated by Thomas Tilling. The Transport Committee wrongly believed that Southdown would be willing to hand over existing rights in return for a reasonable consideration although in practice they hung on to these routes until the formation of Brighton Area Transport Services in 1961!

In 1933 there were plans for a merger of Brighton Corporation's transport undertaking with that of Thomas Tilling Ltd or even the outright purchase of the Tilling company although both met with opposition. On this occasion Southdown does not seem to have been involved but in March 1934 Brighton Town Council convened a conference of representatives of East and West Sussex County Councils and

Brighton, Hove, Portslade, Southwick and Shoreham Corporations to consider transport matters in the area. The object was to prepare a scheme under which a joint transport board could be set up, involving the purchase, either by consent or compulsion, of the local businesses of Thomas Tilling Ltd and Southdown Motor Services Ltd. An approach was also made direct to Southdown asking them to advise the sum that they would be require to sell their Moulscombe and Bevendean operations to the Corporation. The response was that Southdown would not consider disposing of these services! This was the third attempt by Brighton Corporation to establish a local transport board and whilst the scheme rumbled on through 1934 it once again failed.

Thomas Tilling had been operating their last surviving Tilling-Stevens TS3A on relief workings between Old Steine and Rottingdean via Marine Parade during summer of 1935. Its open top proved popular on warm days and on two previous occasions Thomas Tilling had suggested to Brighton Corporation the idea of operating a summer service along the full length of the sea front from Hove to Rottingdean. On both occasions Brighton Corporation declined the proposition. By July 1935 Tilling applied to the Traffic Commissioners for a licence to operate a summer open top sea front service between Hove, Boundary Road and Rottingdean. Brighton Corporation's Tramways Sub-Committee recommended the Council to apply for a similar licence from Hove Lagoon to Saltdean involving the purchase of eight single deck sunshine roof sun saloons. Thomas Tilling's application was supported by Southdown, but both Hove Council and East Sussex County Council objected to the Corporation's application. A three day hearing took place in September 1935 and the outcome was that Thomas Tilling was granted its licence and Brighton Corporation had their application refused. Things were just not going according to plan for Brighton Corporation! The new service 17 commenced on Good Friday 10 April 1936 using seven cream coloured open top double-deck buses and quickly became very popular despite the fact that such vehicles were fast disappearing from normal bus services. No doubt Southdown was influenced by this success to retain the open top Leyland Titans dating from 1929. On 26 November 1935 Thomas Tilling Ltd launched a new subsidiary company called Brighton, Hove and District Omnibus Company Limited and referred to in this text as BH&D.

Brighton Council had voted in favour of the promotion of another Trolleybus Bill and as was normal in Brighton, the scheme was controversial with strong arguments for and against the proposal. It was, however, widely recognised that the existing tramway system – operated entirely with open top cars – was fast becoming outdated with diminishing passengers while in contrast Southdown and BH&D were expanding their

services with much improved covered top buses on a profitable basis. The Brighton Corporation Bill was taken before the House of Lords commencing on 5 May 1936 with formidable opposition. The hearing lasted six days, with the Lords' Committee finally rejecting the Trolleybus Bill and throwing out the remainder of the Transport proposals which included the operation of Corporation vehicles outside the Borough boundary.

Following the rejection of the Corporation's Trolleybus Bill, Brighton Town Council voted by 44 votes to three on 29 July 1937 to approve an agreement between the Corporation and BH&D for a co-operative working of the passenger transport in the town. The Agreement, subject to sanction by Parliament and not directly involving Southdown, would commence on 1 April 1939 and operate for 21 years. But, in a later press statement it was announced that negotiations were to be instituted for the acquisition of the interests of Southdown in the services provided by them for short distance passengers.

The Brighton Corporation (Transport) Bill was published on 7 December 1937 and a town poll held on 5 January 1938. Ratepayers were urged to vote in favour if they did not wish to retain a stagnant tramway system which would become a ratepayer's burden, whilst the bus companies still continued to expand into the new housing estates. A majority of 11,429 voted in favour of the Bill which must have pleased members of Brighton Council. The proposals involved pooling the receipts of BH&D with those from the Corporation's proposed new trolley and motor bus fleet in a ratio of 72½ per cent and 27½ per cent respectively, with each party operating that same percentage of mileage The operation of trolleybuses and the Brighton Corporation vehicles were to be confined to the Borough of Brighton. It meant that a Tilling group company would, for the first time, operate a small number of trolleybuses.

The Brighton Transport Bill was approved on 14 May 1938 with operations due to commence on 1 April 1939. Under the area agreement of 1916 between Thomas Tilling Limited and Southdown Motor Services Limited, those parts of Brighton added to the borough in 1928 were to be developed by Southdown and a supplementary

An interesting study in rear end designs as Southdown's Leyland Titan TD1 with Short Bros body – car 926 (UF 7426) – operating on service 31 towards Pool Valley in Brighton follows a Thomas Tilling AEC Regent with open staircase bodywork by Tilling east along the sea front. Meanwhile Brighton Corporation's fleet of tramcars were all open top! No wonder they were concerned about the progressive expansion of motorbus services in the area. *Alan Lambert Collection*

agreement was signed with Southdown on 19 July 1938 in respect of these matters. For some reason it was anticipated that the new Brighton Transport pool would share these areas with Southdown although in practice they did not until the 1961 agreement.

Whilst the Bill was progressing Southdown applied to the Traffic Commissioners to provide a service between Brighton Railway Station and a new housing development in Saltdean. At the hearing in May 1938, BH&D objected on the grounds that the proposal would cause wasteful competition with their existing service to Rottingdean while Brighton Corporation objected on the grounds that the service could be better supplied by BH&D! The Counsel representing Southdown stated that Saltdean was outside of the BH&D area and that the Corporation's Bill did not affect the proposed service as the Bill did not extend beyond Rottingdean cross roads. The application was granted to Southdown and the new service began operating from 4 June 1938.

The implementation of the new and revised services along with the withdrawal of tram services were finalised by the Advisory Committee during February 1939, the actual introductory dates depending on delivery of the new Corporation fleet. In co-operation with Southdown, service numbers had been chosen for the new routes which did not conflict with those of existing Southdown services working in the town. The new era of agreement began on Saturday 1 April 1939. On 27 April 1939 tram route N was withdrawn and replaced by two new Corporation motor bus services 51 and 52 between Old Steine and Dyke Road, Tivoli Crescent. These were co-ordinated with Southdown service 12 and the same fares were charged between Clock Tower, Seven Dials and Dyke Road. A composite timetable was included in the Southdown bus timetable book for 13 July 1939. Further conversions took place throughout the summer until Thursday 31 August 1939 which was the last day for the remaining tram-cars. Next morning they were replaced by smart new Corporation trolleybuses on routes 41 and 42 which later on that fateful day were forced to endure blackout conditions as war with Germany grew ever more likely.

Portsmouth

The situation faced by Portsmouth Corporation was arguably even more difficult. Traditionally the commercial and residential districts as served by the Corporations tramways and buses were situated on Portsea Island with a short extension northwards across the only bridge to the mainland at Cosham. By the 1920s new resi-dential developments were appearing both east and west along the main A27 coast road and also in the villages to the north of Cosham along the A3 London Road. These were beyond the Portsmouth boundary but soon attracted new motor bus services which needed to take their

passengers to the shops and businesses on Portsea Island. Following boundary extensions in 1925 the Corporation tried extending some services from Cosham to Drayton charging fares lower than Southdown.

The early irregular country bus services were not seen as much of a threat to the frequent tram services provided by the Corporation but, by the late 1920s and the introduction of greatly improved, reliable and comfortable buses running at more regular intervals, some people were even prepared to pay higher fares to use these often faster country buses. With local authorities still acting in a licensing capacity there was pressure to restrict the new services with higher fares and fewer permitted stopping places.

Following lengthy negotiations new arrange-ments came into force in the Portsmouth area as from Wednesday 1 January 1930 as outlined in the special Southdown bus timetable issued for the occasion. In future fares in the City would apply as follows:

In the City of Portsmouth Southdown buses will accept short distance passengers at the same fares as the Corporation trams and buses and the money from these fares handed over to the Corporation. Passengers getting up (boarding) in the city and going to points outside the boundary where the fare is less than 9d, or on services 40, 41, 42 where the fare is less than 10d will require two tickets, one for the portion of journey inside the city and a second ticket for the portion of journey outside the city. If they are going into the city from those same places, they will require two tickets, a Southdown ticket to take them to the City boundary, and a Corporation ticket to take them from City boundary to their destination. If the fare paid is 9d single or over on the Havant and Fareham routes, or is 10d or over on the Horndean and Clanfield routes, the Southdown ticket is sufficient and no Corporation ticket is necessary. Similarly if a passenger takes a return ticket or is returning with an exchange ticket, where the return fare is 1/3 on the Havant and Fareham routes or 1/4 on the Horndean and Clanfield routes, no Corporation ticket is necessary.

In compensation for paying over revenue for short distance passengers Southdown was paid a fixed sum per mile operated. The arrangement continued in force until 1 January 1932 after which time a protective fare was again intro-duced and continued in force until May 1947. In most cases, Southdown fares became 2d higher than Corporation fares within the Portsmouth boundary.

In early 1934 the Corporation again applied to run bus services beyond Cosham to the city boundary at Farlington (Rectory Avenue) in the east and just beyond to Portchester (Railway Hotel) in the west and Purbrook Common to the north. The applications aroused considerable public interest with most expressing satisfaction with the existing Southdown services. After a lengthy Public Inquiry all were refused with the Commissioners stating that the routes were adequately served and rejecting any claim the corporation might make for preferential treatment, having already overruled a similar claim by Eastbourne Corporation. The Commissioners considered that any additional services in the area should be operated by Southdown.

In July 1934 it was announced that within the next two years Portsmouth Corporation's tramways would be replaced by trolleybuses. The corporation also decided to oppose the renewal of existing Southdown Stage Carriage services in Portsmouth to South Harting, Westbourne, Emsworth, Petersfield, Horndean (via two routes), Warsash, Fareham and Hayling Island. The Commissioner dismissed the objection and continued the existing level of protective fares but refused any increased protection for the Portsmouth transport undertaking. The Corporation appealed against the decision claiming that inadequate protection was provided for the corporation's transport undertaking but the Minister decided that no case had been made for increased protection. Trolleybus operations in Portsmouth began on 4 August 1934 and the final trams were withdrawn after 10 November 1936.

In 1920 Portsmouth Council had decided to build an estate on land at Wymering just to the north of Southampton Road along which Southdown ran its service 45 to Fareham. It was initially planned to build 300 houses there but another 200 houses followed in 1927-29. At this time there was an urgent need to demolish the dreadful slums in Portsea and in 1931 the council decided to build a further 410 new houses at Wymering. More houses followed between 1935 and 1939 but no bus service was provided apart from the Southdown service 45 which had admittedly been much enhanced since 1920.

In February 1939 Portsmouth Corporation Transport Committee announced that better transport facilities for residents on the northern outskirts of the city had been under consideration for some time. Following recent visits to the Highbury (just south east of Cosham Station) and Wymering Estates the Committee proposed that application be made to the South Eastern Traffic Commissioner to run a bus service serving both of these estates. They proposed to run a 20 seater bus from Washbrook Grove along the north of the Wymering Estate through the proposed link road to Cosham and then via the High Street to the Highbury Estate as far as Highbury Grove. This would allow passengers to access the Cosham shopping centre and change to other services at Cosham. While there had been problems with Southdown in the past when attempting to run Corporation services beyond Cosham the Committee now felt that the proposed service would have little impact on the existing Southdown services. It was important

for them to provide adequate transport to the new and expanding Council estates to which many people were being moved from slum homes on Portsea Island.

The Passenger Transport Committee reported on 1 August 1939 that on 16 June they had made an application to the Traffic Commissioners for a new bus service to the Portsdown Hill (North) Estate – better known locally as Wymering. The Committee proposed to operate this as an extension of the Highbury Estate service.

In the meantime Southdown had on 8 June already made an application for a new Daily service between Farlington, Station Road/Grove Road (known locally as Drayton) and Washbrook Road (North) via Station Road, Havant Road, Spur Road, Northern Road, Southampton Road, Sixth Avenue, Whitstable Road, Clacton Road, Washbrook Road, Lowestoft Road and Wymering Lane. This in fact extended further into the estate than the Corporation proposal. Both applications were opposed by the other applicant. The new estate, which was entirely within the City boundaries, was planned to have almost 1500 houses and provide accommodation for some 7000 people who would be removed from the clearance areas of the City and who had previously relied on Corporation services. No decisions appear to have been announced before the outbreak of war and the early introduction of fuel rationing dashed hopes of starting a new bus service. It was not until 31 May 1943 that the Corporation was finally permitted to extend its service to the Wymering Estate although it must have been successful as an increased service was introduced on 19 July 1943. Southdown continued to provide a frequent service along Southampton Road but did not actually serve the estate roads.

Relations between Southdown and the Corporation were never cordial even during the extremely dark days of the war and it required the Regional Transport Commissioners to knock some sense into the situation once the blitz on Portsmouth started in earnest in late 1940 and early 1941.

* * * *

One newcomer that appeared during the 1930s was to upset the regulated scene. This was Basil Williams who at a very young age had some ambitious plans to fill what he perceived to be gaps in Southdown's network in the Emsworth area. He formed a company with the impressive name of Hants & Sussex indicating that his ambitions extended far and wide from Emsworth. Southdown had no intentions of allowing any such upstart to compete with them and battles through the Traffic Courts continued even in wartime when such things were officially suspended. Generally Southdown was successful in thwarting any serious advance by Hants & Sussex but arguably they responded by introducing some very marginal rural services that even struggled in the post war travel boom years.

8 FARES

The most striking fact about Southdown bus fares in the 1930s is that they hardly increased at all over the decade and many were even reduced despite the lack of competition following the Road Traffic Act 1930. In most cases Single and Return fares were available although on very short routes no Return fare was shown. Through fares were available for some connecting services including several which involved other neighbouring companies such as Portsmouth to Winchester or Brighton to Guildford. Fares do not appear to be calculated according to any strict mileage scale and the relationship between the Single and Return fare is variable. Full fare tables were included in the bus timetables throughout the 1930s up to the outbreak of war. A sample of Adult Single and Return fares is shown below:

	1 January 1930		15 October 1934		16 July 1939	
	S	R	S	R	S	R
Brighton to Worthing	1/4	2/-	1/2	2/-	1/1	1/9
Brighton to Portsmouth	5/-	7/-	5/-	6/6	4/9	6/6
Brighton to Haywards Heath	2/-	2/9	2/-	2/8	1/8	2/8
Brighton to Lewes	1/-	1/4	1/-	1/4	1/-	1/4
Brighton to Horsham	2/10	4/-	2/9	4/-	2/6	3/6
Eastbourne to Brighton	2/10	4/-	2/6	4/-	2/6	4/-
Eastbourne to Heathfield	1/2	1/10	1/6	2/3	1/6	2/3
Eastbourne to Uckfield	2/-	3/-	2/-	3/3	2/-	3/3
Worthing to Horsham	2/3	3/6	2/3	3/6	2/3	3/-
Worthing to Arundel	1/4	2/3	1/1	2/-	1/1	2/-
Worthing to Chichester	2/6	4/6	2/6	4/6	2/4	4/-
Bognor to Portsmouth	2/9	4/-	2/8	4/-	2/8	4/-
Bognor to Littlehampton	1/-	1/6	1/-	1/6	11	1/6
Bognor to Brighton	3/3	5/-	3/2	5/-	2/10	4/6
Portsmouth to Chichester	1/9	2/9	1/9	2/9	1/9	2/8
Portsmouth to Fareham	10	1/6	8½	1/2	8½	1/2
Portsmouth to Clanfield	1/-	1/9	1/-	1/9	1/-	1/9
Portsmouth to Petersfield	1/9	3/-	1/8	3/-	1/8	3/-

In January 1930 children's fares applied to children over 3 and under 12 years of age

Adult	Child
1	1
1½	1
2	1
2½	1½
3	1½
3½	2
4	2

And then half adult single fare to the nearest penny. The Traffic Commissioners later ruled that children should be carried free of charge up to the age of 3. Throughout the 1930s the school leaving age was 14 and by 14 April 1930 Southdown had raised the upper age limit for children to under 14 years of age. By summer 1939 children's fares remained on the same scale except that additional higher fares had been added as follows:

Adult	Child
4½	2
5	3
5½	3
6	3

And then half adult single fare to the nearest penny

Season Tickets

Adult Season Tickets were issued for one month or three months and calculated according to the normal single fare. They were available for travel any day except on Bank Holidays. Children's and Scholars' tickets were issued for the School Term and again based on the single fare. These could be used on Saturdays if the Scholar had to attend school on that day. There were specific variations in Portsmouth, Brighton and East Grinstead presumably to take account of other operator's conditions.

Workmen's tickets

With few industrial areas outside Portsmouth served by Southdown there were only very limited schemes in operation. By 1 January 1930 Workmen's tickets were available on service 40 leaving Theatre Royal or Clanfield before 0800. On service 45 up to the 0728 from Portsmouth or 0738 from Fareham a fare of 1/- return was available for any distance. Wymering to Portsmouth or Southsea was available for 6d return. By 1939 Workmen's tickets were valid on services 31, 31A, 31C, 43 and 47 as far as Havant, services 39 to 42 as far as Clanfield or Snells Corner and service 45 as far as Fareham. They were issued for travel on any buses departing Theatre Royal or Fratton Bridge at or before 0800 and those arriving at Theatre Royal or Fratton Bridge at or before 0830.

In Eastbourne a Workmen's return ticket costing 1/3 was available on certain early journeys on service 15 between Eastbourne and Herstmonceux or on service 92 between Eastbourne and Golden Cross in January 1930. A 6d return was introduced between Polegate and Eastbourne on services 91 and 94 by January 1933. Reduced fares were later extended to Brighton from 20 July 1931 but only covering services 12 (Seaford to Brighton), 13, 13B and later 13E and 13F. From 29 March 1934 special return fares were introduced on service 11 journeys at 0700 and 0730 from Worthing towards Brighton. Workmen's return tickets were only valid for travel on the day of issue.

Dogs

Dogs were carried, subject to the usual conditions about behaviour, at a rate of a quarter of the single fare in each direction, fractions of 1d to count as a 1d.

Luggage

Personal hand luggage was carried free of charge – at Owner's risk – but where more than two such articles were brought by one passenger then a charge would be made based on the single fare. This ranged from 2d where the single fare was up to 1/- and 4d where the single fare was above 2/-. Bicycles were carried, but only on singe deck buses, at a rate of 6d where the single fare was up to 1/6 and at a rate of 1/- for fares over 1/6.

Parcels

Southdown had offered a parcel service from the very beginning in 1915. The conveyance of parcels by bus was an important service in rural areas in the days before many had access to their own personal transport. Buses ran to set timetables and delays were rare so the service was reliable and simple. Parcels could be handed to the conductor of a bus and delivered to a place along the route on the understanding that the bus was met at the appropriate place. They could also be handed into local agents across the Southdown area or the company's own offices.

All charges had to be prepaid. The cost was based on approximate weight – obviously conductors did not have access to scales – and the normal single fare for the journey. It must be remembered that at this time the fares were not calculated according to a strict mileage scale!

In 1931 certain Southdown offices started to accept parcels for conveyance by the Southern Railway. These included Eastbourne, Brighton (Pool Valley), Worthing, Bognor, Chichester, Portsmouth, Arundel, Hailsham, Havant, Horsham, Lewes, Midhurst and Littlehampton. Passenger tickets for the Southern Railway could also be issued at the same offices and at Steine Street, Brighton.

Connecting Services

Southdown had long been renowned for its system of connecting services. The list below shows those connections which were advertised in the last prewar Bus Timetable dated 13 July 1939. Reference to the company's Traffic Notices which have survived for this period show that in addition to the advertised connections a large number of other connections were observed. For instance service 31 buses connected at Rustington Church or Woodbine Corner with service 68 or 68A buses but these were not included in the public timetable. In most cases the connections were only to be held for two or three minutes unless the other vehicle was in sight. A few rail or last bus connections were to be held for up to 15 minutes in certain circumstances. Even after the savage service cutbacks of 1971, buses continued to connect at places such as Golden Cross, Chailey and Cowfold just as they had throughout the 1930s.

In the foreground at Pool Valley, Brighton is car 829 (UF 5429) shown working on service 16 which, despite the destination screen, only actually ran as far east as Golden Cross where hourly connections were made with service 92 towards both Eastbourne and Uckfield. These connections continued until the severe cutbacks in April 1971. Car 829 is a Leyland Titan TD1 with Leyland lowbridge body new in 1929 and sold in May 1938. *A.Duke, Omnibus Society*

Service	at	with	for
1	Storrington	22	Pulborough, Midhurst
	Worthing Station	Trains	London
2	Washington	22	Steyning, Brighton
	Horsham	LPTB 414	Dorking
	Horsham	A&D 33	Cranleigh, Guildford
13A	Lewes	various	Brighton
	Newhaven	12	Brighton
16	Golden Cross	92	Hailsham, Eastbourne
17	Cowfold	81	Haywards Heath or Billingshurst
	Horsham	LPTB 414	Dorking
	Horsham	A&D 33	Cranleigh, Guildford
18	Hawkhurst	M&D	Battle, Maidstone or Chatham
119	Tunbridge Wells	M&D 7	Maidstone
20	Chailey	89	Haywards Heath or Uckfield
22	Petworth	59	Midhurst
	Petworth	A&D 51	Haslemere
25	Berwick	26	Alfriston
26	Seaford	12	Newhaven, Brighton
	Berwick	25	Lewes
30	Chelwood Common	92	East Grinstead
34	Hassocks	23/30	Brighton
40/42	Petersfield	60	Midhurst
	Petersfield	61	South Harting, Elstead
	Petersfield	A&D	Farnham, Aldershot
43	Churchers Corner	54	Compton or Funtington
45	Fareham	H&D	Southampton or Winchester
48	Horndean	40/42	Petersfield
	Havant	47	Hayling Island
52	Chichester Station	Trains	London, Bognor or Portsmouth
53	Chichester Station	Trains	London, Bognor or Portsmouth
54	Churchers Corner	43	Havant, Westbourne
56	Chichester Station	Trains	London
59	Midhurst	60	Petersfield
		A&D 19	Hindhead
	Petworth	22	Pulborough, Brighton
		63	Billingshurst, Horsham
60	Petersfield	40/42	Portsmouth
	Midhurst	59	Petworth
62	Arundel	10	Worthing, Brighton
63	Petworth	59	Midhurst, Singleton
64	Yapton/Ford	31	Littlehampton
65	Storrington	1/22	Worthing
70	Storrington	1	Worthing
	Pulborough	Trains	London
80	Steyning	22	Brighton
81	Cowfold	17	Henfield or Horsham
88	Turners Hill	LPTB 434	East Grinstead
89	Chailey	20	Lewes, Brighton
92	Golden Cross	16*	Lewes, Brighton
	Uckfield	89*	Chailey, Haywards Heath
	East Grinstead	LPTB*	Purley, Croydon

A&D – Aldershot & District   H&D – Hants & Dorset
LPTB – London Passenger Transport Board   M&D – Maidstone & District
* – Detailed timings not included

9 SOUTHDOWN COACHING IN THE 1930s

THE LONDON EXPRESS SERVICES

By the start of 1930 the history of Southdown's Express Services only dated back some ten years and came about largely by accident. In September 1919 the National Union of Railwaymen went on strike against the threat of a wage reduction and several bus and coach companies within range of London saw their opportunity to make some extra money. Southdown ran a service between Brighton and London and Chapman & Sons of Eastbourne were one of the many operators who came to the aid of stranded holidaymakers during the eleven days of the strike. Whilst the Government soon agreed to the NUR's terms the operators had quickly discovered just how easy it was to run limited stop services to London and there was plenty of demand from the travelling public.

Clearly Southdown could not ignore these apparently successful operations and in 1920 nine companies pooled their express coaching interests and formed London & Coastal Coaches. This led to the establishment, in April 1925, of London Coastal Coaches Ltd, an organisation specifically designed to apportion mileage, charges and departures, and, most importantly get the coaches off their congested roadside stands and into a specially provided coach park at the London end. Locating a suitable site for a permanent coach station proved more difficult than first envisaged and it was not until April 1928 that, as a temporary measure, a two acre site in Lupus Street near Vauxhall Bridge was allocated by the London County Council.

Thanks to improvements in vehicle design in the 1920s there had been a rapid growth of coach services in a relatively short time. The public were very happy to embrace the travel opportunities which the new road services offered and the railways soon lost passenger traffic as a result. It was claimed in 1929 that rail fares had been increased by 100% since 1918 and as a consequence the motor travel industry had seized its opportunity. It could now proudly claim to be the 'poor man's' friend offering first class comfort at less than half the railway third class fare! But, there were strong railway interests which considered motor coach services were 'unnecessary and undesirable in the public interest' and would use this argument once the Road Traffic Act 1930 took effect. Inevitably a few unprincipled owners provided unreliable services leading to severe criticism in the press but most would be swept away once services and vehicles came under much closer scrutiny.

At the start of 1930 Southdown was providing regular departures to the Lupus Street terminal from:

Eastbourne via Uckfield and East Grinstead
Brighton via Bolney or Burgess Hill
Littlehampton and Worthing via Horsham and Crawley
Bognor Regis via Chichester and Midhurst
Portsmouth and Southsea via Petersfield

A map of services shown for the winter of 1929/30 also included a daily service from Brighton to London running via Lewes to Uckfield and then via the A22 but this appears to have been withdrawn by the start of 1930. The Bognor Regis via Littlehampton and Arundel service was also shown on the map but not operating at this time and reintroduced from April 1930. The Worthing via Dorking service was new and commenced in June 1930.

Details of timings and route developments, where known, have been listed below under each individual service rather than chronologically for all services lumped together. The services are listed in geographical order from Eastbourne in the east to Gosport in the west. It is clear that before the need for all services to be licensed by the Traffic Commissioners the timetables altered at frequent intervals and, to make research even more difficult, only very basic information was included in the Southdown bus timetable books which were published monthly at the start of the 1930s. This means that there is a reliance on surviving leaflets, most of which only included a starting date and then ran until further notice. Departure times were shown from terminal points but no arrival times were included although from April 1930 some additional intermediate timing points were included – but noted as approximate! To further confuse matters a 1930 leaflet for Bognor Regis states that 'Coaches will stop to pick up at any point on route providing arrangements are made at time of

A busy scene at Lupus Street as car 427 (UF 2027) prepares to depart for Brighton. This vehicle had a long life with Southdown and was a Tilling-Stevens Express B9B with Harrington 29-seat bodywork rebuilt in February 1930 with fixed back and folding roof as shown. It went on to be rebodied by Harrington in 1935 and then survived until being requisitioned by the Military Authorities in July 1940. *Alan Lambert Collection*

This map of services appeared in a booklet dated April 1930 and includes the link from Brighton via Lewes to Uckfield which was suspended at this time. The Worthing to London via Dorking route which began in June had obviously not been finalised at this time.

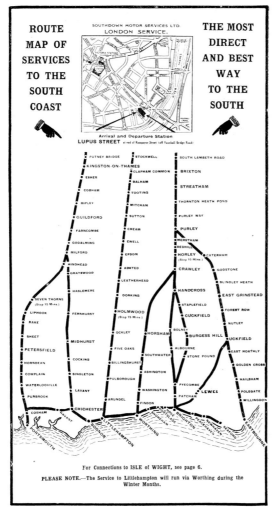

some contemporary leaflets as service E but probably not displayed as such on coaches. Fares to London from Eastbourne at this time were 5/6 (28p) Single, 6/6 (33p) Day Return and 9/- (45p) Period Return. From **1 April 1930** the service was increased to three journeys each way per day departing Eastbourne at 0930, 1415 and 1730 and London at 0930, 1430 and 1830. Coaches also ran to Charing Cross and on the return journey departed ten minutes before the times at Lupus Street. It is likely that services also called at Pevensey Road Bus Station in Eastbourne. At this date it is believed that coaches picked up in the London area at Charing Cross, 1A Lupus Street, South Lambeth Road, Brixton, Streatham, Thornton Heath Pond, Purley Way and Purley. The enhanced timetable continued until 1932 with only minor alteration – the 0830 from Eastbourne becoming 0900 on Sundays. The Refreshment Stop was at East Grinstead, The Crown by October 1931.

Commencing **10 March 1932** the service was significantly enhanced following the takeover of both Chapman's and Southern Glideway services and now departed from Royal Parade Garage at 0815, 0945, 1400 and 1745 calling at Archery, Leaf Hall and Cavendish Place. The 0815 and 1745 coaches continued from Victoria to Kings Cross Coach Station. Southbound services departed from the new Victoria Coach Station at 0930, 1400, 1830 and 2100 with the first two journeys starting from Kings Cross 30 minutes earlier.

Starting on **21 April 1932** the basic service was revised and augmented following the attempted takeover by Southdown of part of G.B. Motor Tours Ltd operations and became very complicated! Northbound coaches now departed Royal Parade at 0800 to Kings Cross, 0945 to Paddington, 1345 and 1445 to Victoria, 1715 to Hammersmith and Chiswick and 1815 to Kings Cross. The 1715 service connected at Victoria at 2045 with a 1730 service from Worthing and Brighton where passengers for Paddington, Kilburn and Willesden Green could change. From London coaches departed at 0900 from Kings Cross, 0915 from Chiswick via Hammersmith, 1315 from Kings Cross, 1445 from Paddington and 1830 and 2100 from Victoria. Again a connection was made at 1000 with a coach from Willesden Green, Kilburn and Paddington to Brighton and Worthing. Journey time to Victoria was three hours 30 minutes at this time.

Fortunately things returned to normal from **17 October 1932** with only the twice daily extension to Kings Cross and minor alterations to departure times but from **2 June 1933** a slightly simpler form of 1932 summer timetable commenced. Departures from Royal Parade were at 0800, 0945, 1345, 1445 and 1815, all to Victoria, plus an extra journey at 1715 to Paddington and Kings Cross. The latter connected at Victoria with a service from

booking'! Brief details are included for summer 1930 and matters became clearer when Express Carriage licences were issued by 1932. Full details of the advertised picking up points are shown for late 1933 by which time they were formally licensed and those deemed by the Metropolitan Traffic Commissioners to be in excess of demand or causing undue congestion had been removed. No refreshment halt details were included on early leaflets although it is likely that a half way stop would have been made. Details are included under each route where known and they were always included from about 1932.

Eastbourne via Uckfield

On **1 January 1930** the Eastbourne service ran just once daily in each direction following a halving in frequency from this date. The London bound coach left from what Southdown called 1 Cavendish Place but actually 2A Cavendish Place at 0900 and returned from 1A Lupus Street at 1830 daily, the 1630 from Eastbourne and 0930 from London having been withdrawn after 31 December 1929. The company faced strong competition on this route both locally and from numerous London operators. It was shown on

Only very brief details were included in timetable leaflets of the early 1930s and before the Road Traffic Act. This is an extract from a leaflet issued in conjunction with London Coastal Coaches including all London services at 1 June 1930 and shows the three times daily Eastbourne service. It does not include all the stops in Eastbourne including the ones nearest the sea front!

By October 1933 the picking up points in the Metropolitan Traffic Area had finally been settled and this extract from a composite leaflet including all London services shows the London area points in detail but, unhelpfully, still fails to include all the stops within Eastbourne.

LONDON to EASTBOURNE

Depart	a.m.	p.m.	p.m.		Notes.
Charing Cross	9 20	2 20	6 20	...	
LUPUS STREET ...	9 30	2 30	6 30	...	With connections by Bus to Eastdean, Heathfield, Herstmonceux and Pevensey.
Brixton (433 Brixton Road)	9 50	2 50	6 50	...	
Purley (Fountain) ...	10 10	3 10	7 10	...	
East Grinstead ...	11 0	4 0	8 0	...	

EASTBOURNE to LONDON

Depart	a.m.	p.m.	p.m.		Notes.
EASTBOURNE (Pevensey Rd. Stn)	9 30	2 15	5 30	...	
Hailsham (High Street) ...	9 55	2 40	5 55	...	With connections by Bus from Eastdean, Heathfield, Herstmonceux and Pevensey.
Uckfield (200 High Street)	10 25	3 10	6 25	...	
East Grinstead ...	11 0	3 45	7 0	...	

LONDON to EASTBOURNE

Depart	a.m.	p.m.	p.m.	p.m.				Notes.
VICTORIA COACH STATION ...	9 30	1 45	6 30	9 0	...	...	...	
Brixton (Church Road) ...	9 45	2 0	6 45	9 15	...	...	...	
Streatham (Chimes Garage) ...	9 55	2 10	6 55	9 25	...	...	...	
Thornton Heath (Pond) ...	10 2	2 17	7 2	9 32	...	...	...	
Waddon (Cross Roads) ...	10 7	2 22	7 7	9 37	...	...	...	Notes.
Purley (Railway Arch) ...	10 15	2 30	7 15	9 45	...	...	...	With connections by Bus to Eastdean, Heathfield, Herstmonceux and Pevensey.
Caterham (Croydon Road) ...	10 28	2 43	7 28	9 58	...	...	...	
Godstone (High Street) ...	10 35	2 50	7 35	10 5	...	...	...	
Felbridge (Co.'s Stn. and Star) (s)	10 55	3 10	7 55	10 25	...	...	...	(s) 10 minutes stop.
East Grinstead (High Street) ...	11 10	3 25	8 10	10 40	...	...	...	
Forest Row (Swan) ...	11 18	3 33	8 18	10 48	...	...	...	
Nutley (The Stores) ...	11 32	3 47	8 32	11 2	...	...	...	
Uckfield (High Street) ...	11 45	4 0	8 45	11 15	...	...	...	
East Hoathly (King's Head) ...	11 58	4 13	8 58	11 28	...	...	...	
Hailsham (High Street) ...	12 20	4 35	9 20	11 50	...	...	...	
EASTBOURNE (Cavendish Place)	12 45	5 0	9 45	12 15	...	...	...	

EASTBOURNE to LONDON

Depart	a.m.	a.m.	p.m.	p.m.				Notes.
EASTBOURNE (Cavendish Place)	8 15	10 0	2 0	5 30	...	...	...	
Hailsham (High Street) ...	8 40	10 25	2 25	5 55	...	...	...	
East Hoathly (King's Head) ...	9 2	10 47	2 47	6 17	...	...	...	
Uckfield (High Street) ...	9 15	11 0	3 0	6 30	...	...	...	
Nutley (The Stores) ...	9 28	11 13	3 13	6 43	...	...	...	Notes.
Forest Row (Swan) ...	9 42	11 27	3 27	6 57	...	...	...	With connections by Bus from Eastdean, Heathfield, Herstmonceux and Pevensey.
East Grinstead (High Street) ...	9 50	11 35	3 35	7 5	...	...	...	
Felbridge (Co.'s Stn. and Star) (s)	9 55	11 40	3 40	7 10	...	...	...	(s) 10 minutes stop.
Godstone (High Street) ...	10 25	12 10	4 10	7 40	...	...	...	
Caterham (Croydon Road) ...	10 32	12 17	4 17	7 47	...	...	...	
Purley (Railway Arch) ...	10 45	12 30	4 30	8 0	...	...	...	
Waddon (Cross Roads) ...	10 53	12 38	4 38	8 8	...	...	...	
Thornton Heath (Pond) ...	10 58	12 43	4 43	8 13	...	...	...	
Streatham (Chimes Garage) ...	11 5	12 50	4 50	8 20	...	...	...	
Brixton (Church Road) ...	11 15	1 0	5 0	8 30	...	...	...	
VICTORIA COACH STATION ...	11 30	1 15	5 15	8 45	...	...	...	

Worthing via Brighton which continued to Hammersmith. From London coaches departed at 0930, 1345, 1445, 1830 and 2100 plus a 0930 from Kings Cross via Paddington which connected at Victoria at 1000 with the 0930 from Hammersmith to Brighton and Worthing.

The extension of some journeys to Kings Cross was abandoned for the winter timetable commencing on **16 October 1933**. Four journeys now ran in each direction leaving Royal Parade at 0800, 0945, 1345 and 1715 and London at 0930, 1345, 1830 and 2100. From this date the Refreshment Stop moved to The Star at Felbridge and stayed there to the end of Southdown's operations on the London to Eastbourne service. The summer timetable of 1934 began a pattern that was to remain a feature of this service for many years. This was the departure from Victoria at 15 minutes past the hour.

By the end of 1933 the picking up points allowed for this service in the London Passenger Transport Area (LPTA) were:

Victoria Coach Station
Brixton, Church Road
Streatham Common, Chimes Garage
Thornton Heath, Pond
Waddon, Cross Roads
Purley, Railway Arch
Caterham, Croydon Road
Godstone, High Street
Felbridge, The Star
East Grinstead, High Street

Southbound passengers were not permitted to alight before East Grinstead, College Lane and the first fare stage from London was now at Ashurst Wood. This was despite the fact that the town centre of East Grinstead was outside the area under which LPTB enjoyed monopoly powers.

Starting on **18 May 1934** timings from Royal Parade became 0800, 1000, 1400, 1500, 1800 and 1900. From London coaches departed at 0915, 1015, 1415, 1515, 1815 and 2115. Winter timings were now regularised to bring them into line with the previous summer becoming 0800, 1000, 1400 and 1800 from Eastbourne and 0915, 1415, 1815 and 2115 from London, a far cry from what was on offer in January 1930. Both summer and winter services for 1935, 1936 and 1937 remained exactly the same as those provided in 1934.

Car 1079 (UF 9779) was a Leyland Tiger TS4 with Harrington body equipped with a roof luggage rack for operation on the company's Express Services. New in 1933 it is seen at the refreshment halt on the London to Eastbourne service at The Star Hotel at Felbridge north of East Grinstead. This coach was requisitioned by the Military Authorities in June 1940 but re-acquired by Southdown in July 1943 and subsequently fitted with a more modern Covrad radiator. It survived without a post war rebuild until being sold for scrap in July 1953.
S.L.Poole

Car 1135 (CCD 735) was part of a batch of twelve Leyland Tiger TS7s with Beadle 32-seat rear entrance bodywork and typical of the coaches employed on the London Express Services in the late 1930s and 1940s. Delivered in 1936 they were fitted with folding sunroof and roof luggage rack and remained petrol engined until conversion to diesel in 1950/1. Car 1135 is seen laying over after the war in the bomb damaged streets around Victoria before a return journey to Eastbourne. *Alan Lambert Collection*

SOUTHDOWN
MOTOR SERVICES, LTD.
(In association with the Southern Railway Company)

Express Coach Service
LONDON (TWO ROUTES)
NUTLEY—UCKFIELD—HAILSHAM, or
LEWES—NEWHAVEN—SEAFORD
EASTBOURNE

LONDON

STREATHAM

CROYDON
Air Port

PURLEY

E. GRINSTEAD

WYCH CROSS
Ashdown Forest

UCKFIELD

LEWES

HAILSHAM

NEWHAVEN
Harbour

SEAFORD

EASTBOURNE

25th MAY to 10th SEPTEMBER, 1939
LONDON DEPARTURES FROM
VICTORIA COACH STATION, S.W.1.   'Phone: Sloane 0202
EASTBOURNE DEPARTURES FROM
CAVENDISH COACH STATION, 32, CAVENDISH PLACE
Phone: Eastbourne 3540
SEAFORD DEPARTURES FROM
5, CLINTON PLACE   -   -   'Phone: Seaford 2817

By the summer of 1939 Southdown were actively promoting the choice of routes between London and Eastbourne no doubt hoping at the same time to boost loadings on the service via Seaford. As emergency timetables were not introduced until 18 September there is no evidence to prove that the timetable did not run its course despite the outbreak of war.

The summer timetable which began on **3 June 1938** was the same as for 1934 but extra journeys were run on Saturdays at 1200 from Royal Parade and 0815 and 1615 from London. Winter 1938 was the same as 1934 and summer 1939 starting on **26 May 1939** the same as that operated in 1938. Fares to London from Eastbourne were now 6/- (30p) Single, 6/6 (33p) Day Return and 10/9 (54p) Period Return but premium rates applied for travel on Saturdays, Sundays and Bank Holidays in high summer with the Day Return increasing to 7/- (35p).

Following the outbreak of war, emergency timetables were introduced on **18 September 1939** with just three journeys operated each way. Coaches departed Cavendish Place at 0900, 1400 and 1800 and London at 0915, 1415 and 1815. The first wartime leaflet was issued to commence on **10 December 1939** with the same level of service except that the last journey from Eastbourne was advanced by one hour to 1700.

Eastbourne via Seaford
The first London service to provide a direct link from Seaford started on **1 July 1932** running daily to 27 September except on Wednesdays and Thursdays. Until this time passengers from Seaford and Newhaven could use the local bus service 12 and change at Brighton where a frequent service ran to London. The new service ran via Newhaven to Lewes and then along the A275 through Chailey and across Ashdown Forest to Forest Row before joining the Eastbourne via Uckfield route to London. Apart from Lewes it did not serve much promising territory! Seaford was not a thriving seaside resort attracting lots of summer visitors and

The cover of the four page leaflet that marked the introduction of the new service between Seaford and London. Car 1044 (UF 7344) was now the standard for leaflet covers of this era.

while Newhaven was a busy port it was also well served by the Southern Railway so opportunities for new business did not seem good. Coaches started from Seaford Clinton Place at 0900, 1400 and 1830 with southbound departures from London at 0915, 1415 and 1930. Fares to London from Seaford were 6/- (30p) Single, 7/6 (38p) Day Return and 11/- (55p) Period Return but had been reduced by 1939! Journey time was three hours and a Refreshment Stop of ten minutes was taken at East Grinstead, The Crown.

Despite these unlikely beginnings it reappeared on **7 July 1933** running to the same schedule as in 1932 and continuing until 26 September. By 1934 the picking up points for this service within the London Passenger Transport Area were as follows:

Victoria Coach Station
Brixton, Church Road
Streatham Common, Chimes Garage
Thornton Heath, Pond
Waddon, Cross Roads
Purley, Railway Arch
Caterham, High Street
Godstone, High Street
Felbridge, The Star
East Grinstead, High Street

Southbound passengers were not permitted to alight before East Grinstead, College Lane and the first fare stage from London was at Ashurst Wood.

For the following three summers it ran between similar dates as in 1933 except that the refreshment halt was moved in line with the Eastbourne via Uckfield service to Felbridge, The Star. But, starting from **3 July 1937** the service was completely revised and some journeys extended to and from Eastbourne. It was a very complicated pattern and from this distant perspective it is very hard to visualise the intended market! Journeys were as follows:

0900 from Seaford on Saturdays, Sundays and Mondays from 1 August to 12 September

1415 from Eastbourne Cavendish Place on Saturdays from 3 July to 12 September plus Sundays and Mondays from 1 August to 12 September

1815 from Eastbourne Cavendish Place daily from 3 July to 12 September

0915 from London daily from 3 July to 12 September to Eastbourne

1415 from London Saturdays from 3 July to 12 September plus Sundays and Mondays from 1 August to 12 September to Eastbourne

1815 from London Saturdays, Sundays and Mondays from 1 August to 12 September to Seaford

Apart from the one round trip from Seaford to London it was presumably now possible to use the journeys to and from Eastbourne as reliefs to the main service.

Not surprisingly this arrangement did not find favour and for the summer of 1938 the whole service was extended to and from Eastbourne. The service started from **2 July 1938** and continued until 11 September. Coaches now departed Eastbourne Cavendish Place at 0915 and 1345 (both Saturdays and Sundays only) and 1745 daily. From London departures were at 0945 daily plus 1345 and 1845 on Saturdays and Sundays only. This same operation was repeated in 1939 but extended to start earlier from **24 June 1939** and run until 10 September. By this time war had been declared and it is likely the service ran as scheduled until its advertised finishing date. Fares to London from Seaford in 1939 were 5/6 (28p) Single, 6/6 (33p) Day Return and 10/- (50p) Period Return and premium rates applied only for journeys between London and Eastbourne.

Brighton

As might be expected the winter timetable introduced on the Brighton service on **3 October 1929** was by far the most frequent of all Southdown's London services. Coaches departed from Steine Street daily at 0800, 0815 (via Lewes, Uckfield and East Grinstead), 0900, 0930, 1000, 1100, 1430, 1700, 1900 and 2000. Southbound services from London 1A Lupus Street were at 0930, 1030, 1200, 1400, 1500, 1645, 1845, 1845 (via East Grinstead, Uckfield and Lewes), 2055, 2340.

Some of the single deck buses delivered in 1929 were intended for use on the company's Express Services. Car 639 (UF 4239) was a Tilling-Stevens Express B10A2 with Harrington 30-seat bodywork incorporating special features such as arm rests between the back seats, glass topped mahogany seat back tables and curtains. This posed photograph was used on the covers of leaflets issued in 1930 but the delivery of new coach bodied Leyland Tigers meant that their stay on the London services was soon curtailed.
Alan Lambert Collection

By **1 January 1930** this service was shown on leaflets as service A and some journeys had been withdrawn. From Brighton the 0800 and 0900 journeys were projected to start from Portslade at 0740 and 0840 running via Hove and this became a feature for the rest of the 1930s and beyond. All journeys had run via Bolney and the A23 but the 0900 from Brighton was now diverted via Burgess Hill and Cuckfield. The 0815 service via Lewes and Uckfield was withdrawn along with the 2000. From London coaches ran at 0930, 1100, 1400, 1645, 1845 via Cuckfield and Burgess Hill, 2055 and 2340, the last two continuing to Portslade. The 1845 via Uckfield and Lewes was also withdrawn although the link appeared on a map of services for April 1930. All services were extended to Charing Cross, Great Scotland Yard Street departing from there 10 minutes earlier than Lupus Street. Early leaflets do not state the location of a Refreshment halt but it is believed to have been at Horley, The Chequers or Lowfield Heath, White Lion until the opening of the Crawley Station. Fares at the start of 1930 from Brighton

to London were 4/- (20p) Single, 5/- (25p) Day Return and 8/- (40p) Period Return.

The summer timetable commenced on **1 June 1930** with an hourly service from Steine Street starting from 0800 and ending with the 2000 except there were no journeys at 1300 and 1600. The 0900 and 1900 both now ran via Burgess Hill and Cuckfield. From Lupus Street the hourly service began at 0900 and continued to 2100 with no journeys at 1300, 1600 or 2000. In addition there was a journey at 2340 and the 1100 and 1900 journeys now diverted via Cuckfield and Burgess Hill. It is believed that coaches picked up in the London area at Charing Cross, 1A Lupus Street, South Lambeth Road, Brixton, Streatham, Thornton Heath Pond, Purley Way and Purley.

No doubt influenced by the forthcoming Road Service licensing and wishing to establish their place on the route this very generous level of service was continued for the winter commencing **1 October 1930**. The summer timetable began on **15 May 1931** with the same frequency but an additional journey was introduced each way on Wednesdays running from Brighton via Henfield and Cowfold to rejoin the main route at Handcross. This left Brighton at 0830 and returned from London at 1930 and remained a feature of the timetable for many years. The 2340 from London was retimed to 2350 and then stayed the same until the outbreak of war.

The existing Refreshment stops on this route were often unable to cope at busy times and in 1930 the company considered the facilities at Horley to be unsatisfactory. By 1931 traffic on the Brighton and Worthing via Crawley routes had reached such proportions that Southdown decided to open their own coach station at County Oak one mile north of Crawley. It was conveniently situated approximately halfway between London and the south coast and the 'Crawley Station', as it became known, opened for business on 1 August 1931 with the capacity to handle up to 12 coaches arriving at the same time. Given the scheduled stop of just ten minutes, speed of service was obviously essential. Coaches reversed on to one of the six stands, arranged in herringbone fashion, to enable passengers to alight from the rear door of the coach and remain under cover before entering the building. With over 1,000 passengers per day carried on these routes, a million passengers used the new premises during their ten minutes break in the first four years of operation. As many of the passengers were requesting alcoholic drinks to accompany their snacks, Southdown applied for a liquor licence but this was strongly opposed. The case was the subject of a long and well publicised legal battle, eventually involving the High Court, before alcohol could be served to Southdown's customers.

Apart from the move to Victoria Coach Station opened on 10 March 1932 the same timetable remained until **21 April 1932** when additional

LONDON to BRIGHTON

DEPART	a.m.	a.m.	a.m.	a.m.	p.m.	p.m.	p.m.	p.m.	p.m.	p.m.	p.m.
Charing Cross	8 50	9 50	10 50	11 50	1 50	2 50	4 50	5 50	6 50	8 50	11 30
LUPUS STREET	9 0	10 0	11 0	12 0	2 0	3 0	5 0	6 0	7 0	9 0	11 40
Brixton (*433 Brixton Road*) ...	9 10	10 10	11 10	12 10	2 10	3 10	5 10	6 10	7 10	9 10	11 50
Purley (*Fountain*) ...	9 30	10 30	11 30	12 30	2 30	3 30	5 30	6 30	7 30	9 30	12 10
					A					A	

BRIGHTON to LONDON

DEPART	a.m.	a.m.	a.m.	a.m.	a.m.	p.m.	p.m.	p.m.	p.m.	p.m.	p.m.
Portslade (*Station Road*) ...	7 40	8 40	...	...	...	...	...	...	...	...	...
BRIGHTON (*Steine Street*) ...	8 0	9 0	10 0	11 0	12 0	2 0	3 0	5 0	6 0	7 0	8 0
Bolney (*Cross Roads*) ...	8 30	...	10 30	11 30	12 30	2 30	3 30	5 30	6 30	...	8 30
Burgess Hill (*The George*) ...	...	9 25	...	...	...	...	...	...	...	7 25	...
Cuckfield (*The Clock*) ...	...	9 35	...	...	...	...	...	...	...	7 35	...
Handcross (*Red Lion*) ...	8 45	9 45	10 45	11 45	12 45	2 45	3 45	5 45	6 45	7 45	8 45

NOTES.
A.—*Via* Cuckfield and Burgess Hill, with connections to Haywards Heath.
All Coaches from LONDON, except the 9 p.m. and 11.40 p.m. connect at BRIGHTON with Buses for HOVE, LEWES, NEWHAVEN, PEACEHAVEN, PORTSLADE, ROTTINGDEAN and SEAFORD.

journeys were added in connection with the attempted takeover of some services previously operated by G.B. (Motor Tours) Ltd. These were a northbound coach at 1815 which left Worthing at 1730 and then continued beyond Victoria via Paddington and Kilburn to Willesden Green. From London the 1000 journey started from Willesden Green at 0915 and continued via Kilburn and Paddington to Victoria and then to Worthing via Brighton. Connections at Victoria Coach Station were made with coaches operating between Chiswick and Hammersmith to Eastbourne.

A full hourly service commenced from **13 May 1932** with departures from Steine Street between 0800 and 2100 plus a new Monday only journey at 0700. From Victoria departures were hourly between 0900 and 2100 plus the 2350 and all coaches departed Charing Cross 10 minutes before the Victoria times. From **5 July 1932** the journeys to and from Willesden Green were

shown as not serving Victoria Coach Station and as operated by G. B. Motor Tours Ltd. Surviving leaflets indicate that the extension to Willesden Green ended by 12 September 1932 on this service but not for the northward projections to the Eastbourne service.

The winter timetable of **17 October 1932** reverted to the nearly hourly service with no journeys either way at 1300 and 1600 but the Monday 0700 from Brighton was withdrawn. From **2 June 1933** the same timetables as in summer 1932 was reintroduced except that the projections north of Victoria were changed. The 1815 northbound now ran to Hammersmith and the 1000 southbound started from Hammersmith at 0930.

Following a long drawn out battle to reduce the number of coaches in Central London, restrictions were imposed which resulted in the Brighton service only operating to and from Charing Cross on Saturday afternoons and all

Judging by the unfinished borders this is an early view of the Crawley Station soon after its opening in August 1931. An interesting selection of three Tilling-Stevens and two Leyland Tiger coaches await departure for Brighton or London as passengers enjoy their ten minute refreshment break. The Leyland Tigers are cars 1044 (UF 7344) and 1048 (UF 7348) delivered in May/June 1931 with Harrington 30-seat coach bodywork and both were requisitioned by the Military Authorities in July 1940. *West Sussex County Council*

Car 1062 (UF 8832) was one of twelve Leyland Tiger TS2s with Harrington 32-seat bodywork delivered for the 1932 season. All but one were intended for the London Express Services with folding sunroof and roof luggage rack but also featuring a neater side display for the route details. This particular coach was requisitioned by the Military Authorities in June 1940 and not returned to Southdown after the war. It went on to be rebodied and was not eventually scrapped until March 1961! *Alan Lambert Collection*

LONDON to BRIGHTON

On Sundays, all Coaches start from Charing Cross 15 minutes earlier than the times shown for Victoria Coach Station. On Saturdays, they start from Charing Cross 15 minutes earlier than from Victoria, from 2.45 p.m. From Mondays to Fridays the only departure from Charing Cross is at 11.40 p.m.

DEPART	a.m.	a.m.	a.m.	a.m.	p.m.	p.m.	p.m.	p.m.	p.m.	W.O p.m.	p.m.	p.m.
Charing Cross [Horse] Daily	...	...	...	...	...	2 45	4 45	5 45	6 45	...	...	1140
Charing Cross {Guards} Saturdays	...	...	...	...	...	...	...	...	...	...	8 45	1140
Charing Cross [Avenue] Sundays	8 45	9 45	1045	1145	1 45	2 45	4 45	5 45	6 45	...	8 45	1140
VICTORIA COACH STATION	9 0	10 0	11 0	12 0	2 0	3 0	5 0	6 0	7 0	7 30	9 0	1150
Brixton (Church Road)	9 10	1010	1110	1210	2 10	3 10	5 10	6 10	7 10	7 40	9 10	12 0
Streatham (Chimes Garage)	9 20	1020	1120	1220	2 20	3 20	5 20	6 20	7 20	7 50	9 20	1210
Thornton Heath (Pond)	9 27	1027	1127	1227	2 27	3 27	5 27	6 27	7 27	7 57	9 27	1217
Waddon (Cross Roads)	9 32	1032	1132	1232	2 32	3 32	5 32	6 32	7 32	8 2	9 32	1222
Purley (Fountain)	9 38	1038	1138	1238	2 38	3 38	5 38	6 38	7 38	8 8	9 38	1228
Coulsdon (Red Lion)	9 45	1045	1145	1245	2 45	3 45	5 45	6 45	7 45	8 15	9 45	1235
Redhill (Market Hall)	10 0	11 0	12 0	1 0	3 0	4 0	6 0	7 0	8 0	8 30	10 0	1250
Crawley (Company's Station) (s)	1020	1120	1220	1 20	3 20	4 20	6 20	7 20	8 20	8 50	1020	1 10
Handcross (Red Lion)	1045	1145	1245	1 45	3 45	4 45	6 45	7 45	8 45	...	1045	1 35
Henfield (George)	...	...	...	...	...	...	...	...	...	9 45	...	...
Cuckfield (Clock)	...	...	...	1255	...	...	...	...	...	8 55	...	...
Burgess Hill (George)	...	...	...	1 7	...	...	...	...	...	9 7	...	...
Bolney (Cross Roads)	1057	1157	...	1 57	3 57	4 57	6 57	7 57	...	...	1057	1 47
BRIGHTON (Steine Street)	1130	1230	1 35	2 30	4 30	5 30	7 30	8 30	9 35	1020	1130	2 20

All Coaches except the 9 p.m. and the 11.50 p.m. connect at BRIGHTON with buses for HOVE, LEWES, NEWHAVEN, PEACEHAVEN, PORTSLADE, ROTTINGDEAN and SEAFORD.
W.O.—Wednesdays only. (s) 10 minutes stop.

BRIGHTON to LONDON

DEPART	a.m.	W.O a.m.	a.m.	a.m.	a.m.	a.m.	p.m.	p.m.	p.m.	p.m.	p.m.	p.m.
Portslade (Station Road)	7 40	...	8 40	...	...	...	...	...	...	...	...	...
BRIGHTON (Steine Street)	8 0	8 30	9 0	10 0	11 0	12 0	2 0	3 0	5 0	6 0	7 0	8 0
Bolney (Cross Roads)	8 33	...	...	1033	1133	1233	2 33	3 33	5 33	6 33	...	8 33
Burgess Hill (The George)	...	...	9 28	...	...	...	...	...	...	...	7 28	...
Cuckfield (The Clock)	...	...	9 40	...	...	...	...	...	...	...	7 40	...
Henfield (George)	...	9 5	...	...	...	...	...	...	...	...	...	...
Handcross (Red Lion)	8 45	9 35	9 50	1045	1145	1245	2 45	3 45	5 45	6 45	7 50	8 45
Crawley (Company's Station) (s)	9 0	9 50	10 5	11 0	12 0	1 0	3 0	4 0	6 0	7 0	8 5	9 0
Redhill (Market Hall)	9 30	1020	1035	1130	1230	1 30	3 30	4 30	6 30	7 30	8 35	9 30
Coulsdon (Red Lion)	9 45	1035	1050	1145	1245	1 45	3 45	4 45	6 45	7 45	8 50	9 45
Purley (Fountain)	9 52	1042	1057	1152	1252	1 52	3 52	4 52	6 52	7 52	8 57	9 52
Waddon (Cross Roads)	9 58	1048	11 3	1158	1258	1 58	3 58	4 58	6 58	7 58	9 3	9 58
Thornton Heath (Pond)	10 3	1053	11 8	12 3	1 3	2 3	4 3	5 3	7 3	8 3	9 8	10 3
Streatham (Chimes Garage)	1010	11 0	1115	1210	1 10	2 10	4 10	5 10	7 10	8 10	9 15	1010
Brixton (Church Road)	1020	1110	1125	1220	1 20	2 20	4 20	5 20	7 20	8 20	9 25	1020
VICTORIA COACH STATION	1030	1120	1133	1230	1 30	2 30	4 30	5 30	7 30	8 30	9 33	1030
Charing Cross {Hrse. Gds.} Sats.	...	...	...	...	...	2 45	4 45	5 45	7 45	8 45	9 45	1045
Charing Cross {Avenue} Suns.	1045	...	1145	1245	1 45	2 45	4 45	5 45	7 45	8 45	9 45	1045

On Sundays all Coaches go to Charing Cross. On Saturdays all Coaches except the 8.0, 9.0, 10.0 and 11.0 a.m.
Mondays to Fridays all Services terminate at Victoria Coach Station.
W.O.—Wednesdays only. (s) 10 minutes stop.

day Sunday plus the nightly 'Theatre' coach at 2340 as from **11 September 1933**. For more details see later in this chapter under *'Restrictions on Coaches in London'*.

Apart from the changes outlined above as far as restrictions at Charing Cross the winter time-table commencing **16 October 1933** was the same as that for winter 1932. As this remained virtually unaltered until winter 1938 it is perhaps appropriate to restate the service in detail. Coaches departed from Steine Street at 0800 (start Portslade 0740), 0830 (Wednesdays via Henfield), 0900 (start Portslade 0840 and running via Burgess Hill and Cuckfield), 1000, 1100, 1200, 1400, 1500, 1700, 1800, 1900 (via Burgess Hill and Cuckfield) and 2000. All journeys on Sundays and Bank Holidays also from the 1200 departure on Saturdays continued to Charing Cross. From London coaches departed at 0900, 1000, 1100 (via Cuckfield and Burgess Hill), 1200, 1400, 1500, 1700, 1800, 1900 (via Cuckfield and Burgess Hill), 1930 (Wednesdays via Henfield), 2100 and 2350 (both to Portslade).

All journeys on Sundays and Bank Holidays plus departures from 1500 on Saturdays departed Charing Cross 15 minutes earlier than Victoria. Additionally the 2350 departed Charing Cross at 2340 daily.

By the end of 1933 the picking up points for this service in the London Passenger Transport Area were as follows:

Charing Cross, Horse Guards Avenue (at restricted times as above)
Victoria Coach Station
Brixton, Church Road
Streatham Common, Chimes Garage
Thornton Heath, Pond
Waddon, Cross Roads
Purley, Fountain
Coulsdon, Red Lion
Redhill, Market Hall
Horley, Albert Road Corner
Crawley, Southdown Station
Crawley, Imperial Cinema south of level crossing
The first setting down point was at Crawley

Railway Station – probably by the Imperial Cinema – just a little south of the old town centre and, along with Horley, outside the area in which LPTB had a complete monopoly. With a fare stage at Crawley Southdown could offer a reasonable alternative to Green Line given the regular service provided.

The summer timetable started on **18 May 1934** and with minor modification was the same as 1933 but no projections beyond Victoria – apart from Charing Cross – were featured although the Worthing via Brighton journey in each direction continued. Charing Cross was only served as shown above for winter 1933. The summer timetable introduced on **7 June 1935** became the standard up to 1939 and is probably worth repeating here for clarity. Services departed hourly from Steine Street between 0800 and 2100 but the 0700 on Mondays did not reappear. In addition there was the 0830 on Wednesdays via Henfield and a 1730 journey which started from Worthing at 1700 and was the only reminder of the brief northward extensions associated with G.B. Motor Tours Ltd. Southbound services departed from London

hourly between 0800 and 2100 with an additional 1930 journey on Wednesdays via Henfield and the 1000 being extended to Worthing. Charing Cross extensions were as shown under October 1933.

Timetables for summer and winter were now continued unchanged each year until the outbreak of war with only minor changes. Starting on **1 February 1938** Southdown finally abandoned the Charing Cross extension and all services now terminated at Victoria Coach Station throughout the week. From **3 June 1938** an extra journey was added from Steine Street at 2200 on Bank Holiday Mondays and this reappeared for 1939. Fares to London from Brighton were now 5/- (25p) Single, 5/6 Day (28p) Return and 8/9 (44p) Period Return but premium fares applied for travel on Saturdays, Sundays and Bank Holidays in high summer with the Day Return increasing to 6/- (30p).

Despite the outbreak of war, a new leaflet was issued for the winter service commencing **11 September 1939** which would have continued the same level of service as previous winters but this was soon overtaken by events and an Emergency schedule was introduced starting on **18 September 1939**. Despite very heavy loadings especially at weekends, services were significantly reduced with departures from Steine Street at 0800, 0900 (via Burgess Hill and Cuckfield), 1000, 1400, 1700 and 1800 (via Hurstpierpoint, Burgess Hill and Cuckfield). From London coaches now ran at 0800, 0900, 1000 (via Cuckfield and Burgess Hill), 1400, 1700 (via Cuckfield and Burgess Hill) and 1800. The first wartime leaflet for the Brighton service was dated **17 December 1939** and continued the same timetable as September 1939 except that the 0900 service from London ran via Cuckfield and Burgess Hill instead of the 1000.

Car 1207 (EUF 107) was one of five Leyland Tiger TS8s with Park Royal 32-seat bodywork delivered for the 1938 season. These were last coaches to be delivered to the company with a straight and parallel waist beading. Although clearly intended for work on the Express Services no roof luggage rack was fitted. By this time Southdown had finally accepted that it was worth specifying diesel engines for its main coach fleet. *Southdown Enthusiasts Club – Clark/ Surfleet Collection*

SOUTHDOWN
MOTOR SERVICES, LTD.
(In association with the Southern Railway Company)

Express Coach Service
BETWEEN

LONDON
AND
BRIGHTON

"Every Hour at the Hour"

TIME & FARE TABLE

11th SEPTEMBER, 1939 until WHITSUN, 1940

BRIGHTON DEPARTURES FROM
STEINE STREET COACH STATION. Telephone: **Brighton 4033**

LONDON DEPARTURES FROM
VICTORIA COACH STATION, S.W.1. Telephone: **Sloane 0202**

As this leaflet rolled off the presses the likelihood of war must have loomed large and its shelf life was reduced to a single week as emergency timetables were introduced from 18 September 1939. Despite the banner claiming 'Every Hour at the Hour' there were the usual gaps in the winter timetable after 25 September although this small point was overtaken by world events and a significantly reduced level of service introduced.

Worthing via Crawley

As at **1 January 1930** this service ran three times daily departing from Worthing Marine Parade at 0900, 1415 and 1800. The 0900 service started from Littlehampton at 0830. From London 1A Lupus Street coaches departed at 0930, 1430 and 1800 with the final service continuing to Littlehampton. It is shown on some contemporary leaflets as service W and ran from Worthing north along the A24 to Horsham before turning east to Crawley and then following the Brighton route to London. Fares for Winter 1929/30 to London from Worthing were 5/- (25p) Single, 6/- (30p) Day Return and 8/6 (43p) Period Return and from Littlehampton were 6/- (30p) Single, 7/6 (38p) Day Return and 10/6 (53p) Period return. It is believed that in April 1930 coaches picked up in the London area at 1A Lupus Street, South Lambeth Road, Brixton, Streatham, Thornton Heath Pond, Purley Way and Purley. The Refreshment halt was at Horley until the opening of Southdown's own facilities at Crawley on 1 August 1931.

Apart from some minor changes to the last journey of the day these times continued until **21 April 1932** although services were diverted to the new Victoria Coach Station on 10 March 1932. From this date departures from Marine Parade were at 0900 (0830 from Littlehampton), 1415 and 1815 plus a 1730 coach to Willesden Green via Brighton which ran as part of the former G.B. Motor Tours Ltd operation already referred to. From London coaches departed at 0930, 1430 and 1800 with the latter continuing to Littlehampton. In addition a service started from Willesden Green at 0915 and ran via Victoria at 1000 where it connected with a service to Eastbourne before continuing to Worthing via Crawley and Brighton. From **5 July 1932** the journeys to and from Willesden Green are shown as not serving Victoria Coach Station and are marked as operated by G. B. Motor Tours Ltd. The extension to Willesden Green ended by **12 September 1932** and the normal three times daily service continued through the winter. Journey time between Worthing and Victoria via Crawley was three

hours 15 minutes. From **2 June 1933** an additional service was run at 1730 from Worthing via Brighton to Hammersmith connecting at Victoria with a service from Eastbourne. The additional morning service left Hammersmith at 0930 and Victoria at 1000 before running via Brighton to Worthing.

By October 1933 the picking up points for this service in the London Passenger Transport Area were as follows:

Victoria Coach Station
Brixton, Church Road
Streatham Common, Chimes Garage
Thornton Heath, Pond
Waddon, Cross Roads
Purley, Fountain
Coulsdon, Red Lion
Redhill, Market Hall
Horley, Albert Road Corner
Crawley, Southdown Station

The first set down point on this service was at Crawley Imperial Cinema but the first fare stage from London was to Horsham. Both were outside the area in which LPTB had a complete monopoly.

The journeys to and from Hammersmith ceased with the winter timetable introduced from **16 October 1933** and the usual three journeys each way continued. But, significant changes occurred on **18 December 1933** with Southdown's takeover of the London to Worthing service of Fairway Coaches Ltd of London SW9. This ran via Dorking and Horsham with local fare stages on some sections and meant that the Dorking route would in future become the dominant service between London and Worthing. In consequence the departures on the Crawley route reduced to 0900 (0830 from Littlehampton) and 1900 from Worthing and 1000 and 1900 from London with the last coach continuing to Littlehampton.

Timings were revised for the summer timetable commencing **18 May 1934** as the service via Dorking was increased to run every two hours. Coaches now departed from Marine Parade at 0900 (0830 from Littlehampton), 1500 and 1900 plus a service at 1730 via Brighton but only running as normal route to Victoria with no onwards projections. From London departures were at 0900, 1000 via Brighton, 1500 and 1900 which continued to Littlehampton.

The winter timetable commencing **15 October 1934** reverted to the two journeys each way as introduced in December 1933 although extra facilities were advertised by use of connecting buses at Brighton. The summer timetable was introduced from **7 June 1935** and remained the same as 1934 except that the journey from Worthing via Brighton was advanced to 1700 and this became the standard for summer until 1938. The winter timetable had now stabilised at two journeys each way and was reintroduced for 1935 and 1936 remaining the same as December 1933. Starting on **27 September 1937** the Littlehampton journeys were cut back to start

A view of two Leyland Tigers at the Southdown Station just north of Crawley. In the foreground is car 1065 (UF 8835) with Harrington 32 rear entrance bodywork new in July 1932. It was one of many petrol engined Tigers to be requisitioned for Military used in summer 1940, most of which never returned to the company at the end of the war. *Alan Lambert Collection*

LONDON to WORTHING

DEPART	D a.m.	C a.m.	D p.m.	C p.m.	C p.m.	¶ p.m.	D p.m.	
VICTORIA COACH STATION ...	9 0	9 30	2 0	2 30	6 0	6 30	7 0	...
Brixton (*Church Road*) ...		9 40	...	2 40	6 10	...	...	...
Streatham (*Chimes Garage*) ...		9 50	...	2 50	6 20	...	...	...
Thornton Heath (*Pond*) ...		9 57	...	2 57	6 27	...	...	...
Waddon (*Cross Roads*) ...		10 2	...	3 2	6 32	...	...	...
Purley (*Fountain*) ...		10 8	...	3 8	6 38	...	...	...
Coulsdon (*Red Lion*) ...		1015	...	3 15	6 45	...	...	...
Putney Bridge (*Underground Station, Hurlingham Road*)	9 15	...	2 15	...	T	6 45	7 15	...
Richmond (*General Omnibus Station*)	9 30	...	2 30	...	...	...	7 30	...
Kingston (*Fairfield West*)	9 45	...	2 45	...	...	7 15	7 45	...
Leatherhead (*Church*) ...	10 5	...	3 5	...	...	7 35	8 5	...
Dorking (*9 High Street*)	1017	...	3 17	...	...	7 47	8 17	...
Holmwood (*Holly and Laurel*) (s)	1025	...	3 25	...	...	7 55	8 25	...
Redhill (*Market Hall*) ...		1030	...	3 30	7 0	...	...	...
Crawley (*Company's Station*) (s)		1050	...	3 50	7 20	...	...	...
Horsham (*The Carfax*)	11 0	1125	4 0	4 25	7 55	...	9 0	...
Washington (*Company's Office*)	1130	1155	4 30	4 55	8 25	...	9 30	...
Steyning (*Woods Garage*) ...						9 0		...
WORTHING (*23 Marine Parade*)	1150	1215	4 50	5 15	8 45	...	9 50	...
Littlehampton (*East Street*)					9 15			...

NOTES.

C—*Via* Crawley.

D—*Via* Dorking.

T—Through Coach to Littlehampton *via* Goring and Ferring. All other Coaches connect with Buses for Angmering, Ferring, Goring and Rustington.

(s)—10 min. stop at Holmwood (Holly and Laurel) and Crawley (Company's Station).

¶ Special Service (**Thursdays only**) *via* Partridge Green and Burrell Arms.

WORTHING to LONDON

DEPART	¶ a.m.	C a.m.	D a.m.	C p.m.	D p.m.	C p.m.	D p.m.	
Littlehampton (*East Street*) ...		8 30	...	...	...	...	...	...
WORTHING (*23 Marine Parade*) ...		9 0	10 0	2 0	2 0	6 15	6 15	...
Steyning (*Woods Garage*) ...	8 30	...	...	...	...	...	...	...
Washington (*Company's Office*) ...		9 20	1020	2 20	2 20	6 35	6 35	...
Horsham (*The Carfax*) ...		9 50	1050	2 50	2 50	7 5	7 5	...
Crawley (*Company's Station*) (s) ...		1015	...	3 15	...	7 30	...	...
Redhill (*Market Hall*) ...		1045	...	3 45	...	8 0	...	...
Holmwood (*Holly and Laurel*) (s)	9 35	...	1115	...	3 15	...	7 30	...
Dorking (*9 High Street*)	9 43	T	1133	...	3 33	...	7 48	...
Leatherhead (*Church*) ...	9 55	...	1145	...	3 45	...	8 0	...
Kingston (*Fairfield West*)	1015	...	12 5	...	4 5	...	8 20	...
Richmond (*General Omnibus Station*)	...	...	1220	...	4 20	...	8 35	...
Putney Bridge (*Underground Station, Hurlingham Road*)	1045	...	1235	...	4 35	...	8 50	...
Coulsdon (*Red Lion*) ...		11 0	...	4 0	...	8 15	...	...
Purley (*Fountain*) ...		11 7	...	4 7	...	8 22	...	...
Waddon (*Cross Roads*) ...		1113	...	4 13	...	8 28	...	...
Thornton Heath (*Pond*) ...		1118	...	4 18	...	8 33	...	...
Streatham (*Chimes Garage*) ...		1125	...	4 25	...	8 40	...	...
Brixton (*Church Road*) ...		1135	...	4 35	...	8 50	...	...
VICTORIA COACH STATION ...	11 0	1145	1250	4 45	4 50	9 0	9 5	...

NOTES.

With connections by Bus from Angmering, Ferring, Goring and Rustington.

(s)—10 min. stop at Crawley (Company's Station), and Holmwood (Holly and Laurel).

T—Through Coach from Littlehampton.

C—*Via* Crawley.

D—*Via* Dorking.

¶ Special Service (**Thursdays only**) *via* Partridge Green and Burrell Arms.

This timetable shows both the London to Worthing services at October 1933 by which time the picking up points in the Metropolitan Traffic Area had finally been settled. This was the last before the takeover of Fairway Coaches service in December 1933 that altered the balance in favour of the route via Dorking which then became the company's principal service.

Car 1113 (CCD 713) was one of an order for 38 Leyland Tiger TS7s delivered during 1935 and 1936. It was fitted with a Harrington 32-seat bodywork and was one of twelve which arrived between October and December 1935 but then stored until March or May 1936 before entering service. All were fitted with folding sunroof and roof luggage rack for use on the London Express Services. *Alan Lambert Collection*

and finish at Goring. An alternative facility was provided by a journey each way on the Bognor Regis via Littlehampton service. The Littlehampton journeys were reinstated from **14 April 1938** but cut back to Goring again for the winter 1938 timetable.

Some minor timing changes occurred from **6 April 1939** as all departures from Worthing were made five minutes later to improve connections with service 31 buses. Departures from Marine Parade were now at 0905 (0835 Littlehampton) and 1905 but southbound timings

NIGHT of 11th-12th MAY only			12th, 13th, 16th, 17th, 19th & 23rd MAY only.	Day Return Fares to London
Read Down			**Read Up**	
Mid't.	a.m.		a.m.	
12. 0	—	LITTLEHAMPTON (East Street) ...	—	} 7/- A.
12. 6	—	**Rustington** (The Church)	—	
12.20	—	Goring (The Church)	—	} 6/6
12.30	3.30	**WORTHING** (Marine Parade) ...	2.20	
12.43	3.43	Findon (The Gun Inn)	2. 7	
12.50	3.50	**Washington** (Southdown Office) ...	2. 0	} 6/-
12.56	3.56	Ashington (The Stores)	1.54	
1. 4	4. 4	**Dial Post** (The Crown Inn) ...	1.46	} 5/6
1.10	4.10	West Grinstead (Buck Barn X Rds.)	1.40	
1.15	4.15	**Southwater** (The Cock Inn) ...	1.35	5/-
1.25	4.25	HORSHAM (S'down Office, Carfax)	1.25	} 4/6
1.45	4.45	Crawley (Imperial Cinema)	1. 5	
a.m.	a.m.		p.m.	
3. 5	6.20	LONDON (Victoria Coach Stn.) ...	11.30	—

A.—6d. extra on 15th, 16th and 17th May.

All the additional Worthing services run in connection with the Coronation operated via Crawley as shown in this extract from a special leaflet covering all London services.

remained the same. The full summer timetable was introduced on **26 May 1939** and northbound departures from Marine Parade became 0905 (0835 from Littlehampton), 1505, 1700 via Brighton and 1905. Southbound services from London remained as in 1938. Fares to London from Worthing were now 5/6 (23p) Single, 6/6 (33p) Day Return and 10/- (50p) Period Return and from Littlehampton were 6/- (30p) Single, 7/- (35p) Day Return and 10/6 (53p) Period return. Premium fares applied for travel to Littlehampton on Saturdays, Sundays and Bank Holidays in high summer with Day and Period Return fares increased by 6d (less than 3p).

Following the outbreak of war this service was suspended after **17 September 1939** but in order to satisfy the needs of families visiting their evacuated children a Sunday journey in each direction was introduced as from **1 December 1939**. This departed from London at 0830 and returned from Worthing at 1730.

Worthing via Dorking

This was a new service introduced on **1 June 1930** which followed the Bognor Regis via Chichester route from London to Kingston before turning south through Leatherhead and Dorking to Horsham and Worthing. A refreshment halt was made at the Holly & Laurel at Holmwood just south of Dorking. At first the number of journeys matched the existing service via Crawley but following the absorption of the Fairways Coaches Ltd operation it became the principal route between Worthing and London. At the start coaches departed from Worthing

Marine Parade at 0915, 1400 and 1830 with southbound services departing from London 1A Lupus Street at 0930, 1400 and 1830.

Apart from some minor changes to the last coach from London this level of service continued until **17 March 1932** although all services were transferred to the new Victoria Coach Station from 10 March 1932. Southdown acquired the Express Carriage service of C. F. Wood & Sons of Steyning and added journeys on Thursdays only at 0830 from Steyning via Partridge Green and Horsham to London returning at 1830 to Steyning. The summer timetable commenced on **13 May 1932** with journeys from Marine Parade at 1000, 1400 and 1800 plus the 0830 from Steyning on Thursdays. From London coaches departed at 0930, 1400 and 1900 plus the 1830 to Steyning on Thursdays and this timetable ran throughout the year with only minor alterations until late 1933.

By October 1933 the picking up points for this service in the London Passenger Transport Area were as follows:

Victoria Coach Station
Walham Green, Barclay Road
Putney Bridge Station, Hurlingham Road
Richmond, LPTB Bus Station
Kingston, Fairfield West
Leatherhead Church
Mickleham, King William 1V
Dorking, 9 High Street
Holmwood, Holly & Laurel
Capel, The Crown
Kingsfold, The Wheatsheaf
Warnham, Corner

The first set down point and fare stage from London on this service was at Horsham Carfax which along with Kingsfold and Warnham were outside the area in which LPTB had a complete monopoly.

On **18 December 1933** Southdown acquired the London to Worthing service of Fairway Coaches Ltd. This service had run from Kings Cross Coach Station and included local fares such as London to Dorking for 2/- (10p) and Kingston to Leatherhead for 1/- (5p) which Southdown continued at first. The local stage carriage section between London and Horsham was subsequently sold to LPTB to form their Green Line route K2 resulting in a drop in revenue for this service. Coaches now departed from Marine Parade at 1000, 1400, 1600 and 1800 all to Kings Cross. From London Kings Coach Station departures were at 0830, 1130, 1330 and 1730. The Thursday journeys to and from Steyning continued as before.

For the summer timetable commencing **18 May 1934** extra journeys were introduced to provide a two hourly frequency departing from Marine Parade between 0800 and 2000 all through to Kings Cross. From Kings Cross coaches departed every two hours between 0730 and 1930. The Steyning service was obviously not proving very successful and was revised to

A tranquil scene in the early 1930s at the Holly & Laurel at Holmwood on the main A24 road just south of Dorking. This was the refreshment stop for the services via Dorking and car 640 (UF 4240), a Tilling-Stevens Express B10A2 with Harrington 30-seat bodywork, is seen taking a break on a northbound service to London. *Alan Lambert Collection*

SOUTHDOWN
MOTOR SERVICES. LTD.
INCORPORATING FAIRWAY COACHES LTD.

Express Coach Services
BETWEEN
WORTHING
AND
LONDON

TIME & FARE TABLE
From DECEMBER 18th 1933 until further notice

WORTHING DEPARTURES FROM
THE DOME, 23 MARINE PARADE Phone : Worthing 1016

LONDON DEPARTURES FROM
VICTORIA COACH STATION, S.W.1. Phone : Sloane 0202
and
KINGS CROSS COACH STATION, N.W.1
Phone : Terminus 6420

depart Steyning at 0810 and London at 1800 running both ways in the times of the main service between Horsham and London. It is likely that it was sometimes operated as a feeder between Steyning and Horsham only.

The winter timetable starting on **15 October 1934** was the same as that introduced on 18 December 1933 except that the northbound Steyning journey was altered to 0910 and run via Crawley so it could still be a feeder to Horsham! The return left London at 1900 via Crawley but by 10 January 1935 it had been withdrawn and replaced by bus connections at Horsham. Apart from the loss of the Steyning service the summer and winter timetables continued unaltered to **28 September 1936** when the service was curtailed for the winter at Victoria and no longer served Kings Cross. It ran as before every 2 hours to and from Kings Cross in the summers of 1937 and 1938. From **6 April 1939** northbound departures from Worthing were made five minutes later but otherwise remained unaltered. The new timings allowed improved connections with service 31 due at 1 minute past the hour from Brighton and 3 minutes past the hour from Littlehampton. The summer timetable introduced from **26 May 1939** was the same as 1938 except for the northbound departures being five minutes later. Fares to London from Worthing were now 5/6 (28p) Single, 6/6 (33p) Day Return and 10/- (50p) Period Return with no premium fares applied on Saturdays, Sundays and Bank Holidays in high summer.

Following the outbreak of war and Southdown's introduction of Emergency timetables from **18 September 1939** the service was revised and no longer ran between Victoria and Kings Cross.

The takeover of Fairway Coaches service between London Kings Cross and Worthing confirmed the route via Dorking as Southdown's principle service for the future. Four journeys a day were provided in winter and a two hourly all day frequency in summer while the route via Crawley was reduced, particularly in winter. Car 1044 (UF 7344) continued to adorn the covers until 1935/6.

Typical of the coaches being used on the London Express Services in the mid-1930s was car 1112 (BUF 412) a Leyland Tiger TS7 with Harrington 32-seat bodywork to Southdown's standard design and new for the 1935 season. The centre section of the side destination board can be reversed to show the alternative route via Redhill and Crawley when required. This coach was one of 24 converted for use as Ambulances just before the outbreak of war. *Alan Lambert Collection*

Departures from Marine Parade were now at 0905 (0830 from Littlehampton), 1405 and 1705 and from London at 0900, 1400 and 1800 with the final journey continuing to Littlehampton. This was the first time that the service via Dorking had been extended to and from Littlehampton but resulted from the withdrawal of all Worthing via Crawley journeys. The first wartime leaflet appeared dated **1 December 1939** but the timetable introduced in September continued through the winter.

Bognor Regis via Littlehampton

This service was suspended in winter 1929/30 but appears to have been reintroduced from **17 April 1930** with a departure from Beach House, Esplanade at 1700 and a morning service from London 1A Lupus Street at 0930 obviously designed for day trippers to the coast. The service was routed from Littlehampton via Arundel, Pulborough and the A29 to Holmwood and then through Dorking to Leatherhead before turning north east through Epsom, Sutton and

Clapham Common. It is believed that coaches picked up in the London area at 1A Lupus Street, Brixton, Clapham Common, Balham, Tooting, Mitcham and Sutton. A refreshment halt was made at the Holly & Laurel at Holmwood just south of Dorking and the journey time was three hours and 40 minutes. The summer timetable began on **1 June 1930** when the service was increased to depart from Beach House, Esplanade at 0930 on Saturdays only, 1400 and 1800 and return from London at 0930, 1400 and 1830. As this was before the advent of Road Service Licensing it is not known why the morning journey from Bognor Regis only ran on Saturdays!

The winter service of one round trip from London resumed from **1 October 1930** and was repeated for the winters of 1931 and 1932 whilst summer 1931 followed the same as 1930. The service transferred to Victoria Coach Station from its opening on 10 March 1932 and from **13 May 1932** the afternoon journey from Beach House, Esplanade was advanced to 1330 but times were otherwise unchanged. By 1 January 1933, but possibly earlier, the service was diverted at Pulborough to run via Petworth and Wisborough Green. The summer timetable of **2 June 1933** introduced some further revisions to times and coaches now left Beach House, Esplanade daily at 0830, 1330 and 1800 with southbound services from London at 0900, 1400 and 1830.

By the end of 1933 the picking up points for this service within the London Passenger Transport Area were reduced to:

Victoria Coach Station

Clapham Common, Old Town

This timetable dated October 1933 shows the complete service between London and Littlehampton including bus connections from Worthing. The Bognor Regis via Littlehampton service had suffered more than most when the picking up points in the London area were reviewed in 1933 being left with just Clapham and Sutton after leaving Victoria Coach Station. As a result future developments tended to favour the alternative service from Bognor Regis via Chichester.

LONDON and LITTLEHAMPTON

DEPART	D a.m.	C a.m.	C p.m.	C p.m.	DEPART	C a.m.	C p.m.	C p.m.	D p.m.
VICTORIA COACH STATION ...	9 30	9 30	2 30	6 0	**LITTLEHAMPTON** (*East Street*) ...	8 30	*1 5*	*5 5*	6 20
Clapham (*Old Town*) ...	9 40	...	...	...	**Worthing** (*Marine Parade*) ...	9 0	*2 0*	*6 15*	...
Sutton (*Hill Road*) ...	10 2	...	...	...	**Washington** (*Company's Office*)	9 20	2 20	6 35	...
Leatherhead (*Church*) ...	1023	...	...	...	**Horsham** (*Carfax*)	9 50	2 50	7 5	...
Dorking (*9 High Street*) ...	1033	...	...	...	**Arundel** (*Square*)	...	...	...	6 30
Brixton (*Church Road*) ...	...	9 40	2 40	6 10	**Pulborough** (*Swan*)	...	...	...	6 50
Streatham (*Chimes Garage*)	...	9 50	2 50	6 20	**Petworth** (*Square*)	...	...	...	7 5
Thornton Heath (*The Pond*)	...	9 57	2 57	6 27	**Billingshurst** (*Post Office*) ...	...	...	...	7 30
Waddon (*Cross Roads*) ...	...	10 2	3 2	6 32	**Holmwood** (*Holly and Laurel*) (s)	...	...	...	8 10
Purley (*Fountain*) ...	...	10 8	3 8	6 38	**Crawley** (*Company's Station*) (s)	1015	3 15	7 30	...
Coulsdon (*Red Lion*) ...	...	1015	3 15	6 45	**Redhill** (*Market Hall*) ...	1045	3 45	8 0	...
Redhill (*Market Hall*) ...	...	1030	3 30	7 0	**Coulsdon** (*Red Lion*) ...	11 0	4 0	8 15	...
Crawley (*Company's Station*) (s) ...	...	1050	3 50	7 20	**Purley** (*Fountain*)	11 7	4 7	8 22	...
Holmwood (*Holly and Laurel*) (s) ...	1040	...	...	...	**Waddon** (*Cross Roads*) ...	1113	4 13	8 28	...
Billingshurst (*Post Office*) ...	1130	...	...	...	**Thornton Heath** (*The Pond*)	1118	4 18	8 33	...
Petworth (*Square*) ...	1155	...	...	...	**Streatham** (*Chimes Garage*) ...	1125	4 25	8 40	...
Pulborough (*Swan*) ...	1210	...	...	...	**Brixton** (*Church Road*) ...	1135	4 35	8 50	...
Arundel (*Square*)	1230	...	...	...	**Dorking** (*9 High Street*) ...	...	...	...	8 27
Horsham (*Carfax*)	...	1125	4 25	7 55	**Leatherhead** (*Church*) ...	...	...	...	8 37
Washington (*Company's Office*) ...	...	1155	4 55	8 25	**Sutton** (*Hill Road*) ...	...	...	...	8 58
WORTHING (*Marine Parade*) ...	...	1215	5 15	8 45	**Clapham** (*Old Town*) ...	...	...	...	9 20
LITTLEHAMPTON (*East Street*) ...	1240	*1 2*	*6 2*	9 15	**VICTORIA COACH STATION** ...	1145	4 45	9 0	9 30

D—*via* Dorking.   C—*via* Crawley.   (s) 10 minutes stop.

The Littlehampton times in Italics are of connections by Service Bus to and from Worthing.

Sutton, Hill Road
Epsom, Clock Tower
Leatherhead Church
Mickleham, King William 1V
Dorking, 9 High Street
Holmwood, Holly & Laurel

The first fare stage and set down point from London on this service was at Slinfold.

This pattern of operation continued with minor timing alterations until **7 June 1935** when the route was revised so that Pulborough was only served when required by prebooked passengers to pick up or set down at Stopham, Pulborough, Hardham or Coldwaltham. Coaches now started from the impressive new bus and coach station in High Street, Bognor Regis. Winter 1935 and summer 1936 followed the same pattern as before but from **28 September 1936** the service was revised to run a round trip from the Bognor Regis end rather than from London which seems more sensible. It now departed from the Southdown Station at 0900 and returned from London at 1930 and this remained the winter timetable until the outbreak of war.

The summer timetable which began on **8 May 1937** was the same as for 1935 and this also remained in place until the war. But, there were some interesting additions with special journeys to and from Rustington Lido from 1938 which were shown on a separate leaflet and did not appear in the main timetable. Coaches departed from London on Maundy Thursday 14 April at 1930, Good Friday 15 April at 0930 and then every Saturday from 4 June to 17 September at 0930 and 1330. From Rustington Lido there were departures on Tuesday 19 April at 0900, Tuesday 7 June at 0900 and then every Saturday

Car 1122 (CCD 722) was part of a large batch of Leyland Tiger TS7 coaches delivered in 1935/6 with bodies by Harrington, Beadle and Burlingham. Had the war not intervened these coaches would have had a maximum expected life with Southdown of around 12 years but as with many of the buses and coaches delivered at this time Harrington bodied car 1122 survived in service until January 1956. The driver is in full summer uniform and appears to be returning to his cab after setting down passengers opposite Littlehampton garage on a southbound service from London to Bognor Regis via Littlehampton. The fine building on the right survives to this day although no longer as a public house. *A.Duke, Omnibus Society*

The opening of the new holiday camp at Rustington Lido brought welcome new summer traffic to the service although in fact Rustington was not on the line of route. Details appeared on a special leaflet but were never included as part of the main timetable.

from 11 June to 24 September at 0900 and 1430. It is interesting to note that Rustington was not on the route of this service but was served by the daily Littlehampton via Worthing journey. A similar service ran for summer 1939 suitably adjusted for Easter dates.

Fares to London from both Bognor Regis and Littlehampton were now 6/- (30p) Single, 7/- (35p) Day Return and 10/6 (53p) Period return. Premium fares applied for travel on Saturdays, Sundays and Bank Holidays in high summer with Day and Period Return fares increased by 6d (3p) to Littlehampton and by 1/- (5p) to Bognor Regis. From **6 April 1939** an additional journey was added to the winter timetable providing a day return facility from London. This departed from Victoria at 0930 and returned from Bognor Regis at 1730. Under the Emergency timetable introduced following the outbreak of war this service was suspended after **17 September 1939**. Alternative facilities were available from Bognor Regis via Chichester and from Littlehampton via Worthing.

Bognor Regis via Chichester
On **1 January 1930** this service, which ran twice daily and was shown on leaflets as service B, departed from Bognor Regis, Beach House, Esplanade at 0830 and 1630 returning from London 1A Lupus Street at 0930 and 1800. From Chichester the service ran north via Midhurst, Guildford and Kingston to London. Once Green Line was established at Guildford the remainder of the places served between there and Chichester did not offer great traffic potential although this route became firmly established as the main service between Bognor Regis and London. Fares from Bognor Regis or Chichester to London were shown as 6/6 Single (33p), 7/6 (38p) Day Return and 10/6 (53p) Period Return. The first reference to a Refreshment halt in 1932 refers to Guildford but this could mean the Green Man at Burpham just to the north of the town and this is where the service stopped for the rest of 1930s.

With effect from **1 April 1930** the service was improved to three coaches daily with departures from Beach House, Esplanade at 0830, 1400 and 1800 returning from 1A Lupus Street at 0930, 1400 and 1830. It is believed that coaches picked up in the London area at 1A Lupus Street, Walham Green, Fulham, Putney Bridge, East Sheen, Richmond and Kingston. With only very minor alterations to timings this became the established pattern until summer 1932 when some enhancement was considered necessary. Starting on **13 May 1932** northbound services became 0830, 1330, 1630 and 1800 with services from London (now from Victoria Coach Station since 10 March 1932) at 0900, 1030, 1400 and 1830 and stayed the same for summers 1933 and 1934. Journey time was now 3 hours 30 minutes.

The winter timetable of **17 October 1932** was similar to winter 1931 with departures from Beach House, Esplanade at 0830, 1330 and 1700

and from Victoria at 0930, 1400 and 1830 and this, with minor amendments to times, became the standard until the war.

By the end of 1933 the picking up points for this service within the London Passenger Transport Area were:
Victoria Coach Station
Putney Bridge Station, Hurlingham Road
Richmond, LPTB Bus Station
Kingston, Fairfield West
Esher, Bear Hotel
Cobham, White Lion
Ripley, Anchor
Burpham, Green Man
Guildford, A & D office, Onslow Street
On this service the first fare stage and setting down point from London was Godalming.

Starting with the winter timetable commencing on **15 October 1934** an additional stop was introduced at King Edward VII Sanatorium north of Midhurst. At this time the hospital was mainly used for the treatment of tuberculosis patients and the coach service provided a convenient service for those visiting friends and relatives.

This is the timetable which applied at the start of 1930 showing the twice daily service which already followed the route that became the established main service between Bognor Regis and London throughout the 1930s and beyond.

LONDON to BOGNOR REGIS

DEPART	L a.m.	C a.m.	C p.m.	C p.m.					
VICTORIA COACH STATION	9 30	9 30	2 0	6 30	...	...	...	...	...
Putney Bridge (*Underground Station, Hurlingham Road*)	...	9 45	2 15	6 45	...	...	...	...	...
Richmond (*General Omnibus Station*) ...	...	10 0	2 30	7 0	...	...	...	...	...
Kingston (*Fairfield West*) ...	...	1015	2 45	7 15	...	...	...	...	...
Cobham (*White Lion*)	...	1035	3 5	7 35	...	...	...	...	...
Clapham (*Old Town*)	9 40	...	...	...	...	...	...	...	...
Sutton (*Hill Road*)	10 2	...	...	...	...	...	...	...	...
Leatherhead (*Church*)	1023	...	...	...	...	...	...	...	...
Dorking (*9 High Street*)	1033	...	...	...	...	...	...	...	...
Holmwood (*Holly and Laurel*) (s) ...	1040	...	...	...	...	...	...	...	...
Guildford (*Green Man*) (s) ...	...	11 0	3 30	8 0	...	...	...	...	...
Guildford (*Aldershot Co., Onslow St.*) ...	...	1115	3 45	8 15	...	...	...	...	...
Midhurst (*North Street*)	...	1210	4 40	9 10	...	...	...	...	...
Chichester (*West Street*)	...	1240	5 10	9 40	...	...	...	...	...
Billingshurst (*Post Office*) ...	1130	...	...	...	...	...	...	...	...
Petworth (*Square*)	1155	...	...	...	...	...	...	...	...
Pulborough (*Swan*)	1210	...	...	...	...	...	...	...	...
Arundel (*Square*)	1230	...	...	...	...	...	...	...	...
Littlehampton (*East Street*) ...	1240	...	...	...	...	...	...	...	...
BOGNOR REGIS (*Esplanade*) ...	1 0	1 0	5 30	10 0	...	...	...	...	...

C—*Via* Chichester.

L—*Via* Littlehampton.
(s)—10 mins. stop.

With connections by Bus to Pagham, Selsey and Wittering.

BOGNOR REGIS to LONDON

DEPART	C a.m.	C p.m.	C p.m.	L p.m.					
ᴮⁿNOR REGIS (*Esplanade*) ...	8 30	1 30	5 0	6 0	...	...	...	...	...
ᴸittlehampton (*East Street*) ...	...	...	...	6 20	...	...	...	...	...
Arundel (*Square*)	...	...	...	6 30	...	...	...	...	...
Pulborough (*Swan*)	...	...	...	6 50	...	...	...	...	...
Petworth (*Square*)	...	...	...	7 5	...	...	...	...	...
Billingshurst (*Post Office*) ...	...	...	...	7 30	...	...	...	...	...
Chichester (*West Street*) ...	8 50	1 50	5 20	...	...	...	...	...	...
Midhurst (*North Street*)	9 20	2 20	5 50	...	...	...	...	...	...
Guildford (*Aldershot Co., Onslow St.*) ...	1015	3 15	6 45	...	...	...	...	...	...
Guildford (*Green Man*) (s) ...	1020	3 20	6 50	...	...	...	...	...	...
Holmwood (*Holly and Laurel*) (s) ...	...	...	...	8 10	...	...	...	...	...
Dorking (*9 High Street*) ...	...	...	...	8 27	...	...	...	...	...
Leatherhead (*Church*)	...	...	...	8 37	...	...	...	...	...
Sutton (*Hill Road*)	...	...	...	8 58	...	...	...	...	...
Clapham (*Old Town*)	...	...	...	9 20	...	...	...	...	...
Cobham (*White Lion*)	1055	3 55	7 25	...	...	...	...	...	...
Kingston (*Fairfield West*) ...	1115	4 15	7 45	...	...	...	...	...	...
Richmond (*General Omnibus Station*)	1130	4 30	8 0	...	...	...	...	...	...
Putney Bridge (*Underground Station, Hurlingham Road*)	1145	4 45	8 15	...	...	...	...	...	...
VICTORIA COACH STATION ...	12 0	5 0	8 30	9 30	...	...	...	...	...

C—*Via* Chichester.

L—*Via* Littlehampton.

(s)—10 mins. stop.

With connections by Bus from Pagham, Selsey and Wittering.

By October 1933 the timetable for the route via Chichester had become established and only began to alter in summer as holiday camps developed around Chichester harbour and new direct services were introduced.

It looks as though the unthinkable has occurred and, after completing a Brighton to London service, car 1000 (JK 1098) has been sent off to Bognor Regis without the side boards being changed! Car 1000 started its life in 1930 with Southern Glideway Coaches of Eastbourne fitted with a Duple rear entrance coach body. Acquired with the business in March 1932 it was rebodied with a new Park Royal body in 1935 and seen here at West Street, Chichester on a London to Bognor Regis service. A.Duke, Omnibus Society

The summer service commencing on **7 June 1935** now from the new bus and coach station in Bognor Regis High Street was slightly amended to run northbound at 0830, 1330, 1630 and 1830 with southbound departures now at 0830, 1030, 1430 and 1830. There were no changes for 1936 but with the introduction of the summer time-table from **8 May 1937** some additional facilities were introduced to meet the growing needs of the new holiday camps being established in the area. An extra journey left Bognor Regis at 1030 plus a new service at 1345 from Selsey, Bracklesham Bay and Wittering on Saturdays from 15 May. Passengers would previously have travelled by Southdown bus services 52 and 53 to and from Chichester to board the London coach. In addition to the four daily departures from Victoria there were new journeys at 0945 and 1445 to Selsey, Wittering and Bracklesham Bay on Saturdays from 15 May plus a new 2230 departure on Sundays from Victoria to Bognor Regis.

The new direct services had obviously proved

New for the 1935 season car 1102 (BUF 402), was a Harrington bodied Leyland Tiger TS7 to Southdown's standard design with folding sunroof and roof luggage rack, and typical of the coaches to be found on the London Express Services in the late 1930s. If required the centre section of the side destination board could be reversed to show the alternative route via Littlehampton. This coach was converted from petrol to diesel in 1951 and sold for scrap in October 1953 although some prewar Tigers remained in the fleet until 1957.
Southdown Enthusiasts Club – Clark/Surfleet Collection

successful as from **3 June 1938** there were departures at 1000, 1430 and 1845 from Selsey, Bracklesham Bay and Wittering on Saturdays although the 1000 and 1845 did not start until 2 July. From London the 0945 and 1445 were joined by a new 1830 journey to Selsey, Wittering and Bracklesham Bay on Saturdays between 2 July and 27 August. For the final summer of peace all of these facilities were repeated as in 1938 with relevant alterations to operating dates. Fares to London from Bognor Regis were 6/- (30p) Single, 7/- (35p) Day Return and 10/6 (53p) Period return but premium fares applied for travel on Saturdays, Sundays and Bank Holidays in high summer with Day and Period Return fares increased by 1/- (5p).

As already referred to in previous sections the company introduced Emergency wartime schedules from **18 September 1939** with coaches on this route departing from both ends of route at 0830, 1330 and 1730. These timings continued in the first wartime leaflet dated **1 December 1939**.

Hayling Island

Southdown had expanded its bus operations on Hayling Island in 1933 and next year began operating a new direct coach service from London to the many holiday camps on Saturdays. Starting on **19 May 1934** and continuing until 22 September 1934 a coach departed from Hayling Beach (Fountain) at 0945 returning from London Victoria Coach Station at 1415. Coaches stopped on request at Eastoke Post Office, Mengham Corner and Northney Holiday Camp before calling at Havant Church and then Guildford and Kingston, Putney Bridge and Walham Green to Victoria.

The service returned in 1935 for the Easter period running from London at 1830 on Maundy Thursday 18 April and at 0900 on Good Friday 19 April and Saturday 20 April only. There was just one return service at 1815 from Hayling Beach on Easter Monday 22 April. A similar level of service, but excluding the operation on Easter Saturday, was provided over the Easter holiday period in subsequent seasons up to the outbreak of war.

This slimline leaflet introduced the new direct coach service between London and Hayling Island in 1934. It obviously proved very successful and further travel opportunities followed in later years. The service ceased in September 1939 and did not reappear until 1948.

The timetable for 1935 which began on **7 June 1935** was altered to provide earlier arrivals at the holiday camps on the outward journey. Coaches now departed from Hayling Beach at 1545 every Saturday and at 1845 on the Whitsun and August Bank Holiday Mondays. From London departures were at 0930 and 1430 on Saturdays plus a journey at 1830 on Friday 7

SOUTHDOWN
MOTOR SERVICES Ltd.

A New Express Coach Service
——— BETWEEN ———

LONDON
AND

HAYLING ISLAND

**Will operate from Whitsun till September 22nd,
EVERY SATURDAY - - as follows:**

HAYLING BEACH (Fountain)...		dep.	**9.45**
HAVANT (Church)		,,	**10.5**
Guildford (Park Street)...		arr.	12. 0
Ripley (High Street)		,,	12.14
Cobham (White Lion)		,,	12.23
Esher (Bear Hotel)		,,	12.33
Kingston (Fairfield West)		,,	12.45
Putney Bridge (Underground Station, Hurlingham Road)		,,	1. 0
Walham Green (Barclay Road) ...		,,	1. 5
LONDON (Victoria Coach Station)		,,	**1.15**

LONDON (Victoria Coach Station)		dep.	**2.15**
Walham Green (Barclay Road) ...		,,	2.25
Putney Bridge (Underground Station, Hurlingham Road)		,,	2.30
Kingston (Fairfield West)		,,	2.45
Esher (Bear Hotel)		,,	2.57
Cobham (White Lion)		,,	3. 7
Ripley (High Street)		,,	3.16
Guildford (Park Street)		,,	3.30
HAVANT (Church)		arr.	**5.15**
HAYLING BEACH (Fountain) ...		,,	**5.35**

On August Bank Holiday an additional journey will run leaving Hayling Beach at 6.15 p.m. and Havant at 6.35 p.m.

All Coaches will stop if required to pick up or set down passengers at Eastoke Post Office, Mengham Corner, Gable Head, and Northney Camp in addition to the points shown above.

FOR FARES AND BOOKING AGENTS SEE OVER.

June only which marked the start of the Whitsun holiday weekend. In view of the limitations on vehicle size due to the weight restricted Langstone Bridge the new 20 seater Leyland Cubs were really the only suitable coaches that could cross the bridge at this time.

From **30 May 1936** the route on Hayling Island was amended to start at Eastoke and then call at Hayling Beach, Sunshine Holiday Camp and Northney Holiday Camp before heading north to Havant and Horndean. Departures from Eastoke were at 1540 on Saturdays from 6 June to 19 September and at 1840 on Whit Monday 1 June only. From London coaches left at 0930 and 1430 every Saturday from 30 May to 19 September. The service was obviously proving a great success and from **15 May 1937** the route was again altered to serve additional points and a new Sunday service added. Coaches now started from Elm Grove, Southdown Garage and ran via Coronation Holiday Camp and Eastoke House to Hayling Beach and then continued via Bank Corner (for Civil Service Camp), Sunshine Camp and Northney Camp. Northbound coaches left Elm Grove at 1030 on Saturdays from 3 July to 4 September, 1530 on Saturdays throughout and at 1830 on Sundays from 4 July to 19 September. From Victoria departures were at 0930 and 1430 on Saturdays throughout and also at 0930 on Sundays from 4 July to 19 September. The new Sunday journeys ran in the paths of Portsmouth journeys and therefore could be worked as feeders to and from Horndean if loadings did not support a through coach. No refreshment halt is stated but there were timing points at Hindhead and Burpham, Green Man which were used by the Portsmouth and Bognor Regis via Chichester services respectively so it is likely that they stopped where space was available on busy Saturdays.

There were just minor changes to timings starting on **4 June 1938** with the afternoon service from Elm Grove retarded to 1530 and the southbound Saturday journeys advanced to 0915 and 1415. Five new lightweight Leyland Cheetah coaches with Park Royal 24-seat bodies were delivered just in time for the 1938 peak holiday season. Fares had not changed since the service commenced and the period return fare from London to Hayling Island by either direct coach or connection at Cosham remained at 12/6 (63p). The same timetable was offered for the 1939 season commencing **26 May 1939** although this was to be the last year of operation until 1948. Services were due to run until 23 September 1939 but the Emergency schedules introduced from **17 September 1939** do not include the Hayling service so it must be assumed that through coaches were suspended after this date. Alternative facilities could easily have been provided by running a feeder coach to Horndean for those brave souls that stayed on until the very last Saturday – assuming, of course, the Holiday Camps remained open!

Car 34 (CCD 704) was one of six Leyland Cub KP3As with attractive Harrington 20-seat coach bodies delivered for the 1936 season. Although usually found on Private Hire and Excursion duties they could often be seen on Relief Duties to London as shown here. With their low seating capacity most were stored for periods out of use during the war although car 34 remained licensed except during 1940 and was finally sold for scrap in 1954. *Southdown Enthusiasts Club – W.J.Haynes Collection*

During 1938/9 Southdown took delivery of eleven Leyland Cheetahs with lightweight Park Royal 24-seat centre entrance coach bodies especially for use on Hayling Island. Car 506 (FUF 506) was one of the six petrol engined LZ4 models delivered in May 1939 which enjoyed only one summer on their intended excursion and London Express Service duties before the war closed down the holiday camps on Hayling Island. It is seen here after the war on arrival at Victoria Coach Station. In 1948 the batch was renumbered by adding 100 to the fleet numbers and the seating capacity increased to 25. All Cheetahs were sold in October 1956 after the opening of the new bridge linking Hayling Island with the mainland. *Alan Lambert Collection*

Portsmouth & Southsea

The service between Portsmouth and London was another that faced strong competition in the early 1930s until Southdown was able to acquire the services and consolidate its operations. The timetable for **3 October 1929** shows three coaches each way daily with departures from Hyde Park Road at 0830, 1300 and 1800 and from London 1A Lupus Street at 0930, 1500 and 1830. In addition to attracting local passengers it was also important for those arriving on one of the Southern Railway's ferries from the Isle of Wight. At this time these served Clarence Pier and the Portsmouth Harbour station all year and some coaches called at these points to provide connections for those wishing to travel onward by road. Of course the majority of passengers transferred to trains at Portsmouth Harbour but as tourism to the island grew so more coach services were extended to cater for them. This is a very complex service and it has been necessary to exclude most minor changes. Not all of the surviving timetable leaflets show full details of the joining points in the Portsmouth area but these are included where known. Fares for Winter 1929/30 from Portsmouth to London were 5/- (25p) Single, 5/6 (28p) Day Return and 8/6 (43p) Period Return.

By **1 January 1930** this service was shown on some leaflets as service P and the same timetable continued in force except that the 1500 from London had been advanced to 1430. Starting on **1 April 1930** the southbound timings were altered to 0900, 1400 and 1900. It is believed that coaches picked up in the London area at 1A Lupus Street, Walham Green, Putney Bridge and Kingston. The summer timetable commenced on **1 June 1930** and more details were included of points served in Portsmouth. There were departures at 0745 from the Harbour Station (0815 Hyde Park Road), 0800 from Hyde Park Road via Havant, 0945 and 1245 from Clarence Pier, 1630 and 1830 from Hyde Park Road. From London coaches ran at 0900, 1200 and 1430 (all with IoW connections but actual point of changeover is not stated), 1700, 1830 via Havant and 2030, all of which terminated at Hyde Park Road. At this time coaches also picked up at Cosham Post Office and Red Lion, Petersfield, Guildford, Kingston and Putney en route to London. The refreshment stop was at The Seven Thorns south of Hindhead.

Starting from **1 October 1930** the winter service was reduced and the journeys via Havant withdrawn. Journeys ran at 0745 from the Harbour Station, 0945 and 1245 from Clarence Pier and 1830 from Hyde Park Road. Southbound departures were at 0900 and 1430 (both with IOW connection but actual point is not stated), 1830 and 2100, both of which terminated at Hyde Park Road. The 2100 now commenced from Charing Cross at 2050. With only minor timing changes the summer timetable starting on **15 May 1931** was the same as in 1930 except for the journeys via Havant which did not reappear. An additional journey left London at midnight on Sundays and there were some slight variations for early northbound Sunday journeys due to the need to connect with the IoW ferries.

Most journeys were extended to start from Clarendon Road Garage in Southsea with the winter timetable commencing **1 October 1931**. It was similar to the previous winter but coaches now departed Clarendon Road Garage at 0735 via Harbour Station, 0935 and 1235 via Clarence Pier. The 1830 continued to start at Hyde Park Road. Southbound journeys stayed the same with the addition of the new midnight journey on Sundays which remained a feature of this service until the outbreak of war. For the summer timetable starting **13 May 1932** the same level of service continued with the addition of a 1630 journey from Hyde Park Road to London and a 1230 down from London – Victoria Coach Station since its opening on 10 March 1932. It now became easier to identify terminal points for southbound journeys with the 0900 terminating at Clarence Pier and the 1330 and 1430 going to the Harbour Station, all for Isle of Wight connections. The 1830, 2100 and 2400 all terminated at Hyde Park Road. It is interesting to note that Southsea did not seem to be of much importance

DAILY SERVICE
TO
PORTSMOUTH
AND
SOUTHSEA
For the ISLE OF WIGHT

Route—PUTNEY, KINGSTON, GUILDFORD, LIPHOOK, RAKE, SHEET, PETERSFIELD, HORNDEAN, COWPLAIN, WATERLOOVILLE, PURBROOK, COSHAM.

COACHES LEAVE 1A LUPUS STREET, VICTORIA,
For PORTSMOUTH and SOUTHSEA,
Connecting With Boats To
RYDE, for SANDOWN, SHANKLIN, VENTNOR,
And All Stations on the Island.

Boats Leave Portsmouth Harbour for Isle of Wight

p.m.	p.m.	p.m.	p.m.	p.m.	p.m.	p.m.	p.m.
1.55	3.15	3.50	4.55	5.50	7.0	8.50	(11.35 Thurs. only)

From LONDON

	A.M.	P.M.	P.M.
1a LUPUS STREET (MOTOR COACH STATION)	9.30	2.30	6.30
VICTORIA ... ... (7b LOWER BELGRAVE ST.)	9.32 ...	2.32 ...	6.32

From PORTSMOUTH

	A.M.	P.M.	P.M.
HYDE PARK ROAD (MOTOR COACH STATION)	8.30	1.0	6.0

FARES
DURING WINTER SERVICE.

LONDON To or From	Single Adult	Single Child	Day Return Adult	Day Return Child	Period Return Adult	Period Return Child
PORTSMOUTH	5/-	3/3	5/6	3/9	8/6	5/6
PETERSFIELD	5/-	3/3	5/6	3/9	8/6	5/6

This is the timetable shown in a London Coastal Coaches publication for January 1930. As it was intended for distribution in the London area it fails to include all of the stops in the Portsmouth area which is not very helpful for those crossing to the Isle of Wight.

LONDON to PORTSMOUTH and SOUTHSEA

Depart	a.m.	p.m.	p.m.	p.m.	Su.O. Mnt.				Notes
VICTORIA COACH STATION ...	9 0	2 15	6 30	9 0	12 0	...	...	...	
Walham Green (*Barclay Road*) ...	9 8	2 23	6 38	9 8	12 8	...	...	...	Su.O.—Sundays only.
Putney Bridge (*Underground Station, Hurlingham Road*)	9 12	2 27	6 42	9 12	12 12	...	...	...	(s)—Stop 10 mins.
Kingston (*Fairfield West*) ...	9 30	2 45	7 0	9 30	12 30	...	...	...	
Esher (*Bear Hotel*) ...	9 42	2 57	7 12	9 42	12 42	...	...	...	★With connections to Isle of Wight (See Special Leaflet for list of Through Fares).
Cobham (*White Lion*) ...	9 52	3 7	7 22	9 52	12 52	...	...	...	
Guildford (*Aldershot Co., Onslow St.*)	1015	3 30	7 45	1015	1 15	...	...	...	
Hindhead (*Golden Hind Cafe*) (s)	1045	4 0	8 15	1045	1 45	...	...	...	All Coaches except 9.0 p.m. connect with Buses for Emsworth, Havant, Fareham and Hayling Island.
Petersfield (*The Square*) ...	1125	4 40	8 55	1125	2 25	...	...	...	
Horndean (*Ship and Bell*) ...	1145	5 0	9 15	1145	2 45	...	...	...	
Waterlooville (*Heroes*) ...	1152	5 7	9 22	1152	2 52	...	...	...	
Cosham (*P.O. and Red Lion*)...	12 0	5 15	9 30	12 0	3 0	...	...	...	
PORTSMOUTH (*Hyde Park Road*) ...	1215	5 30	9 45	1215	3 15	...	...	...	
Clarence Pier ...	1230	5 45	...	...	...	...	...	...	
	★	★							

PORTSMOUTH and SOUTHSEA to LONDON

Depart	a.m. ★	a.m. ★	p.m.	p.m.					Notes
Harbour Station ...	7 50	...	...	...	...	...	...	...	
Clarence Pier ...	...	9 45	1245	6 20	...	...	...	...	(s)—Stop 10 mins.
PORTSMOUTH (*Hyde Park Road*) ...	8 0	10 0	1 0	6 30	...	...	...	...	
Cosham (*Post Office and Red Lion*) ...	8 15	1015	1 15	6 45	...	...	...	...	★On Sundays only Passengers booking from the Isle of Wight join the Coach at the Harbour Station (Pier) at 8.5 a.m. and 10.5 a.m.
Waterlooville (*Heroes*) ...	8 23	1023	1 23	6 53	...	...	...	...	
Horndean (*Ship and Bell*) ...	8 30	1030	1 30	7 0	...	...	...	...	
Petersfield (*The Square*) ...	8 50	1050	1 50	7 20	...	...	...	...	
Hindhead (*Golden Hind Cafe*) (s)	9 20	1120	2 20	7 50	...	...	...	...	
Guildford (*Aldershot Co., Onslow St.*)	10 0	12 0	3 0	8 30	...	...	...	...	With connections by Bus from Emsworth, Fareham, Havant and Hayling Island.
Cobham (*White Lion*) ...	1023	1223	3 23	8 53	...	...	...	...	
Esher (*Bear Hotel*) ...	1033	1233	3 33	9 3	...	...	...	...	
Kingston (*Fairfield West*) ...	1045	1245	3 45	9 15	...	...	...	...	
Putney Bridge (*Underground Station, Hurlingham Road*)	11 3	1 3	4 3	9 33	...	...	...	...	
Walham Green (*Barclay Road*) ...	11 7	1 7	4 7	9 37	...	...	...	...	
VICTORIA COACH STATION ...	1115	1 15	4 15	9 45	...	...	...	...	

to Southdown in these early years of the London service despite a significant presence by its bus services. The Isle of Wight connections were, however, extensively advertised by special leaflets often with train and bus timings on the island included.

Both the winter service from **17 October 1932** and summer timetable from **2 June 1933** were the same as in the previous years but from **16 October 1933** the last journey northwards was extended to start from Clarence Pier at 1820 while the 2100 from London no longer started from Charing Cross. Journey time between Hyde Park Road and London was 3 hours 15 minutes and the Refreshment halt was now defined as the Golden Hind Café at Hindhead.

By the end of 1933 the picking up points for this service in the London Passenger Transport Area were:

Victoria Coach Station
Walham Green, Barclay Road
Putney Bridge Station, Hurlingham Road
Kingston, Fairfield West
Esher, Bear Hotel
Cobham, White Lion
Ripley, Anchor
Guildford, A & D office, Onslow Street

The first fare stage and setting down point on this service was at Farncombe south of Guildford.

During the 1934/5 period Southdown strengthened its position on the London to Portsmouth road by acquiring its principal rivals. North End Motor Coaches (Portsmouth) Ltd was first in May 1934 followed in May 1935 by Alexandra Motor Coaches Ltd and T. S. Bruce's 'Imperial Saloon Coaches', both based in Portsmouth. Aldershot & District also transferred the Grayshott and Hindhead part of their London service while the London based company A. Timpson & Sons Ltd transferred its winter London to Portsmouth Express Service to Southdown. Finally in June 1935 Southdown acquired the service of Underwood Express Services Ltd of Portsmouth giving it complete mastery of the Portsmouth road for many months of the year.

Starting on **18 May 1934** the northbound timetable was enhanced to provide some additional services via Fratton and Copnor. Coaches now departed from Southsea, Clarendon Road at 0735 via Harbour Station plus 0935 and 1235 via Clarence Pier. Later journeys started from Clarence Pier at 1415 via Fratton, 1615, 1815 and finally 1845 via Fratton. There was also a journey at 0745 from Hyde Park Road via Fratton which ran on the same timings as the 0735 between Hilsea Coach Station and Kingston and then served Richmond and Hammersmith. From London there were departures at 0900 to Clarence Pier, 0930 to Hyde Park Road via Fratton, 1230 to Clarence Pier, 1400 to Hyde Park Road via Fratton, 1415 to Clarence Pier, 1830 to Hyde Park Road, 1900 to Hyde Park Road via Fratton, 2100 and 2400 on Sundays only to Hyde Park Road. No services terminated at Clarendon Road.

Setting down passengers at Hilsea Coach Station is car 1125 (CCD 725), a Leyland Tiger TS7 with Harrington 32-seat rear entrance coach body new in January 1936. As delivered it had a half-length folding canvas roof but was one of several coaches modernised in 1939 with folding sunroof and glass cove panels. It is seen in postwar days on a London to Portsmouth and Southsea service and survived with the company until sale in February 1957. *Southdown Enthusiasts Club – Clark/Surfleet Collection*

It seems likely that the significant increase in service was not justified and the winter timetable from **15 October 1934** was similar to October 1933. But, with further acquisitions of local competitors completed in time for the summer service commencing **23 May 1935** the opportunity was taken to increase frequency along the core route and finally extend to a new terminal in Southsea. Although the Southdown proposals reflected an overall reduction in service the main bone of contention for the London independent operators was the application to continue operating the former Underwood and Imperial Saloon services three times daily throughout the year to and from Kings Cross Coach Station. Despite strong objections the Southdown application was granted. Coaches now started from Southsea, 241 Albert Road – which was the office acquired with Alexandra Motor Coaches Ltd – at 0745, 0845, 0945, 1245, 1345, 1545, 1645, 1745, 1845 and 1945 with the departures at 0745, 1245 and 1745 continuing to Kings Cross. All services ran via Clarendon Road and Clarence Pier to Hyde Park Road and then called at North End, Angerstein Road but an additional journey was provided at 0750 from Clarence Pier via Fratton to Hilsea where it met the 0745 from Southsea. A few early journeys still served Portsmouth Harbour Station for Isle of Wight connections. Following the takeover of the Aldershot & District service there was an additional journey at 0915 from Grayshott which joined the main service at Hindhead. From

Victoria departures were at 0830, 0930, 1030, 1230, 1330, 1430, 1630, 1830 which had a Fratton feeder at Hilsea, 1930, 2100 and finally 2400 which now ran on both Saturdays and Sundays. The services departing Victoria at 0830, 1430 and 1830 all started from Kings Cross 30 minutes earlier. In addition there was a journey at 1815 to Hindhead and Grayshott. Previously services had run from Kingston via Putney Bridge and Walham Green but an alternative route was now introduced via Richmond and Hammersmith with one journey each way serving Kensington High Street and Hyde Park Corner presumably for those seeking some high class 'retail therapy'. This remained the standard pattern of operation up to the start of the war although further enhancement occurred on summer Saturdays as more people were able to take a week's paid holiday. The timing point at Hindhead was changed to the Aldershot & District office at this time – probably for the purpose of connections with buses to Grayshott – and it is believed that the Refreshment halt was now taken at the nearby Royal Huts Hotel.

The winter timetable started on **14 October 1935** with the same timetable as summer but minus the journeys at 0845, 1345, 1645 from Southsea and 1030, 1630 and 1930 from London. Extra journeys were, however, diverted to serve Richmond and Hammersmith plus an extra journey for Kensington High Street and Hyde Park Corner. For the summer timetable which began on **29 May 1936** all northbound journeys departed Southsea 5 minutes earlier but otherwise the same timetable applied as in 1935 with the addition of a 0440 departure on Bank Holiday Saturdays 30 May and 1 August. There were no changes to the southbound times. Obviously the new service was proving successful as no changes occurred for the winter commencing **28 September 1936** but the Grayshott journeys had disappeared by the start of the summer timetable on **8 May 1937**. This introduced additional journeys on Saturdays between 26 June and 4 September which provided hourly departures from Southsea between 0740 and 1940 on these days. From London the extra coaches meant that there were departures hourly from 0830 to 1930 then at 2100, 2230 on Sundays and Bank Holidays and 2400 on Saturdays and Sundays. Otherwise the timetable stayed the same as in 1936.

With just minor timing changes the winter timetable starting on **27 September 1937** remained the same as September 1936 while the summer timetable introduced from **3 June 1938** was as May 1937 suggesting that the hourly service on peak summer Saturdays had proved successful. It should be remembered that the railway line from Hampton Court Junction to Guildford and Portsmouth had been electrified with full services starting on 4 July 1937. On summer Saturdays four fast trains an hour left Waterloo for Portsmouth Harbour to cater for holidaymakers travelling to the Isle of Wight so Southdown were obviously fighting back!

The last winter peacetime service for many years began on **26 September 1938** and was the same as in previous winters except that departures from Southsea were made five minutes later and the 1830 from London no longer had a feeder at Hilsea running via Fratton although the morning operation continued until the war. The summer timetable starting on **25 May 1939** followed the same pattern as in the previous summer and was due to continue until 24 September but following the outbreak of war there were some immediate changes. On **4 September 1939** the last coaches were altered to depart from Hyde Park Road at 1705 and from London at 1630. This is probably due to the specific vehicle lighting problems in the Portsmouth area referred to in chapter 2. Along with other London services an Emergency schedule was introduced from **18 September 1939**. This very significantly reduced the level of service to just three coaches in each direction with departures from Hyde Park Road at 0805 running via the Harbour Station and at 1300 and 1800 from Clarence Pier. From London there were departures at 0830 and 1330 both to Clarence Pier and 1730 to Hyde Park Road with no Isle of Wight connection. All journeys ran via Hammersmith and Richmond. From **1 December 1939** and the first wartime leaflet the northbound service was modified with the 0805 from Hyde Park Road altered to run at

Car 1158 (CUF 158) was one of a batch of nine Leyland Tiger TS7s with Burlingham 32-seat bodywork for use on the company's Express Services although not fitted with the customary roof luggage racks. When introduced in summer 1936 they looked very different to the familiar Tigers with Harrington, Beadle and Park Royal bodies to Southdown's standard design delivered over recent years. Unlike the current Harrington and Beadle bodies they carried a brighter livery with cream roof and deeper than usual waist band. At the outbreak of war all acquired a dark green roof to help make them less conspicuous to enemy raiders. *Alan Lambert Collection*

Coronation of H.M. The King Wednesday, 12th May, 1937

SOUTHSEA, PORTSMOUTH, HINDHEAD & LONDON

NIGHT of 11th-12th MAY ONLY Read Down					12th-19th & 22nd & 23rd MAY ONLY Read Up	Day Return Fares to London
p.m.	p.m.	a.m.	a.m.		a.m.	
—	11.45	—	3.15	**SOUTHSEA** (241, Albert Road)...	**3.15**	7/6
—	11.47	—	3.17	Southsea (Clarendon Rd. Garage)...	3.13	
				PORTSMOUTH		
11.45	12. 0	3.15	3.30	(Southdown Stn., Hyde Park Rd.)...	3. 0	
—	12.10	—	3.40	(North End, Angerstein Road) ...	2.50	
12. 2	—	3.32	—	(Fratton Road, St. Mary's Church)	—	7/6
12. 8	—	3.38	—	(Copnor Rd., Stubbington Ave.)...	—	
12.13	12.13	3.43	3.43	(Hilsea, Southdown Garage) ...	2.47	
12.15		3.45		Cosham (P.O. & Red Lion) ...	2.45	
12.23		3.53		Waterlooville (Heroes) ...	2.37	
12.30		4. 0		Horndean (Southdown Office) ...	2.30	7/-
12.45		4.15		**PETERSFIELD** (S'down Office) ...	**2.15**	6/6
12.48		4.18		Sheet (Half Moon)	2.12	
12.53		4.23		Hillbrow (Jolly Drover)	2. 7	
12.55		4.25		Rake (Flying Bull)	2. 5	6/-
1. 0		4.30		Milland (Black Fox)... ...	2. 0	
1. 5		4.35		Liphook (Royal Anchor Hotel) ...	1.55	5/6
1.10		4.40		Bramshott (Seven Thorns) ...	1.50	
1.15		4.45		**HINDHEAD** (Ald'shot & D. Office)	**1.40**	5/-
1.28		4.58		Thursley (Bus Shelter)	1.32	4/6
1.35		5. 5		Milford (Red Lion)	1.25	
1.39		5. 9		Godalming (Orange Box) ...	1.21	
1.42		5.12		Farncombe (Cinema)	1.18	4/-
a.m.		a.m.			Mid't	
3. 5		**6.35**		**LONDON** (Victoria Coach Stn.)...	**12. 0**	—

Following the outbreak of war in September 1939 services on the Portsmouth route were severely curtailed from 18 September. This was the first of the wartime leaflets which appeared at the start of December 1939 and consisted of a double sided sheet printed in red with timings on one side and fares and booking agents on the reverse. Some augmentation came in 1940 but due to the deteriorating war situation all coach services were withdrawn after 29 September 1942.

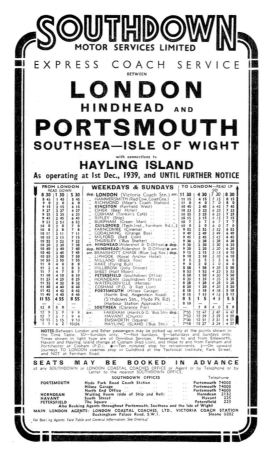

0810 while the journeys from Clarence Pier became 1300, 1600 on Sundays only and 1700. Timings from London remained unaltered. In view of the importance of Portsmouth the level of service is perhaps surprisingly poor but it has to be viewed in the context that this area did not receive any refugees and in fact evacuated its own school children to safer places. Also, that it was feared there could be very heavy bombing raids as soon as hostilities were declared.

Gosport
In July 1934 Southdown acquired the Express Carriage service from Gosport and Fareham to London through the Meon Valley from G. A. Cross of Gosport who traded as 'Perseverance Coaches'. Commencing on **5 July 1934** the new service began with two journeys each way daily.

It ran from Fareham north through Wickham and Droxford to Alton and then onwards through Farnham, Bagshot and Staines to London. A Refreshment halt was made at Bagshot, Fighting Cocks. Coaches departed from Gosport Ferry at 0830 and 1830 and left London at 0915 and 1815. Additional journeys ran from Gosport at 1330 and London at 1415 on 4, 5 and 7 August which was the Saturday, Sunday and Tuesday of what was then the August Bank Holiday. The same timetable applied until **27 June 1935** when Southdown successfully applied to take over the Express Carriage service of Mrs M V Fuger trading as Fareham & District Coaches. Gosport services now departed at 0830, 1330 (Saturdays and Bank Holidays) and 1830 while southbound services to Gosport departed at 0900, 1400 (Saturdays and Bank Holidays) and 1800. To the existing timetable was added a journey starting at 0725 from Fleet End Corner, Warsash running north of Fareham via Bishops Waltham. From London an extra journey ran to Fleet End Corner via Bishops Waltham at 1900.

The winter service was introduced on **16 September 1935** with the same level of service for Gosport but no journeys to Warsash or via Bishops Waltham. For the summer timetable starting on **5 July 1936** the afternoon journeys were run daily in peak summer between 25 July and 29 August and this became a regular feature each year. The evening journeys from London were altered so that the 1830 ran to Gosport and the 1900 to Fleet End Corner via Bishops Waltham. Looking back it is obvious that Southdown were trying hard to make something out of a less than promising operation and for the winter starting on **28 September 1936** the 0830 up from Gosport and 1800 down from London ran via Bishops Waltham on Mondays, Wednesdays and Fridays but served Droxford on other days.

From **8 May 1937** all of the Gosport journeys were diverted to serve Bishops Waltham while the journey each way from Fleet End Corner served Droxford but was reduced to run only between 26 June and 26 September. The winter timetable starting **27 September 1937** was the same as for 1936 except all coaches ran via Bishops Waltham. The extension to Warsash had clearly not proved successful and from **3 June 1938** the additional high season journey was curtailed to run between Fareham and London only. All services ran via Bishops Waltham but on southbound services called only to set down on request. The winter timetable of **26 September 1938** was the same as 1937 and the extra Fareham journeys did not reappear for summer 1939 which began on **26 May 1939**. Fares to London from Gosport were the same as when the service started at 6/- (30p) Single, 7/- (35p) Day Return and 11/- (55p) Period return. No premium weekend fares applied on this service.

What might have happened next will never be

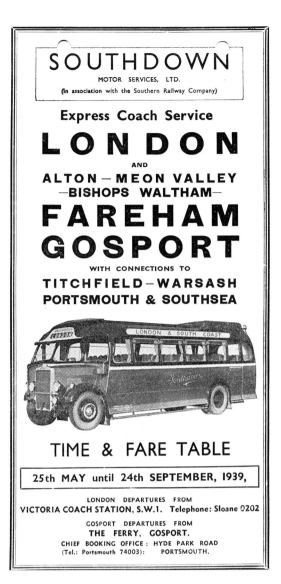

known as following the declaration of war the Gosport service was suspended after operation on **4 September 1939**.

Leaflets and Publicity

At the start of the 1930s leaflets were usually issued for each individual service although both Bognor Regis services (via Chichester or Littlehampton) were included on the same sheet from April 1930. Only the start date was shown, the service generally then running until further notice. Departure times were shown from each end of the route but no arrival times were included although from April 1930 some additional intermediate times were added but noted as approximate. Picking up points gave little or no detail but in the London suburban area were included with a list of booking agents outside which the coaches stopped presumably for prebooked passengers. Southdown booking offices and agents at the coastal end of the services were included in detail. Fares were included but no information about refreshment halts was shown. To add to the confusion some composite leaflets and booklets were produced for distribution in the London area and did not always include full details of points at the coast. For instance, at Eastbourne only Pevensey Road Bus Station was included whereas on other concurrent leaflets coaches were shown picking up at 1 Cavendish Place (Motor Coach Station) and Opposite Leaf Hall by Langney Road Omnibus Station!

Starting from 14 April 1930 a new Brighton leaflet appeared with dark green print and an offside view of a Tilling-Stevens Express on the cover. There was a list of departures and time-table with bus connections to and from Brighton and a diagrammatic route map with picking up points shown. This design continued with a leaflet for the enhanced Worthing routes from 1 June 1930 but with deep pink print although the Portsmouth leaflet for 1 October 1930 featured a nearside view of Leyland Tiger coach 1005 (UF 5805) with London Lorries bodywork. It also included full details of connections with ferry services to the Isle of Wight. The leaflet for the Eastbourne service dated 15 May 1931 featured an unidentified Charabanc on its cover but from the Brighton issue of 1 October 1931 the cover was updated to include a nearside view of Leyland Tiger 1044 (UF 7344) and this became the standard for the next few years.

Starting from the issues dated 1 June 1932 further use was made of standard print colours to identify the individual routes. Among leaflets that have survived brown was used for Bognor Regis, green for Brighton, deep pink for Eastbourne and dark blue for Portsmouth although the latter two would soon change. Full arrival times were included although a note made clear that intermediate times were only approximate. There was detailed reference to the availability of return tickets by rail including the supplements payable. And, the Brighton leaflet gained the banner 'Every Hour at the Hour' for the first time.

During 1933/4 the main London leaflets all reverted to green print although the Brighton

The last prewar timetable leaflet for the London to Gosport service was due to run until 24 September but following the outbreak of war a decision was taken to completely suspend the service after 4 September 1939.

This extract from a leaflet dated 1 June 1930 illustrates the very basic information provided. It was the first leaflet to include the new Worthing to London via Dorking route introduced at this time.

LONDON to WORTHING

DEPART	a.m.	a.m.	p.m.	p.m.	p.m.	p.m.	NOTES.
LUPUS STREET	9 30	9 30	2 0	2 30	6 30	6 30	
Brixton (*433 Brixton Road*) ...	9 40	...	...	2 40	...	6 40	H.—Through Coach to Littlehampton *via* Goring and Ferring. All other Coaches connect with Buses for Angmering, Ferring, Goring and Rustington.
Purley (*Fountain*) ...	10 0	...	...	3 0	...	7 0	
Putney (*Putney Bridge*) ...	...	9 50	2 20	...	6 50	...	
Richmond (*Billiards Hall*) ...	...	10 5	2 35	...	7 5	...	
Kingston (*Coronation Stone*) ...	...	10 20	2 50	...	7 20	...	
Dorking (*27a High Street*) ...	...	11 0	3 30	...	8 0	...	
						H	

WORTHING to LONDON

DEPART	a.m.	a.m.	p.m.	p.m.	p.m.	p.m.	NOTES.
Littlehampton (*East Street*) ...	8 30	...	...	...	...	...	
WORTHING (*23 Marine Parade*)	9 0	9 15	2 0	2 15	6 30	6 30	J.—*Via* Kingston, Richmond and Putney.
Washington (*Company's Office*)	9 20	9 35	2 20	2 35	6 50	6 50	K.—*Via* Crawley, Purley and Brixton.
Horsham (*The Carfax*) ...	9 55	10 10	2 55	3 10	7 25	7 25	With connections by Bus from Angmering, Ferring, Goring and Rustington.
Dorking (*27a High Street*) ...	...	10 45	3 30	...	8 0	...	
	K	J	J	K	J	K	

This cover design with dark green print applied during 1930/1 for leaflets produced in conjunction with London Coastal Coaches for distribution to booking agents in the London area.

The standard cover design that applied from 1932 to 1935 included a nearside view of car 1044 (UF 7344). Note the reference to the takeover of other operators' services which had taken place earlier in the year. A range of different coloured print was used for the leaflets but it was not until 1938 that these were standardised on a regular basis.

From 1935 a new design appeared with a Leyland Tiger of the type being delivered at this time although some leaflets continued to show car 1044! It was customary to produce a Spring edition of the Worthing leaflet at this time as the Littlehampton journeys were curtailed at Goring in mid-winter.

and Portsmouth ones sometimes featured the actual timetables in black print. Through fares with Southdown bus services were now included and the newly introduced Hayling Island service was launched with a non-standard double sided slimline leaflet in red print. The new Gosport service from 5 July 1934 featured car 1044 but with blue print. The Brighton winter leaflet of 15 October 1934 gained a new banner 'Eleven departures daily' which became standard in winter for the rest of the 1930s.

From 23 May 1935 the Portsmouth leaflet was printed red throughout and this became the usual standard colour for this route. The Brighton and Eastbourne leaflets dated 1 January 1936 introduced a new cover design featuring a front nearside view of an unidentified Harrington bodied Leyland Tiger of the type delivered during 1935 and this remained the standard until the wartime leaflets appeared in December 1939.

At last, from the summer leaflets of 3 June 1938 a standard recognisable pattern evolved. Leaflets were now issued for each service or group of services printed in a distinctive colour and these remained the same even for the abridged wartime editions. Eastbourne via both routes were dark blue, Brighton via all routes green, Worthing via both routes orange, Bognor Regis via both routes brown, Hayling Island green, Portsmouth and Southsea red and Gosport purple.

In summer 1939 a comprehensive leaflet

produced for the Hayling Island route was printed in green and included full details of the London service as well as excursions and tours and bus services on Hayling Island. Despite the leaflet cover depicting the customary Leyland Tiger this service was in fact operated by the recently introduced Park Royal bodied Leyland Cheetahs due to the weight restrictions on the only access road to the island.

No leaflets have come to light for the temporary reductions which were introduced at short notice as from 18 September 1939. The notice announcing the reduced services was simply a duplicated sheet and this may have sufficed pending a decision on what level of service could be offered following fuel rationing. Double sided single sheets were produced for the wartime timetables prevailing from December 1939 in the same colours as used pre-war except that the Sunday only service between London and Worthing via Crawley was printed in purple as the Gosport service normally in that colour had been withdrawn from 5 September 1939. These leaflets condensed timetable information to one side of the sheet – usually with 'read up and read down' either side of the timing points – with all the remaining fares, conditions and booking information on the reverse.

Only brief details of coach services were included in the early 1930s bus timetable publications with just departure times from Brighton, Bognor Regis, Chichester, Eastbourne, Littlehampton, Midhurst, Portsmouth and

Worthing along with departures to the same destinations from London. Full London service timetables and fares were included from the issue dated 8 June 1935 although some additional summer services intended mainly for travellers originating in London – such as those to Hayling Island – were never included.

London Terminals

The coach terminal in Lupus Street had always been regarded by London Coastal Coaches as a stop gap measure and from 1300 on Thursday 10 March 1932 the new Victoria Coach Station opened at the corner of Buckingham Palace Road and Elizabeth Street. The impressive new terminal was much more conveniently situated close to bus, tube and rail services and offered greatly enhanced facilities for passengers. It was a sign that long distance coach services had not only come a long way in just thirteen years but were here to stay.

Following the takeover of Chapmans and Southern Glideway in March 1932 the Eastbourne service was extended to serve the new Kings Cross Coach Station situated in Euston Road opposite Kings Cross Railway Station. It occupied a prominent site bounded by Crestfield Street to the east and Belgrove Street to the west and had also been opened in 1932. The acquisition of Fairway Coaches in December 1933 meant that Southdown coaches on the Worthing via Dorking route also served Kings Cross – up to two hourly in summer. In 1935 Southdown successfully applied for the licences of Imperial Saloon Coaches and Underwood Express Services of Portsmouth with three daily journeys extended to and from Kings Cross. This attracted very strong opposition from the

LONDON'S LARGEST
COACH STATION

VICTORIA COACH STATION, BUCKINGHAM PALACE RD. S.W.1.

SOUTHDOWN
MOTOR SERVICES, LTD.

LONDON SERVICE

SPECIAL NOTICE ! !

On and after 1 p.m.
MARCH 10th, 1932

All Southdown Coaches will
arrive at, and depart from

THE NEW
VICTORIA COACH STATION
BUCKINGHAM PALACE ROAD,
VICTORIA, S.W.1.

TELEPHONE - - VICTORIA 2766

MOULTONS (Printers) LTD. 86-86 King Street, Brighton

independent coach operators based in north London who expressed concern at Southdown extending their services northwards from Victoria Coach Station. All Southdown services to Kings Cross ceased by 18 September 1939 and the coach station closed with the gradual run down of services during the war.

Sometimes claimed as the first coach to enter Victoria Coach Station on opening day is car 202 (UF 8032), one of just three TSM Express Six C60A7 models with Harrington 30-seat bodywork delivered in late 1931. Although Southdown had already standardised on Leyland Tigers for its Express Services operation this was the newest coach in the fleet and must have been something of a coup for TSM who were no doubt ever hopeful of new orders. The building to the left is clearly unfinished and the assembled gentlemen – with not a lady in sight – look rather like distinguished invited guests than potential coach travellers even by 1930s dress standards!
Alan Lambert Collection

Restrictions on Coaches in London

In some quarters there was a perceived notion that the traffic congestion in central London was mainly caused by the growing number coaches operating on medium distance services from around outer London. The Traffic Advisory Committee had studied the problem during 1930 and made proposals to the Minister to ban coaches totally from large parts of the West End and City with further restrictions placed on the surrounding areas. Despite the huge popularity of these new services the Committee's view was that coaches should complement the railway services, not compete with them, and that all coaches should terminate at points on the periphery of the central area, off the public highway, in purpose built premises! Stopping places in the central area should be as few as possible and the selection of routes should aim at a wide dispersal of the traffic so as to avoid congestion on particular streets. The Minister announced on 19 December 1930 that he proposed to make restrictions but there were loud protests from the road transport industry – and probably the travelling public who would be most inconvenienced.

Despite the protests the Minister then gave directions to the Metropolitan Traffic Commissioner, Gleeson Robinson, that when considering road service licence applications he should have regard to restricting coach operation in an area within six miles of Charing Cross! The new Commissioner, who did not prove to be much of a fan of coach services in general, favoured terminal locations away from the central area of London despite these usually being sited at inconvenient places away from where most people would choose to arrive on their journey to London! Applications from operators who claimed to have run coach services in this area in the past had to be considered in the light of regulations regarding restricted streets made under the London Traffic Act, 1924 which, it must be admitted, had so far largely been ignored by the new coach services, and the Commissioner should bear in mind the extent to which services had started or developed since the Minister issued warnings on 27 September 1930.

Not surprisingly the many affected operators, including Southdown, lodged appeals to the Minister of Transport over the failure to be granted a licence or the terms of their licence which might include unsuitable terminal points and severely restricted picking up points. After being inundated with appeals the Minister of Transport announced on 18 March 1931 his intention to stop the proposed regulations for restricting the use of motor coaches in the central area of London and to set up a Committee of Inquiry into London motor coach services with Lord Amulree as its chairman.

Its first report was published on 18 June 1932 and dealt with the exclusion of motor coaches from the central area and the limitation of picking up points within the entire Metropolitan Police Area. It recommended that all coach services should terminate off the public highway. The second report was issued on 2 August 1932 and the minister accepted the findings announcing that the new arrangements would apply from 19 September 1932. There was an awful lot at stake for the coach industry and the operators protested loudly. Action was taken in the High Court and a 'rule nisi' was granted against the Metropolitan Traffic Commissioner resulting in the minister suspending his decision to accept the Amulree Committee recommendations and thus allowing the services to continue unchanged for a further period. It was accepted that the Traffic Commissioner's rulings had been too draconian but while the Amulree Committee had allowed some concessions and

This extract from the timetable for 16 October 1933 illustrates the restricted service that was permitted beyond Victoria to Charing Cross after the final implementation of the Amulree Committee recommendations. As was no doubt the hoped for outcome, Southdown abandoned the Charing Cross point as from 1 February 1938.

LONDON to BRIGHTON

On Sundays, all Coaches start from Charing Cross 15 minutes earlier than the times shown for Victoria Coach Station. On Saturdays, they start from Charing Cross 15 minutes earlier than from Victoria, from 2.45 p.m. From Mondays to Fridays the only departure from Charing Cross is at 11.40 p.m.

DEPART	a.m.	a.m.	a.m.	a.m.	p.m.	p.m.	p.m.	p.m.	p.m.	W.O p.m.	p.m.	p.m.				
Charing Cross ⎰ Horse ⎱ Daily	...	...	...	...	...	...	...	...	...	...	...	1140	...	...	...	...
Charing Cross ⎨ Guards ⎬ Saturdays	...	...	...	...	...	...	2 45	4 45	5 45	6 45	...	8 45	1140	...	...	...	...
Charing Cross ⎰ Avenue ⎱ Sundays	8 45	9 45	1045	1145	1 45	2 45	4 45	5 45	6 45	...	8 45	1140	...	...	...	...
VICTORIA COACH STATION ...	9 0	10 0	11 0	12 0	2 0	3 0	5 0	6 0	7 0	7 30	9 0	1150	...	...	...	...
Brixton (Church Road) ...	9 10	1010	1110	1210	2 10	3 10	5 10	6 10	7 10	7 40	9 10	12 0	...	...	...	...
Streatham (Chimes Garage) ...	9 20	1020	1120	1220	2 20	3 20	5 20	6 20	7 20	7 50	9 20	1210	...	...	...	...
Thornton Heath (Pond) ...	9 27	1027	1127	1227	2 27	3 27	5 27	6 27	7 27	7 57	9 27	1217	...	...	...	...
Waddon (Cross Roads) ...	9 32	1032	1132	1232	2 32	3 32	5 32	6 32	7 32	8 2	9 32	1222	...	...	...	...
Purley (Fountain) ...	9 38	1038	1138	1238	2 38	3 38	5 38	6 38	7 38	8 8	9 38	1228	...	...	...	...
Coulsdon (Red Lion) ...	9 45	1045	1145	1245	2 45	3 45	5 45	6 45	7 45	8 15	9 45	1235	...	...	...	...
Redhill (Market Hall) ...	10 0	11 0	12 0	1 0	3 0	4 0	6 0	7 0	8 0	8 30	10 0	1250	...	...	...	...
Crawley (Company's Station) (s)...	1020	1120	1220	1 20	3 20	4 20	6 20	7 20	8 20	8 50	1020	1 10	...	...	...	...
Handcross (Red Lion) ...	1045	1145	1245	1 45	3 45	4 45	6 45	7 45	8 45	9 15	1045	1 35	...	...	...	...
Henfield (George) ...	...	...	...	...	...	...	...	...	...	9 45	...	...	...	...	...	...
Cuckfield (Clock) ...	...	...	1255	...	...	...	...	...	8 55	...	...	...	...	...	...	...
Burgess Hill (George) ...	...	...	1 7	...	...	...	...	...	9 7	...	...	...	...	...	...	...
Bolney (Cross Roads) ...	1057	1157	...	1 57	3 57	4 57	6 57	7 57	...	...	1057	1 47	...	...	...	...
BRIGHTON (Steine Street) ...	1130	1230	1 35	2 30	4 30	5 30	7 30	8 30	9 35	1020	1130	2 20	...	...	...	...

All Coaches except the 9 p.m. and the 11.50 p.m. connect at BRIGHTON with buses for HOVE, LEWES, NEWHAVEN, PEACEHAVEN, PORTSLADE, ROTTINGDEAN and SEAFORD.
W.O.—Wednesdays only. (s) 10 minutes stop.

further negotiations the Minister of Transport announced that the new regulations for motor coach services would apply from 1 October 1933. As a result most operators, including Southdown, found the number of picking up points allowed even in the suburbs was significantly reduced. The Central London restrictions affected Southdown's Brighton service allowing the operation to Charing Cross only on Saturday afternoons and all day Sunday plus the nightly 'Theatre' coach at 2340. Southdown finally gave up the Charing Cross extension as from 1 February 1938.

Fares

It is clear from the early leaflets that fares charged for the London services were not based on any mileage scale. For instance, fares from Littlehampton, Bognor Regis and Chichester, where Southdown encountered little local opposition were higher than those from Portsmouth where several local operators competed for the London traffic. It is obvious that the level of competition played a large part in deciding how much to charge for any particular journey. For those used to 1970s inflation and recurring fare increases it is worth noting that some fares charged in 1939 were actually lower than in 1930! Most stayed around the same level although by the middle of the 1930s it was normal practice to charge premium fares for travel on Saturdays, Sundays and Bank Holidays in high summer between London and the most popular south coast resorts. These were added to Day Return fares where day trippers predominated such as Brighton and to Single and Period Return fares where mainly holidaymakers were concerned such as Portsmouth for the Isle of Wight. Reduced fares were often charged during the winter period when such matters were less contentious.

One of the effects of the Road Traffic Act 1930 was the setting up of Regional Fares Committees which started to function in March 1932. The services radiating from London were divided into zones with No. 2 sub-committee covering the Southdown area between the London to Eastbourne and London to Portsmouth routes. All services, both seasonal or non-seasonal, running between London and these points were required to charge the same fares as 'agreed' by the sub-committee which was inevitably heavily influenced by the large operators. The fare scales had then to be approved by the Traffic Commissioners and the appropriate railway company could make representations if they considered the fares too low! Of course, after agreeing the coach fares, there was nothing to stop the railway companies from offering even cheaper rail fares if they wished!

Until winter 1933 children aged over 3 and under 14 years of age were carried at two thirds the Adult fare with fractions of 3p being charged as 3p but by summer 1934 this was revised to

Southdown Motor Services Limited
Special Arrangements • Coronation Period

London Services

Police Regulations necessitate the following ALTERATIONS to the normal services in the period immediately before and after Coronation Day. The alterations for Coronation Day are shown overleaf. Special ADDITIONAL early and late departures are announced in a separate leaflet, obtainable free of charge from Booking Offices and Agents.

CHARING CROSS (Horse Guards Avenue).
The London-Brighton Service will not take up or set down passengers at Horse Guards Avenue from May 3rd to 23rd, inclusive. Passengers from and to Central London should board and alight at the Victoria Coach Station.

KING'S CROSS COACH STATION.
The Portsmouth-London and Worthing-London Services will not take up or set down passengers at King's Cross Coach Station from May 10th to 15th inclusive, except that the 9.0 a.m., 2.0 p.m. and 6.0 p.m. departures from King's Cross to Portsmouth will be specially maintained on Saturday, May 15th.

HYDE PARK CORNER and KENSINGTON HIGH ST.
The London-Hindhead-Portsmouth Service will not take up or set down passengers at these points from May 8th to 23rd inclusive. All journeys via Hammersmith will run between Victoria and Hammersmith via Chelsea Embankment and Warwick Road.

THESE ARRANGEMENTS WILL NOT BE DEPARTED FROM EXCEPT IN EMERGENCY
For Coronation Day Alterations, Please See Overleaf

The Southern Publishing Co., Ltd., 130, North Street, Brighton—A3524

Southdown Motor Services Limited
SPECIAL NOTICE

CORONATION DAY ⟺ May 12th, 1937
LONDON SERVICES

Subject to the undermentioned alterations, the ordinary Summer Services will run as usual. For particulars of the SPECIAL ADDITIONAL SERVICES, please see the special folder obtainable from Booking Offices free of charge. Alterations for days other than Coronation Day are shown overleaf.

These arrangements will not be departed from except in emergency, but, if in doubt, Passengers should 'phone SLOANE 0202.

KING'S CROSS COACH STATION:
Neither the LONDON-WORTHING nor the LONDON-PORTSMOUTH service will take up or set down passengers at King's Cross Coach Station on this day.

VICTORIA COACH STATION:
All Services will run from Victoria Coach Station except that the undermentioned departures which, owing to Police Regulations, CANNOT RUN FROM THE VICTORIA COACH STATION, will run as follows :—

DEPARTURE ALTERED			ALTERATION
8. 0 a.m. to BRIGHTON			Starts from Clapham, Old Town (a) at 8.10 a.m. ; from Brixton and thereafter as usual.
8. 0 a.m. ,, WORTHING	,,	,,	Walham Green (Barclay Road) (b) at 8.12 a.m.; thence as usual.
8.30 a.m. ,, BOGNOR	,,	,,	Hurlingham Road, nr. Putney Bridge (c) at 8.43 a.m. ; thence as usual.
8.30 a.m. ,, PORTSMOUTH	,,	,,	Walham Green (Barclay Road) (b) at 8.42 a.m. ; thence as usual.
3. 0 p.m. ,, BRIGHTON	,,	,,	Clapham, Old Town (a) at 3.10 p.m. ; from Brixton and thereafter as usual.
3. 0 p.m. ,, WORTHING	,,	,,	Clapham, Old Town (a) at 3.10 p.m. ; from Brixton and thereafter as usual.
3.15 p.m. ,, EASTBOURNE	,,	,,	Clapham, Old Town (a) at 3.25 p.m. ; from Brixton and thereafter as usual.
4. 0 p.m. ,, BRIGHTON	,,	,,	Clapham, Old Town (a) at 4.10 p.m. ; from Brixton and thereafter as usual.
4. 0 p.m. ,, WORTHING	,,	,,	Walham Green (Barclay Road) (b) at 4.12 p.m. ; thence as usual.
4.30 p.m. ,, PORTSMOUTH	,,	,,	Walham Green (Barclay Road) (b) at 4.42 p.m. ; from Hammersmith and thereafter as usual.

NOTES.—(a) Three minutes' walk from Clapham Common Underground Station.
(b) Two minutes' walk from Walham Green Underground Station.
(c) One minute's walk from Putney Bridge Underground Station.
Passengers for these departures are advised to travel to the revised starting points by Underground.

The undermentioned journeys CANNOT RUN TO THE VICTORIA COACH STATION, but will run as far as as the points indicated, whence passengers are advised to proceed by Underground :—

JOURNEYS AFFECTED	Will run as far as	Nearest Underground Station
12 noon 1.0 p.m. 2.0 p.m. } from BRIGHTON	Clapham, Old Town	Clapham Common, 3 minutes' walk
12 noon from WORTHING 1.0 p.m. from PORTSMOUTH }	Walham Green, Barclay Road	Walham Green, 2 minutes' walk

The Coronation of King George VI took place at Westminster Abbey, London, on 12 May 1937 and attracted many visitors from around the world. Throughout May 1937 there was a programme of royal events to commemorate and mark the occasion making it a very busy month for Southdown's London services with full summer timetables being introduced from 8 May instead of the Whitsun holiday as normal. Extra services ran from the coast at Midnight and around 0300 on Coronation Day and later services left London around 2330 for several nights to cater for those who wished to see the floodlit buildings. On Coronation Day itself some journeys were unable to reach Victoria Coach Station and passengers had to make their way by Underground as there was a strike by London busmen in force. There is a pencilled alteration to two journeys shown as affected. No services ran from Kings Cross Coach Station between 10 and 14 May and the Charing Cross extension of the Brighton service was suspended from 3 to 23 May.

FARE TABLES

		Single	Day Return	Period Return
London & Eastbourne		5/6	6/6	9/6

IMPORTANT.—Seats are not reservable in advance on this Service, where the adult single fare paid is less than 3/-, or the adult return fare is less than 3/6.

LONDON — SINGLE FARES

```
LONDON
—  Thornton Heath
—  —  Caterham
—  —  —  Godstone Green
—  —  —  —  Blindley Heath          Children over 3 and under 14
—  —  —  —  —  Felbridge            years, half fare, fractions of
—  —  —  —  —  —  EAST GRINSTEAD     3d. being charged as 3d.
3/-  3/-  2/-  —  —  —  —  Ashurst Wood
3/-  3/-  2/-  2/-  —  —  —  —  Forest Row
3/6  3/6  2/6  2/-  2/-  —  —  —  —  Wych Cross
3/6  3/6  3/-  2/6  2/-  —  —  —  —  —  Nutley
4/-  4/-  3/-  2/6  2/6  2/-  —  —  —  —  —  UCKFIELD
4/6  4/6  3/6  3/-  3/-  2/6  2/6  2/6  2/6  2/6  —  —  East Hoathly
5/-  5/-  4/-  4/-  3/6  3/-  3/-  3/-  3/-  2/6  —  —  Hailsham
5/6  5/6  4/6  4/6  4/6  —  3/6  3/6  3/6  3/6  3/-  —  2/6  EASTBOURNE
6/2  6/2  5/2  5/2  4/8  4/2  4/2  4/2  4/2  4/2  3/8  3/2  Pevensey        ] via
6/1  6/1  5/1  5/1  5/1  4/7  4/1  4/1  4/1  4/1  3/7  3/1  Eastdean        ] Eastbourne
6/2  6/2  5/2  5/2  4/8  4/2  4/2  4/2  4/2  3/8  3/2  Friston
```

LONDON — DAY RETURN FARES

```
LONDON
—  Thornton Heath
—  —  Caterham
—  —  —  Godstone Green
—  —  —  —  Blindley Heath          Children over 3 and under 14
—  —  —  —  —  Felbridge            years, half fare, fractions of
—  —  —  —  —  —  EAST GRINSTEAD     3d. being charged as 3d.
4/-  3/6  2/6  —  —  —  —  Ashurst Wood
4/-  3/6  2/6  2/6  —  —  —  —  Forest Row
4/6  4/-  3/-  3/-  2/6  —  —  —  —  Wych Cross
4/6  4/6  3/6  3/6  3/-  —  —  —  —  —  Nutley
5/-  4/6  4/-  4/-  3/6  3/6  3/-  —  —  —  —  UCKFIELD
5/6  5/-  4/6  4/6  4/-  3/6  3/6  3/6  3/6  —  East Hoathly
6/-  5/6  5/-  5/-  4/6  4/6  4/-  4/-  4/-  3/6  Hailsham
6/6  6/-  5/6  5/-  5/-  4/6  4/6  4/6  4/6  4/-  —  3/6  EASTBOURNE
7/6  7/-  6/6  6/-  6/-  —  6/-  5/6  5/6  5/6  5/6  5/-  4/6  Pevensey     ] via
7/6  7/-  6/6  6/6  6/-  —  6/-  5/6  5/6  5/6  5/6  5/-  4/6  Eastdean     ] Eastbourne
7/8  7/2  6/8  6/8  6/2  6/2  5/8  5/8  5/8  5/8  5/2  4/8  Friston
```

LONDON — PERIOD RETURN FARES

```
LONDON
—  Thornton Heath
—  —  Caterham
—  —  —  Godstone Green
—  —  —  —  Blindley Heath          Children over 3 and under 14
—  —  —  —  —  Felbridge            years, half fare, fractions of
—  —  —  —  —  —  EAST GRINSTEAD     3d. being charged as 3d.
4/6  4/-  3/-  —  —  —  —  Ashurst Wood
5/-  4/6  3/6  3/-  —  —  —  —  Forest Row
5/6  5/-  4/-  4/-  3/-  —  —  —  —  Wych Cross
6/-  5/6  4/6  4/-  3/6  —  —  —  —  —  Nutley
7/-  6/6  5/6  4/6  4/-  4/-  3/6  —  —  —  —  UCKFIELD
8/-  7/6  6/6  5/6  5/-  4/6  4/-  4/-  4/-  —  East Hoathly
8/6  8/-  7/-  6/6  6/-  5/6  5/-  5/-  4/6  4/6  Hailsham
9/6  9/-  8/-  7/6  7/-  —  6/6  6/6  6/6  6/6  6/-  —  4/-  EASTBOURNE
10/6  10/-  9/-  8/6  8/-  7/-  6/6  6/6  6/6  6/-  6/-  5/-  Pevensey    ] via
10/6  10/-  9/-  8/6  8/-  7/-  6/6  6/6  6/6  6/6  6/-  5/-  Eastdean    ] Eastbourne
10/8  10/2  9/2  8/8  8/2  7/2  6/8  6/8  6/8  6/2  6/2  5/2  Friston
```

PLEASE NOTE :—On journeys towards London, passengers may not join this Service after College Lane, East Grinstead ; and towards Eastbourne, passengers cannot be carried whose destinations are short of College Lane, East Grinstead. For intermediate traffic between London and East Grinstead (High Street) a frequent Coach Service is provided by LONDON TRANSPORT.

half the Adult fare with fractions of 3p being charged as 3p. The school leaving age at this time was 14. Dogs were conveyed at a rate of a quarter of the single fare in each direction with fractions of 3d to count as 3d. Not all companies charged for the carriage of dogs at this time.

Advance bookings and Charting

Passengers wishing to travel on Southdown's Express Services were advised to book their seats in advance although tickets were also issued on the coaches subject to accommodation being available. It was not possible to reserve a specific seat. Tickets could be obtained in advance from any Southdown office or one of its many agents throughout the Company's operating area or from a London Coastal Coaches agent in the London area. Many of the agents in country areas were also parcel agents for Southdown and ran small stores, inns and post offices although several did not appear to have a telephone line even by 1939 indicating just how few telephones were in general use in rural areas before the war.

Booking charts were held at Victoria Coach Station and also at the coastal end of each route. Agents in the London area would either telephone for bookings or post a confirmation copy of the ticket if it was not for the following day's travel. In the country areas confirmation copies could be handed to bus or coach conductors to be delivered at a company office for onward transit to wherever the charts were held for the service in question. There were strict guidelines for Agents about which bus services and timings were to be used. For last minute bookings it was always necessary to phone through to the appropriate charting office – assuming you had a phone! Agents between Chelwood Gate and Lewes had to display 'Y' or 'N' signs depending on whether they had any bookings towards London to collect by the 1745 service 28 bus from East Grinstead. Any reservations would be handed in at Lewes office and then transferred to Eastbourne by the 1935 service 25 bus. For any bookings towards Eastbourne these would be collected by the Conductor of the 1610 service 28 from Brighton to be handed over at East Grinstead to the Conductor of the 1745 Eastbourne to London via Seaford service.

An inspector would be responsible for controlling bookings and ensuring the correct number of seats was available. At very busy times it would be necessary to issue a 'stop' notice if all the available capacity – plus a margin for error – had been filled. One disadvantage for Southdown was that often the most significant flow of day return bookings was inevitably FROM London in the morning and TO London in the evening which could mean a good deal of empty running if covered by their own coaches. A London outstation was in operation with drivers and inspectors based at Victoria providing cover for the basic service. These were supplemented at busy times with drivers and coaches based at coastal depots and also coaches hired in from trusted private operators. Certainly I recall in the 1950s Southdown always seemed to be able to conjure up relief vehicles at short notice and no doubt in the 1930s they would be reluctant to turn away business that might otherwise be lost to the many competitors.

One somewhat curious aspect of Southdown's reservations system concerned day and period return tickets. Although return tickets could be issued in advance the return date and time of the journey had to be confirmed on arrival at the destination. This presented little problem for those alighting at Steine Street Coach Station but passengers to an intermediate point were advised to inform the Conductor or Driver of their return details and ensure that their tickets were endorsed accordingly. Alternatively seats could be reserved at the nearest office of the Company or London Coastal Coaches by post, personal call, or telephone subject to sufficient notice being given. It all seems a very cumbersome method of controlling bookings and ensured

the need for Conductors to be carried on service coaches – even in the early 1950s – when almost all express service coaches of the time easily coped with just a driver. Only one Conductor was allocated to each timing and was responsible for checking tickets on all coaches as well as issuing tickets to passengers who had not booked in advance. A special seat was provided for the Conductor with appropriate space underneath for his tickets books.

Bus connections

Even by 1930 Southdown was advertising connections between its local bus services and the London services. As early as April 1930 through fares were included in leaflets but when applications were made to formalise these arrangements they, not surprisingly, attracted a lot of objections from the independent operators who feared more Southdown expansion. The chairman of the South Eastern Traffic Commissioners accepted that such facilities had been in existence for several years and the applications were granted. Even where bus connections were not shown on the coach timetables it was still possible to book through journeys between bus and London Express Services.

The following bus connections were shown in summer 1935:

Eastbourne via Uckfield
From Pevensey Bay and Eastdean to Eastbourne
From Alfriston to Polegate
From Herstmonceux to Hailsham
From Ringmer to Golden Cross

SEAFORD
via NEWHAVEN, LEWES and CHAILEY
to LONDON

Not on WEDNESDAYS & THURSDAYS.   TIME TABLE.

SEAFORD (Clinton Place) .. .. dep.	9 0	2 0	6 30
NEWHAVEN (Bridge Street) .. .. ,,	9 10	2 10	6 40
Laughton (Bus Service 16) .. dep.	8 47	1 53	5 53
Ringmer ,, .. ,,	9 5	2 6	6 6
Lewes .. .. arr.	9 19	2 19	6 19
LEWES (High Street) .. dep.	9 30	2 30	7 0
Cooksbridge (Station Hotel) .. ,,	9 38	2 38	7 8
Piltdown (Bus Service 20) .. dep.	9 10	2 33	6 33
Newick .. ,, .. ,,	9 20	2 38	6 38
Scaynes Hill ,, .. ,,	9 15	2 44	6 44
Chailey .. ,, .. arr.	9 30	2 48	6 53
Chailey (King's Head) .. .. dep.	9 48	2 48	7 18
Haywards Heath (Bus Service 30) dep.	9 15	2 15	6 45
Lindfield ,, .. ,,	9 23	2 23	6 53
Horsted Keynes ,, .. ,,	9 34	2 34	7 4
Danehill .. .. .. arr.	9 42	2 42	7 12
Danehill (Post Office) .. .. dep.	10 1	3 1	7 31
Chelwood Gate (Red Lion) .. ,,	10 6	3 6	7 36
Forest Row (The Swan) .. .. ,,	10 13	3 13	7 43
East Grinstead (The Crown) .. arr.	10 20	3 20	7 50
Godstone .. .. ,,	10 55	3 55	8 25
Purley (Railway Arch) .. .. ,,	11 15	4 15	8 45
LONDON (Victoria Coach Station) .. ,,	12 0	5 0	9 30

Express Service times in heavy type.   Bus Connections in Italic type.

FARE TABLE

FROM	TO	SINGLE Adult	SINGLE Child	DAY RETURN Adult	DAY RETURN Child	PERIOD RETURN Adult	PERIOD RETURN Child
SEAFORD	LONDON ..	6/-	4/-	7/6	5/-	11/-	7/6
NEWHAVEN	LONDON ..	5/6	3/9	7/-	4/9	10/6	7/-
LEWES ..	LONDON ..	5/6	3/9	7/-	4/9	10/6	7/-
CHAILEY ..	LONDON ..	5/-	3/6	6/-	4/-	9/6	6/6
DANE HILL ..	LONDON ..	4/6	3/-	5/6	3/9	8/6	5/9
SEAFORD	Chelwood Gate	4/-	2/9	5/-	3/6	7/-	4/9
,,	East Grinstead	4/6	3/-	5/6	3/9	8/-	5/6
,,	Godstone	5/-	3/6	6/6	4/6	9/-	6/-
NEWHAVEN	East Grinstead	4/-	2/9	5/-	3/6	7/6	5/-
,,	Godstone	4/6	3/-	6/-	4/-	8/6	5/9
LEWES ..	Godstone	4/6	3/-	6/-	4/-	8/6	5/9

Car 1044 (UF 7344) was a Leyland Tiger TS1 with Harrington 30-seat rear entrance body new in June 1931. Intended for use on the London services it was equipped with Walman folding sunroof and rear roof luggage rack. A nearside view of this coach featured on the front covers of London Express Service leaflets for several years. *Alan Lambert Collection*

After a faltering start Southdown, in conjunction with Maidstone & District and East Kent, responded to the new service along the South Coast introduced by Elliott Brothers. The delay in extending west from Portsmouth was probably due to the slow moving licensing system in place at this time.

From Horam and Heathfield to Uckfield
From Chailey to Maresfield
Eastbourne via Seaford
From Ringmer to Lewes
From Newick and Scaynes Hill to Chailey
From Lindfield and Horsted Keynes to Danehill
Brighton
From Seaford, Newhaven, Peacehaven, Rottingdean, Lewes, Worthing, Shoreham, Portslade and Hove to Brighton
From Haywards Heath to Cuckfield
Worthing via Crawley or Dorking
From Steyning and Storrington to Washington
Bognor Regis via Littlehampton
From Pagham to Bognor Regis
Bognor Regis via Chichester
From Pagham, Middleton and Felpham to Bognor Regis
From Old Bosham, Selsey, Bracklesham Bay, Witterings and Tangmere to Chichester
Portsmouth & Southsea
From Fareham, Emsworth, Havant and Hayling Island to Cosham
From Grayshott and Beacon Hill Road to Hindhead (Aldershot & District service)
Gosport
From Southsea, Portsmouth, Warsash, Lee-on-Solent, Hill Head and Stubbington to Fareham

Coach Requirements for summer 1939

The allocation figures for London Express Services shown below are taken from surviving Southdown Traffic Notices and do not include the coaches necessary to cover special weekend or Bank Holiday journeys. These were covered (in the official words of Southdown) by 'the general coach and chara allocation'!

Eastbourne via Uckfield
2 Eastbourne and 2 London
Eastbourne via Seaford
1 Eastbourne and 1 London
Brighton
6 Brighton and 2 London although the 1000 from London counted as a Worthing vehicle.
Worthing via both routes
2 Worthing, 1 Littlehampton and 4 London
Bognor Regis via both routes
2 Bognor Regis and 3 London
Portsmouth & Southsea
4 Portsmouth and 4 London
Gosport
1 Gosport and 1 London

THE SOUTH COAST EXPRESS

On 25 March 1929 Elliott Brothers of Bournemouth, who traded as Royal Blue, began an ambitious new coach service running along the South Coast calling at all the coastal towns between Bournemouth and Margate. Starting on **1 June 1929** Southdown responded by introducing a new 'Limited Stop South Coast Service' between Margate and Portsmouth via Folkestone, Hastings, Eastbourne, Brighton, Worthing, Arundel and Chichester. It was jointly operated by Southdown, Maidstone & District and East Kent. From **9 June 1929** it was extended via Southampton and the New Forest to Bournemouth with westbound journeys at:

0815 and 1015 from Brighton to Bournemouth
1015 from Hastings to Bournemouth
0820 from Margate to Bournemouth
1845 from Brighton to Portsmouth
1645 from Hastings to Portsmouth
1615 from Margate to Brighton

Eastbound departures were at:
0930 from Hastings to Margate
0815 from Portsmouth to Hastings
0800 from Bournemouth to Margate
1115 from Portsmouth to Brighton
1045 and 1415 Bournemouth to Hastings
1730 from Bournemouth to Brighton

LIMITED STOP
SOUTH COAST SERVICE
BETWEEN
MARGATE
AND
BOURNEMOUTH

COMMENCING:
SATURDAY, 1st JUNE, 1929
From MARGATE TO PORTSMOUTH, and on 9th June will be extended to BOURNEMOUTH.

THE ROUTE TAKEN IS VIA:
Ramsgate, Dover, Folkestone, Hastings, Eastbourne, .. Brighton, Worthing, Arundel, Chichester, .. Portsmouth, Southampton and New Forest.

CONVENIENT STOPS ARE ALLOWED FOR MEALS.

Operated Jointly by:
SOUTHDOWN MOTOR SERVICES, LIMITED.,
MAIDSTONE & DISTRICT MOTOR SERVICES, LIMITED,
EAST KENT ROAD CAR COMPANY, LIMITED.

Book at any Southdown, Maidstone or East Kent Office.

Some of these probably involved change of vehicle at places such as Brighton and Hastings – the opposition proudly proclaiming that no changes were required on their service! Conductors were specifically instructed to ensure that passengers required to change were directed to the correct coach – and same seat if possible – and also helped with their luggage. Sample fares were Brighton to Bournemouth 9/- (45p) Single and 15/- (75p) Return, Dover to Portsmouth 11/6 (58p) Single and 18/6 (93p) Return and Margate to Brighton 9/6 (48p) Single and 15/- (75p) Return. Timings were revised from **1 July 1929** with new journeys shown running at 0900 from Portsmouth to Weymouth and returning at 1700 although it is believed that these did not commence until **25 July 1929** when yet another timetable was issued.

From **23 September 1929** Southdown altered their service to run between Hastings and Bournemouth with East Kent providing connecting services from Hastings to Margate. It was now described as 'Coastal Express Service' and there was a generous level of service for winter with westbound departures at:

0815 and 1015 from Brighton to Bournemouth
1130 and 1415 from Hastings to Bournemouth
1700 from Hastings to Portsmouth
2030 from Hastings to Brighton

Eastbound departures were at:
0850 from Brighton to Hastings
0815 from Portsmouth to Hastings
0815 and 1015 Bournemouth to Hastings
1445 and 1715 from Bournemouth to Brighton

Although the leaflet proclaimed that the service was jointly operated with East Kent all of these journeys were listed as Southdown coaches.

It appears that passenger loadings failed to live up to expectations and the service was suspended by 1 January 1930. Services resumed from **14 April 1930** with Southdown running between Bournemouth and Hastings and East Kent between Hastings and Margate. It appears that problems in obtaining licences under the old system had prevented the operation by Southdown of a through service to Margate. Westbound journeys ran at:

1035 from Portsmouth to Bournemouth
1040 from Brighton to Bournemouth
1130 and 1405 Hastings to Bournemouth
1705 and 1930 from Hastings to Brighton

Eastbound departures were at:
0850 and 1030 from Brighton to Hastings
0845 and 1045 Bournemouth to Hastings
1415 from Bournemouth to Brighton
1715 from Bournemouth to Portsmouth

From the summer timetable starting on **23 June 1930** Southdown coaches were extended to run between Bournemouth and Dover with East Kent still providing the Hastings to Margate connections. This appears to have been the best compromise that could be reached. East Kent retained all receipts over the section from Hastings to Dover and paid Southdown running costs at a rate of 11.28 pence per mile. A similar arrangement applied to Maidstone & District between Hastings and Pevensey. At this time all services operated via Arundel with bus connections for Littlehampton and Bognor. There were eight westbound services and five eastbound departures including five each way through to Bournemouth. Clearly this was always a very seasonal service and commencing with the winter timetable of **22 September 1930** just

Car 1011 (UF 5811) is a Leyland Tiger TS2 with Harrington C26R body new April 1930 and seen on South Coast Express duties heading towards Hastings. The well-dressed lady standing beside the coach appears to have alighted by the front door which was normally only used in emergency. A new Harrington C32R body to Southdown's standard prewar style incorporating half folding roof replaced the original at the start of 1936. Car 1011 enjoyed a long life with Southdown and was finally withdrawn in July 1953. *C.F.Klapper, Omnibus Society*

two journeys were provided each way. The westbound departures were at 0910 from Eastbourne to Bournemouth and 0900 from Dover to Bournemouth while eastbound services were at 0845 from Bournemouth to Dover and 1415 Bournemouth to Eastbourne all with East Kent connections to Margate. Elliott Bros of Bournemouth continued to run four journeys each way in competition. By **1 January 1931** an extra journey was added at 0900 from Brighton to Dover returning at 1657 from Dover to Brighton but generally the winter service was always much reduced on summer operations as compared to the London services.

From **23 May 1931** six journeys were introduced each way along the same lines as summer 1930 but starting on **1 August 1931** through services began between Margate and Bournemouth with joint operation by Southdown and East Kent. Westbound services were at:

0915 from Portsmouth to Bournemouth
0815 from Brighton to Bournemouth
0900 from Eastbourne to Bournemouth
0910 from Folkestone to Brighton
0815 and 1015 from Margate to Bournemouth
1215 and 1315 from Margate to Portsmouth
1525 Margate to Brighton

Eastbound services were at:
0900 from Brighton to Margate
0815 and 0945 from Portsmouth to Margate
0830 and 1030 from Bournemouth to Margate
1700 from Brighton to Folkestone
1415 from Bournemouth to Eastbourne
1645 from Bournemouth to Brighton
1845 from Bournemouth to Portsmouth

Although not part of the joint operation at this time Southdown introduced a new limited stop service between Brighton (Steine Street) and Portsmouth (Hyde Park Road) via Worthing Dome, Rustington Church, Littlehampton (East Street), Middleton Post Office, Felpham Post Office, Bognor Pier, Chichester (West Street) and Havant Post Office. It ran from 1 August to 20 September 1931 with departures from Brighton at 0930, 1030, 1130, 1215, 1330 and then hourly to 1930. From Hyde Park Road there were departures at 0940, 1040, 1140, 1310 and then hourly to 2010.

The winter service which began on **19 October 1931** also featured through coaches but was reduced to just three services each way including two to Bournemouth. It seems unlikely that the two competing services could ever really prosper and in March 1932 an agreement was reached between Southdown, East Kent and Royal Blue which made Portsmouth the dividing point with coaches connecting at Southdown's Hyde Park Road depot. Royal Blue vehicles would

The spring timetable leaflet issued for 10 April 1933 first introduced the familiar South Coast Express name by which title it was known until National Travel days.

Service to be operated from 10th April, 1933, until Further Notice

SOUTH COAST EXPRESS SERVICE

With connections at Portsmouth from Bath, Bristol, Exeter, Ilfracombe, Plymouth, Salisbury, Torquay and Weston-super-Mare.

Royal Blue Coaches :							
Ilfracombe (134 High Street)...	... dep.	...	...	...	...	8 0	...
BOURNEMOUTH (Square Station)	... arr.	...	...	...	...	**3 6**	...
Weston-super-Mare	... dep.	...	...	...	...	9 40	...
BOURNEMOUTH (Square Station)	... arr.	...	...	...	...	**3 10**	...
Bristol (Prince Street) ...	... dep.	...	...	...	...	8 45	2†30
Bath (Cleveland Place) ...	... ,,	...	...	...	...	9 28	3†13
Salisbury (Market Place) ...	... ,,	...	...	...	...	11 46	5†30
BOURNEMOUTH (Square Station)	... arr.	...	...	...	...	**1 25**	...
Plymouth (Sherwell Arcade) ...	... dep.	...	...	...	...	8 0	10 15
Torquay (Town Hall)	... ,,	...	...	...	...	8 35	11 54
Exeter (Paul Street)	... ,,	...	...	...	...	10 0	1 17
BOURNEMOUTH (Square Station)	... arr.	...	...	...	...	**2 10**	**5 14**
BOURNEMOUTH (Square Station)	... dep.	...	...	**8 15**	**11 15**	**3 15**	**5 30**
Lyndhurst (Imperial Motor Works)	... ,,	...	...	9 10	12 10	4 10	6 25
Southampton (Grosvenor Square)	... ,,	...	...	9 36	12 36	4 36	6 51
Fareham (High Street) ...	... ,,	...	...	10 15	1 15	5 15	7 30
PORTSMOUTH (Hyde Park Road)	... arr.	...	...	**10 45**	**1 45**	**5 45**	**8 0**
South Coast Express Coaches :							
PORTSMOUTH (Hyde Park Road)	... dep.	...	...	**11 0**	**2 30**	**6 15**	...
Havant (High Street)	... ,,	...	...	11 30	3 0	6 45	...
Emsworth (The Square) ...	... ,,	...	...	11 37	3 7	6 52	...
Bognor (Beach House, Esplanade)	... ,,	...	...	*11 10*	*2 40*	*6 10*	...
CHICHESTER (West Street)*	... ,,	...	...	**11 55**	**3 25**	**7 10**	...
Bognor (Beach House, Esplanade)	... ,,	...	...	*12 53*	*4 23*	*7 53*	...
Arundel (The Square)** ...	... ,,	...	...	12 25	3 55	7 40	...
Worthing (Marine Parade) ...	... ,,	*8a 0*	10 25	12 55	4 25	8 10	...
Shoreham (High Street) ...	... ,,	*8a22*	10 40	1 10	4 40	8 25	...
BRIGHTON (Steine Street) ...	.. arr.	*8a55*	10 59	**1 29**	**4 59**	**8 44**	...
BRIGHTON (Steine Street) ...	... dep.	**9 0**	**11 0**	**2 0**	**5 30**	...	...
Peacehaven (South Coast Road)	... ,,	9 15	11 15	2 15	5 45	...	...
Newhaven (Bridge Street) ...	... ,,	9 25	11 25	2 25	5 55	...	...
Seaford (Clinton Place) ...	... ,,	9 35	11 35	2 35	6 5	...	...
EASTBOURNE (Pevensey Road)	... arr.	**10 4**	**12 4**	**3 4**	**6 34**	...	...
EASTBOURNE (Pevensey Road)	... dep.	**10 5**	**12 5**	**3 5**	...	...	...
Bexhill (Marina)	... ,,	10 35	12 35	3 35	...	...	...
HASTINGS (Railway Station) ...	... arr.	**10 55**	**12 55**	**3 55**	...	...	...
HASTINGS (Railway Station) ...	... dep.	**11 0**	**2 15**	**4 30**	...	...	...
Winchelsea (New Inn)	... ,,	11 25	2 45	4 55	...	...	...
Rye (Company's Office) ...	... ,,	11 35	2 55	5 5	...	...	...
New Romney (Ship)	... ,,	12 12	3 35	5 42	...	...	...
Dymchurch (Bus Station) ...	... ,,	12 25	3 48	5 55	...	...	...
Hythe (Red Lion Square) ...	... ,,	12 39	4 2	6 9	...	...	...
FOLKESTONE (Sandgate Road)	... arr.	**12 55**	**4 19**	**6 25**	...	...	...
FOLKESTONE (Sandgate Road)	... dep.	**1 0**	**4 20**	**6 30**	...	...	...
DOVER (Market Square) ...	... arr.	**1 25**	**4 42**	**6 55**	...	...	...
DOVER (Market Square) ...	... dep.	...	**4 43**	**7 0**	...	...	...
Deal (Parade)	... ,,	...	5 11	7 27	...	...	...
Sandwich (Cattle Market) ...	... ,,	...	5 31	7 47	...	...	...
Ramsgate (Harbour Parade) ...	... ,,	...	5 55	8 10	...	...	...
Broadstairs (Pierremont Hall)	... ,,	...	6 4	8 19	...	...	...
MARGATE (The Parade) ...	... arr.	...	**6 15**	**8 30**	...	...	...

Times shown in italics are Ordinary Bus Services on which tickets of the South Coast Express Service will be accepted.
*For Bognor, change on to Ordinary Service Bus at Chichester.
**For Littlehampton, change on to Ordinary Service Bus at Arundel.
a Not Sundays. † *Via* Romsey to Southampton, arrive Portsmouth 7.45 p.m.

P(B)L—31367 [P.T.O.

Express Service. **BRIGHTON, WORTHING, LITTLEHAMPTON, BOGNOR, CHICHESTER and PORTSMOUTH.**

WEEKDAYS and SUNDAYS

BRIGHTON (Steine St.) ...	Dep.	**9 30**	**10 30**	**11 30**	**12 30**	**1 30**	**2 30**	**3 30**	**4 30**	**5 30**	**6 30**
Worthing (Dome) ...	,,	10 5	11 5	12 5	1 5	2 5	3 5	4 5	5 5	6 5	7 5
Rustington (Church) ...	,,	10 30	11 30	12 30	1 30	2 30	3 30	4 30	5 30	6 30	7 30
Littlehampton (East St.)	,,	10 40	11 40	12 40	1 40	2 40	3 40	4 40	5 40	6 40	7 40
Middleton (Post Office)...	,,	10 55	11 55	12 55	1 55	2 55	3 55	4 55	5 55	6 55	7 55
Felpham (Post Office) ...	,,	11 0	12 0	1 0	2 0	3 0	4 0	5 0	6 0	7 0	8 0
Bognor (Pier) ...	Arr.	11 7	12 7	1 7	2 7	3 7	4 7	5 7	6 7	7 7	8 7
BOGNOR (Pier) ...	Dep.	**11 10**	**12 10**	**1 10**	**2 10**	**3 10**	**4 10**	**5 10**	**6 10**	**7 10**	**8 10**
Chichester (West Street)	,,	11 33	12 33	1 33	2 33	3 33	4 33	5 33	6 33	7 33	8 33
Havant (Post Office) ...	,,	11 55	12 55	1 55	2 55	3 55	4 55	5 55	6 55	7 55	8 55
PORTSMOUTH (Hyde Park Road)	Arr.	**12 25**	**1 25**	**2 25**	**3 25**	**4 25**	**5 25**	**6 25**	**7 25**	**8 25**	**9 25**
PORTSMOUTH (Hyde Park Road)	Dep.	**10 0**	**10 30**	**12 0**	**1 0**	**2 0**	**3 0**	**4 0**	**5 0**	**6 0**	**7 0**
Havant (Post Office) ...	,,	10 30	11 0	12 30	1 30	2 30	3 30	4 30	5 30	6 30	7 30
Chichester (West Street)	,,	10 52	11 22	12 52	1 52	2 52	3 52	4 52	5 52	6 52	7 52
Bognor (Pier) ...	Arr.	11 17	11 47	1 17	2 17	3 17	4 17	5 17	6 17	7 17	8 17
BOGNOR (Pier) ...	Dep.	**11 20**	**11 50**	**1 20**	**2 20**	**3 20**	**4 20**	**5 20**	**6 20**	**7 20**	**8 20**
Felpham (Post Office) ...	,,	11 27	11 57	1 27	2 27	3 27	4 27	5 27	6 27	7 27	8 27
Middleton (Post Office)...	,,	11 30	12 0	1 30	2 30	3 30	4 30	5 30	6 30	7 30	8 30
Littlehampton (East St.)	,,	11 45	12 15	1 45	2 45	3 45	4 45	5 45	6 45	7 45	8 45
Rustington (Church) ...	,,	11 55	12 25	1 55	2 55	3 55	4 55	5 55	6 55	7 55	8 55
Worthing (Dome) ...	,,	12 20	12 50	2 20	3 20	4 20	5 20	6 20	7 20	8 20	9 20
BRIGHTON (Steine St.) ...	Arr.	**12 55**	**1 25**	**2 55**	**3 55**	**4 55**	**5 55**	**6 55**	**7 55**	**8 55**	**9 55**

not operate east of Portsmouth – until July 1933! From **9 May 1932** the three companies launched their new joint service between Bournemouth, Southampton, Portsmouth, Brighton and Margate and in 1933 it gained the more familiar title of South Coast Express. On the eastern section there were eight journeys each way including a new innovation which saw the previously Hastings based coach projected back to begin and end its day at Rye.

Southdown reintroduced their limited stop service between Brighton and Portsmouth from 18 June until 18 September 1932 with an hourly service daily. From Brighton there were departures at 0930 and hourly until 1830 with eastbound departures from Hyde Park Road at 1000, 1030, 1200 and hourly to 1900.

For the winter service commencing **1 October 1932** five services ran each way including an unusual Worthing to Hastings round trip. From 1933 onward it became customary to have a spring timetable which was only a slightly enhanced version of the winter service before introducing a full summer timetable in July. The new timetable commencing on **15 July 1933** also included Southdown's Brighton to Portsmouth via Bognor Regis journeys which had been kept separate since it began in 1931. Also two new through journeys between Brighton and Bournemouth were introduced on Saturdays only, calling at Hilsea but not Hyde Park Road. In total there were 18 journeys each way.

In the Southdown area services now ran via Arundel or Bognor Regis and Littlehampton. Royal Blue connections were advertised from Bournemouth to Ilfracombe, Plymouth, Torquay, Exeter, Bristol, Bath and Salisbury. The winter service starting **16 October 1933** reverted to four journeys each way and Royal Blue working all Portsmouth to Bournemouth journeys. Onward connections from Bournemouth were only available on the Brighton to Portsmouth journeys. This was a more leisurely era when a journey from Brighton to Plymouth with changes at Portsmouth and Bournemouth would have taken 11 hours 30 minutes! Apart from some minor retiming which saw the loss of the journeys starting and finishing at Rye the summer timetable beginning **14 July 1934** followed the same pattern as introduced in 1933. Towards the end of 1934 Elliott Bros decided to sell the business and from 1 February 1935 the Royal Blue express services passed to Western National.

In an attempt to provide better services for passengers travelling to the Isle of Wight all daytime journeys to Portsmouth were extended from Hyde Park Road to serve Clarence Pier as from **8 June 1935**. The full summer timetables commenced on **13 July 1935** with some minor changes and now included 16 journeys in each direction. Clearly the enhanced timetable was proving a success and starting from **11 July 1936** further through coaches were introduced although no East Kent journeys went west of

Portsmouth. As this became the pattern of summer service until the outbreak of war it seems worth describing in detail.

Westbound journeys:
0810 Portsmouth – Bournemouth
1015 Portsmouth – Bournemouth
0800 Brighton – Bognor Regis – Portsmouth – Bournemouth
0800 Eastbourne – Brighton – Arundel – Portsmouth
0915 Brighton – Arundel – Portsmouth – Bournemouth *(Saturdays only)*
0930 Brighton – Bognor Regis – Portsmouth – Bournemouth
1030 Brighton – Bognor Regis – Portsmouth – Bournemouth
0830 Hastings – Brighton – Arundel – Portsmouth
1330 Brighton – Bognor Regis – Portsmouth – Bournemouth
0900 Folkestone – Brighton – Arundel – Portsmouth
0815 Margate – Brighton – Arundel – Portsmouth
1500 Brighton – Bognor Regis – Portsmouth – Bournemouth
1630 Brighton – Arundel – Portsmouth

Royal Coronation Naval Review
at Spithead, Thursday, May 20th, 1937
Also the Assembly and Dispersal of the Fleet, May 13th to 23rd
Summary of augmented Coach Services between
SOUTHSEA AND SOUTH COAST TOWNS
including special late departures on May 20 in connection with
THE ILLUMINATION OF THE FLEET

(Timetable: TO SOUTHSEA—EACH DAY and FROM SOUTHSEA Each Day)

Places served — TO SOUTHSEA: BRIGHTON (Steine Street), Hove (7 St. Aubyns Gardens), Shoreham (High Street), Worthing (Marine Parade), Littlehampton (East Street), Arundel (The Square), Bognor (Coach Stn., High St.), CHICHESTER (West Street), Emsworth (The Square), Havant (High Street), Hilsea (Southdown Station), PORTSMOUTH (HydePk.Rd.)

FROM SOUTHSEA: SOUTHSEA (Clarence Pier), PORTSMOUTH (Hyde Pk.Rd.), Havant (High Street), Emsworth (West Street), CHICHESTER (West Street), Bognor (Coach Stn., High St.), Littlehampton (East Street), Arundel (The Square), Worthing (Marine Parade), Shoreham (High Street), Hove (7 St. Aubyns Gardens), BRIGHTON (Steine Street)

† These journeys will operate on Review Day, Thursday, May 20th ONLY

Notes:— ★ These journeys will be run only on Thursday night, May 20/21, for the use of visitors staying to view the illumination of the Fleet.

For full list of departure times, intermediate fares, etc., please see separate handbills.

The journeys from Southsea at 11.50 p.m. will run on Thursday night, May 20/21 only

SPECIAL EXCURSIONS
will also be run to Southsea on May 13th to 23rd, from many other towns in the Southdown Area, including:
EASTBOURNE, HAYWARDS HEATH, HORSHAM, BILLINGSHURST, PULBOROUGH, PETWORTH, etc., etc.
For full details of Times & Fares please apply at the local offices

The Southern Publishing Co., Ltd., 130, North Street, Brighton—A3732

Through the 1930s special journeys were run in conjunction with the very popular Naval Reviews held at Portsmouth including some late facilities to allow visitors the chance to return after viewing the Illuminations.

During the high summer period Southdown provided additional services between Brighton, Portsmouth and Bournemouth which were eventually incorporated into the South Coast Express timetable although also shown on this separate leaflet for 1938. All of these journeys ran via Bognor and Littlehampton but most South Coast Express journeys called at Arundel instead.

– Bournemouth *(Saturdays only)*
1730 Brighton – Bognor Regis – Portsmouth – Bournemouth
1045 Margate – Brighton – Arundel – Portsmouth
1830 Brighton – Bognor Regis – Portsmouth – Bournemouth
1545 Folkestone – Brighton – Bognor Regis – Portsmouth
1530 Margate – Brighton

Eastbound journeys:
0900 Brighton – Margate
0800 Portsmouth – Bognor Regis – Brighton – Margate
0930 Portsmouth – Bognor Regis – Brighton – Margate
1110 Portsmouth – Arundel – Brighton – Margate
0815 Bournemouth – Portsmouth – Bognor Regis – Brighton
1015 Bournemouth – Portsmouth – Arundel – Brighton *(Saturdays only)*
1330 Portsmouth – Arundel – Brighton – Folkestone
1015 Bournemouth – Portsmouth – Bognor Regis – Brighton
1200 Bournemouth – Portsmouth – Bognor Regis – Brighton
1500 Portsmouth – Arundel – Brighton – Folkestone
1445 Bournemouth – Portsmouth Arundel – Brighton *(Saturdays only)*
1445 Bournemouth – Portsmouth – Bognor Regis – Brighton
1745 Portsmouth – Arundel – Brighton – Hastings
1545 Bournemouth – Portsmouth – Arundel – Brighton
1830 Portsmouth – Arundel – Brighton – Eastbourne
1730 Bournemouth – Portsmouth – Bognor Regis – Brighton
1845 Bournemouth – Portsmouth
2030 Bournemouth – Portsmouth

At Bournemouth connections were available with Royal Blue services to Salisbury, Bath, Bristol, Exeter, Torquay, Plymouth, Weston-Super-Mare and Ilfracombe. The through coaches across Portsmouth ceased with the Autumn timetable as from **21 September 1936** and just three journeys each way were offered for the winter starting on **12 October 1936** including two each way serving Margate.

From this point until summer 1939 it was normal for the service to consist of 18 journeys each way in high summer – roughly early July to mid-September – with several through journeys between Brighton and Bournemouth. Six journeys on the eastern section of route were sufficient for the spring and autumn whilst winter was generally three or four journeys each way. Since Elliott Bros sale in early 1935 the South Coast Express timetable leaflets had shown Western National as the operator at the Bournemouth end of the route despite their

SOUTHDOWN MOTOR SERVICES, Ltd.

EXPRESS SERVICE

Brighton, Worthing, Bognor, Portsmouth, Southampton, Bournemouth
Commencing SATURDAY, 11th JULY, 1936

Timetable: Brighton, Bognor, Portsmouth, Southampton & Bournemouth (Week Days and Sundays, 11th July to 20th September, 1936)

Timetable: Bournemouth, Southampton, Portsmouth, Bognor and Brighton (Week Days and Sundays, 11th July to 20th September, 1936)

coaches used on the service being in Royal Blue livery. From 14 April 1938 leaflets were sensibly altered to show the operating name as Royal Blue Coaches.

Starting on 1 May 1939 the South Coast Express terminal in Eastbourne was transferred from Pevensey Road Bus Station to Cavendish Place Coach Station. The attention of drivers was directed to the limited clearance at the Susans Road entrance being only 11 feet 3 inches and the need to take special care when bulky luggage was being carried in the roof luggage container! The last full summer timetable for seven years began on **8 July 1939** and was due to end on 17 September. It contained the usual 18 journeys each way and through running across Portsmouth although this was certainly not a service designed for anyone in a hurry as the overall journey time from Margate to Portsmouth was 9 hours 31 minutes eastbound and 9 hours 15 minutes westbound. The through fare from Margate to Portsmouth was 14/- (70p) Single and 22/- (£1.10) Period Return and to Bournemouth was 18/6 (93p) Single and 30/- (£1.50) Period Return. At Bournemouth connections were shown for Royal Blue services onward to Weymouth, Exeter, Torquay and Plymouth, Yeovil, Taunton and Ilfracombe. At Hyde Park Road connections were made with Associated Motorways services to Salisbury, Bath, Bristol, Devizes, Swindon, Stroud and Cheltenham.

A total of 18 coaches were required to operate the full summer service of which 11 were provided by Southdown. One was based at

South Coast Express Coaches :							
MARGATE (The Parade) ... dep.	...	...	...	...	8 30	11 30	
Broadstairs (Pierremont Hall) ,,	...	...	...	...	8 43	11 43	
Ramsgate (Harbour Parade) ... ,,	...	...	...	...	8 53	11 53	
Sandwich (Cattle Market) ,,	...	...	...	...	9 15	12 15	
Deal (The Parade) ... ... ,,	...	...	...	...	9 33	12 33	
DOVER (Market Square) ... ,,	...	...	...	...	9 58	12 58	
FOLKESTONE (Sandgate Road) ,,	...	...	...	...	10 25	1 25	
Hythe (Red Lion Square) ... ,,	...	...	...	...	10 39	1 39	
Dymchurch (Bus Station) ... arr.	...	...	...	...	10 53	1 53	
Dymchurch (Bus Station) ... dep.	...	...	...	...	11 1	2 1	
New Romney (Ship) ... ,,	...	...	...	...	11 11	2 11	
Rye (Company's Office) ... ,,	...	...	...	...	11 44	2 44	
Winchelsea (New Inn) ... ,,	...	...	...	...	11 52	2 52	
Hastings (White Rock) ... arr.	...	...	...	...	12 19	3 19	
HASTINGS (White Rock) ... dep.	...	...	...	...	12 20	4 30	
Bexhill (Marina) ... ,,	...	...	...	...	12 40	4 30	
Eastbourne (Pevensey Road) ,, arr.	...	...	...	...	1 9	4 59	
EASTBOURNE (Pevensey Rd.) dep.	...	...	...	...	1 55	5 0	
Seaford (Clinton Place) ... ,,	...	...	8z20	...	2 20	5 25	
Newhaven (Bridge Street) ... ,,	...	...	8z35	...	2 30	5 35	
Peacehaven (South Coast Road) ,,	...	...	8z48	...	2 40	5 45	
Brighton (Steine Street) ... arr.	...	...	9z 9	...	2 54	6 0	
BRIGHTON (Steine Street) dep.	...	...	9 15	...	3 0	6z 5	
Hove (7 St. Aubyns Gardens) ,,	...	...	9 20	...	3 5	6z14	
Shoreham (High Street) ... ,,	...	...	9 31	...	3 16	6z35	
Worthing (Marine Parade) ... ,,	...	...	9 45	...	3 30	6z57	
Littlehampton (East Street) ,,	...	...	10 15	...	4 0	...	
Arundel (The Square) ... ,,	...	...	* *	...	* *	...	
Bognor (Coach Station, High St.) ,,	...	...	10 40	...	4 25	...	
CHICHESTER (West Street) ,,	...	...	11 5	...	4 50	...	
Emsworth (The Square) ... ,,	...	...	11 23	...	5 8	...	
Havant (High Street) ... ,,	...	...	11 30	...	5 15	...	
Hilsea (Southdown Station) ... arr.	...	...	11§45	...	5§30	...	
PORTSMOUTH (Hyde Pk. Rd.) ,,	...	...	12 0	...	5 45	...	

Western National Royal Blue Coaches :							
PORTSMOUTH (Hyde Pk.Rd) dep	8 20	11 45	2 0	6 0	...		
Hilsea (Southdown Station) ,,	8 35	12§ 0	2 15	6§15	...		
Fareham (Bus Stn., West St.) ,,	8 43	12 13	2 28	6 28	...		
Wickham ... ... ,,	...	12 23	2 38	6 38	...		
Bursledon ... ... ,,	9 4	...	...	...	...		
Southampton (Grosvenor Sq) ,,	9 24	12 55	3 10	7 10	...		
Lyndhurst (Imp. Motor Wks.) ,,	9 46	1 17	3 30	7 32	...		
BOURNEMOUTH (Sq.Stn.) ,,	10 47	2 18	4 31	8 33	...		

	PORTSMOUTH (Hyde Pk.Rd) dep	7 53	12 55	...	...	...		
Motorways	Hilsea (Southdown Station) ,,	8 8	1 10	...	...	...		
	Salisbury (Market Place) ... arr.	10 3	3 9	...	...	...		
	Bath (Riverside Car Park) ,,	11 50	5 25	...	...	...		
	Bristol (Prince Street) ,,	12 30	6 4	...	...	...		

	PORTSMOUTH (Hyde Pk.Rd) dep	7 53	12 55	...	...	...		
Associated	Hilsea (Southdown Station) ,,	8 8	1 10	...	...	...		
	Devizes (Chandler's Garage) arr.	...	4 20	...	...	...		
	Swindon (Regent Circus) ... ,,	11 36	5 28	...	...	...		
	Stroud (King Street Parade) ,,	1 6	6 39	...	...	...		
	Cheltenham (Motor Coach Stn.) ,,	1 15	7 32	...	...	...		

BOURNEMOUTH (Square Stn) dep	11 0	2 40	4A50	...			
Exeter (Paul Street) ... arr.	3 10	6 36	8B36	...			
Torquay (New Town Hall) ,,	4 39	8 15	10C8	...			
Plymouth (Sherwell Arcade) ,,	6 16	8 45	...	...			

BOURNEMOUTH (Square Stn) dep.	...	2 35	6S 0	...			
Yeovil (Vincent's Garage) ... arr.	...	4 46	8S11	...			
Taunton (Billet St. Coach Station) ,,	...	6 17	9S43	...			

BOURNEMOUTH (Square Stn) dep.	...	2 35	...	...			
Ilfracombe (Cleave Ho Wilder Rd.) arr.	...	9 30	...	...			

BOURNEMOUTH (Square Stn) dep.	...	2 50	...	...			
Weymouth (Edward Street) ... arr.	...	4 40	...	...			

A—Operates 15 minutes earlier from 7th Nov. to 16th Dec., and from 2nd Jan. to 2nd April.
B—Operated at 8.58 p.m. by Southern National and Devon General Joint Service No. 42 from 7th Nov. to 16th Dec., and from 2nd Jan. to 2nd April.
C—Operated by Devon General, Service No. 46.

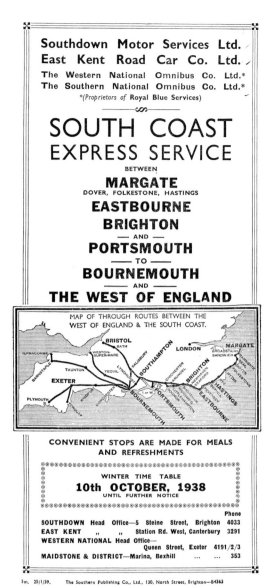

Southdown Motor Services Ltd.
East Kent Road Car Co. Ltd.
The Western National Omnibus Co. Ltd.*
The Southern National Omnibus Co. Ltd.*
*(Proprietors of Royal Blue Services)

SOUTH COAST EXPRESS SERVICE

BETWEEN

MARGATE
DOVER, FOLKESTONE, HASTINGS

EASTBOURNE
BRIGHTON
— AND —
PORTSMOUTH
TO
BOURNEMOUTH
— AND —
THE WEST OF ENGLAND

MAP OF THROUGH ROUTES BETWEEN THE WEST OF ENGLAND & THE SOUTH COAST.

CONVENIENT STOPS ARE MADE FOR MEALS AND REFRESHMENTS

WINTER TIME TABLE
10th OCTOBER, 1938
UNTIL FURTHER NOTICE

			Phone
SOUTHDOWN Head Office—5 Steine Street, Brighton			4033
EAST KENT ,, ,, Station Rd. West, Canterbury			3291
WESTERN NATIONAL Head Office—			
Queen Street, Exeter			4191/2/3
MAIDSTONE & DISTRICT—Marina, Bexhill			353

3m. 25/1/39. The Southern Publishing Co., Ltd., 130, North Street, Brighton—B4363

Far left This leaflet shows the westbound winter service which commenced on 10 October 1938. All services west of Portsmouth were run by Royal Blue in winter and passengers travelling across Portsmouth were required to change coaches at Hilsea. This proved to be last winter timetable until 1946 as the service east of Portsmouth was completely withdrawn on 4 September 1939.

The cover design eventually standardised on this format with dark blue print but the Western/Southern National names varied. This was despite the fact that their coaches used on these services were in Royal Blue livery and only the legal owner panel – not easily observed by intending passengers – would have shown the full company name!

Eastbourne, five at Brighton – including one outstationed overnight at Folkestone – and five were based at Portsmouth including one garaged overnight at Folkestone and one at Margate. East Kent provided three coaches of which one was outstationed overnight at Portsmouth and Royal Blue supplied four coaches, one of which was outstationed overnight at Portsmouth.

Following the outbreak of war the complete service east of Portsmouth was abandoned after operation on **Monday 4 September 1939** although Royal Blue continued to run between Portsmouth, Southampton and Bournemouth throughout the war latterly as a Stage Carriage facility.

Coastal Express and South Coast Express Leaflets

As with the services themselves the leaflets issued for the Coastal Express and later South Coast Express were complex although they were far advanced compared to contemporary London leaflets! The first leaflet issued for 1930 was dated 14 April 1930 and titled Coastal Express Service with Southdown and East Kent as operators. It was a four page slimline with dark green print and included full detailed timetables with departure points and times and also a faretable with through fares. Southdown times were shown between Bournemouth and Hastings, East Kent between Hastings and Margate. The summer leaflet dated 23 June 1930 was similar but expanded to six pages and showing Southdown coaches now running between Bournemouth and Dover. Also included were connections from Weymouth, Dorchester, Bridport, Exeter, Torquay and Plymouth to Bournemouth. By the timetable of 1 August 1931 through services were shown between Margate and Bournemouth without any distinction as to operator but no connecting services were included at Bournemouth.

Southdown's new Express Service from Brighton to Portsmouth starting on 1 August 1931 was shown in a separate four page leaflet in blue print but not included on the Coastal Express leaflet until 1933. Following the new agreement with Elliott Bros the new summer timetable running from 9 May to 30 September 1932 appeared in red print and now included Royal Blue connecting services. From 10 April 1933 the leaflet was titled South Coast Express.

A ten page leaflet was issued for summer 1933 in green print with a map on the front cover showing routes between the West of England and South Coast. It included timetables for early and late summer covering 1 June to 14 July and 18 September to 15 October 1933 along with high summer from 15 July to 17 September 1933. The South Coast Express services from Portsmouth to Margate included the Brighton to Portsmouth Express journeys for the first time. The Maidstone & District name was shown on the cover but it not believed that they had any part in the new joint service other than providing relief coaches when required. Apart from changes in print colour – which became mostly dark blue – this was the standard leaflet style until the outbreak of war in 1939.

OTHER SERVICES

East Grinstead to Brighton
In the summer of 1931 the Traffic Commissioners for the South Eastern Area refused to grant an Express Carriage licence application by H J Sargent of East Grinstead (trading as East Grinstead Motor Coaches) to continue operation of their coach service between Felbridge, East Grinstead and Brighton. The decision was made after a hearing which had been adjourned following a complaint regarding alleged irregularities in the issuing of tickets. Despite an existing railway service the Commissioners considered that there was need for a limited stop service between East Grinstead and Brighton, and asked Southdown and East Surrey to make applications in the next few days. Following this Southdown was licensed to provide a Sunday service between East Grinstead and Brighton starting on 23 August 1931. This ran on short term licences each covering a single day's operation until 25 October 1931 departing East Grinstead, Crown at 1015 and returning from Brighton, Steine Street at 2042. The through journey time was 1 hour 40 mins with intermediate stops allowed at Ashurst Wood, Forest Row, Chelwood Gate, Danehill, Sheffield Arms, Chailey and Lewes. Unlike East Surrey, Southdown had no base in East Grinstead at this time but no record has been found of East Surrey ever running over this service or providing a weekday operation.

At a further attempt Sargent was granted a short term Express Carriage licence from East Grinstead to Brighton to operate daily from 27

October to 2 November 1931. Passengers could only be picked up at East Grinstead, Ashurst Wood or Forest Row and set down at Lewes or Brighton. Departures from East Grinstead were at 0905 and 1505 and from Brighton at 1210 and 2040. Fares to Lewes were 1/8 (9p) single and 2/6 (13p) return and to Brighton were 2/- (10p) single and 3/- (15p) return. Further short-term licences were granted from 3 to 9 November, 10 to 16 November and 17 to 23 November 1931. A full licence was then granted with additional stops allowed at Chelwood Gate, Danehill, Sheffield Green and Sheffield Park – but not Chailey which was served by Southdown – and times revised to depart East Grinstead at 0900 and 1500 on Weekdays and 1005 on Sundays returning from Brighton at 1210 and 2040 on Weekdays and 2030 on Sundays. Southdown's short-term licence for Sunday 1 November 1931 was then revoked.

As part of a number of changes taking place as a result of the formation of the London Passenger Transport Board Southdown acquired the service although other local bus services to the east of the town continued under Sargent control until after the war. Starting on **30 June 1933** the un-numbered Limited Stop service ran between BRIGHTON (STEINE STREET) and EAST GRINSTEAD (CROWN HOTEL) via Falmer, Lewes, Offham, Cooksbridge, South Common, Chailey, Sheffield Park, Danehill, Chelwood Gate, Wych Cross, Forest Row and Ashurst Wood. With a journey time of 1 hour 30 minutes there were two journeys each way daily. Coaches were

A leaflet for a single day's operation has fortunately survived although it is not known if this was repeated throughout the period whilst operating on short period licences.

SOUTHDOWN MOTOR SERVICES LTD.

Having acquired the EXPRESS SERVICE of EAST GRINSTEAD MOTOR COACHES

BETWEEN

EAST GRINSTEAD

AND

BRIGHTON

they will operate the following Service as from 30th JUNE, 1933

WEEKDAYS and SUNDAYS.

	a.m.	p.m.		noon	p.m.
EAST GRINSTEAD, The Crown	9 0	2 0	BRIGHTON, Steine St. Station	12 0	8 40
Ashurst Wood, Three Crowns	9 5	2 5	Falmer, The Swan	12 14	8 54
Forest Row, The Swan	9 10	2 10	LEWES, Co's Office, High St.	12 24	9 4
Wych Cross	9 17	2 17	Cooksbridge, Station Hotel	12 34	9 14
Chelwood Gate, Red Lion	9 22	2 22	Chailey, Post Office	12 45	9 25
Danehill, Post Office	9 28	2 28	Chailey, King's Head	12 50	9 30
Sheffield Arms	9 32	2 32	Sheffield Park Station	12 55	9 35
Sheffield Park Station	9 35	2 35	Sheffield Arms	12 58	9 38
Chailey, King's Head	9 40	2 40	Danehill, Post Office	1 2	9 42
Chailey, Post Office	9 45	2 45	Chelwood Gate, Red Lion	1 8	9 48
Cooksbridge, Station Hotel	9 56	2 56	Wych Cross	1 13	9 53
LEWES, Co's Office, High St.	10 6	3 6	Forest Row, The Swan	1 20	10 0
Falmer, The Swan	10 16	3 16	Ashurst Wood, Three Crowns	1 25	10 5
BRIGHTON, Steine St. Station	10 30	3 30	EAST GRINSTEAD, The Crown	1 30	10 10

FARE TABLE

From	To	Singl Adult	Child	Day Return Adult	Child	Period Rtn Adult	Child
East Grinstead	Sheffield Arms or Station	1/6	1/-	2/-	1/6	2/6	1/9
"	Lewes	1/8	1/3	2/6	1/9	3/-	2/-
"	Brighton	2/-	1/6	3/-	2/-	3/6	2/6
Ashurst Wood or	Sheffield Arms or Station	1/6	1/-	2/-	1/6	2/6	1/9
Forest Row	Lewes	1/8	1/3	2/6	1/9	3/-	2/-
Chelwood Gate	Brighton	2/-	1/6	3/-	2/-	3/6	2/6
"	Lewes	1/-	9d.	1/6	1/-	2/-	1/6
Danehill	Brighton	3/-	2/-	4/6	3/-	5/-	3/6
"	Lewes	1/-	9d.	1/6	1/-	2/-	1/6
Sheffield Arms or Station	Brighton	2/10	2/-	4/3	3/-	4/9	3/3
"	Lewes	1/-	9d.	1/6	1/-	2/-	1/6
Warren Villa Pillar Box	Brighton	1/6	1/-	2/6	1/9	3/-	2/-
"	Lewes	1/3	1/-	2/-	1/6	2/6	1/9
"	Brighton	2/3	1/6	3/6	2/6	4/-	2/9

BOOK YOUR SEAT IN ADVANCE
at any Southdown Office or Agent

SOUTHDOWN BOOKING OFFICES.

Lewes—174 High Street			Lewes	250
Brighton—5 Steine Street			Brighton	4033

BOOKING AGENTS.

East Grinstead—Miss E. Miller, 11 High Street	E. Grinstead	498
Ashurst Wood—Mr. Frost's Stores		
Forest Row—Castle's Stores	Forest Row	7
Chelwood Gate—Ashdown Garage	Chelwood Gate	9
Danehill—Post Office	Danehill	1
Sheffield Arms—Hotel	Danehill	46
Chailey—Chailey Motor Company	Newick	5
Chailey—Post Office	"	35

RETURN TICKETS.

Passengers booking PERIOD RETURNS are asked to state at time of booking date of return, or to give 24 hours notice, otherwise seats cannot be guaranteed.

Dogs are charged for at quarter single passenger fare each way.

Moulton (Printers) Ltd., 55-56 King Street, Brighton.   P.T.O.

Road at 0856 (via Godalming), 1126, 1411, 1811 (all via Shalford, Bramley). With a journey time of around two hours it would appear that both the Southdown and Aldershot & District buses could complete two round trips each day. Seats could be reserved in advance and a full range of Single, Day Return and Period Return tickets were available. Fares between Brighton and Horsham were marginally higher than those applying to bus service 17.

At this time the Southern Railway had lines linking Horsham with Guildford and Brighton and this new service appeared to work against the spirit of road/rail co-ordination enshrined in the 1930 Act. Certainly the Southern Railway would have strongly objected to anyone else attempting such an operation! It was seasonally withdrawn after close of service on 19 September 1933. The service ran for the same duration each summer to a similar timetable with only minor timing changes until 20 September 1938. Whilst most services were prospering by the late 1930s it did not reappear for the 1939 season although for many years Southdown bus timetables included connections at Horsham between Aldershot and District service 33 from Guildford and Southdown service 17 to Brighton and through tickets were available.

generally used on the service and local fares were often higher on this route than on parallel services and period return tickets were available. It was licensed as a Stage Carriage service from **19 May 1934** and gained the number **28** with northbound journeys from Brighton diverted via Pool Valley. Further history is included in chapter 2.

Brighton to Guildford

A new Express Service operated jointly with Aldershot & District started on **30 June 1933** between BRIGHTON (Steine Street) and GUILDFORD (Aldershot & District Garage, Woodbridge Road) via Patcham, Pyecombe, Poynings, Henfield, Cowfold, Monks Gate, Horsham Carfax, Bucks Green, Bramley and Guildford, although one journey each way operated via Godalming instead of Bramley. Four journeys were provided each way daily with departures from Brighton Steine Street at 0915, 1130, 1415 (all via Bramley, Shalford), 1815 (via Godalming) and from Guildford Woodbridge

BRIGHTON
AND
GUILDFORD

WEEKDAYS AND SUNDAYS.   TIME TABLE.

	a.m.	a.m.	p.m.	p.m.
BRIGHTON (Southdown Stn., Steine Street)	10 0	11 30	2 30	6 15
Patcham, Fountain	10 10	11 40	2 40	6 25
Pyecombe, Plough	10 16	11 46	2 46	6 31
Poynings, Cross Roads	10 21	11 51	2 51	6 36
Henfield, George	10 31	12 3	3 3	6 48
Cowfold, Post Office	10 41	12 15	3 15	7 0
Monks Gate	10 51	12 26	3 26	7 11
HORSHAM, Carfax	11 0	12 35	3 35	7 20
Broadbridge Heath	11 5	12 40	3 40	7 25
Bucks Green, Queen's Head	11 16	12 52	3 52	7 37
Hascombe Corner	11 28	1 5	4 5	7 50
Bramley, Grange Hotel	11 40	1 18	4 18	..
Shalford, Station	11 44	1 23	4 23	..
Godalming, Wharf Car Park	..	..	..	8 15
GUILDFORD (JACKSON'S GARAGE, ONSLOW STREET)	11 50	1 30	4 30	8 27
GUILDFORD (ALDERSHOT CO.'S GARAGE, WOODBRIDGE ROAD)	11 53	1 34	4 34	8 31

FARE TABLE

FROM	TO	SINGLE Adult	Child	DAY RETURN Adult	Child	PERIOD RET'N Adult	Child
BRIGHTON	Cowfold	2/3	1/3	3/-	1/6	4/-	2/-
"	Horsham	3/-	1/6	3/6	1/9	5/-	2/6
"	Bucks Green	3/6	1/9	4/9	2/6	6/6	3/3
"	Hascombe Corner	3/9	2/-	5/-	2/6	7/-	3/6
"	Bramley	4/-	2/-	5/6	2/9	7/6	3/9
"	Guildford	4/-	2/-	5/6	2/9	7/6	3/9
HENFIELD	Horsham	1/6	9d.	2/9	1/6	2/9	1/6
"	Hascombe Corner	2/9	1/6	4/-	2/-	5/-	2/6
"	Bramley	3/3	1/9	4/6	2/3	5/6	2/9
"	Guildford	3/3	1/9	4/6	2/3	6/-	3/-
COWFOLD	Hascombe Corner	2/3	1/3	3/3	1/9	4/-	2/-
"	Bramley	2/6	1/3	3/9	2/-	4/6	2/3
"	Guildford	2/9	1/6	4/-	2/-	5/-	2/6
HORSHAM	Guildford	2/3	1/3	3/3	1/9	4/-	2/-

An extract from the northbound timetable which applied during the summers between 1936 and 1938. There were minor timing alterations during the years of operation but four round trips were provided each day jointly with Aldershot & District.

Hove to Hellingly Hospital

The bus timetable for **1 January 1937** included details of a new group of services operating between various points in the Southdown area and Hellingly Hospital. Opened in 1903 as the East Sussex County Asylum, Southdown offered a network of services which catered for patients from across East Sussex including:

Hove – Brighton – Lewes – Golden Cross – Hellingly (main route)

Seaford – Eastbourne – Hellingly (appears to be a second main route)

Alfriston Cross – Berwick – Polegate – Hailsham – Hellingly (connection by 26 and 25 to Polegate)

East Grinstead – Uckfield – Hellingly (connection by service 92 to Golden Cross)

Hurstpierpoint – Hassocks – Ditchling – Lewes – Hellingly (special connection to Lewes)

Hastings – Bexhill – Herstmonceux – Hailsham – Hellingly (connection by service 15)

The new services ran every Wednesday and on the first Sunday of each month and appear to have been covered under existing Stage Carriage licences as no separate Express Carriage licence has been traced in Notices & Proceedings for this period. These services, normally worked by coaches, are included here as only return fares are quoted and all are over 1/- suggesting an Express Carriage operation.

SOUTHDOWN MOTOR SERVICES LTD.

Commencing TUESDAY, 24th AUGUST, 1937, a SPECIAL COACH will run EVERY TUESDAY to HELLINGLY HOSPITAL at the following times :—

HOVE (Company's Office)		Hellingly (Hospital)	dep. 5.15
dep. 12.40		Horsebridge ... ... „ 5.20	
Brighton (Pool Valley) „ 12.50		Golden Cross... ... arr. 5.30	
Lewes (Company's Office) „ 1.15			
Golden Cross ... arr. 1.46		Golden Cross ... dep. 5.46	
		Uckfield ... ... arr. 6.15	
East Grinstead ... dep. 12.19		East Grinstead ... „ 7.15	
Uckfield ... ... „ 1.20			
Golden Cross ... arr. 1.46		Golden Cross... ... dep. 5.30	
		Lewes (Company's Office)	
Golden Cross ... dep. 1.46		arr. 6. 0	
Horsebridge ... ... „ 1.55		Brighton (Pool Valley) „ 6.25	
Hellingly (Hospital) arr. 2. 0		**Hove** (Company's Office) „ 6.35	

RETURN FARES TO HELLINGLY

EAST GRINSTEAD.....................3/9
HOVE...3/6
BRIGHTON.................................3/6
FOREST ROW.............................3/6
CHELWOOD GATE....................3/-
MARESFIELD..............................2/6
UCKFIELD....................................2/3
LEWES...2/2
GOLDEN CROSS.........................1/6

This service is additional to that already operated

The Southern Publishing Co., Ltd., Brighton—A5768

This leaflet was issued for the additional service on Tuesdays. The connection at Golden Cross from East Grinstead was provided by existing service 92 journeys.

In August 1937 Southdown acquired from H. K. Hart of Brighton the goodwill for an excursion from Hove Station and Brighton to Hellingly Hospital limited to run on the first Sunday of each month. From 24 August 1937 Southdown added a Tuesday service from Hove with a connection from East Grinstead.

In the days when hospital visiting times were much more restricted than the present, the services operated on specified weekdays (such as alternate Wednesdays) and one or two Sundays in each month although the pattern of operation changed over the years. They continued throughout the war years and proved to be long lasting.

Hove to Darvell Hall Sanatorium

In April 1939 Southdown successfully acquired from C. R. Shorter of Brighton, who traded as Blue Bird Motor Coaches, an Express Service between Hove, Brighton and Darvell Hall Sanatorium at Robertsbridge which specialised in the treatment of patients suffering from TB. It ran on Sundays departing Hove Station at 1215 returning from Robertsbridge at 1700 and the company had been operating the service under short period licences since 8 January 1939. After picking up at Seven Dials, Preston Circus and Lewes Road/Bear Road it proceeded via Lewes, Ringmer, Blackboys, Cross-in-Hand, Heathfield and Burwash.

Starting on **9 April 1939** Southdown extended the service by also providing a link to and from Robertsbridge Station. On arrival at Darvell Hall the coach worked light to the Station and then departed at 1415 after connecting with a train from Hastings due at 1407 and one from Tunbridge Wells due at 1412. At the end of visiting the coach worked a 1625 journey from the Sanatorium to the Station to connect with the 1635 train to Hastings then ran light to the Sanatorium to provide a 1650 journey to the Station for those returning by the 1719 train to Tunbridge Wells. A fare of 3d (less than 2p) single was charged for adults on the Station journeys so this section was worked under Stage Carriage licence conditions. A day return fare from Hove cost 5/6d (28p) and coaches or 1400 class saloons were normally used on the service with conductors to collect the fares.

Starting on **16 July 1939** the service was revised beyond Heathfield to run via Punnetts Town, Woods Corner and Brightling instead of Burwash. Bus connections were introduced from Seaford, Newhaven, Haywards Heath and Chailey to Lewes and from East Grinstead and Uckfield to Heathfield or Cross-in-Hand with through fares available in advance through company offices and agents or from conductors. As a result of changes to train connections the shuttle coach from the station now departed at 1410 and returned from the Sanatorium to the station for both trains at 1640.

Services to Race Meetings

Southdown had also been granted Express Carriage licences to operate services between railway stations and racecourses in its area. All were to be operated for Race Meetings only and included:

Lewes Railway Station – Lewes Racecourse

Barnham Junction Railway Station – Fontwell Racecourse

Singleton Railway Station – Goodwood Racecourse

Chichester Railway Station – Goodwood Racecourse

Brighton Central Railway Station – Brighton Racecourse

Coach Cruises

It is generally recognised that the first long distance coach touring holiday was operated by Sussex Tourist Coaches from Worthing to Devon and Cornwall departing on 14 June 1913. Despite a few teething problems it proved a great success and attracted a lot of attention on the way. Other tours ran in 1914 to Devon and Cornwall, Wales and the Lake District but such pioneering activities were brought to an end by The Great War. Southdown ran their first coach cruise, as they preferred to call them, to North Wales in September 1922 but none operated in the following two years. The takeover of Southsea Tourist Company Ltd in 1925 included an established tour organisation and so a small

---

SOUTHDOWN MOTOR SERVICES, LTD.

Programme of Motor Coach
Holiday Tours, 1930

The Itineraries given are liable to slight alteration.
Night Accommodation is provided at the Hotels given in italics.

THREE DAYS   **Tour S**

TOUR TO THE
SHAKESPEARE COUNTRY

A tour specially suitable for those who cannot be away for a long time. Ample time is given to visit STRATFORD-ON-AVON.

STARTING ON
THURSDAYS.   June 5th and September 4th.
MONDAYS.   June 30th and July 14th.

Inclusive Cost £5 5s. 0d.

Day.   ITINERARY.
1st.   BRIGHTON, Hindhead, Reading, Dorchester, Oxford, BANBURY *(White Lion Hotel).*
2nd.   BANBURY, Stratford-on-Avon, Anne Hathaway's Cottage, Warwick, Guy's Cliffe, Kenilworth, LEAMINGTON *(Manor House Hotel).*
3rd.   LEAMINGTON, Aylesbury, Marlow, Windsor, Aldershot, Hindhead, BRIGHTON.

FOUR DAYS   **Tour W**

Tour to WYE VALLEY

This tour embraces the most beautiful river scenery, passing CHELTENHAM, GREAT MALVERN, ROSS, SYMONDS YAT, TINTERN ABBEY, CHEPSTOW, GLOUCESTER, BATH and STONEHENGE.

STARTING ON
MONDAYS.   May 12th, June 2nd, June 23rd and July 7th.
TUESDAY.   June 10th.
WEDNESDAYS.   August 27th and September 17th.

Inclusive Cost £7 5s. 0d.

Day.   ITINERARY.
1st.   BRIGHTON, Chichester, Cosham, Winchester, Andover, Swindon, Cricklade, Cirencester, CHELTENHAM *(Queens Hotel).*
2nd.   CHELTENHAM, Tewkesbury, Great Malvern, Ross, Monmouth, TINTERN *(Beaufort Arms).*
3rd.   TINTERN, Chepstow, Forest of Dean, Gloucester, Stroud, BATH *(Pulteney Hotel).*
4th.   BATH, Devizes, Stonehenge, Salisbury, Winchester, Fareham, Cosham, BRIGHTON.

A couple of shorter tours from the 1930 programme. Note the modest distances travelled each day!

New in 1928, car 480 (UF 3080) was one of the four shorter Tilling-Stevens Express B9BL lorry type chassis fitted with luxurious 20-seat rear entrance Harrington bodies which became known as Devon Tourers as they were able to cope with narrow bridges and steep hills in the South West. It is seen here picking up passengers at Worthing on a tour from Brighton to the Wye Valley. *Alan Lambert Collection*

programme was offered that year with a full range of three, seven, ten and fourteen day coach tours starting in 1926.

In 1930 the company was asked by American Express, Frames Tours and Dean & Dawson to arrange a programme of tours starting and finishing in London which was clearly intended for incoming tourists. Following competition from Elliott Bros of Bournemouth on the Coastal Express Service a further programme of tours was planned from Bournemouth. Southdown were also successful in operating an Easter Tour for the first time. By summer 1930 the programme had been expanded and the following coach cruises were being offered:

SHAKESPEARE'S COUNTRY	3 days	£5.5.0 (£5.25)
WYE VALLEY	4 days	£7.5.0 (£7.25)
NORTH & SOUTH DEVON	6 days	£10.10.0 (£10.50)
NORTH & SOUTH DEVON	7 days	£11.11.0 (£11.55)
NORTH WALES	6 days	£11.0.0 (£11)
LANDS END	9 days	£15.10.0 (£15.50)
LAKE DISTRICT	10 days	£17.0.0 (£17)
YORKSHIRE & DERBYSHIRE	9 days	£15.15.0 (£15.75)
YORKSHIRE & DERBYSHIRE	10 days	£17.0.0 (£17)
SCOTTISH HIGHLANDS	17 days	£28.15.0 (£28.75)
SCOTTISH HIGHLANDS	19 days	£32.15.0 (£32.75)

In March 1932 Southdown acquired the coach business of Chapman & Sons (Eastbourne) Ltd which had built up the largest fleet of charabancs in the resort. The company had commenced operating holiday tours by coach in 1914 and enjoyed a very good reputation. Despite the vehicle standards of the day and the poor state of many roads some ambitious tours were being offered to Scotland and Wales by 1920 and even France and Switzerland were included in the programme. The business expanded through the 1920s and by Easter 1925 the fleet consisted of 37 Dennis charabancs and tours to Italy and the north and west of Ireland had been added with over 100,000 passengers being carried each year. Chapman's business had already established a lucrative London departure point for its tours which helped to attract foreign travellers. They also had a London office at 17 Ebury Street, SW1 close to Victoria. In 1932 Southdown acquired the goodwill of the business and certain leasehold premises in Eastbourne and London along with 44 coaches helping to substantially expand their coaching operations in Eastbourne along with the Coach Cruise programme. Southdown even advertised its tours using the offshore Radio Normandy Broadcasting Station in 1932 prompting Brighton Corporation to thank the company for the publicity which the resort had enjoyed.

The front cover of Chapman's 1932 brochure which has been overprinted following the takeover by Southdown.

In 1930 Southdown started to take delivery of new Leyland Lioness coaches to update and expand their fleet of touring coaches. Delivered in 1933, car 314 (UF 8828) was a Lioness LTB1 model with luxurious Harrington rear entrance bodywork seating just 20 in 2+1 layout. The appearance of these vehicles changed over the years as they were rebuilt with an electrically operated folding sunroof and cove windows in 1937. After wartime storage car 314 was renumbered to 1814 and returned to touring duties after the war. It was further modified with the entrance door moved from the rear to centre in 1948 before withdrawal in 1952.
Alan Lambert Collection

Following the takeover of Chapman & Sons the programme for 1933 commencing at Easter was even more ambitious with a choice of four tours to Scotland and a new 20 day holiday to John o' Groat's costing £30 – a sum equivalent to well over 10 weeks' wages for most ordinary working people at this time! Southdown's coach cruises now covered the country from Lands End to John O'Groats stopping overnight only in first class hotels. With a dedicated fleet of modern Leyland Lioness and Cub coaches they cruised at a leisurely average speed of 22 mph covering no more than 100 miles per day and the drivers were chosen from among the best of the long serving employees and wore a chauffeur's uniform.

By 1934 Southdown had become the largest operator of long distance coach tours in Great Britain and, as tension increased across continental Europe in the late thirties, many travellers accustomed to foreign travel chose coach cruising in Britain providing Southdown with its best year so far in 1939. For the last summer season before the war the programme of cruises started with four Easter tours in April and then ran from the middle of May until late September with a final 'Autumn' departure on 2 October at a specially reduced rate. Tours departed from either London or Brighton but a few travelling northbound served both and included the following destinations:

Car 319 (CUF 319) was one of six Leyland Tigress RLTB3 models with luxurious Burlingham 20-seat bodywork which joined the fleet for the 1936 season of Coach Cruises. They were fitted with an electrically operated folding sunroof and cove windows. This view shows the roof in the open position and also the wrap around rear corner windows. Despite very low mileages following wartime storage all were withdrawn in 1952 by which time modern underfloor engined coaches rendered these fine vehicles obsolete in the eyes of the travelling public. A further image of car 319 appears in chapter 4. *Alan Lambert Collection*

WYE VALLEY	3 days	£5.5.0 (£5.25)
PEAK DISTRICT	4 days	£7.5.0 (£7.25)
WYE VALLEY	4 days	£7.5.0 (£7.25)
NORTH & SOUTH DEVON	6 days	£11.0.0 (£11)
NORTH WALES	6 days	£11.0.0 (£11)
DEVON & CORNWALL	7 days	£13.0.0 (£13)
WYE VALLEY & NORTH WALES	7 days	£13.0.0 (£13)
DEVON & CORNWALL	8 days	£15.0.0 (£15)
LAKE DISTRICT	10 days	£18.0.0 (£18)
YORKSHIRE & DERBYSHIRE	10 days	£17.10.0 (£17.50)
SCOTLAND	12 days	£23.0.0 (£23)
LAKES & SCOTLAND	12 days	£25.0.0 (£25)
WALES, DEVON & CORNWALL	14 days	£26.0.0 (£26)
SCOTTISH (John O'Groats)	15 days	£28.0.0 (£28)
SCOTTISH HIGHLANDS	15 days	£28.0.0 (£28)

The outbreak of war on 3 September 1939 probably caused the cancellation of late season tours including the last departure on 2 October.

Tours & Excursions

Along the promenades of the South Coast from Southsea to Eastbourne demand for coach excursions was so great in the 1930s that the most favoured places on the stands were often allocated by rotation to operators according to the size of fleet. In addition to printed leaflets Southdown advertised its trips by attractively written blackboards placed beside the well-presented coaches with smartly uniformed drivers on hand to assist with enquiries from the passing crowds. Booking kiosks were

The front cover of Southdown's last prewar brochure featuring the picturesque village of Clovelly in North Devon. The programme proved very successful thanks partly to the deteriorating political situation in parts of Europe which made travel abroad less attractive.

Through
ENGLAND
SCOTLAND
AND
WALES
by

SOUTHDOWN
— MOTOR SERVICES LTD. —
COACH CRUISING HOLIDAYS 1939

Car 728 (UF 5831) is a Tilling-Stevens Express B10B2 new in 1929 but rebodied by Harrington in 1934. The new bodies seated 30 and as normal with Southdown a rear entrance was specified. Along with many other Tilling-Stevens buses and coaches in the fleet it was requisitioned by the Military Authorities in summer 1940. Some, including car 728, enjoyed a further period of service after the war although none returned to Southdown. *Alan Lambert Collection*

included Ascot, Brighton with special service and enclosure, Epsom including The Derby with a special package, Folkestone, Fontwell, Gatwick, Goodwood, Hurst Park, Kempton Park, Lewes, Lingfield Park, Plumpton, Sandown Park and Windsor. In 1934 the company reported that 154 vehicles attended The Derby meeting at Epsom and 59 at Royal Ascot.

It might be thought that taking coach parties to Britain's crumbling stately homes and gardens was very much a post-war idea but Southdown were featuring many in their 1930s programme of tours. Among some familiar names were Arundel Castle, Battle Abbey, Beaulieu Abbey & Brockenhurst, Cowdray Park & Midhurst, Goodwood House, Longleat House, Michelham Priory, Petworth House and Windsor Castle.

An afternoon drive by coach was an important part of the day for many holidaymakers and even day trippers of the period. At Brighton, especially, a very impressive line up of coaches along Madeira Drive would be offering a bewildering choice of trips to local beauty spots, neighbouring seaside resorts and places of interest. Obviously

conveniently sited on most of the popular sea front promenades including Southsea, Littlehampton, Brighton and Eastbourne and there was an amazing choice of trips on offer. The examples listed below are from Brighton but all the resorts enjoyed a varied range of excursions.

Among the most ambitious were the Long Day Tours which included a trip to Cheddar Caves stopping for lunch and sightseeing in Wells as well as a tea stop in Salisbury for a fare of 25/- (£1.25). At a time when even a dual carriageway was a novelty on Britain's roads and most towns had not been by-passed the coach left Brighton at 0700 and returned about 2300! Other long tours in the same direction included Marlborough & Savernake Forest at a cost of 21/- (£1.05) and Wookey Hole & Cheddar Gorge. The furthest west along the coast coaches reached was on a tour to Swanage, Corfe Castle & Wareham at a fare of 22/6 (£1.13).

Among the Special Day Tours was a popular trip to Southampton Docks to view the liners with actual visiting ships listed in the programme as part of the attraction. The Isle of Wight tour cost 13/6 (68p) including first class travel on the ferry from Portsmouth to Ryde and an afternoon tour by coach via Ventnor and Blackgang to Alum Bay. Also popular were the Road & River Tours which included travelling by Salter's river steamers from Windsor to Kingston or Henley to Windsor.

The range of day tours included such diverse attractions as Bournemouth, Chislehurst Caves, Frensham Ponds, Lyndhurst and New Forest, Rochester, Stonehenge & Romsey Abbey, Salisbury & Winchester Cathedrals, Winchelsea & Rye and Whipsnade Zoo & Park. Special Events were also very popular and included Aldershot Tattoo, Portsmouth Navy Week, Royal Air Force display at Hendon and the Southdown Hunt Point to Point Steeplechases at Plumpton.

In the 1930s before on line gambling and High Street betting shops coach operators served all the local Race Meetings. Southdown's programme

Just some of the Excursions and Tours available from Brighton in 1936.

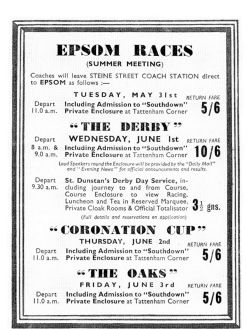

The Epsom summer programme was very popular and Southdown offered a full range of travel opportunities. Note the special package priced in guineas – indicating perhaps that 'drunken riff-raff' was most unwelcome!

Southdown offered a comprehensive range of Excursions from almost all the towns and villages in its operating area. Seen on a trip to Dicker Pottery just north of Hailsham is car 1135 (CCD 735), a Leyland Tiger TS7 with Beadle rear entrance body incorporating a folding sunroof and roof luggage rack. For the return journey the front board would normally be reversed to show the starting point which aided passengers when several Southdown coaches were parked together. *C.F.Klapper, Omnibus Society*

In 1938 Southdown took delivery of its last four Cub coaches. Car 58 (EUF 558) was a Leyland Cub KPZ4 model with Harrington 20-seat body and is seen here at Brighton before setting out on an afternoon drive to Tunbridge Wells. These were versatile coaches that could be found on all kinds of coaching duties until their sale at the end of the 1956 season. *A.B.Cross*

The last batch of prewar Tigers arrived between May and July 1939 and were arguably the most attractive of all. Intended for use on excursions some unfortunately only saw a few weeks in service before the outbreak of war curtailed such activities. Car 1217 (FUF 317) was one of fourteen Leyland Tiger TS8s with Harrington 32-seat bodies to a design developed from that carried by car 1212 delivered a year earlier. After the war several were converted to 21-seat touring coaches to augment the ageing fleet of Lioness and Tigress vehicles and the last was not withdrawn until August 1957. *Alan Lambert Collection*

Car 1071 (UF 8841) was a Leyland Tiger TS4 with Harrington 32-seat rear entrance coach body new in June 1932. It was unusual in being fitted with a full length roof luggage rack to carry band instruments. In addition six rows of seats could be easily removed to allow heavy luggage to be carried inside the coach. At least one such vehicle was retained in the Southdown fleet until the 1950s. Car 1071 was requisitioned by the Military Authorities in July 1940 and later operated by several coach firms until June 1950. *Alan Lambert Collection*

these varied from resort to resort as most travelled fairly short mileages but all would include a tea stop. The Dicker Circular visited Dicker Pottery and had tea at Thornwell Tea Gardens, long since gone. The Horeham Road Circular visited the village of Waldron and took tea in the old Oast House of Horeham Manor while the Chanctonbury Ring & Long Furlong excursion stopped for tea at High Salvington and returned via Worthing. Some went further afield to Ashdown Forest, Hindhead, Reigate, Boxhill & Dorking or Tunbridge Wells but places such as Alfriston, Amberley, Eastbourne & Beachy Head or Wannock Tea Gardens remained popular throughout the 1930s. Many of the more adventurous travellers opted for a Mystery Tour but under the new Act the routes of such tours had to be licensed in the normal way although some enterprising coach drivers no doubt had more lucrative ideas of their own!

In addition the company ran a varied programme of Morning and Evening Drives – often sold as Mystery Tours – which were operated more according to weather and demand. On Summer Saturdays only a very limited Day Tour programme would be available as coaches were required for use on the Express Services and most holidaymakers were anyway arriving or departing on what was then a fairly inflexible changeover day. After the passing of the 1930 Act Southdown acquired many rival operators

and expanded their Excursion and Tour programmes. Details are included in Appendix 4.

The outbreak of war on 3 September 1939 and subsequent introduction of fuel rationing brought a drastic reduction in the number of excursions and tours that could be offered although they were not totally banned at this time.

Private Hire and Contracts

During the 1930s Southdown had a large fleet of coaches and buses of varying types and sizes as well as experienced and courteous uniformed drivers allowing it to provide a high quality service to the most prestigious and discerning of private hire customers. The dramatic improvement in both comfort and reliability of modern coaches in the 1930s along with better roads boosted the demand for travel including party outings which became very popular especially through the summer months. At a time when few had their own car, many companies had staff outings and all kinds of clubs and societies, large and small wanted to enjoy a day out together. To suit their varied requirements Southdown could offer them a choice ranging from a fleet of Leyland Tiger coaches to a single 20-seat Leyland Cub. Quotations were provided by the local area offices which were considered to be more in touch with local needs and probably aware of the local competition. Some private hire business, unfortunately, tended to attract rowdy groups which led to particular problems at the new Road Houses springing up along the main roads from London although it seems unlikely that Southdown would have tolerated such behaviour by its clients!

Prior to the introduction of the Road Traffic Act 1930 the operation of private hire work undertaken by most bus and coach operators was largely unregulated. A price was agreed between the hirer and operator and the exact manner in which the money was paid was of little concern as long as it was paid! The new Act sought to define how this sector would work in future and a Contract Carriage Licence was required to cover those motor vehicles carrying passengers

for hire or reward under a contract for the use of the vehicle as a whole at a fixed or agreed rate. This described in legal terms the nature of a typical private hire operation. It is likely that many smaller operators of the day who were unused to such jargon and not involved with running Stage or Express Carriages carried on just as they always had done collecting payments from a local person or even from among those travelling. But problems started to arise over how parties were brought together, if it was advertised and whether the organiser was entitled to have a free ride!

During 1933 and with most of the initial licensing of Stage and Express services out of the way both the Southern and West Midland Traffic Commissioners turned their attention to Contract Carriages. Eventually, they formulated a most unwieldy scheme for the issue of special Road Services Licences to cover pre-booked parties where passengers were carried for separate payments. This was presumably to distinguish from, say, a staff outing where the company itself paid for the hire. Applicants would have to produce evidence to prove the need for a proposed service and backing licences were required if necessary. One picking up point was permitted within a radius of four miles of the starting point and no advertising to the general public was allowed. An inclusive return fare must be charged which could not be less than the minimum shown on the schedule approved under the licence. The total sum of the fares calculated in accordance with the number of seats occupied had to be paid to the operator without any deduction. Clearly the Commissioners had not the slightest idea how the private hire market worked in practice!

A test case involving Elliott Bros of Bournemouth was heard by the Traffic Commissioners for the Southern area which despite great opposition from operators, including Southdown, was granted. In January 1934 the Minister announced plans to alleviate the difficulties with a so called 'simplified' procedure which involved separate applications for each individual hire! Applications for one day licences would be listed in tabular form in Notices and Proceedings including the date of the service, the name of the operator, terminal points and return fare. Given the many thousands of coaches operating on Private Hire at summer weekends the scale of the task was huge. It would also have prevented any last minute bookings and raised more objections in the Traffic Courts.

Problems continued and later in 1934 the regulations were changed by redefining the functions of the Contract Carriage. The organiser must still not be remunerated for their role in bringing the party together and the trip must not be advertised to the general public but there was no longer the need to make separate application for each private hire operation undertaken.

It specifically excluded operations such as a regular works contract which would still require a Road Service Licence. Meanwhile, it seems likely that the small companies specialising in local Private Hire carried on just as they always had done.

Given that Southdown had enthusiastically embraced the Road Traffic Act and fought hard in the Traffic Courts to protect its operations from what it considered unnecessary competition it must have been somewhat embarrassing to be involved, along with the organiser, in a prosecution by the Metropolitan Traffic Commissioner for Contract Carriage offences! The case involved a trip from Horsham to the Ford works at Dagenham with the hearing taking place at Horsham Sessions. The four coaches which had been hired from Southdown travelled from Horsham to Westminster Pier where the party, who were charged 15s (75p) each, transferred to a river steamer to complete the journey. The trip had certainly been advertised but the organiser's defence was that he thought it was Southdown's responsibility to ascertain whether a licence was required. Payment to Southdown was made in a lump sum and the company was under the impression from past experience of similar trips that it was a works outing. After lengthy legal arguments the case against the company was dismissed and the organiser fined £1.

But, the dismissal was challenged by an examiner for the South Eastern Traffic Area, in a King's Bench Divisional Court who submitted that the company had left the matter to chance and had been guilty of 'permitting' the offence. Fortunately for Southdown the Court dismissed the appeal, with costs, although it can be imagined that for some time afterwards prospective hirers would be questioned in some detail about the nature of their planned outings! No doubt Conditions of Hire were also closely scrutinised. The operation of normal Private Hire work was soon curtailed after the outbreak of war in September 1939 as more important uses were found for the coach fleet.

Delivered in July 1933 car 1 (ACD 101) was one of two Leyland Cubs with Harrington 14-seat bodywork for use on Southdown's Coach Cruises to Devon. It was fitted with luxurious 2+1 seating and is seen here in Bognor High Street close to the company's Bus and Coach Station on Private Hire duties. It can easily be imagined that only thoroughly vetted groups were permitted to hire such vehicles! They retained their folding canvas roofs to the end which came in June 1953 when they were sold for scrap. J.E.Cull, Omnibus Society

The Fleet at 1 January 1930

At the start of the decade most of the Southdown fleet was comprised of vehicles manufactured by Tilling-Stevens or Leyland with Dennis being represented among the smaller buses and charabancs. Apart from some single deck buses and coaches delivered new from 1926 onwards the former were all of the petrol-electric type with some chassis dating back as far as 1914 although often rebodied on several occasions. Tilling-Stevens Motors of Maidstone had pioneered the petrol-electric system of transmission in which a petrol engine was connected to an electricity generator and the current produced passed to a motor which drove the rear wheels. The simpler to operate petrol-electric transmission was popular among bus drivers rather than the often primitive conventional crash gearbox of this period as few bus staff had any previous experience of driving motor vehicles. The decision by the Military Authorities in 1914 not to requisition the petrol-electrics for service in France during The Great War ensured that many enjoyed long lives with bus operators across the country. Southdown continued to take new Tilling-Stevens petrol-electrics into the fleet until 1926 but after this date only buses and coaches based on the new Express models with normal gearbox and conventional transmission were purchased.

Leyland supplied its N and G7 normal control (driver behind engine) models with a variety of single and double deck bodies and many remained in service at the start of the 1930s. Again, most had been rebodied at least once during their lifetime. A small batch of SG11 forward control (driver beside engine) single deck buses were acquired in 1925 but only five remained at the start of 1930.

A number of Dennis vehicles had entered the fleet as a result of operators selling out to Southdown although between 1927 and 1929 some normal control Dennis 30cwt chassis with 19-seat rear entrance bus bodies were bought new and originally used to compete with any small independent operators daring to spring up in the company's territory. Most were to be found at Portsmouth and Eastbourne, the former to compete with Portsmouth Corporation's attempts to extend their services to Drayton! They became

Delivered new in May 1925 car 228 (CD 9228) is a forward control Tilling-Stevens TS6 with Tilling 51-seat body seen at Brighton in June 1925 before conversion to pneumatic tyres. This batch of 14 were the first forward control vehicles to enter the Southdown fleet although the company continued to take deliveries of the TS3 normal control (driver behind engine) models. Car 228 is seen about to embark on a long run to Portsmouth on service 31 and was sold in November 1930 being outlasted by many of the older TS3 models. *Pamlin Prints*

Car 187 (CD 9817) is a forward control (driver beside the engine) Leyland SG11 with Tilling 35-seat rear entrance body new in July 1925 and seen at Uckfield in August 1926 on service 29 which linked Eastbourne and Uckfield via East Hoathly. One of a batch of seven they had a relatively short life with Southdown and car 187's body was removed in September 1930 and the chassis sold in October 1930. *Pamlin Prints*

Car 600 (UF 4300) was a Tilling-Stevens Express B10A2 with all metal body by Short Bros new in March 1929 and seen here reversing on to its stand at Pool Valley on service 11A to Worthing via Sussex Pad Hotel. It enjoyed a relatively long life with Southdown and was placed in store during 1940 but later noted in use as a tree lopper in April 1944. In March 1946 it was renumbered to 0600 in the service fleet and officially designated a tree lopper until being sold to a Showman in February 1950. *C.F.Klapper, Omnibus Society*

known to the staff as 'chasers' but after the passing of the 1930 Road Traffic Act such activities declined and most were quickly sold between 1931 and 1933. The 1928 examples had front entrances and could theoretically be used as one man operated buses on rural routes surviving until 1936 and the arrival of Leyland Cubs. All vehicles in service with Southdown at the start of 1930 had either been fitted or delivered new with pneumatic tyres.

From 1928 some interesting developments occurred. Car 600 dating from March 1929 was one of only two conventional Tilling-Stevens double deckers to be actually purchased by Southdown. Based on the forward control single deck Tilling-Stevens B10A2 lower frame chassis it had an all metal double deck open top body by Short Bros. This form of construction was well ahead of its time and it was claimed that the only

wood in the body was used for the upper deck slatted seats and the non-slip battens in the gangways. Although a further covered top model was acquired in 1932 no further orders followed and future double deck deliveries in the 1930s came exclusively from Leyland.

Southdown began taking deliveries of Leyland Titan TD1s starting in 1929 although the first 23 had rather dated looking Brush O27/24RO bodies and retained open staircases. Following a decision in 1937 to retain them for seasonal use they were to outlive many later covered top examples and all remained in stock at the outbreak of war. There followed an order for 42 Leyland Titan TD1s with standard Leyland lowbridge bodywork seating 48 of which cars 824 to 845 appeared during 1929 with the remainder delivered in 1930. By comparison with the Brush bodied examples these presented a far more

The first delivery of Leyland Titans TDIs in 1929 had 51-seat open top bodies to an outdated design by Brush although Leyland was already offering a closed top version of significantly more modern appearance. This view shows car 804 (UF 4804) before delivery. As the 1930s progressed the use of open top buses in winter became less acceptable and the whole batch was relegated to seasonal use in 1937. During the war they were fitted with temporary top covers but most returned to summer use as open top buses from 1946 until the end of the 1951 season. *Alan Lambert Collection*

Car 841 (UF 5541) was one of a batch of 42 Leyland Titan TDIs with distinctive Leyland 48-seat lowbridge bodywork delivered during 1929/30. They represented the first truly modern double deckers in the fleet and quickly helped to improve comfort and reliability. All were withdrawn and sold for further service by 1938. *Alan Lambert Collection*

modern appearance. The buses had six bay bodies of composite construction with equal width window bays and enclosed staircases. For the first time the bodywork of the upper deck was extended over the driver's cab and a destination display fitted into the front of the upper deck. A roller blind destination display was also fitted at the rear of the upper deck. The seating in the lower saloon was of the normal 2+2 layout but on the upper deck it was arranged with alternately 3 or 4 seats to each row on the nearside and an offside gangway sunken into the lower saloon.

At the end of the 1920s Southdown was in the middle of a large order for Tilling-Stevens Express B10A vehicles which became the company's standard single deck bus until the arrival of the 1400 class Tigers in 1935. Delivery started in 1928 with body orders shared between

Harrington, Short Bros and Thomas Tilling and the class eventually totalled 115. They were built to a distinctive standard rear entrance design and were, effectively, the first modern looking buses to be purchased by the company. As delivered in 1928 the first 38 did not originally have the roof mounted front screen box or roof luggage rack and these were subsequently fitted by Southdown. All later deliveries were fitted from new with elaborate roof mounted destination boxes, curved glass windows at the rear corners of the body and a rear roof luggage rack with access by a ladder at the back of the bus. Most seated 31 for normal stage carriage work but a few were specified as 'dual purpose' vehicles with 30 seats and special fittings such as arm rests between the back seats, glass topped mahogany seat back tables and curtains. There was some difficulty in getting the vehicles licensed for Express Service work because they did not have a separate emergency exit although this was rectified in later deliveries as it was a requirement of the 1930 Road Traffic Act. They were powered by a smooth running 4 cylinder engine and proved reliable in service compared to the variety of vehicles they replaced. Withdrawals started in 1936 but several survived long enough to be requisitioned by the Military Authorities in July 1940.

During 1929 Southdown took delivery of its first examples of the new lower frame Tilling-Stevens Express B10B normal control chassis for coach work. Cars 701 to 710 and 716 to 723 had 30-seat Harrington bodies with normal 2+2 seating. Cars 711 to 715 were similar but fitted with just 20 seats for use on the company's Coach Cruises, being known as Devon Tourers. All were withdrawn during the period 1936 to 1938.

Car 647 (UF 4647) was one of 45 Tilling-Stevens Express B10A2 single deck buses delivered during 1929. This example has a Short Bros 32-seat body but others were bodied by Harrington. All were delivered from new with distinctive roof mounted destination screens and roof luggage racks. Car 647 was finally sold or further service in September 1939 shortly after the outbreak of war.
Alan Lambert Collection

A further 12 chassis were fitted with Harrington charabanc bodies removed from older vehicles. All of this latter batch were rebodied with new Harrington C30R bodies in 1934 and then survived in service until being requisitioned by the Military Authorities in July 1940.

A total of 459 vehicles were in stock at 1 January 1930 of which 15 were chassis only – a detailed fleet list appears in Appendix 1.

NEW DELIVERIES FROM 1930

Double deck buses

As described in Chapter 1 many towns in the Southdown area enjoyed a boom in house construction during the 1930s and the fleet was rapidly expanding to meet the growing demand. During 1930 the replacement of the elderly buses gathered pace and Southdown completed the delivery of an order for 42 Leyland Titan TD1s with standard Leyland lowbridge bodywork which began in 1929. These appeared as cars 846 to 865. Also delivered in 1930 were cars 866-877 – a further twelve Leyland Titan TD1s but this time with standard six bay highbridge Leyland H24/24R bodywork which allowed a central gangway with 2+2 seating on the upper deck. Leyland named this version as 'Hybridge'. Most were sold in 1938 and only seven covered top Leyland bodied TD1s remained in stock at the outbreak of war. In 1943 the three remaining (cars 871/4/6) had their original bodies replaced by new Park Royal utility H30/26R bodies and were finally withdrawn from service in early 1952.

As a result of the large intake of new buses the ranks of the Tilling-Stevens petrol-electrics was thinned with some 27 being withdrawn along with some 10 Leyland N and G7 models. Tilling-Stevens at Maidstone took all the withdrawn petrol-electrics in a dealer capacity as they proved popular with Showmen after their life as buses and some of the Leyland G7 types had their bus bodies removed and replaced with lorry bodies. Cars 146, 150 and 175 remained with Southdown and became, respectively, the Portsmouth, Eastbourne and Bognor breakdown lorries being renumbered 0146, 0150 and 0175. Compared to the old fashioned open top buses that were being replaced the new Titans were a huge advance in terms of appearance, comfort and reliability.

Car 878 (UF 7078) delivered in December 1930 was the first of a batch of 55 Leyland Titan TD1s with distinctive Short Bros 48-seat highbridge bodywork featuring a Walman folding sunroof shown here in open position. The roof was opened and closed from the interior of the top deck by means of chains on each side which moved simultaneously. This vehicle was sold to Wilts & Dorset in June 1939 and rebodied by Eastern Coachworks in October 1941 surviving in this form until May 1961! *Alan Lambert Collection*

Car 892 (UF 7392) delivered in April 1931 was a Leyland Titan TD1 with Short Bros 50-seat highbridge body featuring a Walman folding sunroof. Note the 'piano front' shelf below the upper deck 'vee-front' windows. Car 892 was withdrawn in 1938 and most of the covered top TD1s new in 1930/1 were sold before the outbreak of war but a few lingered on until September 1940. Some enjoyed long lives with their new owners and many were fitted with new utility bodies during the war. *Alan Lambert Collection*

Brief mention should be made of the AEC Regent demonstrator used by Southdown for some months during 1930/1 as it proved to be the only modern AEC double-deck bus ever to run in the company's livery. It was important, though, because the vee-front Short Bros six bay bodywork formed a pattern for future orders.

At the very end of 1930 the company took delivery of one further Leyland Titan TD1 but this time fitted with a Short Bros six bay highbridge composite bodywork which was the first of 55 vehicles numbered 878 to 932 to a new design with vee-front windows to the front upper deck. A new feature of these vehicles was the deep cove panels to the roof as they were fitted with an upper deck folding 'sunshine' roof as an experiment. Many were sold in 1939 to Wilts & Dorset who urgently needed to increase their fleet in connection with the rapid expansion of Military facilities around Salisbury Plain as the prospect of war loomed. Thirteen remained in the fleet at the outbreak of war but all were sold by 1940. Car 928 passed to a dealer at Southampton in

1939 and later saw service with Viceroy Coaches of Saffron Walden, Essex before being acquired for preservation in 1959. It was moved to Amberley Museum in 1987 and has since been fully restored.

The new national Construction and Use regulations introduced under the Road Traffic Act 1930 established uniform maximum weight, length and width dimensions for passenger service vehicles and to satisfy the demand for chassis capable of carrying heavier bodywork Leyland introduced the Titan TD2 in late 1931. The new model had the same 16ft 6ins wheelbase of the TD1 but allowed for bodywork up to 26 feet long, the maximum permitted for a four wheel double decker and about a foot longer than the Titan was originally designed to carry. A larger 7.6 litre overhead camshaft engine was developed, producing 96 bhp at 2200 rpm but the short radiator remained unchanged. The new specification included a fully floating rear axle and introduced the larger rear axle hub by which the new model could be easily distinguished from the earlier TD1. The brakes were also revised to a triple-servo system and larger tyres were also fitted.

The new deliveries allowed the last of the Tilling-Stevens petrol electric double deckers to be taken out of service with some 33 being withdrawn during the year. T.S. Motors at Maidstone (as Tilling-Stevens was now known following Thomas Tilling's disposal of its shareholding in the company) took all the withdrawn petrol-electrics in a dealer capacity. In addition ten Leyland N models were withdrawn from service.

The first vehicle delivered in 1932 proved to be the company's only Tilling-Stevens or T S Motors chassis fitted with a double deck covered top body although the manufacturer no doubt hoped to renew their earlier standing in the Southdown order books. Car 700 was based on an Express Six E60A6 chassis with a Short Bros 48-seat highbridge body similar to those on cars 878-932 – except that it did not have a folding roof. It ran for most of its time with Southdown on service 17 (Brighton – Henfield – Cowfold – Horsham) and was sold early in 1936. Neighbouring Portsmouth Corporation bought a batch of ten with English Electric bodies in 1932 but soon switched to Leyland Titans – including some early diesel engined versions – for future deliveries as the smaller manufacturers struggled to attract orders.

Seen in Pool Valley, Brighton is car 700 (KJ 2919), a TSM Express Six E60A6 with Short Bros 48-seat highbridge body delivered in January 1932. It has just arrived from Horsham on service 17, its regular haunt during the four years it stayed with Southdown. Unfortunately for TSM no further orders followed and with increasing numbers of new Leyland Titans entering service 'this odd man out' was sold to a dealer in Glamorgan in January 1936. *Southdown Enthusiasts Club – Clark/Surfleet Collection*

In April and May 1932 Southdown took delivery of its final batch of Leyland Titan TD1s. Cars 933-943 were again fitted with six bay highbridge bodywork of composite construction by Short Bros and similar to car 700 with fixed roofs and vee-front windows to the top deck but seating for 50 passengers. They were to lead a much fuller life than earlier deliveries thanks to the outbreak of war in 1939. In September 1940 cars 933-6, 941 and 943 were sold for further service to Cumberland Motor Services Ltd of Whitehaven surviving in sometimes rebuilt form until 1950/1 while cars 937-940 and 942 received new utility bodywork in 1943/4. Park Royal H30/26R bodies were fitted to cars 937-939 during 1943 and metal framed East Lancs H26/26R bodies fitted in 1944 to cars 940 and 942. The Park Royal composite bodied examples were withdrawn in 1951/2 but the metal framed East Lancs bodied ones were transferred to wartime delivered Guy Arabs in 1951 and the Leyland chassis scrapped.

In the summer of 1932 Southdown took delivery of six new Leyland Titan TD2s with Short Bros H26/24R bodies to a new design without the distinctive 'piano front' shelf and vee front windows to the top deck. Numbered 944-949 they were not fitted with folding roofs. Cars 944/5 passed for further service to Cumberland Motor Services Ltd of Whitehaven in September 1940 but the remaining three were included in the wartime rebodying programme. Cars 946 and 949 gained very austere L27/24R bodies by Willowbrook in 1943 and car 947 received a metal framed East Lancs H26/26R

body in 1945. All three were withdrawn in 1951 but the East Lancs body on car 947 was transferred to a Guy Arab.

Most of the new deliveries were now intended for expansion of the service network with few of the pre-1929 double deckers remaining in service. Just a handful of Leyland N and G7 models were withdrawn leaving a small number to survive until 1934/5.

A further ten similar Leyland Titan TD2s with Short Bros H26/24R bodies followed in 1933 but this time fitted with the folding 'sunshine roof'. These became cars 950-959 and all survived in Southdown service until 1951 after being rebodied in the wartime programme of 1944/5. Cars 951, 953, 957 were fitted with L27/24R bodies by Willowbrook in 1944 while the remainder received metal framed East Lancs H26/26R bodies. All were withdrawn from Southdown service in 1951 but the East Lancs bodies were transferred to Guy Arabs.

All of the double deckers delivered between 1934 and the end of 1939 were to lead significantly longer lives than expected thanks to major rebuilds or new bodies fitted in the post war period. Between 1944 and 1946 a total of 34 prewar Titans were rebuilt and refurbished mostly retaining their original outline although some work by Beadle produced an almost new body. This work was undertaken by Beadle, Willowbrook, Saunders, Portsmouth Aviation, West Nor and Southdown. At the end of the war the company opted to rebody the majority of its older double deck buses delivered between 1934 and 1939 in order to prolong the life of the

Unfortunately it has not been possible to find a suitable image showing any of the batch of sixteen Short Bros bodied Leyland Titan TD3s in original condition with offside destination and number boxes. In the early part of the war these were panelled over as seen on car 974 (AUF 674) waiting outside Bognor Bus Station whilst on local service 55 in post war days. Rather surprisingly some of this batch, dating from 1934, were included in the final months of the postwar rebodying scheme during 1950 and three – including car 974 – survived with original bodies until withdrawal in 1953, a remarkable life for a composite double deck body of this time.
E.G.P.Masterman, Omnibus Society

chassis. This programme included 152 of the TD3, TD4 and TD5 fleet which received new highbridge bodies by East Lancs, Beadle, Saunders, Park Royal and Northern Counties between 1946 and 1950. As a result many of the prewar Titans were to continue in service until 1958-1962 with some chassis completing 25 years of service. Brief details are included with each batch.

In 1933 Leyland introduced a new Titan TD3 model similar to its immediate predecessors mechanically but with a revised, more compact front end layout which saved 6 inches in engine and cab length. The engine, radiator and driving position were all moved relative to the front axle, with the result that the steering column was more upright. This allowed the front bulkhead to be moved forward by 6 inches and permitted more passenger space and comfort in the lower saloon. The most obvious external change was to the radiator which was much deeper than before, and had parallel sides. Normally a cast plate with the name 'LEYLAND' was fixed to the top tank but Southdown substituted a plate with the company name in the familiar script style. Southdown took delivery of 16 of the new Leyland Titan TD3 chassis in 1934, to two different mechanical specifications.

Cars 960 to 963 had the 7.6 litre petrol engine with Leyland torque converter which provided the first automatic transmission for buses in Europe, and probably first in the world. The function of the converter was to multiply engine torque in much the same way as the gearing of the conventional gearbox. While it was possible to drive through the converter at all times, a direct drive was provided for higher road speeds. The driver used a single lever in place of the conventional gear lever. It had four positions: direct, converter, neutral, and reverse, and when the driver was ready to start he engaged the converter position and built up the engine revs rapidly to approximately 1200 rpm. On reaching a speed of around 20 mph he moved the lever into direct, without the need for a clutch pedal. At the time it was claimed to be ideal for city services as there was no gear changing delay and loss of acceleration as with

conventional buses. Buses with the torque converter had a small suffix letter 'c' added to their designation (TD3c) and in most cases, a 'Gearless Bus' badge, in block letter style was mounted in the lower nearside corner of the radiator grille. They could also be identified by the larger Autovac and the header tank for converter fluid situated on the bulkhead alongside the bonnet. Their performance on hilly routes and during icy road conditions was questionable and all were allocated to Worthing for town services. To reduce fuel consumption cars 960 – 963 were fitted with Leyland 8.6 litre diesel engines early in the Second World War and the torque converters were replaced with conventional gearboxes during 1946 or 1947.

Cars 964 to 975 had conventional transmission but were the first for Southdown to be fitted with Leyland's smooth running and economical 8.6 litre diesel engine (TD3). This engine was directly interchangeable with its petrol counterpart but consumed on average slightly over half the amount of fuel per mile operated as compared with the petrol equivalent. The diesel engined buses were allocated to Portsmouth where they were used on the services which climbed over Portsdown Hill. All 16 were fitted from new with Short Bros 50-seat highbridge bodies similar to those of cars 944 to 959 except that three blind boxes were fitted over the lower deck windows on both sides. As delivered cars 960 – 963 had a fixed roof but cars 964 – 975 were originally fitted with the 'folding sunshine roof'.

In the postwar rebodying programme 13 Leyland Titan TD3s received new bodies including three right at the end in 1950 at which point the Short Bros bodies were 16 years old. Withdrawal of the buses with original bodies occurred in 1953 while the rebodied examples continued in service until 1959 with the very last surviving until January 1960. Two of the TD3s have fortunately survived into preservation – car 966 with a 1949 Beadle body and car 970 with a 1946 East Lancs body.

Although most of the pre-1929 Leyland double deckers had now been withdrawn a few remained into 1934. Cars 131, 135, 145 and 151 passed to Gosport & Fareham Omnibus Company at nearby Hoeford for further service and two of the N types were to lead extended lives. Car 131 remained in service until 1944 and was then stored at the Hoeford depot only to be destroyed during the disastrous fire on 1 June 1957. Car 135 was more fortunate and after the war was restored for preservation and publicity work for Gosport & Fareham. It passed back to Southdown in January 1970 for further preservation and survives to the present time.

The final withdrawals of the Leyland N and G7 types took place in 1935 when cars 125/6, 134, 153 and 155 were taken out of service. Cars 125, 126, 134 and 155 had lorry bodies fitted and became, respectively, the Eastbourne, Bognor, Worthing and Portsmouth breakdown lorries being renumbered 0125, 0126, 0134 and 0155 in the service fleet. Cars 125 and 0134 were sold in 1940 but the other two survived in use with Southdown until after the war.

Early in 1935 Leyland further updated their Titan and Tiger models which became the TD4 and TS7 respectively. A minor front end redesign permitted more space in the lower saloon usually allowing 26 seats downstairs in the TD4s. During 1935 Southdown took delivery of 39 of the new Leyland Titan TD4 chassis to three different mechanical specifications and started a new numbering series for double deck buses. Cars 100 to 111 had the 7.6 litre petrol engine with the standard clutch and gearbox while cars 112 to 121 had the 7.6 litre petrol engine with Torque Converter (model TD4c). Finally cars 122 to 138 had conventional transmission but were fitted with the 8.6 litre diesel engine. All these buses were fitted with Short Bros bodies and the elaborate destination display front and rear together with three roller blind boxes over the lower deck windows on each side. These could not be fitted on the offside of lowbridge vehicles due to the sunken gangway. The bodies on the three batches were also to different specifications with cars 100 to 111 having 52-seat lowbridge five bay all metal bodywork. These 12 buses were the first five bay double deckers bought new by the company and the first lowbridge buses since car 865 in 1930. The other 27 buses had 50-seat composite six bay highbridge bodies. Cars 112 to 121 had fixed roof bodywork identical to cars 960 to 963, while cars 122 to 138 were the same as cars 964 to 975 and had the folding 'sunshine roof'. All the Titan TD4s with petrol engines delivered in 1935 were ultimately fitted with diesel engines but cars 112, 115, 116, 117, 119 and 121 reverted to petrol during the period they were converted to run on producer gas in 1943/4. At the end of gas operation they all regained their diesel engines. The Torque Convertors fitted to cars 112-121 were finally removed and replaced by conventional gearboxes in 1946/7.

Those buses still retaining original bodies were withdrawn between 1951 and 1953, a remarkable life for composite framed bodies of the time. Thirty of the 1935 batch received new bodies in the post war programme and the last was withdrawn in June 1961, the chassis being 26 years old at the time!

In 1936 Southdown took delivery of only a dozen double deck buses. These were again Leyland Titan TD4s with two different mechanical specifications. Cars 139 to 144 had 7.6 litre petrol engines with standard clutch and gearbox (TD4) while cars 145 to 150 had 8.6 litre diesel engines with torque converter (TD4c). All were fitted with composite six bay Beadle 52-seat bodies with the standard destination display front and rear and three roller blind boxes over the lower deck windows – nearside only on the lowbridge examples. They were the first double

After withdrawal in 1935 car 125 had its bus body removed and a lorry body fitted becoming the company's Eastbourne breakdown lorry and renumbered 0125 until withdrawal in 1940. The bus body was sold for use as a summer house near Pulborough in 1935 but rescued in 1971 and then fitted to a similar replica Leyland N chassis in 1977. The complete vehicle is now restored as car 125 and owned by the Southdown Omnibus Trust at Amberley where it is seen here in active service. The uniform worn by the Conductress is NOT standard Southdown 1930s style!! *Author's Collection*

In 1935 Southdown took delivery of 39 Leyland Titan TD4 chassis with Short Bros bodywork of both highbridge and lowbridge layout. They were to lead very long lives with the company and many were rebodied in the post war scheme. Southdown usually recorded the delivery of each new type of bus with posed shots such as car 107 (BUF 207) with lowbridge body delivered in October 1935. Its petrol engine was replaced by a diesel engine during the war but unlike most of the batch car 107 was withdrawn and broken up for spares in August 1951. *Southdown Enthusiasts Club – Clark/Surfleet Collection*

Seen at Worthing Garage is car 115 (BUF 215), a Leyland Titan TD4c with Short Bros highbridge body clearly showing its three offside screen boxes. New in May 1935 it was originally fitted with a petrol engine and Torque Converter – the radiator carries the description 'Gearless Bus'. The Torque Converter and original body were removed in October 1946 and car 215 appeared with a new Saunders body in July 1947 being finally sold in January 1961. *S.L.Poole*

Car 139 (CCD 939) was a Leyland Titan TD4 with Beadle 52-seat lowbridge bodywork delivered new in May 1936. It was originally fitted with a petrol engine although after 1936 Southdown only specified new double deckers with diesel engines. In the postwar rebodying programme car 139 received a new Northern Counties highbridge body in March 1950 and remained in the fleet until February 1961. *Alan Lambert Collection*

deck buses delivered with flared skirts and a distinctive small metal sun visor over the driver's windscreen. Cars 139 to 144 had lowbridge bodywork with normal 2+2 seating layout downstairs. On the upper deck the seats were arranged with 4 seats to each row with the offside gangway sunk into the lower saloon. Cars 145 to 150 had highbridge bodywork with the folding 'sunshine roof' – although as with other pre-war Titans these were sealed up during the war. This batch of vehicles marked the end of a number of mechanical and design features for the company. Car 144 was the last double deck bus purchased by Southdown fitted with a petrol engine and car 150 was the last delivered fitted with a 'sunshine'

sunroof and also last newly delivered with a torque converter.

Cars 139-144 were fitted with 8.6 litre diesel engines during the war and the Torque Convertors fitted to cars 145-150 were finally removed and replaced by conventional gearboxes in 1946/7. At the end of the war five of the batch were rebuilt with cars 142 and 144 surviving until 1956 and the end of lowbridge buses in the Southdown fleet. Eight of the batch received new bodies in the post-war programme and the last survived until February 1961 at which point the chassis was almost 25 years old. Car 140 with 1950 East Lancs body has fortunately survived into preservation.

Southdown took delivery of just four new double deckers in 1937, all diesel engined Leyland Titan TD5 models with Park Royal highbridge bodies similar to the Beadle examples of 1936. Car 151 (DUF 151) shows off the three nearside roller blind boxes which were a feature of Southdown deliveries in the 1930s. It was rebodied by East Lancs in June 1949 and finally sold for scrap in March 1961. *Southdown Enthusiasts Club – Clark/Surfleet Collection*

Seen laying over in West Street, Chichester whilst operating on service 52 is car 810 (UF 4810) a Leyland Titan TD1 with Brush open top body dating from 1929. Following the decision to retain these buses for summer use they could be found on a variety of operations and although service 52 was not specifically a seasonal service it would certainly have carried plenty of visitors and tourists to the beaches and holiday camps at Selsey. *Alan Lambert Collection*

During 1937 Leyland again updated their Titan range with the new TD5 design incorporating minor alterations to the chassis frames, and worm and nut steering replacing the cam and roller assembly. The new model could easily be recognised by the front chassis dumb irons which were now square rather than rounded. Based on Titan TD5 chassis with the 8.6 litre diesel engine and composite six bay 52-seat highbridge bodies by Park Royal, cars 151 to 154 were the only double deck buses delivered in 1937. The bodies were similar in outline to the Beadle examples on cars 145 to 150 and were the last Southdown vehicles delivered with the three roller blind boxes over the offside lower deck

windows. They were also the first double deckers since the TD1s of 1929 to have plain front and rear destination displays without the illuminated Southdown name. All received new bodies in the post war programme and three survived until 1961.

By 1937 the 23 open top Leyland Titan TD1s dating from 1929 would have been due for withdrawal but instead the company decided to retain them for seasonal use. In this form they gained cream upper deck panels and went on to outlive all later covered top TD1s that retained their original bodies. During the war they were fitted with temporary top covers enabling them to be used throughout the year. Most were then

converted back for use as open top vehicles and survived in summer service at Brighton, Worthing and Hayling Island until the end of the 1950 season. Fortunately car 813 was stored at Portslade after being withdrawn in 1951 and later restored by the company making occasional appearances at special events such as the Brighton Coach Rally. In July 1971 it was used on a Vintage Bus Service 100 between Brighton and Hove after full restoration. It passed into Stagecoach ownership in August 1989 when they acquired Southdown but remains in traditional livery making occasional appearances at bus rallies.

Against the background of a worsening political situation in Europe, Southdown purchased no fewer than 133 new vehicles during 1938 including a further 52 Leyland Titan TD5 double deckers. The company had now standardised the mechanical specification for its double deck buses and all the TD5s were fitted with smooth running and economical 8.6 litre diesel engines from new. Cars 155 to 180 had lowbridge

bodywork by Park Royal while cars 181 to 200 were identical but had bodywork by Beadle. Cars 201 to 205 and 209 had similar, but highbridge, bodywork by Park Royal. Fourteen of the Beadle lowbridge bodied TD5s in this batch were rebuilt by Beadle between March 1945 and April 1946 allowing many to continue running in Southdown service until the mid-1950s. After withdrawal in 1956/7 cars 181, 182, 184 and 198 had their Beadle bodies removed and breakdown tender bodies fitted becoming 0181, 0182, 0184 and 0198 in the service fleet. The latter bodies had been removed from Leyland Titan TD1s. After being withdrawn in the 1970s all four passed into preservation and survive to the present day. A total of 39 of the 1938 batch received new bodies after the war and most remained in service until 1961 with the final withdrawal of East Lancs bodied car 170 in January 1962. Two buses from the 1938 delivery have fortunately survived into preservation – car 196 with its original, but rebuilt, Beadle body and car 204 with 1949 Park Royal body.

Given that the normal lifespan for a composite construction double deck body of the time was around eight years, the year 1938 marked the start of the withdrawal of covered top Leyland Titan TD1s delivered in 1929/30. A total of 53 were taken out of service including all of the Leyland bodied batches 824-845 from 1929 along with 846-865 new in 1930 although most found ready buyers and, thanks to the war, continued in service for many years. Most passed through the dealer Milburn Motors of Glasgow who resold them to operators in Scotland. Car 873 lasted long enough to be rescued for preservation and is now owned by the Southdown Omnibus Trust at Amberley.

Seen here at Storrington Square on service 1 bound for Worthing is car 210 (FCD 510), a Leyland Titan TD5 with Park Royal 52-seat highbridge bodywork delivered new in February 1939. A new East Lancs body was fitted in February 1950 and the vehicle passed to Brighton Corporation for further service in June 1961.
Alan Lambert Collection

Car 229 (FUF 229) was a Leyland Titan TD5, part of batch of twelve with Beadle 52-seat highbridge bodywork new in July 1939 and seen here after the war in West Street, Havant heading west on service 31. Apart from the addition of a front spotlight it remains in original condition although the side screens appear to have been wound to white blanks! In the postwar rebodying programme a new East Lancs body was fitted in May 1950 and the vehicle was sold in December 1961.
Southdown Enthusiasts Club – Clark/Surfleet Collection

Car 265 (GCD 365) was a Leyland Titan TD5 with Park Royal 52-seat lowbridge bodywork new at the end of December 1939 and numerically the last of the prewar Titans. It is seen after the war in West Street in Chichester on a southbound service 59 which did not have any low bridges but interworked with other routes that did. A new East Lancs body was fitted in May 1950 and the vehicle was sold in March 1962
Southdown Enthusiasts Club – W J Haynes Collection.

In the final months before the second major European war in twenty years the company took delivery of a further 43 Leyland Titan TD5 double-deck buses Once again, all were fitted with 8.6 litre diesel engines and composite six bay 52-seat bodies similar to those purchased since 1936. As in the previous year there were three body types with cars 206, 207, 208, 210, 211, 218 to 227 and 240 to 249 having highbridge bodywork by Park Royal, while cars 228 to 239 had identical highbridge bodies by Beadle. Cars 212 to 217 had lowbridge bodies by Park Royal with the usual 4 seats to each row on the upper deck and offside gangway sunk into the lower saloon. All of the 1939 delivery were included in the post war rebodying programme and several survived into 1962. Car 248 with 1950 Park Royal body has fortunately survived into preservation.

During 1939 a large number of the remaining Leyland TD1s were withdrawn with some 39 passing to Wilts & Dorset, Salisbury to be used in connection with the transport of construction workers to the rapidly expanding military facilities in the area. At the outbreak of war only 24 covered top Leyland Titan TD1s along with 16 TD2s all with Short Bros bodywork remained in stock.

Sixteen Leyland Titan TD5s with Park Royal bodies remained on order for delivery at the outbreak of war and cars 250-265 arrived between October and December 1939 with the last four registered as from 30 December 1939. All were included in the post-war rebodying programme and all survived until at least 1961. Finally, the very last of the prewar Titans to be sold was car 257 in October 1962 some 23 years after its delivery in the early months of the war.

Car 165 (EUF 165) was one of the large batch of Leyland Titan TD5s delivered in 1938. It has a Park Royal lowbridge body and is seen on service 91 which then ran hourly between Uckfield and Eastbourne via Heathfield but did not pass under any low bridges. It received a new body by the same coachbuilder in May 1949 and survived with Southdown until withdrawal in March 1961. S.L.Poole

Lowbridge Buses

Some 70 prewar Titans were fitted with lowbridge bodies for operation on routes where railway over bridges had restricted headroom. By 1939 these were situated at:

Eastbourne, between Stone Cross and Friday Street (B2104) – services 92, 92A and 94

Lewes, Cliffe High Street – services 13, 16, 18, 20, 25 and 119

Shoreham, Old Shoreham Road (A283) – services 9, 10, 22

Due to interworking, other services such as the 15, 91 and 93 in Eastbourne regularly featured lowbridge buses although they had no physical restrictions requiring their use. During the early months of the war an 'H' or 'L' suffix was added to the fleet numbers of double deck buses in order to help identify their height in the blackout. The suffix letters continued in use after the war whilst lowbridge vehicles remained in the fleet.

Single deck buses

At the start of the 1930s Southdown was part way through an order for 115 Tilling-Stevens Express B10A vehicles with bus bodies to a distinctive design. Some 26 examples with Short B31R bodies numbered 678/80/81/86-88/90-99 and 1200-09 were delivered in 1930 all fitted with a front nearside emergency door which was about to become a requirement under the new 1930 Road Traffic Act. The new buses allowed the withdrawal of some eight petrol-electrics of which four dated from 1920 and retained their original bodies. Four of the Leyland SG11 dating from 1925 were also withdrawn during the year.

In 1931 Southdown made its final purchase of six forward control Tilling-Stevens Express B10A2 chassis with Short Bros all metal lightweight single deck rear entrance bodies. Cars 1210-1215 (later renumbered 710-715), were saloons to the standard design except that these bodies had a shorter overhang at the rear and only 26 seats. They were intended specially for use on services to Hayling Island where severe weight restrictions imposed on the timber toll bridge at Langstone did not allow the passage of fully laden normal sized buses. The new deliveries allowed most of the remaining Tilling-Stevens petrol electric single deckers to be taken out of service although five remained until 1933/4. By 1932 most of the small Dennis 30 cwt buses introduced in 1927 were sold with many having the bodies removed and the chassis fitted with lorry bodies. The advent of regulations under the 1930 Road Traffic Act meant that their original use as 'chasers' to try and deter new competitors was no longer necessary.

To provide additional capacity and expansion of the Hayling services Southdown purchased six TSM Express B39A6 saloons fitted with Short Bros 26-seat lightweight rear entrance bodies to the same style as the 1931 batch. After Thomas Tilling disposed of its shareholding in Tilling-Stevens the chassis were badged as TSM. Delivered in 1933 cars 1216 to 1221 were the very last chassis purchased new by Southdown from Tilling-Stevens/TSM ending a link from the very earliest days of the company. They were renumbered 716-721 in 1938 and along with the 1931 batch all were requisitioned for war service in July-August 1940. Ironically 1933 marked (almost) the end for the Tilling-Stevens petrol-electrics with cars 58 and 59 dating from 1914, car 72 from 1919 and car 88 from 1920 finally being withdrawn. All had been rebodied by Short

Bros in 1927/8. Few of the many and varied buses delivered in 1914 lasted more than five years in service so the long lives of these unconventional vehicles bears testimony to the Southdown maintenance of the period.

In 1934 Leyland introduced the three-axle Tiger TS6T with the suffix letter indicating that the second rear axle was undriven. Of similar mechanical specification to the TS6, this chassis had an 18ft 10in wheelbase, intended for 30 foot long bodywork with up to 43 seats. Southdown bought two TS6T chassis for its popular service 97 from Eastbourne Redoubt to the Top of Beachy Head which was considered by the Traffic Commissioners to be unsuitable for operation by double deck buses. Cars 50 and 51 had impressive 40-seat centre entrance Short Bros bodywork and were built in the style of the company's coaches with a folding 'sunshine roof', air-smoothed luggage pannier to the rear of the roof, sliding centre door and a sun visor over the driver's cab windscreen. They were renumbered to 550/1 in 1937 and the petrol engines replaced by 8.6 litre diesel engines early in the war. Following the wartime suspension of service 97 at the end of July 1940 cars 550/1 were redeployed on service 30 (Brighton–Haywards Heath–Chelwood Common). The bodies were rebuilt after the war losing the roof luggage rack and had their seating reduced to 39. They were finally withdrawn in 1952.

In March 1934 car 61, the very last of the Tilling-Stevens petrol electrics, was sold marking the end of an era dating back to the very earliest days of Southdown. It was a normal control TS3 model delivered new in March 1919 and at various times carried both double and single deck bodies until being finally rebodied by Short Bros in 1928.

Southdown acquired the business of W.H. Rayner & Son trading as the Horsham Bus Service of Barns Green as from 15 January 1935 along with a Dennis 30 cwt with Harrington B18F body – the sole surviving member of the fleet following a fire in July 1934. It became car 538 (PX 5776) and survived until October 1936 by which time new Leyland Cubs were being introduced.

A total of eleven Thornycroft buses joined the fleet when Southdown acquired the business of F. G. Tanner who traded as Denmead Queen Motor Services based at Denmead on 21 March 1935. They were new between 1927 and 1933 and numbered cars 39 to 49 – full details appear in Appendix 3. The survivors were renumbered 541-3/5-7 in 1936 after 39/40/4 were quickly withdrawn during 1935. Unlike most other acquisitions at this time which were quickly sold off, cars 545-7 survived until sale to Wilts & Dorset in July/August 1939 at a time when that company was under great pressure due to the expansion of Military camps in their area.

Until the mid-1930s Southdown had only purchased Leyland Tigers for coach work but in

Part of a batch of six buses for Hayling Island services, car 1215 (UF 7315) was a TSM Express B10A2 with lightweight Short Bros 26-seat all metal bodywork delivered in April 1931. Similar to the large batches already in service with Southdown these buses were shorter and lighter allowing them to carry a full load of holidaymakers across the weight restricted bridge to the mainland. The complete batch survived until summer 1940 when they were requisitioned by the Military Authorities. *Alan Lambert Collection*

Not quite what it seems! The original Short Bros B19R body of car 517 (UF 1517) was sold in December 1932 but discovered in a garden at Fulking in Sussex in 1949. It was acquired for preservation in 1982 and taken to the Amberley Museum where it was eventually fitted to a Dennis 30 cwt chassis similar to the original and fully restored. It is seen here operating around the roads at Amberley displaying route details for service 81 which in the 1930s wandered across Sussex from Haywards Heath to Billingshurst through mostly very remote countryside. *Author's Collection*

Car 51 (AUF 851) is one of two Leyland Tiger TS6Ts with Short Bros 40-seat 'coach style' centre entrance bodywork complete with folding sunroof and roof luggage rack. They were delivered new in August 1934 for operation on the busy service 97 between Eastbourne and the top of Beachy Head and were unusual in carrying script fleet names normally found only on coaches. They also carried coach style livery with dark green roofs rather than the cream applied to other saloons of this period. *J.F. Higham*

In 1935 Southdown chose Leyland Tigers for its new fleet of single deck buses when the first 24 of what generally became known as the 1400 class entered service. Car 1402 (BUF 982) a Leyland Tiger TS7 with stylish Harrington DP31R bodywork was the first to appear in September 1935. The informative side destination screens – which were fitted on both sides – were a new feature on single deckers that had previously relied on side boards. The batch had a number of modifications during and after the war and car 1402 was withdrawn in January 1956. *Alan Lambert Collection*

1935 took delivery of 24 of the new Leyland Tiger TS7 chassis fitted with Harrington 31-seat rear entrance single deck dual purpose bodywork to a very luxurious specification. Among many distinctive features were three roller blind boxes fitted over the lower deck windows on both sides, a Walman half-length sliding roof and an air smoothed roof luggage rack with rear access ladder. Curved glass windows were fitted on both the rear corners of the body although many of these features disappeared with wartime and post war rebuilding. Originally powered by 7.6 litre petrol engines they represented a great advance on the previous standard set by the Tilling-Stevens Express saloons dating from 1928 to 1930 which they replaced on some important services. Known generally as the 1400 class these buses started a new numbering system for single deckers becoming 1400 to 1423, part of a class that eventually totalled 86 by early 1940. At the end of the 1938 season they were reseated to B32R. As delivered they carried a striking livery with light green body sides, cream roof and a cream band below the windows although, in an attempt to make the buses less visible from

the air, roofs were repainted dark green at the start of the war. A number of other modifications were made in the early months of the war with use of the three roller blind boxes on the offside of these buses being discontinued from late 1939 and the glass being over painted to show 'Southdown/(blank)/Services' in script lettering on a cream background. The rear corner curved glass windows on most of these vehicles were replaced with normal panelling starting early in the war, although some retained this feature until they were rebuilt in the post war period. By the end of the war these saloons would, in normal circumstances, have been nearing the end of their lives with Southdown but it was decided instead to undertake a full refurbishment programme. All but car 1421 were rebuilt and this included removal of the rear luggage locker, offside blind boxes, roof luggage rack and ladder and sealing shut the Walman sliding roof. Although displaced from the most important routes, several remained in service until 1957 which marked the final year for the 1400 class with car 1405 being the last when sold in June 1957.

Also in 1935 Southdown purchased two more of the three axle saloons with Short Bros 40-seat centre entrance bodies for use on service 97 between Eastbourne and the Top of Beachy Head. Cars 52 and 53 were based on the updated specification Leyland Tiger TS7T but otherwise were virtually identical to the earlier pair. They were renumbered to 552/3 in 1937 and were similarly converted to diesel engines early in the war and then redeployed and rebuilt after the war as cars 550/1 before being withdrawn in 1952.

In 1936 Southdown took into stock 82 new Leyland vehicles which included a number of Leyland Cubs for use as one man operated buses to replace various acquired buses and the time expired front entrance Dennis 30cwt (cars 522 to 526) used on short local services or those traversing very narrow roads. The first three (cars 13 to 15) were type KP3A and the remainder (cars 16 to 18) were of type KPZ2. All six normal control buses were powered by 4.7 litre petrol engines and had Park Royal 20-seat bodywork suitable for one man operation and fitted with a two leaf jack-knife folding door which was lever operated by the driver. They saw service on some lightly loaded rural routes but all were withdrawn by 1956. Three further Cubs in the 1936 delivery (cars 10 to 12) were of the longer forward control SKPZ2 type and were purchased specifically for use on services crossing the weight restricted Langstone Bridge to Hayling Island. They were fitted with half cab 26-seat rear entrance bus bodies by Park Royal and included a rear roof luggage pannier.

Also in 1936 came six more 1400 class petrol engined Leyland Tiger TS7s fitted with Harrington rear entrance single deck dual purpose bodywork numbered 1424 to 1429. Unlike the earlier batch no rear roof luggage pannier was fitted. Three were included in the post war rebuilding programme but the three unrebuilt buses unusually retained their offside destination screen boxes to the end. Most of the 1936 batch left the fleet in 1952/3 but car 1426 survived until sale in September 1956.

During the year some 23 of the 1928 batch of Tilling-Stevens buses were withdrawn with most passing for further service with other operators. Two had been sold to Southern National in 1935 but otherwise the 1929/30 batches remained intact until 1939 despite the arrival of many new Tigers.

Three more Leyland Cub SKPZ2s for Hayling Island services arrived in 1937. These were cars 7 to 9 with Park Royal B26R bodies identical to cars 10 to 12 of 1936 and survived in service until 1956. Also during 1937 Southdown took delivery of a further eight Leyland Cub KPZ2 buses with Park Royal B20F bodies designed for one man operation on lightly loaded routes. These cars were numbered 19 to 26 and were identical to cars 16 to 18 of 1936 except that they were the first single deckers to be delivered with

Car 53 – later renumbered 553 – (BUF 553) was one of the four 3 axle Leyland Tigers acquired specially for use on the busy service 97 between Eastbourne and Beachy Head. This vehicle is a Tiger TS7T model with 40-seat bodywork by Short Bros new in August 1935 and is seen at the terminus opposite the Royal Parade garage in Eastbourne. Wartime suspension of service 97 saw the four Tigers move to service 30 between Brighton and Chelwood Common where their extra capacity was much needed. All four were withdrawn and sold for scrap in 1952 after Guy Arab open top double deckers were allowed to operate on service 97. A.Duke, Omnibus Society

Car 14 (CUF 314) was one of three Leyland Cub KP3As with Park Royal 20-seat bodywork delivered new in May 1936. They were suitable for one man operation with the jack-knife folding door lever operated by the driver. It is seen here at Horsham Carfax on local service 72 to Orchard Road although this was later upgraded to larger buses after the war. The one man operated Cubs did not see a lot of use in their later days with Southdown and all left the fleet by the end of 1956. Alan Lambert Collection

plain front and rear destination displays without illuminated Southdown fleet names. Despite the rural nature of Southdown's operating territory away from the coastal belt these buses seem to have been restricted to a small number of routes such as the 34 (Hassocks), 44 (Emsworth), 48 (Havant), 72, 73, 78, 79 and 80 (Horsham). All were withdrawn from service by 1956 but car 24 survives in preservation with the Southdown Omnibus Trust at Amberley.

Car 9 (DUF 9) was one of three additional Leyland Cub SKPZ2s with Park Royal 26-seat bodywork added to the fleet in 1937 to augment services on Hayling Island which required small lightweight buses. These were used extensively in summer on the very busy route 47 which then ran to Havant and Southsea and finally withdrawn in October 1956 after the opening of the new bridge. *Southdown Enthusiasts Club – Clark/Surfleet Collection*

Given that very few suitable prewar photographs showing the offside of the 1400 class Tigers exist, it is necessary to include this view of car 1428 (DCD 328) taken after the war in Pool Valley. It was one of the very few that retained the offside destination screen boxes to the end of its life which came in February 1952. As delivered it would have had a cream roof, rear corner windows and Walman sliding roof but not the front nearside spotlight. Early in the war the cream roofs were painted dark green in an attempt to reduce their visibility to marauding German aircraft but unfortunately never restored. *Alan Lambert Collection*

During 1938 Southdown added 39 more buses to its 1400 class of saloons but this time on Leyland Tiger TS8 chassis and powered by 8.6 litre diesel engines. Cars 1430 to 1467 and 1470 had basically the same body specification as cars 1424 to 1429 new in 1936 except that no triple roller blinds were fitted on the offside. Also cars 1442 to 1467 and 1470 were not fitted with an opening sunshine roof. The three buses – 1468, 1469 and 1471 – outstanding from the 1938 delivery arrived in January 1939. On Saturday 2 November 1940 car 1443 was seriously damaged near Rushlake Green when bombs exploded close to the nearside rear wheel. The body was subsequently removed and replaced by a spare prewar 32-seat centre entrance coach body by Metcalfe. In the postwar rebuilding programme 27 vehicles from this batch were included. Withdrawals started in 1951 and gathered pace during 1952 but cars 1451 and 1455 were the last to be sold in April 1957.

On 1 April 1938 Southdown purchased the Tramocars business from W.R. Gates along with two local services in Worthing and a fleet of 11 rather quaint looking Shelvoke & Drewry Freighter buses delivered between 1924 and 1935. They were numbered T3 to T13 in the Southdown fleet and full details are in Appendix 3. The S & D chassis were usually found as the basis for municipal refuse vehicles but with small wheels they offered a low entrance step and easy access for the elderly residents in the town. Late

In July 1938 two further Shelvoke & Drewry Freighter buses joined the Southdown fleet. These were very different to earlier models in the Tramocars fleet and featured stylish full fronted Harrington 26-seat centre entrance bodywork. Although full Southdown livery was carried the Tramocar name is prominently displayed at the front. Car T17 (FCD 17) is seen at the Splash Point terminus in Worthing although its operating life with Southdown proved to be very short as all of the remaining six S&D buses were rendered surplus by June 1940. After a period of storage it passed to Arlington Motor Company in July 1942. *Alan Lambert Collection*

Car 81 (FUF 181) was one of two Dennis Falcons acquired for the former Tramocars services in May 1939. Although painted in normal livery they carried Tramocars names at the front and also featured script fleet names normally only found on coaches. It is seen waiting at the terminus of services T1 and T2 at Splash Point in Worthing during the summer of 1939 in front of the more traditional Tramocars vehicles. Early in the war the Falcons became surplus to requirements and were stored for the duration. *C.F.Klapper, Omnibus Society*

The remaining Tilling-Stevens Express buses were withdrawn in 1940 and requisitioned by the Military Authorities. After war service and use as a hen house, car 705 (originally 1205) was acquired for preservation in 1977 and subsequently fully restored by the Southdown Omnibus Trust at Amberley. Seen at Amberley in 2015 this example with Short Bros body dating from 1930 shows off the distinctive wrap around rear windows and rear luggage rack so typical of these buses. *Author's Collection*

The final batch of fourteen Leyland Tiger buses did not arrive until after the start of the war. Car 1476 (GCD 376), a Leyland Tiger TS8 with Harrington 32-seat bodywork was delivered in November 1939 and is seen here after the war at Shoreham operating on local service 21A. This route proved to be an early casualty due to wartime service reductions but reappeared in September 1945. Although some members of the 1400 class survived until 1957 car 1476 was withdrawn in 1953. *Southdown Enthusiasts Club – W J Haynes Collection.*

in July 1938 Southdown took delivery of two S & D Freighters to an advanced design. Cars T16 and T17 retained the smaller wheels and a transverse engine but in this model the engine was at the rear of the chassis allowing Harrington to design a modern looking full front 26-seat body with a porch style centre entrance. Car T4 was partly stripped and not used in service by Southdown but apart from cars T3 and T5 withdrawn in early 1939, the remainder were in service up until the start of the war. The Shelvoke & Drewry buses were replaced by 1400 class Leyland Tigers in the summer of 1940 although due to wartime restrictions on the sale of buses some remained in stock until 1942.

Three further Leyland Tiger TS8s with Harrington B34R bodies numbered 1468/9/71 remaining from the 1938 batch were delivered in January 1939. All were rebuilt after the war and withdrawn during 1953/4.

In July 1939 Southdown took delivery of two more vehicles for use on the Worthing Tramocars services. Cars 80 and 81 were based on a newly introduced Dennis Falcon chassis powered by the Dennis 3.77 litre petrol engine and fitted with Harrington porch style centre entrance bus bodywork seating 30. The chassis frame was raised over the axles to give a lowered floor level suitable for these routes. The outbreak of war two months later meant their stay on the Tramocars routes was short as they were stored out of use by August 1940. Both returned to use at Worthing in June 1945 but in June 1950 they were transferred to the Portsmouth area to join the postwar Dennis Falcons working on Hayling Island. They became redundant after the opening of the new Langstone Bridge in September 1956 but car 81 was stored at Southdown's Hambledon garage until sale in May 1958. It subsequently passed into preservation.

During 1939 a large number of Tilling-Stevens buses left the fleet including the 13 remaining of the 1928 batch, 31 from 1929 and eight from 1930. At the outbreak of war some 36 dating from 1929/30 plus the 12 shorter buses for Hayling Island new in 1931/3 remained in service with Southdown and many then went on to be requisitioned for military use in 1940.

A further 14 diesel engined Tiger TS8 buses with Harrington rear entrance bodywork were on order but delivered after the outbreak of war. On these cars – numbered 1472 to 1485 – the body style was similar to the 1938 deliveries but the front dash panel was flush with the driver's cab giving a neater appearance to the final batch of this very well regarded class of buses. Ten buses arrived during November and December 1939 but four – 1480, 1481, 1484 and 1485 – were delayed until 1940 and the final one – car 1485 – was delivered on 15 March 1940. All except car 1483 were included in the postwar rebuilding programme. Withdrawals began in 1953 and the final member of this batch to be sold was car 1474 in May 1957.

Coaches

At the 1927 Commercial Motor Show Leyland had introduced its new Tiger TS1 single deck chassis suitable for either bus or coach work. It had a low frame chassis and was fitted with the smooth and quiet running Leyland six cylinder 6.8 litre overhead camshaft petrol engine. The Tiger marked the beginning of the end for Tilling-Stevens as main supplier of coaches to Southdown and in 1930 the company took delivery of their first modern forward control half cab coaches for use on the London Express Services. Cars 1001-28 had Tiger TS2 chassis and Southdown began to develop their own easily recognisable standard design for these coaches with a straight roof and waistline. They were the first in the fleet to be fitted with bodies that had enclosed roofs and fixed cove panels and 'sunshine roofs' – as Southdown described them – with only the centre part of the roof folded into the space over the rear entrance. Although the

bodies were classed as C26R they had an extra front door which was only for use in an emergency although both doors could be used for loading and unloading at terminal coach stations. All had brackets to hold side destination boards for express services and were fitted with short roof luggage racks at the rear reached by a fixed ladder.

As delivered cars 1001-5/9 had bodies by London Lorries but these were replaced by new Harrington C32R bodies in 1935 of the then standard design. These had a folding sunroof and roof luggage rack and were intended for use on the company's Express Services surviving until 1951-3. Eleven of the Harrington bodied coaches – cars 1007/08/10/11/16-19/21/24/26 were fitted with new Harrington C32R bodies with half-length folding roofs in 1936 and were then used on excursions with some remaining in service until 1953. The unrebodied coaches were sold in 1936.

Car 1005 (UF 5805) was one of six Leyland Tiger TS2s new in early 1930 with London Lorries 26-seat rear entrance coach bodywork. They were fitted with a roof luggage rack and 'Plein-Azur' flexible folding sunshine sunroof which it was claimed could be closed by the driver in only 20 seconds should a sudden downpour occur! The front opening door was normally only used in emergency. The bodies did not endure with all six being rebodied by Harrington in 1935 and in that form car 1005 survived in the Southdown fleet until July 1953. *Alan Lambert Collection*

Also part of the 1930 delivery of 28 Leyland Tigers was car 1021 (UF 6621), a Leyland Tiger TS2 with Harrington 26-seat rear entrance bodywork. It is seen here with destination screen and side boards for the London to Eastbourne service and brought a vast improvement in passenger comfort as compared to all its predecessors on the London services. The front hinged door was normally only used in emergency. A new Harrington body was fitted in 1936 and car 1021 survived in the fleet until July 1953. *Author's Collection*

Car 1026 (UF 6926) illustrates the new Harrington body style as fitted to some of the 1930 Leyland Tiger TS2s in 1935/6. This was now Southdown's standard design coach body for its general purpose fleet and included a half-length folding sunroof. Coaches intended mainly for use on the London Express Services had a rear roof luggage rack. Car 1026 survived in the fleet until July 1953 when it was sold for scrap. *Alan Lambert Collection*

During 1929 Southdown had ordered 12 Tilling-Stevens Express B10B chassis on which they fitted Harrington charabanc bodies from older acquired Dennis vehicles in the fleet as follows:

723	body removed from car 364 (BK 4502)
724	body removed from car 355 (BK 4432)
725	body removed from car 359 (BK 4433)
726	body removed from car 342 (BK 2880)
727	body removed from car 362 (BK 4501)
728	body removed from car 353 (BK 4294)
729	body removed from car 361 (BK 4500)
730	body removed from car 378 (CD 6203)
731	body removed from car 367 (BK 4435)
732	body removed from car 377 (CD 5095)
733	body removed from car 360 (BK 4530)
734	body removed from car 341 (BK 2879)

Cars 341/2 had been acquired from South Coast Tourist Co Ltd, Littlehampton 1/24, car 377 from G.W. Miskin, Littlehampton 5/25, car 378 from S. Foard, Eastbourne 12/26 and cars 353/5/9-62/4/7 from Southsea Tourist Co Ltd, Southsea 2/25. All of the bodies were first rebuilt to C30R with a fixed back and folding roof. Eight of these, cars 723, 727-732 and 734 arrived in 1929 while cars 724-726 and 733 were delivered in 1930. All were rebodied with new Harrington C30R bodies incorporating a half-length folding canvas roof in 1934. The complete batch was requisitioned on 4 July 1940 and as with the other Tilling-Stevens vehicles none returned to Southdown after the war.

Two further batches of Tilling-Stevens Express B10B2 normal control coaches entered service in 1930. Cars 735-746 were fitted with Harrington C30R bodies incorporating a fixed back and canvas folding roof. As with many others of this type the driver's position remained uncovered when the hood was folded back. Cars 747-63 were fitted with Short Bros C30R bodies

Car 744 (UF 5846) was one of a batch of 12 Tilling-Stevens Express B10B2 models with Harrington 30-seat rear entrance bodywork new in May 1930. All had a fixed back, glass side screens and folding sunroof and were generally used on excursions and private hire duties. Car 744 was sold for further service in October 1937 and survived until 1953. *Alan Lambert Collection*

including a fixed back and half-length folding roof. None were rebodied and all had departed from the fleet before the 1938 season.

To further consolidate their position Southdown acquired two coach operators running Excursions and Tours in the Brighton and Hove area in 1930. The first was J. Poole who traded as Royal Red Coaches of Hove on 28 March 1930 with a mixed fleet of Charabanc type vehicles including a Chevrolet (which became car 29), four Fiats (cars 31-34), a Thornycroft (car 384) and a Dennis 30 cwt (car 500). Most were quickly sold, but car 29 survived until 1932 and car 500 until May 1933. From A. Potts trading as Potts Motor Services of Brighton acquired on 5 June 1930 came two elderly Daimlers (cars 28 and 36), one Fiat (car 30) and six Dennis (cars 393-396 and 536/7) mostly dating from 1929. The Daimlers and Fiat were quickly withdrawn but Southdown had the two normal control Dennis GLs – cars 536/7 – rebodied with new Harrington C18R bodies for the 1931 season. They remained in the fleet until sale in 1936/7. Further details are included in Appendix 3. With the intake of modern coaches to the fleet all of the remaining normal control Leyland N and most of the G7 vehicles fitted with Charabanc type bodies were withdrawn during the year. Many of the chassis were subsequently fitted with lorry bodies for further use.

Southdown's 1931 delivery of 32 Leyland Tiger coaches was based on the TS1 chassis with bodies by Harrington (cars 1029/31-33/35/36/42-1055) or Hoyal (cars 1030/34/37-41/56-1060) of which the latter were specifically for the 'Coastal Express Service'. The chassis specification was similar to the TS2 model previously taken by Southdown, except that the TS1 allowed a longer overhang behind the rear wheels. Cars 1029-1060 had a single rear doorway with a hinged door allowing 30 luxurious seats in 2+2 format. After only seven months in service cars 1056-1060 were sold to East Kent for use on the Coastal Express Service now running between Margate and Bournemouth.

In 1931 T S Motors (as successors to Tilling-Stevens) introduced an entirely new range of 'Express' chassis. Although by now committed to the Leyland Tiger for its full size single deck chassis, Southdown took three of the new C60A7 'Express Six' models – cars 200-202 – fitted with 30-seat Harrington coach bodies of very similar style to those on the Tiger TS2s, except that the passengers' baggage was carried in an air smoothed pannier at the rear of the roof. They did not prove entirely successful with Southdown and were sold in January 1936.

Ironically at the start of 1931 the very last of the Tilling-Stevens petrol electrics with a charabanc body was finally withdrawn. The chassis had started life with Worthing Motor Services in November 1914 and in its final form had carried a Harrington body new in 1924 but rebuilt to Ch30R two years later. The year also marked the

The seventeen Tilling-Stevens Express B10B2s bodied by Short Bros looked very different to those with Harrington bodies. Car 761 (UF 6361) with 30-seat rear entrance bodywork delivered new June 1930 illustrates the prominent front roof canopy with destination screen and half-length folding sunroof. The batch were sold in 1937/8 with some passing to Jersey and eventually being requisitioned by the German Occupation Forces. Car 761 stayed in the London area and survived until 1946. *Alan Lambert Collection*

New in June 1931, car 1044 (UF 7344) was a Harrington bodied Leyland Tiger TS1 with 30-seats, rear entrance, Walman folding sunroof and rear roof luggage rack. This vehicle featured on the front covers of London Express Service leaflets for several years. The seating capacity was increased to 32 in 1933 and, along with several other members of this batch, car 1044 was requisitioned by the Military Authorities in the dark days of July 1940.
Alan Lambert Collection

Car 202 (UF 8032), was one of three TSM Express Six C60A7 models with Harrington 30-seat bodywork delivered in late 1931. They had a folding sunroof and improved roof luggage pannier rather than the open cage type previously fitted to some coaches. Southdown had already decided to standardise on Leyland Tigers for its Express Services and all three were sold for further service in early 1936. No further vehicles were ever purchased by Southdown from TSM/Tilling-Stevens.
Author's Collection

Car 1067 (UF 8837) was a Leyland Tiger TS4 with Harrington 32-seat rear entrance body new in June 1932 and destined to have a long life. It featured a folding sunroof and the same type of roof luggage rack as introduced on the TSM coaches. In June 1940 it was requisitioned by the Military Authorities but returned to Southdown in September 1946 and converted to a lorry based at Portslade Works. It then remained in the service vehicle fleet until 1970 when it was sold for preservation.
Alan Lambert Collection

end for the last Leyland G7 types dating from 1925 when cars 178 and 180 were finally withdrawn. With the massive advances in modern enclosed coaches these elderly charabancs must have seemed very outdated!

In 1932 Leyland introduced the Tiger TS4 with fully floating rear axle and more powerful 7.6 litre petrol engine. It was also fitted with a redesigned and longer radiator than those still fitted to Titan TD2s. In other respects it retained the dimensions of the TS1 with a 17ft 6ins wheelbase allowing bodywork up to the maximum permitted length of 27ft 6ins. Southdown's 1932 delivery of 12 Tiger coaches – numbered 1062-1073 – was based on the new TS4 chassis with Harrington bodywork for 32 passengers. All were requisitioned in June-July 1940 but car 1067 was returned to the fleet in September 1946. The body was removed and scrapped and a lorry body fitted and in this form it was based at Portslade Works and used to deliver parts to the main depots until 1965 before being sold for preservation in 1970.

Southdown purchased two coach operators based in Eastbourne, Sussex in March 1932, of which the first and smaller concern was Southern Glideway. The mixed fleet of ten coaches included examples by GMC (car 30), ADC (car 31), Morris (32), Gilford (cars 37-40), Dennis (car 371) and Leyland (cars 1000/61) with full details shown in Appendix 3. Most were quickly replaced but their two Leyland Tiger TS2s were rebodied with new Park Royal 32-seat bodies in 1935. Car 1000 was requisitioned on 4 July 1940 but car 1061 enjoyed a long life with Southdown, being rebuilt in 1948 and finally sold in August 1955.

The other Eastbourne company was Chapman & Sons which operated an express service to London but in addition ran extended tours with luxury coaches and also local excursions. Chapman's still favoured the by now outdated normal control chassis, and most of its large fleet had gangway charabanc bodies with full length folding roofs. The fleet acquired consisted of 24 Maudslay (becoming cars 318-341), 18 Dennis (cars 372-83/5-90) and two Lancia (cars 41-42) but many were taken out of service within the first year. Some were converted by the company for use as lorries and six Tilling-Stevens Express B9B chassis new in 1927/8 were purchased from The Thames Valley Traction Co Ltd and fitted with Park Royal bodies dating from 1930 and transferred from Chapman vehicles. The latter became cars 490 to 495 and survived in service until sale between 1936 and 1938. Full details can be found in Appendix 3.

The coach fleet gained another 12 Leyland Tiger TS4 coaches with Harrington C32R bodywork incorporating folding sunroof and roof luggage rack in 1933 which became cars 1074-1085. The last two of the batch introduced a new design with wider windows and one less bay. All were requisitioned on 28 June 1940 although six – cars 1075/6/9 and 1083-5 – were later repurchased by the company from the Ministry of Supply. After the war all except car 1079 were rebuilt and modernised with the last two – cars 1084/5 – surviving in the fleet until the start of 1957.

Southdown acquired the London to Worthing Express Service of Fairway Coaches Ltd of Stockwell, London SW9 on 18 December 1933 along with five Maudslay and three Dennis Lancet coaches new in 1929-32. The Maudslays became cars 342-346 but were quickly sold while the newer Dennis numbered as cars 397-399 lasted until November 1934. Full details are shown in Appendix 3.

In 1934 Southdown took just three of the new Tiger TS6 chassis fitted with Harrington C32R

bodies incorporating folding sunroof and roof luggage rack which were numbered cars 1086-1088. These were similar in outline to the last two of the 1934 batch and established the company's standard coach design until 1938. All three avoided the requisitioning authorities in 1940 and survived long enough to be fitted with 8.6 litre diesel engines in 1950. Cars 1086/8 were rebuilt in the post-war programme but all were withdrawn by 1955.

For the 1935 season Southdown took delivery of 36 of the new petrol engined Leyland Tiger TS7 chassis and fitted with the now standard rear entrance 32-seat coach body. Thirty were bodied by Harrington – cars 1089 to 1100 and 1107 to 1124 – to the design introduced the previous year. The other six – cars 1101 to 1106 – were built by Park Royal and while very similar could be distinguished from the others by their flared skirts and differently shaped glass rain shields over the opening side windows. Cars 1116/7 were sold to Samuelson New Transport at Victoria in March 1938 and subsequently requisitioned by the Military Authorities in 1940 although returned to Samuelson after the war. In late August 1939 just before the actual declaration of war Southdown converted a total of 24 Leyland Tiger TS7 coaches for work as Ambulances – including cars 1089 to 1096, 1101, 1102, 1104, 1106 to 1115, 1120, 1123. Several from this batch survived in service until 1956/7 with car 1099 the last to be sold on 1 June 1957. This was a truly remarkable service life for a vehicle built in the mid-1930s!

To update its 'small coach' fleet Southdown took delivery of eight Leyland Cub coaches in 1936. The first six – cars 30 to 35 – were of the longer KP3A type with fully enclosed Harrington coach bodywork and 20 generously spaced seats in 2+2 layout. Two more coaches – cars 36 and 37 – had identical Harrington C20F bodies on the later KPZ2 chassis. Car 37 was requisitioned

Southdown took delivery of just three new coaches in 1934, all based on the new Leyland Tiger TS6 chassis and fitted with Harrington 32-seat rear entrance bodywork incorporating a folding sunroof and roof luggage rack. This became Southdown's standard design for coaches used on the London Express Services until 1938. Car 1088 (AUF 787) was rebuilt by Portsmouth Aviation after the war and was the last of the trio to be sold in January 1955. *Alan Lambert Collection*

Car 1094 (BCD 894) was a Leyland Tiger TS7, one of thirty with Harrington 32-seat rear entrance bodywork new for the 1935 season. It is seen after the war – during which time it was converted for use as an Ambulance – whilst operating on the London to Fareham and Gosport service probably at the refreshment halt although as this changed on several occasions the exact location has not been identified. It was sold for scrap in October 1953. *A.J.Higham*

Southdown took into stock a total of twenty Leyland Cubs during 1936. This photograph illustrates one of the batch of six KP3A models – cars 30 to 35 (CCD 700-705) – fitted with Harrington 20-seat bodies and delivered in early 1936. All had a folding sunroof and could be seen on a wide variety of coaching work throughout the company's territory. Due to their low seating capacity most were stored for varying periods during the war but five survived in service until 1956. *Alan Lambert Collection*

Car 1130 (CCD 730) was a Leyland Tiger TS7 with Harrington 32-seat rear entrance bodywork new in March 1936. It is shown here with the half-length folding roof in the open position. In October 1940 it was requisitioned by the Military Authorities and resold to a coach operator in Staffordshire in 1943 who had a new body and Gardner 5LW engine fitted as late as 1955! *Alan Lambert Collection*

on 24 June 1941 and did not return to the company after the war. With their small capacity some of the Leyland Cub coaches were stored out of use during the war but most enjoyed long lives with Southdown, the last being withdrawn at the end of the 1956 season.

A further 38 full size coaches joined the fleet in 1936 based on Leyland Tiger TS7 chassis and becoming cars 1125 to 1162. Of these 32 had the 7.6 litre petrol engine – cars 1125 to 1153 and 1160 to 1162 – but for the first time six had 8.6 litre diesel engines – cars 1154 to 1159. Previously Southdown had chosen petrol engines for its coach fleet partly due to the fact that the relatively low mileages that most of the coaches operated did not justify the increased cost of specifying diesel engines. Fifteen of these coaches – cars 1125 to 1130, 1132, 1133, 1147 to 1150 and 1160 to 1162 – were for use on excursions and had rear entrance 32-seat Harrington bodies with flared skirts and half-length folding roofs. Cars 1145 and 1146 were similar but had only 26 seats and a full length folding canvas roof along the top of the window line. In 1939

eight of these coaches – cars 1125, 1126, 1128, 1132, 1133, 1145, 1146 and 1147 – were rebuilt with an enclosed roof incorporating glass cove windows between the front bulkhead and rear entrance, and a folding 'sunshine roof'. A further dozen all purpose coaches – cars 1131 and 1134 to 1144 – were fitted with the standard rear entrance 32-seat coach body but built by Beadle. Cars 1151 to 1159 had elegant Burlingham rear entrance 32-seat bodies to that company's then standard design and were used on Express Services and based at Portsmouth and Brighton. These cars were fitted with a half-length sliding roof panel but were, unusually, not fitted with roof luggage racks. Car 1131 was converted for use as an ambulance in August 1939 and was restored to normal coaching duties in March 1946. Cars 1160-2 were requisitioned on 7 March 1940 while cars 1127/9/30 and 1150 followed on 10 October 1940 with only 1129 being returned to Southdown. After the war almost all the surviving petrol engine coaches were fitted with Leyland 8.6 litre diesel engines and most of this year's coaches had very long lives with

An interesting rear view of car 1137 (CCD 737), a Leyland Tiger TS7 new in May 1936 with Beadle 32-seat rear entrance bodywork equipped with folding sunroof and roof luggage rack. This shows the standard rear end layout of coaches used on the London Express Services delivered at this time. Alongside is a 1400 class Tiger bus showing the rear destination screen box fitted to these vehicles and, as it has a green roof, this photograph was clearly taken after the war. Car 1137 was finally sold in February 1956. *J. V. Short*

After taking delivery of many coaches based on their standard design the batch of nine bodied by Burlingham were certainly very different to anything that had been seen before. Car 1158 (CUF 158) was one of nine Leyland Tiger TS7s with rear entrance 32-seat bodywork new in July 1936 for use on the London Express Services. As delivered they had a deep cream waistband and cream roof but the latter was painted dark green after the outbreak of war. Six were fitted with Leyland 8.6 litre diesel engines, the first to be specified for coaches in the Southdown fleet. All lasted until sale in 1956/7. *Southdown Enthusiasts Club – W J Haynes Collection.*

To upgrade its fleet of small coaches Southdown took a further 17 Leyland Cubs into stock for the 1937 season. Car 52 (DUF 52) is a KPZ2 model with attractive Harrington 20-seat front entrance bodywork and seen after the war on Excursion duties at Worthing. It was sold along with the remaining Cubs in 1956 and ended its days as a Mobile Shop in Lancashire. *A.B.Cross*

Southdown. Several remained in the fleet until summer 1957 with the last – car 1158 – being sold in August.

Cars 38 to 54 were a further batch of 17 Leyland Cub KPZ2 coaches with Harrington C20F bodies, similar to cars 36 and 37. Cars 39 and 49 were requisitioned on 24 June 1941 and car 46 on 30 July 1941 with the first two returned to Southdown at the end of the war. As with the other Leyland Cub coaches many were stored for periods out of use during the war but with the return of peace were used on a wide variety of work and most survived until the end of the 1956 season.

Also for the 1937 season Southdown also took delivery of a further 16 petrol engined Leyland Tiger TS7 excursion coaches fitted with Harrington 32-seat bodies with half-length folding roofs. Cars 1163 to 1178 were identical to cars 1160 to 1162 which arrived at the end of 1936. Later in 1937 Southdown took its final Tiger TS7 and its first two Tiger TS8 chassis – cars 1179-81. All three had 32-seat rear entrance all purpose coach bodies by Harrington to the standard design incorporating a half-length

sliding 'sunshine roof'. Cars 1177 and 1178 were fitted with only 26 seats from new and in 1939 were rebuilt by Harrington with an enclosed roof incorporating glass cove windows between the front bulkhead and rear entrance, and a folding sunroof. On 7 March 1940 cars 1160-76 were requisitioned and only cars 1166/8/72-4/6 returned to Southdown. Many of the survivors remained in service until the mid-1950s and, at a time when the private preservation of buses and coaches was almost unknown, car 1179 was sold directly to an enthusiast on withdrawal in May 1957 and fortunately still makes occasional appearances.

Several of the Tilling-Stevens Express B9B and B10B normal control vehicles with Harrington or Short coach bodies withdrawn at this time found their way to Jersey between 1936 and 1938 mostly joining Mascot Motors Ltd. In late June 1940 following the German invasion of the Channel Islands these passed to the German Occupation Forces. Many were transferred to France for scrap but four survived to be repurchased in 1946 and returned to service until 1949/50.

Car 1173 (DUF 173), a Leyland Tiger TS7 with Harrington 32-seat rear entrance bodywork new in early 1937, was one of 17 intended for use on Excursion duties and therefore fitted with a half-length folding roof. Some of the batch were upgraded in 1939 with glass cove windows. Car 1173 was requisitioned by the Military Authorities in March 1940 but re-acquired by Southdown in May 1943. It is seen here soon after the war in a bomb damaged area near Victoria Coach Station while on London Express Services and sold for scrap in 1952. *Southdown Enthusiasts Club – W J Haynes Collection.*

Seen after the war at Eastbourne Pier helping out on the busy service 97 to Beachy Head is car 1183 (EUF 83), a Leyland Tiger TS8 with Harrington rear entrance coach body new in 1938. It was one of many intended for use on Excursions and fitted with half-length folding canvas roof which could be opened on warm summer days. During the war its diesel engine was exchanged for a petrol unit from a 1400 class bus although it reverted to diesel at the end of its service life. *Author's Collection*

Among the 1938 delivery of new coaches were five diesel engined Leyland Tiger TS8s with Park Royal 32-seat rear entrance bodywork similar to Southdown's standard design. As general purpose coaches they were fitted with half-length sliding sunroof but no roof luggage racks. Although marking the end of the line for the traditional straight waistrail design they introduced a curving side flash which was later applied to some earlier deliveries. Car 1210 (EUF 110) was new in June 1938 and withdrawn in October 1953. *Southdown Enthusiasts Club – Clark/Surfleet Collection*

In 1938 the company took delivery of 31 of Leyland's new Tiger TS8 with rear entrance bodies and all had 8.6 litre diesel engines from new. Cars 1182 to 1205 were for use on excursions and had Harrington C32R bodies with half-length folding roofs. These vehicles were the last 'rag top' coaches delivered to Southdown, and although cars 1182, 1184, 1193 and 1199 were rebuilt after the Second World War all of this batch retained folding roofs whilst with the company. Cars 1206 to 1210 were further all purpose coaches fitted with C32R bodies but built by Park Royal. The bodies were very similar to those on cars 1101-6 of 1935 but fitted with sliding rather than folding sunshine roofs and no roof luggage rack. They were the last coaches delivered to the company with a straight and parallel waist beading although a chrome beading formed a side flash that swept down from the waist at the front bulkhead line, back and over the rear wheel arch to the bottom of the coach. Several earlier coaches had a similar flash added in an attempt to modernise their appearance. Finally cars 1211 and 1212 introduced to the fleet a more elegant and rounded style of Harrington body and the following year's coach deliveries followed this design. Car 1211 had a fixed roof with a full length luggage container for band instruments whilst car 1212 had a sliding sunroof and no roof luggage rack.

In the early years of the war Southdown decided that all of the 1400 class buses would be fitted with diesel engines removed from coaches including cars 1182 to 1209. Unfortunately some of this batch that had already been converted to petrol, as preferred by the Military Authorities,

were requisitioned with 1193/9, 1200 on 19 September 1940, 1185 on 17 October 1940 and 1184 and 1197 on 31 March 1941. Fortunately all except car 1185 returned to Southdown. The last two in service were cars 1193 and 1199 which survived until sale in August 1957.

The last four Leyland Cubs for Southdown – cars 55 to 58 – were of the KPZ4 type with attractive Harrington C20F bodies similar to cars 36 to 54 except that the waistline curved down slightly to the rear. These versatile small coaches were used on private hire, excursions and even express relief work and lasted until the end of the 1956 season. In order to provide suitable modern vehicles for the many Holiday Camps on Hayling Island lightweight vehicles were needed which could pass over the restricted Langstone Bridge. For the 1938 season Southdown took delivery of five petrol engined Leyland Cheetah LZ3 coaches with rather bus-like Park Royal 24-seat centre entrance coach bodies – cars 500 to 504 – suitable for both local excursions and the weekend Hayling Island to London express service. They were often stored out of use during the war although occasionally used on bus services. The batch was renumbered to 600 to 604 and altered to C25C in 1948 surviving until the end of the 1956 season and the opening of the new Langstone Bridge.

For the final summer season before the outbreak of war Southdown took delivery of 14 Tiger TS8 coaches, again with 8.6 litre diesel engines and Harrington bodywork developed from the stylish curved waist rail design introduced on car 1212 in the previous year. Cars 1213 to 1226 arrived during June and July and

In July 1938 Southdown took into stock two further Leyland Tiger TS8s with Harrington 32 rear entrance bodywork to a completely new design with a slightly curved waist rail. Although many attempts at streamlining coach designs in the 1930s were often short lived and soon dropped, the restrained outline of these two coaches formed the basis for Southdown's next year's coach deliveries. Car 1211 (EUF 511) was equipped with a full length roof luggage rack for carrying band instruments and survived in the fleet until August 1957.
Southdown Enthusiasts Club – Clark/Surfleet Collection

Car 55 (EUF 555) was a Leyland Cub KPZ4 with Harrington 20-seat front entrance coach body new in 1938 and shows the final design for this type with sloping window line towards the rear. There was a good demand for small coaches from private parties but they were also often to be found on local excursions and Express Service reliefs. Many of the Cubs were stored during the war years and all were withdrawn by the end of the 1956 season. *Author's Collection*

New for the 1939 season were fourteen Leyland Tiger TS8s with elegant Harrington 32 rear entrance bodywork incorporating cove windows and a Walman half-length sliding sunroof. Delivered in June and July for Excursion duties they enjoyed just a few weeks in service before the outbreak of war curtailed such activities. Car 1214 (FUF 314) is seen after the war in what appears to be an officially posed photograph taken on a very nasty wet day and lasted in service until March 1957. *Alan Lambert Collection*

were for use on excursions being fitted with half-length sliding sunroof and cove windows. There was no provision for the fitting of a coach service roof board. Their life on front line duties was to be very short as within just a few weeks their intended duties were severely curtailed by the outbreak of war. They were to be the last new coaches delivered to Southdown until 1947. During the early years of the war the diesel engines were exchanged with the petrol engines from cars 1400 to 1429 although all were reconverted by 1951. After the war these coaches were held in such high esteem that during 1949 and 1950 nine of them – 1218 to 1226 – were reseated to C21R at Portslade Works to operate a new programme of European luxury tours and to

augment the ageing Lionesses and Tigresses then used on luxury tours in the UK. Cars 1221 and 1223 were sold in 1951/2 to the Ulster Transport Authority and used exclusively on Southdown's Northern Ireland tours until replaced by Leyland Royal Tigers in 1956. Several continued in service until 1957 with car 1213 the last to depart on 19 August.

Another six similar lightweight vehicles for Hayling Island were purchased for the 1939 season. Cars 505 to 510 were Cheetah LZ4 coaches with the same 4.7 litre petrol engines and again fitted with Park Royal 24-seat centre entrance bodywork. They were renumbered to 605 to 610 and altered to C25C in 1948 continuing in service until the end of the 1956 season.

During 1938/9 Southdown took delivery of eleven petrol engined Leyland Cheetahs with lightweight Park Royal 24-seat centre entrance coach bodies especially for use on Hayling Island. Car 502 (EUF 502) was a LZ3 model delivered in May 1938. This rear view shows that despite a rather basic bus style outline at the front they had a more pleasing rear! The batch was renumbered in 1948 by adding 100 to the fleet numbers and the seating capacity increased to 25.
Alan Lambert Collection

In 1928 Southdown took delivery of four shorter Tilling-Stevens Express B9BL lorry type chassis fitted with luxurious 20-seat rear entrance Harrington bodywork for use on the company's Coach Cruises. With a 13 feet wheelbase they were the first vehicles in the fleet to be fitted with power assisted brakes and became known as Devon Tourers, being capable of handling the narrow bridges and steep hills found in Devon. It is seen here on a six day tour to North and South Devon. After sale in 1937 all four passed to Jersey and after the occupation of the Channel Islands were eventually requisitioned by the German Forces.
Alan Lambert Collection

At the outbreak of war the Southdown fleet included a total of 313 coaches of which 28 were specially designed for touring work. The oldest vehicles remaining in the fleet were 18 normal control Tilling-Stevens Express B9B new in 1926-7 and rebodied with new Harrington C30R bodies in 1935 and a further 18 normal control Tilling-Stevens Express B10B2 new in 1929-30 and rebodied with new Harrington C30R bodies in 1934. All but two were requisitioned for military use in July 1940 with the remainder sold for further service.

Touring Coaches

During the second half of the 1920s Southdown had successfully established a programme of extended 'coach cruises'. In 1930 yet another Leyland model was introduced to the fleet in the form of the normal control Lioness LTB1. Cars 301-11 had Harrington C20R bodywork with luxurious seating in a 2+1 layout for use on the coach cruises which ran between Easter and late September with the coaches safely stored each winter. As delivered these quiet, impressive vehicles had fixed backs, glass side screens and a canvas hood which folded along the top of the window line into a short roof space. The driver's position remained completely uncovered when the hood was folded back. Although soon looking rather outdated in appearance they offered a massive advance in terms of passenger comfort over the Tilling-Stevens B9B types with 2+2 seating previously used on the tours.

A further six Leyland Lioness touring coaches of similar type were acquired in 1933 (cars 312-317) which were rebuilt by Harrington in 1937 with an enclosed roof, glass cove windows and electrically operated folding 'sunshine roof' although at this stage cars 301-311 remained in original condition. Soon after the outbreak of the war the coach cruise programme was suspended and all of the touring coaches were put into store for the duration. During 1940 the Lioness tourers were renumbered as 1801-1817 so that the 3xx numbers could be used for the twenty Leyland Titans on loan from East Kent Road Car Co Ltd. Cars 1801 and 1805 were sold to the United States Army on 12 August 1943 but the remainder returned to service with the reintroduction of the coach cruises from May 1947. The surviving coaches which had not been modernised in 1937 were rebuilt with cove windows and folding roof after the war and all converted to C20C layout in 1948/9. Some were fitted with a longer and more modern looking Covrad radiator and all remained in service until sale in 1952.

Leyland had introduced its Cub range of small normal control chassis for both passenger and goods use in 1931. For the 1933 season Southdown took two Leyland Cub KP2 touring coaches with 2+1 seating in Harrington 14-seat

Car 310 (UF 6510) was one of eleven Leyland Lioness LTB1 models fitted with Harrington 20-seat bodywork and delivered during 1930 for use on the company's expanding Coach Cruise programme. After wartime storage the survivors were all renumbered into the 18xx series and subject to a modernising rebuild with a folding roof and cove panels. The rear entrance was also moved to a central position ahead of the rear wheels.
Alan Lambert Collection

In July 1933 Southdown took delivery of two Leyland Cub touring coaches and started a new numbering series for small coaches and buses at number 1. Car 2 (ACD 1021) was a Leyland Cub KP2 with Harrington body fitted with just 14 luxurious seats in 2 + 1 layout. They proved especially useful on the company's Coach Cruises to Devon and Cornwall where their compact size allowed them to access the narrow roads and bridges. During the war years they were stored out of use but unlike other coaches with full length folding roof these were not modernised or rebuilt in later years. They were converted to 20 normal coach seats in 1949 and then used on excursions and relief workings on Express Services before sale for scrap in June 1953.
Alan Lambert Collection

front entrance bodies (cars 1 and 2). They proved ideal for crossing the very narrow bridges found in Devon. These were the last new vehicles purchased by the company to have the, by then, old fashioned fixed backs, glass side windows and canvas hood which folded along the length of the body into a short roof space and uncovered driver's position. For many years to come front entrance bodywork was only specified by Southdown on smaller coaches. Cars 3 to 5 were three further additions to the touring fleet in 1936. Based on the short KPZ1 chassis, these small 14-seat coaches were of similar layout to cars 1 and 2 of 1933 except that the luxurious Harrington front entrance bodies were this time enclosed at the front and rear, and a folding canvas roof bridged the gap along the top of the window line. They were rebuilt by Harrington in 1939 with an enclosed roof incorporating glass

cove windows, but it is thought that due to their small capacity all of the Cub touring coaches were mostly stored out of use during the war. Cars 1 and 2 were converted to C20F in normal 2+2 layout during 1949 but otherwise remained in original condition until sale in 1953. Cars 3-4 were also converted to C20F in 1950 and sold to Jersey Motor Transport in 1953/4. The luxury seats removed from cars 1-4 were used in the conversion of the 1939 Leyland Tiger coaches to 21 seaters. Fortunately car 4 was acquired for preservation in 1962 and returned to the mainland. Finally, car 5 remained as a 14 seater to the end in 1953.

By the mid-1930s there was little demand in the home market for full size normal control coaches although Leyland still offered the mainly export Tigress RLTB3 model and Southdown chose six of these massively bonneted and elegant

Car 5 (CUF 405) was one of three additional Leyland Cub touring coaches added to the fleet in 1936. Based on the KPZI model with Harrington 14-seat bodywork and 2+1 seating these vehicles were modernised in 1939 with folding sunroof and cove windows. Whilst some Cubs were reseated with 20 standard coach seats towards the end of their lives car 5 remained as a 14 seater touring coach until being sold for scrap in June 1953. *Alan Lambert Collection*

Six Leyland Tigress RLTB3 models were added to the touring coach fleet in 1936 including car 319 (CUF 319) with Burlingham touring coach body seating just 20 passengers in a 2+1 layout. Progress was at a leisurely pace in the days of a 30 mph speed limit and hardly any by-passes and certainly no Motorways! All were sold for scrap in 1952 after the delivery of new underfloor engined Leyland Royal Tigers. *Alan Lambert Collection*

Amongst the oldest vehicles in the fleet at the outbreak of war were 18 Tilling-Stevens Express B9B models dating from 1926/7 which had been rebodied by Harrington in 1935. Typical of these coaches is car 423 (UF 2023) although this one only lasted until July 1939 when it was sold to Wilts & Dorset and later requisitioned by the Military Authorities in July 1940.
Alan Lambert Collection

machines in 1936 to add to its fleet of touring coaches. Slightly larger than the earlier Lioness tourers, cars 318 to 323 were fitted with petrol engines and fully enclosed 20-seat Burlingham centre entrance bodywork. Additional refinements included six glass cove windows on each side and an electrically operated 'sunshine roof', as well as the luxurious seats arranged in the usual 2+1 format. As with the Lioness and Cub tourers they were stored during the war, being at some time renumbered to 1818-1823 and then returned to service in 1947. The complete batch was withdrawn in 1952 and, despite their relatively low mileages thanks to wartime and winter storage, all went for scrap.

* * * * *

At the company Board Meeting held on Thursday 31 August just days before the start of hostilities it was reported that the following rolling stock had been ordered: 26 Leyland Titan and 14 Leyland Tiger.

The Titans presumably refer to the batch – in fact 27, due to have been cars 266-292 – that were diverted elsewhere in 1940 as a result of the deteriorating wartime situation. The 14 Tigers were delivered in late 1939 and early 1940 as cars 1472-1485. In addition the following additional orders were authorised: 13 single deckers and 27 coaches.

None of these latter orders were fulfilled and no further single deck buses arrived until the Dennis Falcons in 1948/9 and no new coaches until 1947. The Southdown fleet at 31 December 1939 consisted of the following vehicles:

244	Double deck buses comprising:
1	Tilling-Stevens Express B10A2 open top new 1929
23	Leyland Titan TD1 open top new 1929
22	Leyland Titan TD1 covered top new 1930-2
16	Leyland Titan TD2 new 1932-3
16	Leyland Titan TD3/TD3c new 1934
51	Leyland Titan TD4/TD4c new 1935-6
115	Leyland Titan TD5 new 1937-9

163	Single deck buses comprising:
33	Tilling-Stevens Express B10A2 new 1929-30
6	TSM Express B10A2 for Hayling Island services new 1931
6	TSM Express B39A6 for Hayling Island services new 1933
14	Leyland Cub suitable for one person operation new 1936-7
6	Leyland Cub for Hayling Island services new 1936-7
30	Leyland Tiger TS7 new 1935-6
52	Leyland Tiger TS8 new 1938-9
4	Leyland Tiger TS7T/TS8T for service 97 new 1934-5
10	Shelvoke & Drewry new 1930-8 (ex Tramocars)
2	Dennis Falcon new 1939

313	Coaches comprising:
18	Tilling-Stevens B9B new 1926-7 (rebodied in 1935)
18	Tilling-Stevens B10B2 new 1929-30 (rebodied 1934)
46	Leyland Tiger TS2 new 1930-1 (19 rebodied in 1935-6)
24	Leyland Tiger TS4 new 1932-3
3	Leyland Tiger TS6 new 1934
89	Leyland Tiger TS7 new 1935-7 (including 24 converted to ambulances August 1939)
47	Leyland Tiger TS8 new 1937-9
5	Leyland Cub touring coaches new 1933-6
29	Leyland Cub new 1936-8
11	Leyland Cheetah LZ3/LZ4 for Hayling Island services new 1938-9
17	Leyland Lioness LTB1 touring coaches new 1930-3
6	Leyland Tigress RLTB3 touring coaches new 1936

The grand total of 720 vehicles meant that Southdown was now the sixth largest bus company in the country with annual revenue exceeding one million pounds and an operating territory covering some 1500 square miles.

Full details of vehicles that still survive from the 1930s can be found in the Southdown Enthusiasts' Club book titled 'Southdown Survivors'.

Wartime – Blackout

As dusk fell on the evening of Friday 1 September, two days before the actual declaration of war, Britain was plunged into complete darkness as wartime blackout regulations were introduced. Devastating air attacks by enemy bombers were expected at any time and no light was allowed on the streets. To improve their visibility in the darkened streets all vehicles were required to have white markings added. Southdown buses and coaches had white paint applied to the edge of the front wings and at the bottom of the rear panel including the platform area on double deckers. A large white circular disc was painted on the back, normally below the window but sometimes on the offside corner. It took some months before a satisfactory headlight mask was developed and at the start of the war most vehicles used during hours of darkness were fitted with a single hooded nearside headlamp to direct a reduced beam downwards. Usually the bulb was removed from the offside headlamp and side and rear lamp glasses were partially masked using the equivalent of two layers of newsprint. Lighting of destination indicators had to be extinguished completely making it very difficult for passengers to identify an oncoming vehicle. The interior lighting of buses and coaches also proved a problem – especially in Portsmouth – which took some time to properly solve. The large expanse of glass at the rear of Southdown's 1400 class saloons was a particular difficulty.

Often the stairs and platform area of double deckers were unlit making fare collection a major headache for bus conductors. By the middle of October 1939 approved headlight masks that permitted a little more light were becoming available and from Monday 22 January 1940 a much improved headlight mask became compulsory for all civilian vehicles.

During the war years many Southdown vehicles were delicensed and put in store at various times although they could still be used in emergency when required by the Military or civilian authorities. These included most of the Leyland Cub coaches, some of the Leyland Cheetahs, all of the Leyland Lioness and Tigress touring coaches, the two Dennis Falcons, the unique open top double deck Tilling-Stevens (car 600) and the open-top Leyland Titan TD1s until they were later fitted with temporary canvas tops. In the case of the Cubs and Cheetahs these changed from year to year to even out their mileage.

Coaches to Ambulances

In early 1939 the Government turned its attention to the provision of an adequate number of ambulances which might be required to move large numbers of casualties in the event of war. It was imperative that there should be sufficient large stand by ambulances for the transport of injured civilians to first aid posts and hospitals as aerial bombardment was expected within hours of the start of hostilities. During the Munich crisis of September 1938, a number of London Transport's Green Line coaches had been prepared for conversion and had proved very suitable for the work. Later the Ministry of Health approached large passenger transport companies to determine whether they were

willing to place vehicles at the disposal of the Government in a national emergency. Southdown was one of those that agreed to provide drivers and maintain and garage the vehicles. Arrangements were completed in March 1939, so that several months before war was declared, there were hundreds of coaches and single deck buses in regular service with fittings which, at very short notice, would enable them to be converted into stretcher carriers.

In late August, Southdown received the 'Stand to' order, and work began on the conversion of the vehicles. This required the removal of seats and parcel racks, windows made opaque and fitting of supports for ten stretchers plus other equipment to enable them to serve as civilian ambulances. Modifications were also made to the rear of the coach to enable the loading of stretchers through the luggage locker which could then be pushed along a special ramp fixed to the floor. Southdown converted 24 Leyland Tiger TS7 coaches for this work – cars 1089 to 1096, 1101, 1102, 1104, 1106 to 1115, 1120, 1123 and 1131 – including examples with Harrington, Park Royal and Beadle bodies. Most companies were able to complete the work within a few days of the outbreak of war although fortunately, after being used for initial evacuation duties, they were not required for civilian use for some months to come.

Whilst parked at the Royal Hospital, Portsmouth two of the fourteen ambulances based at Portsmouth – cars 1089 and 1092 – were totally destroyed during an air raid on the night of 10/11 January 1941. The surviving ambulances were released during 1945/6 and converted for normal coach operation with the first appearing in service during July 1945.

Car 1089 (BCD 889) was a Leyland Tiger TS7 with Harrington 32-seat body delivered in April 1935. Fitted with a folding sunroof and roof luggage rack it was used on the London Express Services until being chosen as a suitable candidate for conversion to an Ambulance. After conversion in August 1939 it was based at Portsmouth and was one of two coaches that were completely destroyed during an air raid on the night of 10/11 January 1941. *Alan Lambert Collection*

DESTINATION DISPLAYS

Buses

By comparison with most operators Southdown's destination displays during the 1930s were comprehensive and very informative. Starting in October 1928 the company had introduced the first of its standard service information displays with a sight opening measuring 41 inches x 10 inches. This was shown in a separate large screen box fitted in the centre at the front above the driver's cab. From 1930 the destination information was displayed on top of a separate glass panel on which the company name was painted either on a cream background or reversed out on a dark background. Most service buses entering the fleet from this time had screen boxes to these standards although the 1400 class Tigers had the Southdown name above the destination similar to the coach displays of the time. They were also fitted by Portslade Works to some other earlier vehicles such as the B10A2s and Dennis 30cwt buses. In addition a few of the older normal control double deck buses had a plain version of this display box but without the company name. These were separately fitted beneath the front of the canopy outside the windscreen on double deckers. Rear boxes of similar dimensions were also fitted from 1930 on double deckers or the end of 1934 on single deckers.

In addition Southdown continued to fit a route board to each side of the bus just below the saloon or lower deck windows. These were 5 feet

Car 838 (UF 5538) was a Leyland Titan TD1 with Leyland lowbridge body new in December 1929 and is seen here laying over in Pool Valley, Brighton between journeys on the short local service 13B to North Moulscombe. The side destination board illustrates the spelling of Moulscombe as used by Southdown at this time – even though it differed from contemporary OS maps. The bus was sold in March 1938 and saw service with several East Anglian independent operators ending up with Osborne of Tollesbury until final sale in October 1951. *Author's Collection*

Seen on a very wet day at Hailsham in May 1938 is car 174 (EUF 174), a Leyland Titan TD5 with Park Royal lowbridge body delivered just one month earlier. It is operating a southbound journey on service 92 from East Grinstead which does require the use of lowbridge buses due to a restricted bridge near Stone Cross. Note the detachable plate fitted at the bottom of the 14 inch screen box to enable the continued use of 10 inch screens. *S.L.Poole*

6 inches long showing intermediate points, service number and final destination and fitted into three brackets each side. From 1934 onwards the side boards were discontinued on new vehicles and were replaced by three boxes on each side above the lower deck windows. These consisted of a centre number box flanked by a destination box and a box showing via points. Although they were normally fitted to both sides of the vehicle, it proved impossible to accommodate them on the offside of lowbridge vehicles due to the sunken gangway.

In 1938 it was decided to increase the depth of the destination box to 14 inches and this new size was applied to all new buses delivered from this date except cars T16, T17, 80 and 81 which retained the 10 inch box. The latter also retained side boards mounted above the windows on both sides showing the principal places on the routes. To allow the use of the old 10 inch screens in the new buses, a 4 inch plate could be slotted in the bottom of the 14 inch box reducing it to 10 inches. This meant that the Southdown fleet name was no longer shown adjacent to the destination box. Also from this time new deliveries of both double deckers and single deckers were not fitted with the three displays on the offside although retaining this feature on the nearside.

During 1938 new designs of 14 inch screens came into use, but they were all for single deck routes and initially just sufficient to fit all the new 1400 class saloons delivered that year. New 14 inch screens for double deckers were

also introduced in Eastbourne for interworked services 16 and 25, but other garages had to wait until 1940 before new designs were brought into use.

There were very strict instructions to staff about what route information to show. For instance in the January 1939 changes in which service 9 was extended from Angmering Village via Littlehampton to Arundel conductors were advised that buses leaving Worthing must not show 'Arundel' as their destination because there was an alternative service 10 following a more direct route. Starting from Shoreham buses were to show:

NORTH LANCING
WORTHING
ANGMERING GREEN

From East Worthing, Half Brick Hotel to Angmering Village blinds or boards were altered to show:

PATCHING
ANGMERING GREEN
LITTLEHAMPTON

Finally from Angmering Village to Arundel blinds or boards were to show:

RUSTINGTON
LITTLEHAMPTON
ARUNDEL SQUARE

On leaving Arundel on the return journey they must not show any destination or via points beyond Angmering Village.

On the longer services such as the 31 it was necessary for the conductors to change the displays at designated points as the bus progressed along the route. For example on through westbound journeys the first display applied from Brighton to East Worthing, Half Brick Hotel and showed:

WORTHING
LITTLEHAMPTON
BOGNOR SOUTHSEA

From East Worthing to South Downs Hotel, Felpham blinds were changed to show:

LITTLEHAMPTON
BOGNOR &
PORTSMOUTH

Between South Downs Hotel, Felpham and Chichester, West Street blinds were changed to show:

CHICHESTER
PORTSMOUTH
SOUTHSEA

And, from Chichester to Southsea buses were to show:

PORTSMOUTH
GUILDHALL
SOUTHSEA

On journeys terminating in Portsmouth the final line was altered to THEATRE ROYAL. There were lots of other displays covering all the usual short workings at the start and finish of day.

With the changes of January 1939 services 31, 31F and 31G interworked at Brighton and new blinds and sideboards were required. Buses from

Car 150 (CCD 950) was a diesel engined Leyland Titan TD4c with Beadle 52-seat highbridge body delivered in July 1936. Buses fitted with a torque convertor were normally allocated only to Worthing where they ran on the easily graded town services so this must be a rare appearance by car 150 which is believed to be at Warsash at the far western end of service 45 – although this was also flat! Portsmouth bound buses did not at this time show a separate service number as seen here.
Frank Case

the 31 changed to a 31F or 31G at Pool Valley and Conductors were instructed to change the blinds at the last eastbound stop by the Savoy Cinema. Even in 1939 side boards had to be produced for these in case earlier TD1s and TD2s found their way on to the route. As many buses did not return to their home depot each night it was especially important to keep track of the side boards required for specific journeys and instructions were issued detailing which buses were to carry which boards! For example when the 1750 bus left Bognor for Brighton it had to be carrying the special side boards for a short working as it ended its day on the 2145 departure as far as Bognor. The Traffic Notice demanded strict adherence to the instructions but it is hard to imagine that, even in those days, mistakes were not made. New screens or side boards were produced even where they applied to just one journey per day – just showing 'Service' or 'Relief' was not acceptable for Southdown at this time! A special screen was even produced for the single late evening journey provided by service 9B which ran to Angmering Green via Angmering-on-Sea.

On service 59 which passed both ways through West Street in Chichester on its way between Bognor and Midhurst Conductors were instructed to turn the front side screen to blank before reaching Chichester Cross to avoid any confusion to waiting passengers. As all the intermediate points included had been passed the screens were to remain blank for the remainder of the journey. Along with the connections to be observed along the route Southdown Conductors had plenty to learn and commit to memory!

From 1940 onwards all of the older buses that were still in service had their boxes altered to take the new 14 inch designs, which meant removing the Southdown name from the box. Those which had the three boxes on the offside had them painted out in the case of single deckers or panelled over in the case of double deckers at the same time. Apart from car 8 the Leyland Cubs so fitted retained their Southdown names above the destination to the end. The Dennis Falcons, Shelvoke & Drewry, Leyland Tiger TS6T/TS7T and remaining Leyland Titan TD1 and TD2s were not altered and retained their existing boxes. After the war some of the Titans fitted with three nearside boxes had these replaced by a single box over the platform but the programme was never completed and a few Titan TD3s not rebodied in the post war scheme

retained them until withdrawal in 1953. Also most of those 1400 class Tigers fitted with the, now unused, three offside boxes had them removed in the post war rebuilding programme.

Coaches

These were generally fitted with a shallower destination box with the Southdown name below the display as on buses of the time. On those vehicles with a fully folding roof such as the Lioness and Cub touring coaches there was no space for a destination display. From 1934 the Southdown name was placed above the destination display and this continued into the 1950s. Coaches that were intended to be used on the company's Express Services were also fitted with removable side boards including service details such as:

EXPRESS LONDON AND BRIGHTON SERVICE

From the 1932 deliveries these could be fitted into a recess in the roof coving on both sides of the coach.

Liveries and fleet names

Southdown's famous livery during this period was apple green and cream with some dark green relief on the front wings and around the rear wheel arches. Dark green lining was also applied to double deck buses. Single deck buses were cream above the bottom of the window line and the 1400 class also had a separate cream band. Coaches had a cream band below the window line and dark green above. A single gold line was also applied below the lower deck windows on both buses and coaches. To reduce their visibility to enemy aircraft the roofs of both double deck and single deck buses were painted dark green at the start of the war, but otherwise vehicles continued to be repainted as normal, until supplies of cream paint ran low which is thought to be around 1942. There is photographic evidence to suggest that some vehicles retained a cream roof for several months as no air attacks materialised until June 1940.

Block style fleet names were applied to buses and a script style fleet name for coaches. There were a few exceptions and the Tigers for the Beachy Head service – cars 50-53 – and the two Dennis Falcons for the former Tramocars services – cars 80 and 81 – had script style fleet names from new. Fleet numbers were applied towards the rear on the nearsides and offsides of buses using black edged gold numerals. They were not applied to coaches during this period.

Southdown's impressive bus and coach station in Pevensey Road, Eastbourne opened for business in 1929 and in this view of the exit, probably posed soon after opening, are four Tilling-Stevens Express B10A2 saloons dating from 1928/9. On the left car 472 (UF 3072) is just leaving on service 91 to Uckfield via Heathfield while on its right is car 642 (UF 4642) on service 12 to Brighton via Seaford. In the right hand exit is car 473 (UF 3073) on service 92 to Chailey via Uckfield along with car 471 (UF 3071) on service 25 to Brighton via Lewes. All had rear entrance bodywork by Short Bros. Buses entered from Langney Road but most coach services transferred to nearby Cavendish Place when the new Coach Station opened in 1933. Although long closed the frontage is still easily recognizable to the present day. *Stilltime Images*

With a long and narrow operating territory Southdown divided the day to day management of the company into five separate geographical areas each of which was responsible for Stage Carriage bus services including Duty Schedules, Coach Services, Tours and Excursions programmes along with Private Hire quotations and engaging Drivers and Conductors. The five areas had their own local Manager and were based, from east to west, in Eastbourne (code E), Brighton (code A), Worthing code W), Bognor Regis (code B) and Portsmouth (code P). Vehicles were allocated to a specific area and the letter code was affixed somewhere in the driver's cab. On occasions the outstations changed between adjoining areas to meet operating requirements. The headquarters staff and organisation was based in Brighton.

During the 1920s Southdown had built many fine garages and small but practical 'dormy' sheds as the fleet expanded and this programme continued during the 1930s. The so called 'dormy' sheds were usually in country districts and held just one or two buses for overnight parking which then returned to the principal depots each day for fuelling, cleaning and maintenance. Many of these continued to function into the 1960s. Other overnight parking was rented in open yards and also at railway stations by arrangement with the Southern Railway.

A comprehensive central overhaul works was located in Victoria Road, Portslade opened in 1928 and further extended in 1931 by covering the area known as the 'Paddock'. This was staffed and designed to handle just about every part or function that was ever likely to be needed for the maintenance of the fleet. A significant proportion of the fleet was laid up during the winter months and some fifty 'dual purpose' employees who worked on overhauls at Portslade during the winter were transferred to the depots as drivers, conductors or tradesmen in summer.

The 1930s saw further improvements and expansion. To cater for passengers on the London to Brighton and Worthing via Crawley express services Southdown decided in 1931 to open their own refreshment facilities at County Oak one mile north of Crawley. Following the takeover of Chapmans in Eastbourne in March 1932 the Victoria Garage in Susans Road was rebuilt and became known as Cavendish Coach Station in 1933 providing much improved facilities for passengers on the London services. The company's association with East Grinstead began in July 1933 following the extension of services northwards on the establishment of the London Passenger Transport Board and a new garage in Chequer Road was opened for business on 9 January 1934 with an enquiry office at 11 High Street following in December 1937. This lasted until October 1938 when the office at 33 High Street opened for business.

Expansion in the Portsmouth area demanded a large new garage and coach station which was opened at London Road, Hilsea on the northern edge of Portsea Island in May 1934. This was followed by an especially impressive new bus and coach station in High Street, Bognor Regis in January 1935 and, to cater for growing seasonal demand, a garage was opened at Elm Grove on Hayling Island in September 1935. A new garage at Bedford Row in Worthing with accommodation for a further 50 buses and modern offices for staff was finally opened in May 1940 and proved to be the last major work built on Southdown's behalf until the 1950s. The company established offices for enquiries, bookings and parcels throughout its operating area and this continued during the 1930s. It was not so keen on providing off street bus and coach stations in the main towns although new premises were established in Eastbourne, Bognor Regis and Uckfield. Pool Valley in Brighton had become the new departure terminal for stage services in the town in July 1929 but congested on street departure points in Lewes and Chichester were not resolved until the 1950s.

GARAGES, BUS & COACH STATIONS AT 1 JANUARY 1930

Head Office: 5 Steine Street, BRIGHTON

EASTBOURNE	**(E)**	Pevensey Road Bus Station
		Royal Parade *extension planned 24/2/1930 completed 7/30*
		Langney Road Bus Station *closed 9/35*
ALFRISTON		West Street
HEATHFIELD		Tilsmore Road
LOWER DICKER		Hellingly Garage
SEAFORD		Richmond Road *closed 4/32 and replaced by Dane Road*
UCKFIELD		Mill Road *closed 4/36 and replaced by High Street*
BRIGHTON	**(A)**	Freshfield Road. *Adjacent land and property acquired 9/38 extension agreed 3/39*
		Royal Mews, Steine Street Coach Station
		Manchester Street
		Edward Street. *Extension 3/30 completed by 7/30*
BOLNEY		London Road, A23
CHELWOOD GATE		Beaconsfield Road
EAST HOATHLY		Routh & Stevens
HANDCROSS		Unknown location. *New garage at London Road, A23 (1/37)*
HAYWARDS HEATH		Gordon Road. *Additional land purchased 9/31, extension nearing completion 9/32*
HENFIELD		Unknown location possibly station yard. *New garage at Station Road (9/30) authorised 1/31, building extended and completed 1/33*
LEWES		Eastgate
SCAYNES HILL		On A272 *closed 4/36*
STEYNING		Star Inn
WORTHING	**(W)**	Steyne Mews. *New garage (extension) authorised in Library Place 4/32 nearing completion 9/32 fully occupied by 1/33*
HORSHAM		Denne Road *but let to Fry & Co. 6/35*
LITTLEHAMPTON		19/21 East Street
PULBOROUGH		Unknown location possibly SR station yard. *London Road (12/35) garage opened 6/36*
STORRINGTON		Amberley Road
BOGNOR REGIS	**(B)**	Fields Garage, Richmond Road
CHICHESTER		Northgate
EAST WITTERING		Longlands Farm. *Garage rebuilt to accommodate double deckers 3/35*
MIDHURST		Unknown location possibly SR station yard
PETWORTH		Angel Street
SELSEY		New Inn
SINGLETON		Unknown location possibly SR station yard
PORTSMOUTH	**(P)**	Hyde Park Road. *Adjacent premises purchase planned 2/30 and authorised 1/31. Improved passenger accommodation following changes to Costal Express service 3/32*
		53 Clarendon Road, Southsea *closed and sold 12/32*
CLANFIELD		Premises acquired from Pinhorn in 7/29. *Garage in North Lane opened 8/30*
EMSWORTH		Fords Lane. *Extension approved 5/34 opened by 6/34*
PETERSFIELD		Station Road
WARSASH		Warsash Road

OFFICES AT 1 JANUARY 1930

ARUNDEL	High Street
BOGNOR REGIS	Beach House, Esplanade *closed c7/35*
BRIGHTON	5 Steine Street
	Aquarium Kiosk, Palace Pier
	West Street Kiosk, Kings Road
CHICHESTER	11 West Street. *Authorised extension of offices 5/31*
EASTBOURNE	1 Cavendish Place
HAILSHAM	43 High Street
HAVANT	3 South Street. *No 1 South Street added 1932 and No 5 South Street added 12/36*
HAYWARDS HEATH	Kiosk, Railway Station. *New office built by SR 12/31 opened 8/32*
HORNDEAN	Ship & Bell waiting room
HORSHAM	22 Richmond Terrace, Carfax
LONDON	7b Belgrave Street, Pimlico, SW1. *Closed by 3/32*
LEWES	174 High Street
NEWHAVEN	1 Bridge Street
PETERSFIELD	27 The Square
PETWORTH	The Square
PORTSMOUTH	Southdown Buildings, North End Junction
	69 Commercial Road
SEAFORD	5 Clinton Place
SHOREHAM-BY-SEA	86 High Street
SOUTHSEA	South Parade Pier Kiosk
	No 5 Kiosk near Canoe Lake
WASHINGTON	Frankland Arms
WORTHING	23 Marine Parade

CENTRAL WORKS Victoria Road, Portslade. *Extension completed 4/31*

Additional premises were acquired during the 1930s and in some cases open parking was used to establish a base before a garage was built although not necessarily on the same site. The dates indicated in brackets are those when the purchase of land or premises took place and not the date they became operational which was often up to 12 months later. Where known, opening dates are shown. Various other pieces of land or premises were leased, purchased or sold from time to time but do not seem to have been directly used in connection with the principal business and are not therefore included.

GARAGES

BARNS GREEN	Two Mile Ash Road (3/35)
BOARHUNT	Unknown location acquired from Blue Motor Services (Southwick) Ltd 8/35. *Closed and buses transferred to Wickham by 9/36*
BOGNOR REGIS	Bus Station, 66-70 High Street (1/34) opened 1/35
BRIGHTON	11/11A/12 Manchester Street (12/32)
COMPTON	Unknown location
DIAL POST	A24 (4/31) Garage being erected 3/33
EASTBOURNE	Victoria Garage, Susans Road (3/32) *(ex Chapman & Sons – after rebuilding in 1933 became known as Cavendish Coach Station). Further work in 1937 and 1938*
	Susans Road *ex Chapman 5/32 rented on a monthly basis pending decision on future needs.*
EAST GRINSTEAD	22/24 Chequer Road (1/34) opened -/34
HAMBLEDON	West Street (3/35) *ex Denmead Queen*
HANDCROSS	London Road, A23 (1/37)
HAYLING ISLAND	59 Elm Grove (9/35) opened 5/36
HORSHAM	Denne Road (1/35) opened 6/35 and known as South Garage
HURSTPIERPOINT	Mansion House, West Furlong Lane (9/38) *(ex L. Cherriman)*
PORTSMOUTH	London Road, Hilsea opened 6/34, extended 1/39
SEAFORD	Dane Road (11/31) open by 3/32
UCKFIELD	High Street (2/35) opened 4/36
WICKHAM	Station Road (5/36) opened 9/36
WIVELSFIELD	Unknown location
WORTHING	Bedford Row (5/31) extension agreed 6/39 opened 5/40

An interesting view of Pool Valley in Brighton sometime between October 1935 and June 1938 illustrates the changing face of the Southdown fleet. On the far left is car 111 (BUF 211) a Leyland Titan TD4 with Short Bros lowbridge body new in September 1935. Next is car 833 (UF 5533) a Leyland Titan TD1 with Leyland lowbridge body new December 1929. Unlike the remainder of the buses present it did not survive until the outbreak of war and was sold in June 1938. In the centre of the picture is car 1409 (BUF 989) a Leyland Tiger TS7 with Harrington body new in October 1935. Three of Southdown's large fleet of Tilling-Stevens Express B10A2 single deck buses dating from 1929/30 complete the scene. Third from left is car 679 (UF 5679) with Short Bros body while to the right of the picture are 1200 (UF 6600) another with Short Bros body and car 675 (UF 5075) with Harrington body. The latter is on service 21 to Bungalow Town as the area of Shoreham Beach was described in the 1930s. All three Tilling-Stevens buses survived until requisitioned by the Military Authorities in July 1940.
A.Norris, Omnibus Society

OFFICES

BOGNOR REGIS	Elmer Bus Stand (7/34)
BRIGHTON	Royal York Buildings, Pool Valley (4/30)
	14/15/16/17 Manchester Street for use as an employees' club (5/31) completed 9/31
EASTBOURNE	Kiosk, Pier Gates (3/32) *(ex Chapman & Sons)*
	Cavendish Place adjoining Claremont Hotel (3/33) *(ex Pratt & Pearce)*
EAST GRINSTEAD	11 High Street (12/37) closed 10/38 and replaced by 33 High Street 10/38
HOVE	7 St Aubyn's Gardens *(ex Poole's Royal Red Coaches in 3/30)*
LONDON	17 Ebury Street, Belgravia, SW1 (3/32) *(ex Chapman & Sons)* closed 1/38 as located too close to Victoria Coach Station and replaced by 27 Princes Street, Hanover Square, W1 12/37
LITTLEHAMPTON	Kiosk, The Parade (5/31)
MIDHURST	North Street (c5/30)
SOUTHSEA	241 Albert Road (5/35) *(ex Alexandra Coaches)*
	Traffic Regulators Kiosk, South Parade (3/37)
UCKFIELD	200 High Street (c4/31) closed 4/36 and replaced by Bus Station, High Street
WORTHING	4 Arcade Buildings (12/33) *(ex Fairway Coaches)* closed 11/35
	2 New Broadway, Tarring Road (7/35)
	5 Arcade Buildings (9/35)
	45 Marine Parade (12/36) *(ex C.J. Landsall)*

ROAD HOUSE/ LICENSED RESTAURANT & BAR

CRAWLEY	London Road, County Oak (9/30). Work commenced 3/31 opened 8/31. Ladies toilet accommodation extended 4/32 and further alterations followed in 1938

An impressive line up of Leyland and Tilling-Stevens coaches at the Crawley Station probably very soon after the opening in August 1931. The new image is represented by car 1048 (UF 7348) on the extreme left of the picture. Delivered in May 1931 it is a Leyland Tiger TS1 with Harrington 30-seat coach body which was requisitioned by the Military Authorities in July 1940. With Southdown opting for rear or centre entrances for all its Express Service coaches until the Beadle-Commers in 1956/7 it made sense for vehicles to be reversed into the bays to allow passengers to alight as close as possible to the covered awning.
Argus

Appendix 1

SOUTHDOWN FLEET AS AT 1 JANUARY 1930

1	CD 5001	DAIMLER CB	HARRINGTON Ch26 (1922)	1914
2	CD 5002	DAIMLER CB	HARRINGTON Ch23C (1922)	1914
27	LP 8233	DAIMLER CB	HARRINGTON Ch18F (??)	1915
35	CD 8569	DAIMLER CK22	DODSON Ch/B28R	1924
48	CD 5648	TILLING-STEVENS TS3A	SOUTHDOWN B30R (1926)	1920
49	CD 349	TILLING-STEVENS TS3	TILLING O27/24RO (1924)	1920
50	CD 5648	TILLING-STEVENS TS3A	SOUTHDOWN B30R (1927)	1920
51	CD 4951	TILLING-STEVENS TS3	HARRINGTON Ch30R (1924)	1914
54	UF 2199	TILLING-STEVENS-SOUTHDOWN	SHORT BROS B25F	1927
55	CD 4855	TILLING-STEVENS TS3A	SOUTHDOWN B30R (1927)	1913
56-57	CD 4856-7	TILLING-STEVENS TS3A	HARRINGTON B31R (1926)	1914
58	CD 4858	TILLING-STEVENS TS3	SHORT BROS B25F (1927)	1914
59	CD 4859	TILLING-STEVENS TS3	SHORT BROS B25F (1928)	1914
60	CD 4860	TILLING-STEVENS TS3	TILLING O27/24RO (1924)	1914
61	CD 4861	TILLING-STEVENS TS3	SHORT BROS B25F (1928)	1919
62	CD 4862	TILLING-STEVENS TS3A	SOUTHDOWN B31R (1926)	1919
63	CD 4863	TILLING-STEVENS TS3	HARRINGTON Ch27C (1923)	1919
64	CD 4864	TILLING-STEVENS TS3A	TILLING O27/24RO (1927)	1919
65	CD 4865	TILLING-STEVENS TS3	HARRINGTON B33R (1923)	1919
67	CD 4867	TILLING-STEVENS TS3A	TILLING O27/24RO (1926)	1919
69	CD 4869	TILLING-STEVENS TS3	HARRINGTON B33R (1923)	1919
70	CD 4870	TILLING-STEVENS TS3A	TILLING O27/24RO (1927)	1919
71	CD 4871	TILLING-STEVENS TS3A	TILLING O27/24RO (1926)	1919
72	CD 4872	TILLING-STEVENS TS3	SHORT BROS B25F (1928)	1919
73	CD 4873	TILLING-STEVENS TS3A	TILLING O27/24RO (1926)	1919
75	CD 4875	TILLING-STEVENS TS3	HARRINGTON B33R (1923)	1920
76-79	CD 4876-9	TILLING-STEVENS TS3	BRUSH B29F	1920
81	CD 1581	TILLING-STEVENS TS3	SHORT BROS B25F (1927)	1920
83	CD 1583	TILLING-STEVENS TS3	SOUTHDOWN B30R (1926)	1920
84	CD 2184	TILLING-STEVENS TS3	HARRINGTON Ch27C (1923)	1920
85	CD 2485	TILLING-STEVENS TS3	SOUTHDOWN B30R (1926)	1920
86-87	CD 5586-7	TILLING-STEVENS TS3A	TILLING O27/24RO (1927)	1920
88	CD 5588	TILLING-STEVENS TS3	SHORT BROS B25F (1927)	1920
89-90	CD 5589-90	TILLING-STEVENS TS3A	TILLING O27/24RO (1927)	1920
94	CD 6894	TILLING-STEVENS TS3A	TILLING O27/24RO	1922
96	CD 6896	TILLING-STEVENS TS3A	TILLING O27/24RO (1923)	1922
100	CD 6900	TILLING-STEVENS TS3A	TILLING O27/24RO (1928)	1922
102	CD 3532	LEYLAND N	TILLING O27/24RO (1928)	1919
105	CD 3535	LEYLAND N	TILLING O27/24RO (1928)	1919
106	CD 3536	LEYLAND N	TILLING O27/24RO (1926)	1919
107	CD 3537	LEYLAND N	TILLING O27/24RO (1923)	1919
109	CD 5109	LEYLAND N	Chassis only	1919
110-111	CD 5110-1	LEYLAND N	TILLING O27/24RO (1926)	1919
112	CD 5112	LEYLAND N	TILLING O27/24RO (1925)	1919
113-114	CD 5113-4	LEYLAND N	HARRINGTON Ch30R (1927)	1919
115-116	CD 5115-6	LEYLAND N	TILLING O27/24RO (1928)	1919
117	CD 5117	LEYLAND N	SHORT BROS O27/24RO (1928)	1919
118	CD 5118	LEYLAND N	TILLING O27/24RO (1923)	1919
119	CD 5119	LEYLAND N	TILLING O27/24RO (1927)	1920
120	CD 5120	LEYLAND N	TILLING O27/24RO (1926)	1919
121-122	CD 5121-2	LEYLAND N	HARRINGTON Ch28R (1927)	1920
123-124	CD 5123-4	LEYLAND N	HARRINGTON Ch28R (1926)	1920
125	CD 5125	LEYLAND N	SHORT BROS O27/24RO (1928)	1920
126	CD 5126	LEYLAND N	SHORT BROS O27/24RO (1928)	1921
128	CD 5128	LEYLAND N	TILLING O27/24RO (1926)	1921
129	CD 5129	LEYLAND N	SHORT BROS O27/24RO (1928)	1921
130	CD 5130	LEYLAND N	TILLING O27/24RO (1926)	1921
131	CD 6541	LEYLAND G7	SHORT BROS O27/24RO (1928)	1921
132	CD 6542	LEYLAND G7	TILLING O27/24RO (1927)	1921
133	CD 6543	LEYLAND G7	TILLING O27/24RO (1923)	1921
134-135	CD 7044-5	LEYLAND N Special	SHORT BROS O27/24RO (1928)	1922

138-142	CD 7138-42	LEYLAND G7		TILLING O27/24RO	1922
144	CD 7144	LEYLAND G7		HARRINGTON B31R (1926)	1922
145	CD 7145	LEYLAND G7		TILLING O27/24RO (1928)	1922
146	CD 7723	LEYLAND G7		HARRINGTON Ch30R	1923
150	CD 7720	LEYLAND G7		Chassis only	1923
152	CD 7722	LEYLAND G7		HARRINGTON Ch30R	1923
153-154	CD 7713-4	LEYLAND G7		SHORT BROS O27/24RO (1929)	1923
155	CD 7715	LEYLAND G7		SHORT BROS O27/24RO (1928)	1923
156	CD 7716	LEYLAND G7		TILLING O27/24RO	1923
158	CD 7718	LEYLAND G7		TILLING O27/24RO	1923
160	CD 9877	LEYLAND G7		HARRINGTON Ch30R	1923
165	CD 8065	LEYLAND G7 Special		TILLING O27/24RO	1923
168	CD 8378	LEYLAND G7 Special		HARRINGTON B31R (1926)	1924
169	CD 8379	LEYLAND G7 Special		HARRINGTON Ch30R	1924
171-172	CD 8381-2	LEYLAND G7 Special		HARRINGTON Ch30R	1924
175	CD 8900	LEYLAND G7		HARRINGTON Ch30R	1924
177	CD 9877	LEYLAND G7 Special		HARRINGTON Ch30R	1925
178-180	CD 9708-10	LEYLAND G7 Special		HARRINGTON Ch30R	1925
181-184	CD 9881-4	LEYLAND G7 Special		HARRINGTON Ch30R	1925
185	CD 9711	LEYLAND SG11		TILLING B35R	1925
186	CD 9712	LEYLAND SG11		TILLING B36R	1925
187	CD 9817	LEYLAND SG11		TILLING B35R	1925
189-190	UF 89-90	LEYLAND SG11		TILLING B36R	1925
192-194	UF 92-4	LEYLAND G7 Special		HARRINGTON Ch30R	1925
195-199	UF 995-9	LEYLAND SG7		TILLING O27/24RO	1926
200	UF 2200	TILLING-STEVENS-SOUTHDOWN		SHORT BROS B25F	1927
204-206	CD 7704-6	TILLING-STEVENS TS3A		TILLING O27/24RO	1923
208-212	CD 7708-12	TILLING-STEVENS TS3A		TILLING O27/24RO	1923
214-216	CD 8014-6	TILLING-STEVENS TS3A		TILLING O27/24RO	1923
217	CD 8417	TILLING-STEVENS TS3A		TILLING O27/24RO	1924
219-224	CD 8419-24	TILLING-STEVENS TS3A		TILLING O27/24RO	1924
225	CD 9225	TILLING-STEVENS TS3A		TILLING O27/24RO	1925
226-236	CD 9226-36	TILLING-STEVENS TS6		TILLING O27/24RO	1925
237	CD 9837	TILLING-STEVENS TS6		TILLING B36R	1925
238	CD 9838	TILLING-STEVENS TS6		TILLING B35R	1925
239	CD 9839	TILLING-STEVENS TS6		TILLING B35R	1925
240	CD 9640	TILLING-STEVENS TS3A		TILLING O27/24RO (1924)	1925
241	CD 9640	TILLING-STEVENS TS3A		TILLING O27/24RO (1927)	1925
242-247	UF 42-7	TILLING-STEVENS TS3A		TILLING O27/24RO	1925
248-257	UF 748-57	TILLING-STEVENS TS3A		TILLING O27/24RO	1926
341	BK 2879	DENNIS 3 ton		chassis only	1919
342	BK 2880	DENNIS 3 ton		chassis only	1919
343	BK 4505	DENNIS 3 ton		HARRINGTON Ch30R (1927)	1920
344	BP 8603	DENNIS 2½ ton		LONDON LORRIES Ch20F	1922
345	BP 8799	DENNIS 2½ ton		LONDON LORRIES Ch20F	1922
349	BK 2881	DENNIS 3 ton		HARRINGTON Ch30R (1927)	1919
350	BK 2883	DENNIS 3 ton		HARRINGTON Ch30R (1927)	1919
351	BK 2884	DENNIS 3 ton		chassis only	1919
352	BK 4051	DENNIS 3 ton		chassis only	1919
353	BK 4294	DENNIS 3 ton		chassis only	1920
355	BK 4432	DENNIS 3 ton		chassis only	1920
356	BK 4379	DENNIS 3 ton		HARRINGTON Ch30R 1927)	1920
357	BK 4394	DENNIS 3 ton		chassis only	1920
359	BK 4433	DENNIS 3 ton		chassis only	1920
360	BK 4530	DENNIS 3 ton		chassis only	1920
361	BK 4500	DENNIS 3 ton		chassis only	1920
364	BK 4502	DENNIS 3 ton		chassis only	1920
365	BK 4504	DENNIS 3 ton		chassis only	1920
367	BK 4435	DENNIS 3 ton		chassis only	1920
368	BK 6585	DENNIS 3 ton		LONDON LORRIES Ch20R	1922
369	BK 6648	DENNIS 3 ton		LONDON LORRIES Ch20R	1922
370	BK 6682	DENNIS 3 ton		HARRINGTON Ch30R 1928)	1922
371	BK 6709	DENNIS 3 ton		LONDON LORRIES Ch20R	1922
372	BK 6747	DENNIS 2½ ton		LONDON LORRIES Ch20R	1922

373	BK 6760	DENNIS 2½ ton	LONDON LORRIES Ch20R	1922
375-376	TP 29-30	DENNIS 4 ton	HICKMAN O26/24RO	1924
381	HC 9385	GRAHAM DODGE TDS	??? B20-	1928
382	JK 88	THORNYCROFT A2	STRACHAN B22R	1929
383	HC 9159	THORNYCROFT A2	??? B20-	1928
391	TP 7485	DENNIS E	DENNIS B32R	1929
392	JK 210	DENNIS E	STRACHAN B31F	1929
401-410	UF 1001-10	TILLING-STEVENS B9B	HARRINGTON Ch30R	1926
411	UF 2011	TILLING-STEVENS B9B	HARRINGTON C29R	1927
412	UF 1814	TILLING-STEVENS B9B	HARRINGTON C29R	1927
413	UF 1813	TILLING-STEVENS B9B	HARRINGTON C29R	1927
414-416	UF 2014-6	TILLING-STEVENS B9B	HARRINGTON C29R	1927
417-430	UF 2017-30	TILLING-STEVENS B9B	HARRINGTON Ch29R	1927
431-437	UF 2031-7	TILLING-STEVENS B9B	TILLING C29R	1927
438	UF 2038	TILLING-STEVENS B9B	HARRINGTON C29R	1927
439-444	UF 2039-44	TILLING-STEVENS B9B	LONDON LORRIES Ch30R	1927
445-459	UF 2945-59	TILLING-STEVENS B9B	HARRINGTON C30R	1928
480-483	UF 3080-3	TILLING-STEVENS B9BL	HARRINGTON C20R	1928
501-518	UF 1501-18	DENNIS 30 cwt	SHORT BROS B19R	1927
519	UF 1519	DENNIS 30 cwt	HARRINGTON Ch18F	1927
520	UF 1520	DENNIS 30 cwt	HARRINGTON B19R	1927
521	UF 1182	DENNIS 30 cwt	HARRINGTON Ch14R	1927
522-526	UF 3022-6	DENNIS 30 cwt	SHORT BROS B19F	1927
527-531	UF 3027-31	DENNIS G	SHORT BROS C18R	1927
532	UF 4532	DENNIS G	SHORT BROS C18F	1929
533	TP 6947	DENNIS 30 cwt	STRACHAN & BROWN B18F	1928
534	TP 7563	DENNIS 30 cwt	STRACHAN B18F	1929
600	UF 4300	TILLING-STEVENS B10A2	SHORT O24/24RO	1929
601-619	UF 3061-79	TILLING-STEVENS B10A2	SHORT B32R	1928
620-621	UF 3824-5	TILLING-STEVENS B10A2	HARRINGTON B30R	1928
622-623	UF 3822-3	TILLING-STEVENS B10A2	HARRINGTON B30R	1928
624	UF 3584	TILLING-STEVENS B10A2	TILLING B32R	1928
625	UF 3585	TILLING-STEVENS B10A2	HARRINGTON B32R	1928
626-631	UF 3586-91	TILLING-STEVENS B10A2	TILLING B32R	1928
632-634	UF 3592-4	TILLING-STEVENS B10A2	HARRINGTON B32R	1928
635-637	UF 3595-7	TILLING-STEVENS B10A2	TILLING B32R	1928
638	UF 3826	TILLING-STEVENS B10A2	HARRINGTON B30R	1928
639-640	UF 4239-40	TILLING-STEVENS B10A2	HARRINGTON B30R	1929
641	UF 4641	TILLING-STEVENS B10A2	HARRINGTON B32R	1929
642-663	UF 4642-63	TILLING-STEVENS B10A2	SHORT B31R	1929
664-671	UF 5064-71	TILLING-STEVENS B10A2	SHORT B31R	1929
672-677	UF 5072-7	TILLING-STEVENS B10A2	HARRINGTON B31R	1929
679	UF 5679	TILLING-STEVENS B10A2	SHORT B31R	1929
682-685	UF 5682-5	TILLING-STEVENS B10A2	SHORT B31R	1929
689	UF 5689	TILLING-STEVENS B10A2	SHORT B31R	1929
701	UF 4001	TILLING-STEVENS B10B2	HARRINGTON C30R	1928
702-711	UF 4502-11	TILLING-STEVENS B10B2	HARRINGTON C30R	1929
712-715	UF 4512-15	TILLING-STEVENS B10B2	HARRINGTON C20R	1929
716-718	UF 4825-17	TILLING-STEVENS B10B2	HARRINGTON C30R	1929
719-722	UF 5019-22	TILLING-STEVENS B10B2	HARRINGTON C30R	1929
723	UF 5423	TILLING-STEVENS B10B2	HARRINGTON C30R (1926)	1929
727-732	UF 5830-5	TILLING-STEVENS B10B2	HARRINGTON C30R (1926)	1929
734	UF 5734	TILLING-STEVENS B10B2	HARRINGTON C30R (1926)	1929
801-823	UF 4801-23	LEYLAND TITAN TD1	BRUSH O27/24RO	1929
824-829	UF 5424-9	LEYLAND TITAN TD1	LEYLAND L24/24R	1929
830-845	UF 5530-45	LEYLAND TITAN TD1	LEYLAND L24/24R	1929

ON ORDER – Six TILLING-STEVENS B10B2 (678/80/1/6/7/80) and four TILLING-STEVENS B10B2 to be fitted with second hand HARRINGTON C30R bodies dating from 1926 (724-6/33) remained outstanding

SOUTHDOWN BUS & COACH SERVICES AS AT 1 JANUARY 1930

All services operate daily except where otherwise stated

1	Worthing Dome – Findon – Storrington
2	Worthing Dome – Findon – Horsham Carfax
3	Elm Grove – Tarring – Worthing Town Hall – East Worthing Half Brick Hotel *(loop in both directions)* – Worthing Pier – Tarring – Elm Grove *(No service until 1400 on Sundays)*
4	Worthing Dome – Thomas A'Beckett Hotel – Durrington – High Salvington
5	Goring Church – Worthing Pier – Broadwater – Wigmore Road *(Weekdays)*
5A	Worthing Town Hall – Sompting *(Weekdays)*
5S	Worthing Pier – Broadwater – Wigmore Road – Sompting *(Sundays – No service until 1400)*
6	Worthing Pier – Broadwater – Thomas A' Becket Hotel – Clifton Arms – Worthing Pier
10	Worthing Dome – Angmering-on-Sea
10A	Worthing Dome – Offington Corner – Patching – Poling – Arundel Square
10B	Arundel Square – Walberton – Middleton-on-Sea – Bognor Pier *(Summer only)*
11	Brighton Pool Valley – Shoreham – Lancing – Worthing – Goring Church OR
11	Brighton Pool Valley – Shoreham – Sussex Pad Hotel – Lancing – Worthing – Goring Church
12	Brighton Station – Newhaven – Seaford – Eastbourne
12	Brighton Pool Valley – Peacehaven Annexe
13	Brighton Pool Valley – Lewes – Newhaven
14	Brighton Pool Valley – Bolney – Haywards Heath Station – Lindfield
15	Eastbourne – Hailsham – Ninfield – Hastings
16	Brighton Pool Valley – Lewes – Laughton – Golden Cross – East Hoathly
17	Brighton Pool Valley – Henfield – Cowfold – Horsham Carfax
18	Brighton Pool Valley – Lewes – Heathfield – Hawkhurst
19	Brighton Pool Valley – Uckfield
20	Brighton Pool Valley – Lewes – Chailey – Haywards Heath – Cuckfield or Borde Hill – Balcombe
21	Southwick (Town Hall) – Shoreham
22	Brighton Pool Valley – Steyning – Pulborough – Petworth – Duncton
23	Brighton Pool Valley – Ditchling – Haywards Heath Station – Handcross
24	Brighton Pool Valley – Lewes – Ditchling – Hurstpierpoint – Henfield
25	Brighton Pool Valley – Lewes – Eastbourne
26	Seaford – Alfriston – Berwick
27	Brighton Pool Valley – Devil's Dyke Hotel – Poynings – Small Dole – Henfield George
30	Brighton Pool Valley – Burgess Hill – Haywards Heath Station – Chelwood Gate
31	Brighton Pool Valley – Worthing – Littlehampton – Bognor – Chichester – Emsworth – Portsmouth Theatre Royal – Southsea South Parade Pier
31A	Westbourne – Emsworth – Havant – Fratton – Southsea South Parade Pier
31B	Havant – Portsmouth Theatre Royal – Southsea South Parade Pier
40	Southsea South Parade Pier – Theatre Royal – Purbrook – Waterlooville – Clanfield – East Meon
41	Southsea South Parade Pier – Fratton – Purbrook – Waterlooville – Horndean
42	Southsea South Parade Pier – Theatre Royal – Purbrook – Waterlooville – Horndean – Petersfield – South Harting
43	Farlington – Portsmouth Theatre Royal
45	Southsea South Parade Pier – Theatre Royal – Fareham – Warsash
46	Churchers Corner – Westbourne – Havant – Portsmouth Theatre Royal – Southsea South Parade Pier
47	Portsmouth Theatre Royal – Havant – Hayling Island – Havant – Portsmouth Theatre Royal (Hayling loop in both directions)
48	Waterlooville – Havant – Hayling Island (loop in clockwise direction)
49	Horndean – Havant – Hayling Island (loop in clockwise direction)
50	Elmer New City – Bognor
51	Bognor Pier – Linden Road – Aldwick Road – Bognor (Circular in both directions)
52	Chichester Station – Hunston – Sidlesham – Selsey Marine Hotel
52	Chichester Station – Donnington – Sidlesham – Selsey Marine Hotel

53	Chichester Cross – Birdham – East Wittering – West Wittering – Birdham – Chichester Cross (Circular in both directions)
53	Chichester Cross – Itchenor
54	Chichester Cross – Funtington – Churchers Corner – Compton
54	Chichester Cross – Funtington – Churchers Corner – Emsworth (Saturdays)
56	Halnaker – Boxgrove – Tangmere – Chichester Cross – Old Bosham
57	Chichester Cross – Tangmere – Westergate – Bognor Pier
58	Chichester Cross – Singleton – East Dean
59	Bognor Station – Chichester – Midhurst – Petersfield
59A	Bognor Station – Chichester – Midhurst – Petworth – Billingshurst – Horsham
61	Bognor – Pagham
64	Chichester Cross – Westergate – Barnham – Yapton Sparks Corner
65	Littlehampton – Arundel – Amberley – Storrington – West Chiltington
66	Littlehampton – Arundel – Slindon Common – Chichester Cross
68	Angmering Green – Littlehampton – Arundel
69	Littlehampton – Arundel – Pulborough – Billingshurst – Horsham Station
81	Haywards Heath Station – Cowfold – Billingshurst – Wisborough Green
82	Haywards Heath Station – Cuckfield – Handcross – Lower Beeding – Horsham
88	Haywards Heath Station – Lindfield – Ardingly – Turners Hill
91	Eastbourne Pevensey Road – Hailsham – Horam – Heathfield – Uckfield
92	Eastbourne Pevensey Road – Stone Cross – Hailsham – Uckfield – Chailey
93	Eastbourne Langney Road – Wannock – Jevington
93B	Eastbourne Langney Road – Polegate Station
96	Eastbourne Pevensey Road – Stone Cross – Pevensey Bay – Pevensey Bay Road – Eastbourne (Circular in both directions)

Services 15 and 18 were operated jointly with Maidstone and District Motor Services Ltd.

EXPRESS SERVICES

Eastbourne – Hailsham – Uckfield – East Grinstead – Caterham – London 1A Lupus Street

Brighton – Lewes – Uckfield – East Grinstead – Caterham – London Charing Cross (Suspended)

Brighton – Bolney – Handcross – Crawley – Redhill – London Charing Cross

Brighton – Burgess Hill – Cuckfield – Handcross – Crawley – Redhill – London Charing Cross

Littlehampton – Worthing – Horsham – Crawley – Redhill – London 1A Lupus Street

Bognor Regis – Littlehampton – Arundel – Dorking – Sutton – London 1A Lupus Street (Suspended)

Bognor Regis – Chichester – Guildford – Kingston – London 1A Lupus Street

Portsmouth – Petersfield – Guildford – Kingston – London 1A Lupus Street

COASTAL EXPRESS SERVICE Hastings – Brighton – Portsmouth – Bournemouth (Suspended)

Appendix 3

VEHICLES ACQUIRED SECONDHAND 1930-1939

From J. POOLE t/a ROYAL RED COACHES, HOVE, SUSSEX – 28 MARCH 1930

29	PN 3091	CHEVROLET LQ	???Ch14	1929
31	BH 8896	FIAT	???Ch14	1922
32	PM 583	FIAT	???Ch14	1922
33	BP 6649	FIAT	???Ch14	1921
34	XK 6897	FIAT	???Ch14	1921
384	PN 3465	THORNYCROFT A2	REDHEAD Ch20F	1929
500	PM 9170	DENNIS 30 cwt	BAKER Ch14	1927

From A. POTTS t/a POTTS MOTOR SERVICES, BRIGHTON, SUSSEX – 5 JUNE 1930

28	CD 6879	DAIMLER Y	???Ch26	1922
30	PC 9910	FIAT	???Ch14	1923
36	CD 4909	DAIMLER CK	???Ch23	1919
393	UF 4501	DENNIS F	DUPLE C30R	1929
394	UF 4516	DENNIS F	DUPLE C30R	1929
395	UF 4925	DENNIS F	DUPLE C30R	1929
396	UF 1832	DENNIS $2\frac{1}{2}$ ton	DUPLE C25R (1929)	1927
536	UF 4867	DENNIS GL	???Ch18F	1929
537	UF 4848	DENNIS GL	???Ch18F	1929

From SOUTHERN GLIDEWAY COACHES LTD, EASTBOURNE, SUSSEX – 1 MARCH 1932

30	JK 857	G.M.C.	???C13R	1930
31	HC 9153	A.D.C. 416	DUPLE C23R	1928
32	JK 1064	MORRIS VICEROY	???C20R	1930
37	JK 1911	GILFORD 168SD	DUPLE C26R	1931
38	JK 1273	GILFORD 168SD	DUPLE C26R	1930
39	JK 1065	GILFORD 168SD	DUPLE C26R	1930
40	JK 473	GILFORD 168SD	DUPLE C26R	1929
371	HC 9817	DENNIS F	HOYAL C20R	1928
1000	JK 1098	LEYLAND TIGER TS2	DUPLE C28R	1930
1061	JK 1266	LEYLAND TIGER TS2	DUPLE C28R	1930

From CHAPMAN & SONS (EASTBOURNE) LTD, EASTBOURNE, SUSSEX – 4 MARCH 1932

41	HC 7507	LANCIA PENTAIOTA	PARK ROYAL Ch18R (1930)	1927
42	HC 7509	LANCIA PENTAIOTA	PARK ROYAL Ch18R (1930)	1927
318	HC 6075	MAUDSLAY ML4	DUPLE Ch22R (1929)	1926
319	HC 9129	MAUDSLAY ML4B	DUPLE Ch22R (1929)	1928
320	HC 9995	MAUDSLAY ML4B	HALL LEWIS Ch22R	1928
321	JK 20	MAUDSLAY ML4B	HALL LEWIS Ch22R	1929
322	JK 21	MAUDSLAY ML4B	HALL LEWIS Ch22R	1929
323	JK 22	MAUDSLAY ML4B	HALL LEWIS Ch22R	1929
324	JK 23	MAUDSLAY ML4B	HALL LEWIS Ch22R	1929
325	JK 24	MAUDSLAY ML4B	HALL LEWIS Ch22R	1929
326	JK 25	MAUDSLAY ML4B	HALL LEWIS Ch22R	1929
327	JK 26	MAUDSLAY ML4B	HALL LEWIS Ch22R	1929
328	JK 27	MAUDSLAY ML4B	HALL LEWIS Ch22R	1929
329	JK 28	MAUDSLAY ML4B	HALL LEWIS Ch22R	1929
330	JK 655	MAUDSLAY ML7A	DUPLE Ch31R	1929
331	TD 5458	MAUDSLAY ML2	KNAPE Ch18	1926
332	TD 5460	MAUDSLAY ML2	KNAPE Ch18	1926
333	JK 1002	MAUDSLAY ML4B	HALL LEWIS Ch26R	1930
334	JK 1003	MAUDSLAY ML4B	HALL LEWIS Ch26R	1930
335	JK 1004	MAUDSLAY ML4B	HALL LEWIS Ch26R	1930
336	JK 1005	MAUDSLAY ML4B	HALL LEWIS Ch26R	1930
337	JK 1006	MAUDSLAY ML4B	HALL LEWIS Ch26R	1930
338	JK 1007	MAUDSLAY ML4B	HALL LEWIS Ch26R	1930
339	JK 1207	MAUDSLAY ML4B	PARK ROYAL Ch22R	1930
340	JK 1208	MAUDSLAY ML4B	PARK ROYAL Ch22R	1930
341	JK 1209	MAUDSLAY ML6B	DUPLE Ch24R	1930

372	HC 2347	DENNIS 4 ton	PARK ROYAL Ch25R (1930)	1923	
373	HC 2349	DENNIS 4 ton	PARK ROYAL Ch25R (1930)	1923	
374	HC 2351	DENNIS 3½ ton	PARK ROYAL Ch22R (1930)	1923	
375	HC 2833	DENNIS 3½ ton	PARK ROYAL Ch22R (1930)	1923	
376	HC 4141	DENNIS 2½ ton	DENNIS Ch22R ?	1924	
377	HC 4143	DENNIS 2½ ton	PARK ROYAL Ch22R (1930)	1924	
378	HC 4145	DENNIS 4 ton	PARK ROYAL Ch30R (1930)	1925	
379	HC 5059	DENNIS 4 ton	PARK ROYAL Ch30R (1930)	1925	
380	HC 5385	DENNIS 3½ ton	PARK ROYAL Ch22R (1930)	1925	
381	HC 2837	DENNIS 3½ ton	PARK ROYAL Ch22R (1930)	1923	
382	HC 6077	DENNIS 30 cwt	DENNIS Ch24R	1926	
383	HC 6079	DENNIS 2½ ton	PARK ROYAL Ch22R (1930)	1926	
385	DB 2209	DENNIS C	PARK ROYAL Ch22R (1930)	1920	
386	DB 2210	DENNIS C	PARK ROYAL Ch22R (1930)	1920	
387	DB 2212	DENNIS C	PARK ROYAL Ch22R (1930)	1920	
388	HC 9131	DENNIS F	PARK ROYAL Ch26R	1928	
389	JK 1008	DENNIS GL	HALL LEWIS Ch14R	1930	
390	JK 1009	DENNIS GL	HALL LEWIS Ch14R	1930	

From THAMES VALLEY TRACTION CO. LTD, READING, BERKSHIRE – APRIL 1932

490	MO 9313	TILLING-STEVENS B9B	chassis only	1927	
491	MO 9314	TILLING-STEVENS B9B	chassis only	1927	
492	RX 1398	TILLING-STEVENS B9B	chassis only	1928	
493	RX 1399	TILLING-STEVENS B9B	chassis only	1928	
494	MO 9312	TILLING-STEVENS B9B	chassis only	1927	
495	MO 9315	TILLING-STEVENS B9B	chassis only	1927	

From G. W. MEEKINGS, BENTLEY, HAMPSHIRE – 3 AUGUST 1933

-	PF 7258	MORRIS COMMERCIAL	B???	1927	(Not operated by Southdown)

From FAIRWAY COACHES LIMITED, STOCKWELL, LONDON SW9 – 18 DECEMBER 1933

342	UL 1509	MAUDSLAY ML3	DODSON C24R	1929
343	UL 8823	MAUDSLAY ML3	DODSON C24R	1929
344	UL 8824	MAUDSLAY ML3	DODSON C24R	1929
345	GU 8930	MAUDSLAY ML4	???C26R	1929
346	GU 8931	MAUDSLAY ML4	???C26R	1929
397	GX 2618	DENNIS LANCET	STRACHAN C30F	1932
398	GX 2619	DENNIS LANCET	STRACHAN C30F	1932
399	GX 2620	DENNIS LANCET	STRACHAN C30F	1932

From W.G. WAUGH t/a REGAL COACHES, BRIGHTON, SUSSEX – 18 DECEMBER 1933

26	UF 5985	AEC REGAL	HARRINGTON C32F	1930

From B.R. ROBERTS, PORTSLADE, SUSSEX – 6 DECEMBER 1934

	PN 3539	CHEVROLET	???Ch14	1929

From W.H. RAYNER & SON t/a THE HORSHAM BUS SERVICE, BARNS GREEN, SUSSEX – 15 JANUARY 1935

538	PX 5776	DENNIS 30 cwt	HARRINGTON (?) B18F	1927

From F. G. TANNER t/a DENMEAD QUEEN MOTOR SERVICES, DENMEAD, HAMPSHIRE – 21 MARCH 1935

39	TP 4760	THORNYCROFT UB	WADHAM B26F	1927
40	TP 6601	THORNYCROFT A6	WADHAM B20F	1928
41	TP 7591	THORNYCROFT A2	WADHAM B20F	1929
42	TP 8693	THORNYCROFT A2	WADHAM B20F	1930
43	TP 9164	THORNYCROFT A2	WADHAM B20F	1930
44	TP 9645	THORNYCROFT A6	WADHAM B20R	1930
45	OU 7856	THORNYCROFT BC	RANSOMES B32R	1929
46	CG 7119	THORNYCROFT CD	BRUSH B32F	1933
47	RV 1844	THORNYCROFT CD	WADHAM B32R	1932
48	JK 88	THORNYCROFT A6	STRACHAN & BROWN B22R	1929
49	HC 9159	THORNYCROFT A2 Long	B20-	1928

Notes: 41-3/5-7 renumbered 541-3/5-7 -/36. 48/9 had previously been acquired by Southdown 9/29 and numbered 382/3, being sold to Tanner 10/31.

From W. F. ROWLAND & G. B. ORR, WORTHING, SUSSEX – 18 MAY 1936

-	PX 5798	DENNIS 30 cwt	Ch18	1927
-	PX 5799	DENNIS 30 cwt	Ch18	1927

From TRAMOCARS LTD, WORTHING, SUSSEX – 1 APRIL 1938

T3	PX 886	SHELVOKE & DREWRY FREIGHTER	HICKMAN B20R	1924
*T4	PX 1593	SHELVOKE & DREWRY FREIGHTER	HICKMAN B20R	1925
T5	PX 6872	SHELVOKE & DREWRY FREIGHTER	HICKMAN B20R	1927
T6	PO 1626	SHELVOKE & DREWRY FREIGHTER	HICKMAN B20R	1930
T7	PO 1748	SHELVOKE & DREWRY FREIGHTER	HARRINGTON B20R	1930
T8	PO 1780	SHELVOKE & DREWRY FREIGHTER	HARRINGTON B20R	1930
T9	PO 7706	SHELVOKE & DREWRY FREIGHTER	HARRINGTON B26R	1933
T10	PO 8014	SHELVOKE & DREWRY FREIGHTER	HARRINGTON B26R	1933
T11	PO 9665	SHELVOKE & DREWRY FREIGHTER	HARRINGTON B26R	1934
T12	PO 9890	SHELVOKE & DREWRY FREIGHTER	HARRINGTON B26R	1934
T13	APX 237	SHELVOKE & DREWRY FREIGHTER	HARRINGTON B26R	1935

*Never operated by Southdown (T4 was partly stripped by the company)

Typical of the Shelvoke & Drewry based buses taken over with the Tramocars' fleet is PO 7706 which became car T9 in the Southdown fleet. It was new in June 1933 and fitted with a Harrington 26 seat body. Although painted into Southdown livery in May 1939 it was placed into store in 1940 but wartime restrictions on the resale of vehicles prevented disposal until July 1942 when all remaining Tramocars passed to the dealer Arlington Motor Company. Due to the extreme shortage of serviceable vehicles PO 7706, along with three other former Tramocars, saw further service with Worthington Motor Tours of Stafford until its withdrawal in December 1944. *Alan Lambert Collection*

Appendix 4

OPERATORS ACQUIRED 1930–1939

J. POOLE t/a ROYAL RED COACHES, HOVE, SUSSEX – 28 MARCH 1930
Excursions & Tours from Hove

A. POTTS t/a POTTS MOTOR SERVICES, BRIGHTON, SUSSEX – 5 JUNE 1930
Excursions & Tours from Brighton

SOUTHERN GLIDEWAY COACHES LTD, EASTBOURNE, SUSSEX – 1 MARCH 1932
Express: Eastbourne–London

CHAPMAN & SONS (EASTBOURNE) LTD, EASTBOURNE, SUSSEX – 4 MARCH 1932
Express: Eastbourne–London
Excursions & Tours from Eastbourne

C. F. WOOD & SONS LTD, STEYNING, SUSSEX – 17 MARCH 1932
Goodwill only – no vehicles
Express: Steyning–London

G B. MOTOR TOURS LTD, LONDON W1 – 14 APRIL 1932
Goodwill only – no vehicles
Express: London–Worthing, London–Brighton, London–Eastbourne. Licences subsequently refused

G. TATE t/a RED ROVER MOTOR SERVICES, FELPHAM, BOGNOR, SUSSEX – 17 OCTOBER 1932
Goodwill only – no vehicles
Stage: Bognor Regis–Pagham

G. H. MEABY, BRIGHTON, SUSSEX – 15 NOVEMBER 1932
Goodwill only – no vehicles
Excursions & Tours from Brighton

J. HAFFENDEN, VINES CROSS, SUSSEX – 15 NOVEMBER 1932
Goodwill only – no vehicles
Stage: Heathfield–Eastbourne

S. S. T. OVERINGTON t/a BLUE BUS SERVICE, HORSHAM, SUSSEX – 14 DECEMBER 1932
Goodwill only – no vehicles
Stage: Horsham–Handcross–Balcombe and Horsham–Maplehurst

KEITH & BOYLE LTD, PROPRIETORS OF PRATT & PEARCE LTD t/a LITTLE VIC ORANGE COACHES, EASTBOURNE – 9 MARCH 1933
Goodwill only – no vehicles
Excursions & Tours from Eastbourne

H. J. SARGENT t/a EAST GRINSTEAD MOTOR COACHES, EAST GRINSTEAD, SUSSEX – 30 JUNE 1933
Goodwill only – no vehicles
Express: East Grinstead–Brighton

LONDON GENERAL COUNTRY SERVICES LTD, REIGATE, SURREY – 1 JULY 1933
Goodwill only – no vehicles
Stage: Uckfield–East Grinstead and Handcross–Crawley

G. W. MEEKINGS, BENTLEY, HAMPSHIRE – 3 AUGUST 1933
Stage: Hayling Ferry–Eastoke

P. C. BELLIER, HAYLING ISLAND, HAMPSHIRE – 3 AUGUST 1933
Goodwill only – no vehicles
Stage: Hayling Ferry–Eastoke
Excursions & Tours

FAIRWAY COACHES LIMITED, STOCKWELL, LONDON SW9 – 18 DECEMBER 1933
Express:London–Worthing

W.G. WAUGH t/a REGAL COACHES, BRIGHTON, SUSSEX – 18 DECEMBER 1933
Excursions & Tours from Brighton

NORTH END MOTOR COACHES (PORTSMOUTH) LTD, NEW CROSS, LONDON SE14 – 4 MAY 1934
Goodwill only – no vehicles
Express: Portsmouth–London

A. D. JESSETT & D. A. FARRANCE t/a JESSETT'S COACHES, HAYWARDS HEATH – 12 JULY 1934
Goodwill only – no vehicles
Excursions & Tours from Haywards Heath

G. A. CROSS t/a PERSERVERANCE BLUE SALOON COACHES, GOSPORT, HAMPSHIRE – 12 JULY 1934
Goodwill only – no vehicles
Express: Gosport–Meon Valley–London

B.R. ROBERTS, PORTSLADE, SUSSEX – 6 DECEMBER 1934
Excursions & Tours from Portslade

HAMPSHIRE LIGHT RAILWAYS (ELECTRIC) CO LTD, t/a PORTSDOWN & HORNDEAN LIGHT RAILWAY, LONDON EC4 – 10 JANUARY 1935
Goodwill only – no vehicles
Tramway Cosham–Horndean replaced by Southdown buses.

W.H. RAYNER & SON t/a THE HORSHAM BUS SERVICE, BARNS GREEN, SUSSEX – 15 JANUARY 1935
Stage: Horsham–Barns Green, Horsham–Coolham, Horsham–St. Leonards, Horsham–The Common and Horsham–Billingshurst

T. W. CARTER t/a CARTER BROTHERS, HORSHAM, SUSSEX – 15 JANUARY 1935
Goodwill only – no vehicles
Stage: Horsham– Steyning

A. TIMPSON & SONS LTD, CATFORD, LONDON SE6 – 11 MARCH 1935
Goodwill only – no vehicles
Express: London–Portsmouth (Winter)

W. F. ALEXANDER t/a COMFY COACHES, HORSHAM, SUSSEX – 20 MARCH 1935
Goodwill only – no vehicles
Excursions & Tours from Horsham

F. G. TANNER t/a DENMEAD QUEEN MOTOR SERVICES, DENMEAD, HAMPSHIRE – 21 MARCH 1935
Stage: Portsmouth–Hambledon

ALDERSHOT & DISTRICT TRACTION CO LTD, ALDERSHOT, HAMPSHIRE – 1 MAY 1935
Goodwill only – no vehicles
Express: Grayshott/Hindhead–London

ALEXANDRA MOTOR COACHES LTD, SOUTHSEA, HAMPSHIRE – 23 MAY 1935
Goodwill only – no vehicles
Express: Southsea–London

T. S. BRUCE t/a IMPERIAL SALOON COACHES, PORTSMOUTH, HAMPSHIRE – 23 MAY 1935
Goodwill only – no vehicles
Express: Portsmouth–London

UNDERWOOD EXPRESS SERVICES LTD, PORTSMOUTH, HAMPSHIRE – 23 MAY 1935
Goodwill only – no vehicles
Express: Portsmouth–London

MRS M. V. FUGER t/a FAREHAM & DISTRICT COACHES, WARSASH, HAMPSHIRE – 27 JUNE 1935
Goodwill only – no vehicles
Express: Warsash–Fareham–London

BLUE MOTOR SERVICES (SOUTHWICK) LTD, BOARHUNT, HAMPSHIRE – 1 AUGUST 1935
Goodwill only – no vehicles
Stage: Hambledon–Droxford–Wickham–Portsmouth

MAIDSTONE & DISTRICT MOTOR SERVICES LTD, MAIDSTONE, KENT – 27 MARCH 1936
Goodwill only – no vehicles
Stage: Uckfield–Tunbridge Wells (joint)

W. F. ROWLAND & G. B. ORR, WORTHING, SUSSEX – 18 MAY 1936
Excursions & Tours from Worthing

G. C. LANDSALL T/A MASCOT SAFETY COACHES, WORTHING, SUSSEX – 6 JANUARY 1937
Goodwill only – no vehicles

H. MILLER t/a MILLER'S COACHES, PORTSLADE, SUSSEX – 6 JANUARY 1937
Goodwill only – no vehicles

H. J. SARGENT t/a EAST GRINSTEAD MOTOR COACHES, EAST GRINSTEAD, SUSSEX – 16 JULY 1937
Goodwill only – no vehicles
Stage: East Grinstead–West Hoathly–Sharpthorne

H. K. HART t/a ALPHA COACHES, BRIGHTON, SUSSEX – 24 AUGUST 1937
Goodwill only – no vehicles
Excursion: Brighton–Hellingly Hospital

R. J. SMART t/a FERRING OMNIBUS SERVICE, FERRING, SUSSEX – 10 NOVEMBER 1937
Goodwill only – no vehicles
Stage: Ferring-on-Sea–Goring-by-Sea Station

F. & H. L. POWNALL, BRIGHTON, SUSSEX – 30 NOVEMBER 1937
Goodwill only – no vehicles

S. W. STEPHENS T/A SYDNEY MOTOR COACHES, EASTBOURNE, SUSSEX – 25 FEBRUARY 1938
Goodwill only – no vehicles
Excursions & Tours from Eastbourne

M. H. W. GARLICK, EAST HOATHLY, SUSSEX – 4 MARCH 1938
Goodwill only – no vehicles
Stage: East Hoathly–Uckfield

H. J. SARGENT t/a EAST GRINSTEAD MOTOR COACHES, EAST GRINSTEAD, SUSSEX – 26 APRIL 1938
Goodwill only – no vehicles
Excursions & Tours from East Grinstead

HARTINGTON MOTORS LTD, EASTBOURNE, SUSSEX – 8 JUNE 1938
Goodwill only – no vehicles
Excursions & Tours from Eastbourne

TRAMOCARS LTD, WORTHING, SUSSEX – 1 APRIL 1938
Stage: Splash Point–Library and Splash Point–West Worthing

L. CHERRIMAN, HURSTPIERPOINT, SUSSEX – 15 SEPTEMBER 1938
Goodwill only – no vehicles
Stage: Hurstpierpoint–Hassocks

C. R. SHORTER, BRIGHTON, SUSSEX – 8 JANUARY 1939
Goodwill only – no vehicles
Express: Hove–Brighton–Robertsbridge Sanatorium
Excursions & Tours from Brighton

HARVEY'S COACHES, EASTBOURNE, SUSSEX – SEPTEMBER 1939
Goodwill only – no vehicles
Excursions & Tours from Eastbourne